Rhode Island

D1008369

Rhode Island

Phyllis Méras & Katherine Imbrie

The Countryman Press ✳ Woodstock, Vermont

FOURTH EDITION

DEDICATION

To the two Toms and Dot
—P. M.

We welcome your comments and suggestions. Please contact Explorer's Guide Editor, The Countryman Press, P.O. Box 748, Woodstock, VT 05091, or e-mail countrymanpress@wwnorton.com.

Copyright © 1995, 1998, 2000 by Phyllis Méras and Tom Gannon

Copyright © 2004 by Phyllis Méras and Katherine Imbrie

Fourth Edition

ISBN 0-88150-516-1
ISSN 1542-4731

Cover and text design by Bodenweber Design
Front cover photograph by Billy Black, courtesy of the Newport, Rhode Island, Convention & Visitor's Bureau, www.GoNewport.com, 1-800-976-5122
Back cover photograph by Kim Grant; www.kimgrant.com
Maps by Mapping Specialists Ltd., Madison, WI, copyright © The Countryman Press
Composition by PerfecType, Nashville, TN

Published by The Countryman Press
P.O. Box 748, Woodstock, Vermont 05091

Distributed by W. W. Norton & Company, Inc., 500 Fifth Avenue, New York, NY 10110

Printed in the United States of America

10 9 8 7 6 5 4 3 2 1

EXPLORE WITH US!

Welcome to the fourth edition of *Rhode Island: An Explorer's Guide,* the first statewide guide to the Ocean State. As in every other book in the Explorer's Guide series, all inclusions—attractions, inns, restaurants—have been chosen on the basis of personal experience, not paid advertising.

We hope you find this guide easy to read and use. We've kept the layout fairly simple, but here are some general tips to help you find your way.

WHAT'S WHERE

In the beginning of the book you'll find an alphabetical listing of special highlights and important information that you may want to reference quickly.

LODGING

When making reservations, especially at B&Bs and smaller inns, we suggest that you inquire in advance about policies regarding smoking, children, the use of credit cards for payment, and any minimum-stay requirements.

RESTAURANTS

In most chapters please note a distinction between *Dining Out* and *Eating Out.* Restaurants listed under *Eating Out* are generally inexpensive and more casual; reservations are suggested for restaurants in *Dining Out.*

PRICES

It is difficult to convey current prices, as changes occur frequently and, especially in popular vacation areas, rates are often adjusted to the season. As always, we suggest that you call ahead. There is a 12 percent state room tax in Rhode Island, added to a 7 percent sales tax. The prices indicated by the rating system used in this book do not include taxes or gratuity.

Lodging (double occupancy, per night): $ means under $95; $$ means $95–125; $$$ means $125–175; $$$$ means over $175.

Eating Out and Dining Out (price of an entrée): $ means under $10; $$ means $10–20; $$$ means $20–30; $$$$ means over $30.

KEY TO SYMBOLS

🏵 The "value" symbol appears next to lodgings, restaurants, and activities that combine exceptional quality with moderate prices.

🐾 The dog paw symbol appears next to lodgings that as of press time accept pets (with prior notification), as well as other places where pets are allowed.

𝄞 The "child and family interest" symbol appears next to lodgings, restaurants, activities, and shops of special appeal to youngsters and families.

♿ The wheelchair symbol appears next to establishments that are partially or fully handicapped accessible.

We would appreciate your comments and corrections about places you discover or know well. Please send your letters to Explorer's Guide Editor, The Countryman Press, P.O. Box 748, Woodstock, Vermont 05091; or use the reply card enclosed in this book.

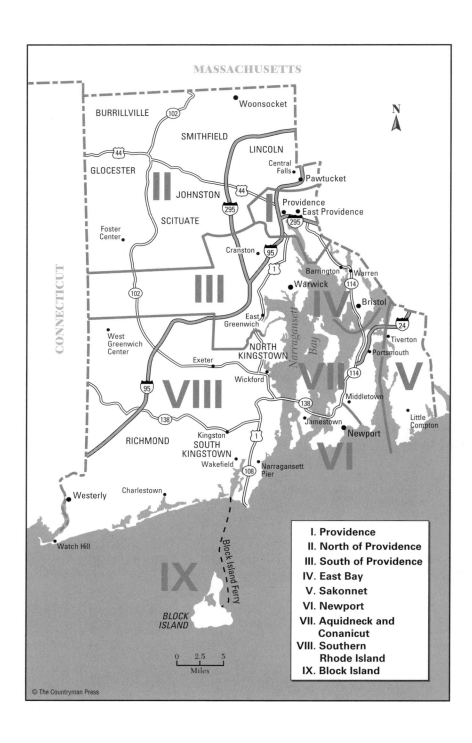

CONTENTS

LIST OF MAPS

ACKNOWLEDGMENTS

The following people have been most generous with suggestions, information, and advice during the preparation of this book: Bob Billington, of the Blackstone Valley Tourist Authority; David de Petrillo, of the Rhode Island Tourism Division; Mark Brouder, of the Rhode Island Welcome Center; Albert Klyberg, of the Rhode Island Historical Society; Leonard Panaggio, formerly of the Rhode Island Tourism Division; the Newport Tourism & Development Council; Deb O'Hara, director of Tiverton Library Services; the Preservation Society of Newport County; Ida Millman, Jean Rossi, Nancy Luedeman, Richard J. Walton, Leigh Diakapolous, Nancy Whitcomb, Thomas D. Stevens, Sal Laterra, the late Edwin Safford, Richard and Janet Wood, Laurinda Barrett, James Dugan; Donald Breed, Lynne Chaput, Channing and Bianca Gray, Ken Weber, Doug Fellow, Alan Kerr, William K. Gale, Andy Smith, Mikki Catanzaro, Janet Butler, Donna Lee, Janina Fera, Rose Lansing, Donna McGarry, Patricia Pothier, Lars Smith, and Jim Seavor of the *Providence Journal.*

Thanks are also due to Brian C. Tefft, of the State Division of Fish, Wildlife, and Estuarine Services; Robert and Betsy Dunley, Katrina Aldrich, Emily Cocroft, Robert Cocroft, William Cocroft, the late Thomas H. Cocroft, David Fowler, Frank and Esther Mauran, Mary McGovern, Joan and Roger Noone, and B. L. Gordon, of the Watch Hill Book & Tackle Shop; Susan Capuano, Wilbur Doctor, Jim and Adelheide Dresser, Carol Hazelhurst, John C. Quinn, Leppy McCarthy, Joan Ress Reeves, Suzanne Jeffers, Caroline Vollmer, Paul Carrick, Ann Lampson, Laura Katz, Anita Pariseau, Lorraine and Jacques Hopkins, Gregory Del Sesto, Gloria Maroni, Chet Browning, the Rhode Island Department of Economic Development; Evan Smith, Newport County Convention & Visitors Bureau; and Kermit Hummel, Jennifer Thompson, and Laura Jorstad of The Countryman Press, for their extraordinary patience.

INTRODUCTION

Welcome to the Ocean State. That may seem like a grand nickname for the country's tiniest state, which measures a mere 48 miles long by 37 miles wide, but with Narragansett Bay slicing it nearly in two, there's no place within Rhode Island's borders that's more than a 20-minute drive from its 400-mile coastline. In fact, with a total of 36 islands, including Aquidneck, second largest (after Long Island) on the East Coast, Rhode Island could almost be classified as an archipelago.

Very much a New England state in many respects, Rhode Island enjoys its own distinct identity—actually several identities, all of which involve a strong sense of independence. Rhode Island was founded in 1636 by religious refugees fleeing the rigid Puritanism of the Massachusetts Bay Colony, and soon became a haven for outcasts of all sorts—Quakers, Jews, Antinomians. Privateering—preying on enemy ships—grew simultaneously with the colony's shipbuilding industry and often was indistinguishable from outright piracy. All of this combined to earn the colony an earlier nickname, Rogue's Island.

The ports of Providence and Newport were heavily engaged in the unsavory slave trade, but the state could also boast some early abolitionists, including Samuel Hopkins and Ezra Stiles, later president of Yale, who helped enact a ban on slave trading in 1774, the first such law in the colonies. Rhode Island's Black Regiment, the nation's first such unit, routed Hessian mercenaries on Aquidneck in 1778, earning members full citizenship in the process.

Rhode Island and Mother England clashed regularly over trade-related issues, and the colony finally declared itself independent of the Crown on May 4, 1776, two months before the remaining colonies issued the Declaration of Independence. After participating enthusiastically in the Revolution—General Nathanael Greene was a native son—Rhode Island typically refused to join the Union, reluctantly becoming the 13th and last colony to ratify the Constitution in 1790, and only after threats of tariff barriers and invasion. That stubborn streak has continued; in the 1920s, when the rest of the nation was dutifully approving the Volstead Act, Rhode Island was one of just two states to reject it. Once Prohibition was a fact, Rhode Islanders quickly moved into rum-running, taking full advantage of the coast's many hidden coves and inlets.

But the long, colorful history is just one aspect of the Ocean State. Blessed with some swift-running rivers that could be harnessed for waterpower, particularly in the Blackstone River region, the state developed into what has been called the birthplace of the industrial revolution. In Pawtucket, Samuel Slater in 1790 started the nation's first successful cotton-manufacturing operation. Peace Dale in South County was the site of the first power loom, in 1814. The textile industry drew thousands of immigrant workers—French Canadians, Irish, English, and Italians, the same groups who make up much of the population today. Rhode Island also got an early start in the jewelry business, perfecting the plating of pot metals in the 1700s and creating an industry that remains an important part of the economy.

Divided as it is by water and geography—the colony at one time had four different capitals—Rhode Island offers much diversity in a small space, from the quiet pastures and woods of South County (the popular name for the southwestern part of the state), home to Swamp Yankees and descendants of the Narragansett tribe; to the urban life of revitalized Providence, now one of the most inviting small cities in America and boasting some of the region's finest restaurants. Its entire downtown has been placed on the National Register of Historic Places. Then there is the sophistication of Newport, summer home to wealthy visitors from the 1700s to the present. The geography is varied as well, with rugged hillsides in the north, barrier beaches along the southern coast, steep headlands in the east, and rolling pastures in the southeast corner. And there is Narragansett Bay, the second largest estuary on the East Coast (after the Chesapeake Bay), which forms a 28-mile wedge cutting into the state and accounts for the two most popular forms of recreation: swimming and boating.

In this book we have done our best to introduce you to the highlights of the smallest state with the longest name (officially Rhode Island and Providence Plantations)—to its history and legends; its 400 miles of shore; its natural areas and winding country roads; and its grand historic houses, mill villages, and immigrant neighborhoods. We urge you to follow us on our exploration and see for yourself what so many travelers miss in their rush from Boston or New York to Cape Cod and northern New England.

Phyllis, born in New York, came to Rhode Island after Wellesley College and the Columbia Graduate School of Journalism. Although she has come and gone from the state many times since then, working for the *New York Times,* the *Vineyard Gazette* on Martha's Vineyard, and a newspaper in Switzerland, she married a Rhode Islander, Thomas Cocroft, and, like the proverbial bad penny, seems always to come back. She has written an earlier guidebook to the state and is the former travel editor of the *Providence Journal.*

Katherine Imbrie has spent summers on the Rhode Island coast since she was a child, and came to live in Rhode Island 35 years ago, as a teenager. She has been a features and local travel writer for the *Providence Journal* for more than two decades, and in that time has come to know just about every nook and cranny of the littlest state.

We hope this guide will help you to discover something new in your backyard or to plan a holiday in the Ocean State. As you follow some of our recommendations and visit our favorite places, please don't forget to send us your own recommendations, so that future editions of this guide are as complete and accurate as possible.

WHAT'S WHERE IN RHODE ISLAND

AGRICULTURAL FAIRS Each August the agriculturally minded head to Richmond for the annual Washington County Agricultural Fair. This is the state's only major old-fashioned country fair, with horse and oxen pulls, animals, fruit and vegetable judging, country-and-western stage shows, and midway games. Smaller fairs include Foster's Old Home Days, in July, and Exeter's Old Home Days, held during the last weekend in June. There are Harvest Fairs held in September at Coggeshall Farm Museum and in October at the Norman Bird Sanctuary in Middletown. For further information, call or write the Rhode Island Division of Agriculture (401-222-2781), 235 Promenade Street, Providence 02908.

AIRLINES AND AIRPORTS **Theodore Francis Green State Airport** on Post Road in Warwick, the state's largest airport, is served by major and commuter airlines. **New England Airlines** offers scheduled flights between **Westerly State Airport** and **Block Island State Airport,** and **Action Airlines** flies to Block Island from **Groton/New London Airport** in Connecticut. **Newport State Airport** in Middletown, **Quonset**

State Airport in North Kingstown, and **North Central Airport** in Smithfield are open to charter and private planes.

AMUSEMENT PARKS **The Enchanted Forest** (401-539-7711) in Hopkinton offers a petting zoo, storyland structures, and, for children under 12, a miniature carousel and roller coaster. The water slides at **Water Wizz** (401-322-0520), at Misquamicut Beach in Westerly, attract adults as well as children. In North Kingstown, **Fiddlesticks Recreation Center** (401-295-1519) has a picturesque miniature golf course and batting cages. More miniature golf and batting cages, as well as bumper boats, can be found in Narragansett at **Adventureland;** and **Yawgoo Valley Ski Area and Water Park** (401-295-5366) in Exeter has water slides, a volleyball court, and horseshoes.

ANTIQUES Like any other New England state, Rhode Island is rich in antiques. And while the dealers are fairly knowledgeable, the prices (especially outside Newport) will surprise visitors from metropolitan areas. Newport, with its Gilded Age artifacts

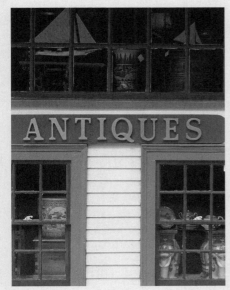

Kim Grant

(401-222-3880). Many galleries are also listed in the *"Providence Journal'*s Summer Guide" published in May by the *Providence Journal* (401-277-7000).

ART MUSEUMS The **Museum of Art, Rhode Island School of Design** (401-454-6500) in Providence is the state's most important museum of art, with a collection that includes ancient and Oriental art, 19th-century French art, modern Latin American work, American furniture, and decorative arts. The **Newport Art Museum** (401-848-8200) offers changing exhibits of historical and contemporary art from Newport and other parts of New England. (See also *Art Galleries* and *Museums.*)

BALLOONING Balloon flights over the southern part of the state are offered by the **Kingston Balloon Company** (401-783-9386).

BEACHES Living up to its nickname of the Ocean State, Rhode Island has more than three dozen saltwater beaches along its hundreds of miles of coastline. Among the largest and most popular of the beaches with surf are **Charlestown Town Beach, Narragansett Town Beach, Watch Hill Town Beach, East Matunuck State Beach,** and **Green Hill** in South Kingstown; **Misquamicut State Beach** in Westerly; and **Scarborough State Beach** in Narragansett. Less accessible but still popular is **Goosewing Beach** in Little Compton. Body surfers find Newport's **First** and **Second Beaches** to their liking, while surfboarders come to ride the waves between the **Narragansett Town Beach** and **East Matunuck State**

and China trade connections, not surprisingly has the biggest selection. You can start your hunt along tiny Franklin Street, aka Antique Row, which runs between Thames and Spring Streets beside the main U.S. post office. For more information, contact the **Newport County Antique Dealers Association,** Box 222, Newport 02940. Warren, particularly the downtown waterfront area, is another trove of antique treasures, along with Providence and South County, especially Wickford village in North Kingstown. But that unheralded shop along a country road may be just the place you've been looking for.

AREA CODE The area code for all Rhode Island is **401.**

ART GALLERIES There are art galleries throughout the state, with major public and private galleries in most communities. Further information may be obtained from the **Rhode Island State Council on the**

Beach. Saltwater bathing facilities for families with small children are best at **Roger Wheeler State Beach** and **Salty Brine Beach** in Narragansett and **Fred Benson Town Beach** (Crescent Beach) on Block Island. **Third Beach** in Middletown is also relatively calm, and popular with children. Farther inland, the best beaches are **Sandy Point** in Portsmouth and **Fogland** in Tiverton, both on the Sakonnet River, and **Bristol Town Beach** and **Colt State Park,** both along upper Narragansett Bay. There are parking fees for both state and town beaches (anywhere from $5 to $20), and parking is always limited, so it's wise on a hot summer's day to arrive at a beach as early as possible. Rates are higher on weekends and for out-of-state residents, and a few beaches charge entrance fees.

BED & BREAKFASTS Rhode Island offers bed & breakfast accommodations by the ocean, in rural villages, and in its capital. A list is printed each year in the **Rhode Island Tourism Division's** *Rhode Island Visitor's Guide,* available at visitors information bureaus throughout the state or by calling 401-222-2601 or 1-800-556-

Kim Grant

2484. Reservation services include **Access to Accommodations** (401-846-9443) in summer only, **Anna's Victorian Connection** (401-849-2489), **Bed & Breakfast of Newport** (401-846-5408), **Bed & Breakfast of Rhode Island** (401-849-1298; 1-800-828-0000), **Bed & Breakfast Referrals of South Coast Rhode Island** (1-800-853-7479), **Block Island Chamber of Commerce** (401-466-2982; 1-800-383-BIRI), **Historic Newport Inns** (401-846-7666), the **Narragansett Chamber of Commerce** (401-783-7121), **Taylor-Made Reservations of Newport** (401-848-0300; 1-800-848-8848), and the **URI Youth Hostel** (401-789-3929).

BIKING Though Rhode Island is a small state, its terrain varies widely—with dense woodlands, sea and bay coastline, flatlands, hills, and rolling farmland. Much of it is interesting for the cyclist to explore. Among the best areas for cycling are along the 14.5-mile **East Bay Bicycle Path** between Providence and Bristol, which sometimes edges Narragansett Bay and at other times passes through towns and villages. A map of the bicycle path is contained in the **Rhode Island Tourism Division's** *Rhode Island Visitor's Guide.* **Block Island's** unspoiled winding roads are also popular with cyclists. A ride along Newport's 15-mile-long **Bellevue Avenue** and **Ocean Drive** will take you past mansions on one side and the ocean on the other. Bristol's **Colt State Park** and remote **Tiverton** and **Little Compton** afford picturesque rides as well. We also recommend Warwick's **Goddard State Park,** the **Greenville** area of Smithfield, and the island of **Jamestown.**

BIRDING Situated as it is directly under the Atlantic Flyway, **Block Island** lures many a birder, especially in fall. There are many other fine birding sites in the state as well: in Middletown, the **Sachuest Point National Wildlife Refuge** and the **Norman Bird Sanctuary;** in South Kingstown, the **Trustom Pond National Wildlife Sanctuary;** in Charlestown, the **Ninigret National Wildlife Area;** in Providence, the **Swan Point Cemetery;** and the many state management areas. Further information is available from the **Audubon Society of Rhode Island** (401-949-5454).

BUS SERVICES **Bonanza** (401-751-8800; 1-800-556-3815) serves Providence from New York, Boston, Cape Cod, and Albany (via Springfield, Massachusetts). **Greyhound** (401-454-0790; 1-800-221-2222) also links Providence with Boston and New York. On both lines there can be intermediate stops in Connecticut.

CAMPING Both private and state camping areas—some sophisticated, some quite primitive—are scattered throughout the rural sections of the state. A *Rhode Island Outdoor Activities Guide* including camping is available from the **Rhode Island Tourism Division** (401-222-2601; 1-800-556-2484).

CANOEING AND KAYAKING Canoe and kayak rentals, lessons, and guided trips are offered by the **Kayak Centre** (401-295-4400) in Wickford, **Hope Valley Bait and Tackle Shop** (401-539-2757) in Wyoming, **Narrow River Kayaks** (401-789-0334) in Narragansett, **Sakonnet Boathouse**

in Tiverton (401-624-1440), **Ocean State Adventures** in Bristol (401-254-4000), and **Quaker Lane Bait and Tackle** in North Kingstown. Further information on canoeing routes and facilities can be obtained from the **Rhode Island Canoe Association** (401-725-3344). A guide to canoeing the Blackstone River is available from the **John H. Chafee Blackstone River Valley National Heritage Corridor** (401-762-0250), Depot Square, Woonsocket 02895. Information on canoeing the Wood and Pawcatuck Rivers is available from the **Wood-Pawcatuck Watershed Association** (401-539-9017), 203 Arcadia Road, Hope Valley 02832.

CHILDREN, ESPECIALLY FOR Throughout this book we have marked a number of sites with particular appeal to children and families with a "🦆." In Providence, the **Providence Children's Museum** (401-331-6588) is a hands-on museum for children 2 to 11 years old. The Newport area's attractions for children include the **Old Colony and Newport Railway** (401-849-0546) and **Green Animals** topiary gardens in Portsmouth (401-847-1000). There are children's carousels at **Roger Williams Park** (401-785-9450) in Providence, **Slater Memorial Park** (401-728-0500, ext. 257) in Pawtucket, and at the site of the former **Crescent Park** (401-433-2828) in East Providence. In Providence, **Roger Williams Park** (401-785-3510) has a zoo. For young students of Native American culture, the **Haffenreffer Museum of Anthropology** (401-253-8388) in Bristol is an attraction, and in Jamestown at the **Watson Farm** (401-423-0005) there are horses, chickens,

Jin McElholm/South County Tourism

and sheep as well as the recently restored **Windmill** (401-423-1798).

CLAM CAKES A Rhode Island phenomenon, the clam cake, or fritter, is an irregular sphere of dough containing bits of clam or, more properly, quahog meat, along with salt and pepper. The cakes are fried so that they are crispy brown on the outside and soft and chewy within. Clam cakes, sold by the dozen or half dozen, are synonymous with summer hereabouts and often served as a complement to chowder, also made from the meat of the quahog.

CLIMATE Narragansett Bay and the Atlantic Ocean play a major role in the climate of the state. During winter the proximity of the water quickly changes many snowstorms to rain, and many hot summer days are cooled by ocean and bay breezes. Extreme temperatures are infrequent in either summer or winter: In January the average temperature is 30 degrees; in July, 72 degrees. Temperatures generally exceed 90 degrees only 2 or 3 days a year.

CRUISES With the water playing such a prominent part in the state,

cruises abound. Among them are **La Gondola** (401-421-8877) in Providence, offering river gondola trips; and **Bay Queen Cruises** (245-1350) in Warren, offering sightseeing, dinner dances, and theme cruises to such special events as Bristol's Fourth of July Parade. The *Viking Queen* (401-847-6921), *Spirit of Newport* (401-849-3575), and **Sight Sailing of Newport** (401-849-3333) all provide narrated tours of Newport's historic harbor during summer. The **Galilee Cruises** (401-783-2954) vessel *Southland* takes 45-minute narrated tours around Galilee, Jerusalem, and Point Judith, while the *Blackstone Valley Explorer* (401-724-1500; 1-800-619-BOAT) cruises the Blackstone River. A complete listing of excursion and sightseeing boats is contained in *Boating and Fishing*, published annually by the **Rhode Island Department of Economic Development,** Rhode Island Tourism Division (401-222-2601; 1-800-556-2484).

EVENTS Major events in the state are listed at the end of each chapter, but seasonal-events booklets are published by the **Rhode Island Tourism Division** (401-222-2601; 1-800-556-2484). Events are also listed in each year's *Rhode Island Visitor's Guide*, available from the Tourism Division. (Also see *Newspapers.*)

FALL FOLIAGE For much of September and October the Blackstone River Valley and the western part of the state are ablaze with color. This is one of the most popular seasons for a boat trip on the *Blackstone Valley Explorer* (401-724-1500; 1-800-619-BOAT).

Kim Grant

Kim Grant

Company (401-783-4613; 1-860-442-7891; 1-860-442-9553) has ferries year-round sailing between Galilee and Block Island and in summer linking Providence, Newport, and New London with Block Island. The **Block Island Hi-Speed Ferry** cuts sailing time between Galilee and Block Island to about 30 minutes (1-877-733-9425). Ferry service (401-253-9808) also links Bristol with Prudence and Hog Islands in Narragansett Bay.

FISHING Fish are plentiful in Rhode Island waters and streams where largemouth bass, northern pike, crappies, trout, and landlocked salmon are stocked. Coastal waters abound with striped bass, bluefish, tuna, and sharks. For freshwater fishing, licenses are required of everyone between 16 and 65. A 3-day resident tourist license is a bargain for short-term visitors. For a complete set of rules and regulations pertaining to freshwater fishing, contact the Division of Licensing of the Department of Environmental Management (401-789-3094; 401-277-3075). No license is required for saltwater fishing unless there are plans to sell the catch. Freshwater

FARMER'S MARKETS Farmers offer their produce for sale not only at roadside stands but also at seasonal markets such as the **Newport Farmer's Market** on Dr. Marcus Wheatland Boulevard, behind the Salvation Café at 140 Broadway on Sunday 9–1; the **South Kingstown Farmer's Market** on Flagg Road at the University of Rhode Island in Kingston on Saturday morning; the **Westerly-Pawcatuck Farmer's Market** in the post office parking lot in Westerly on Wednesday until 2 PM; and the **Block Island Farmer's Market** at Manisses Corner on Block Island on Wednesday morning and at Negus Park on Saturday morning. For further information, call or write the **Rhode Island Division of Agriculture** (401-222-2781), 235 Promenade Street, Providence 02903.

FERRIES The **Rhode Island Public Transportation Authority** (RIPTA) runs a convenient ferry in summer (May through October) between Providence and Newport (401-453-6800). The trip down the bay takes about an hour and costs $6 each way. The **Interstate Navigation**

licenses can be obtained at 235 Promenade Street, Providence 02908 (401-222-3576).

FLORAL EVENTS Spring comes busting out in February when the **Rhode Island Spring Flower and Garden Show** opens at the Rhode Island Convention Center (401-458-6000; 1-800-858-5852) on Sabin Street in Providence. The **Spring Flower Show** comes to Roger Williams Park in Providence April 1–15. From mid-April to mid-May thousands of crocuses, daffodils, and tulips edge the wooded paths at Blithewold Gardens in Bristol for the annual **Spring Bulb Display.** During **Daffodil Week** more than 50,000 daffodils bloom at Blithewold, making it one of the largest daffodil displays in New England. In mid-May find the **Arbutus Garden Annual Plant Sale** at the South Kingstown American Legion Hall in Wakefield. The annual plant sale on Water Street on Block Island is also held in mid-May. In early June a highlight is Newport's **Secret Gardens Tour;** Block Island offers its **Garden Tour** in July. The Indian Run Garden Club presents **Herb Garden Day** in midsummer and an **Herbal Wreath Day** in mid-September, both held at the South County Museum in Narragansett. Also in September see the **Dahlia Society Flower Show** at the Cold Spring House in Wickford, while in November the annual **Mum Show** comes to Roger Williams Park in Providence.

GENEALOGY Although the historical societies of most Rhode Island towns have genealogical records that are open to the public, the best place to begin a quest for genealogical infor-

mation is at the **Rhode Island Historical Society Library** (401-331-8575) in Providence.

GOLF A list of public golf courses, including addresses, telephone numbers, and facilities, is contained in the **Rhode Island Tourism Division's** *Rhode Island Visitor's Guide* (401-222-2601; 1-800-556-2484).

HISTORIC HOUSES The **Rhode Island Tourism Division** (401-222-2601; 1-800-556-2484) provides some information on historic houses in its *Rhode Island Visitor's Guide.* Town historical societies and the **Rhode Island Historical Preservation Commission** (401-222-2678) in Providence are other good sources.

HORSEBACK RIDING **Newport Equestrian Center** (401-848-5440) in Middletown, and **Sandy Point Stables** (401-849-3958) offer riding on Aquidneck Island. The Sakonnet area has **Roseland Farms** (401-624-8866) in rural Tiverton. In West Greenwich there is year-round trail riding at **Stepping Stone Ranch** (401-397-3725).

HOTELS/MOTELS In this guide hotels and motels are listed only in the large cities where they are the principal accommodation and there is little else to offer. Most listings are B&Bs and small, attractive New England inns.

HUNTING Rhode Island offers plenty of opportunity for hunters, with seasons for small game, deer, and waterfowl. Special hunting licenses are required and there are various restrictions, including type of firearms permitted and use of reflective clothing (either 200 or 500 square inches of fluorescent orange, depending on the season). In addition, certain towns have their own ordinances governing hunting. Licenses are available at local town halls and certain authorized agents (Kmart, for example). For more information, contact the Division of Licensing of the **Department of Environmental Management** (401-222-3576), 235 Promenade Street, Providence 02908. Further information is available from the **State Division of Fish and Wildlife** (401-789-3094) in Wakefield.

INFORMATION The **Rhode Island Tourism Division** (401-222-2601; 1-800-556-2484), 7 Jackson Walkway, Providence 02903, publishes an annual *Rhode Island Visitor's Guide.* It also offers publications on boating and fishing, camping, and special events. At the southern approach to the state on I-95 between exits 2 and 3 in Richmond, the **Rhode Island Welcome Center** (401-539-3031) offers assistance to visitors. There are also regional tourism organizations: the **Blackstone Valley Tourism Council** (401-724-2200), 175 Main Street, Pawtucket; the **Providence-Warwick Convention & Visitors Bureau** (401-274-1636; 1-800-233-1636), 1 West Exchange Street, Providence 02903; the **Newport Visitor's Center** (401-849-8048; 1-800-326-6030), 23 America's Cup Avenue, Newport 02840; the **South County Tourism Council** (401-789-4422; 1-800-548-4662), 4808 Tower Hill Road (in the Oliver Stedman Government Center), Wakefield 02879; and the **Warwick Tourism Office** (401-738-2000, ext. 6402; 1-800-492-7942), Warwick City Hall, 3275 Post Road, Warwick 02907.

INNS There are many country inns and bed & breakfasts in Rhode Island. A list of these accommodations, as well as hotels, is included in the **Rhode Island Tourism Division**'s *Rhode Island Visitor's Guide,* available by calling 401-222-2601 or 1-800-556-2484. (Also see *Bed & Breakfasts.*)

INTERSTATES Rhode Island is served by I-95 from Westerly to Pawtucket; I-295 from Warwick around Providence to Attleboro, Massachusetts; and I-195 from Seekonk, Massachusetts, to Providence.

ISLANDS **Block Island** is the most populous and popular of the state's offshore islands, and it remains truly cut off from the mainland. (Aquidneck, site of Portsmouth, Middletown, and Newport, and the island of Conanicut are linked to the mainland by bridges.) Block Island is served by ferry from Galilee year-round and from Newport and New London, Connecticut, and Montauk, New York, in summer. **Prudence** and **Hog Islands** have summer ferry service from Bristol, but—except for the National Marine Estuarine Reserve on the northern part of Prudence—these islands are largely of interest only to their own small summer populations. **Patience Island** also has an Estuarine Reserve, but it is accessible only by private boat.

JONNY CAKES (OR JONNYCAKES) The recipe for these flat cornmeal cakes was originally based on white flint corn, which grows almost exclusively in the acid, salt-tinged soil of Rhode Island. (These days midwestern white dent corn is usually substituted.) Called "journey cakes" by early settlers—who stuffed them in their pockets or saddlebags for sustenance on long treks—jonny cakes are now served warm, often with a coating of maple syrup. According to the Society for the Propagation of the Jonnycake (yes, there is one), there are two versions: The West Bay/South County cake, formed thick, is made with scalding water; the East Bay/Newport preference is for a thinner, crêpelike cake made with cold milk. The cakes are served at area restaurants and at May Breakfasts (in honor of Rhode Island Independence Day) at halls around the state.

LAKES Beside the spectacular Narragansett Bay, Rhode Island's lakes are bound to pale, but there are several that are popular with anglers, many that are enjoyed by boaters, and the largest inland body of water in the state—the **Scituate Reservoir**—is loved simply for its beauty. Among the larger of the state's lakes (though they are sometimes called ponds, their size notwithstanding) are **Worden's Pond** in South Kingstown, **Watchaug Pond** in Charlestown, **Wallum Lake** in Pascoag, **Tiogue Lake** and **Johnson's Pond** in Coventry, **Olney Pond** in Lincoln, **Lake Washington** in Glocester, and **Echo Lake** in Burrillville.

LIGHTHOUSES Twelve working lighthouses blink along the 400 miles of Rhode Island coastline, warning mariners of shoals and rocks and marking harbor entrances. For the most part they are not open to the public except by special request, but two—**Watch Hill** and Block Island's **North Light**—have museums of lighthouse history. **Southeast Light**

on Block Island has a museum as well. At **Castle Hill** in Newport the Coast Guard station is open to the public by request. The other Rhode Island lighthouses are **Beavertail,** off Jamestown, and facilities at Hog Island, Point Judith, Conimicut, Sakonnet, Warwick, Sandy Point, and Goat Island.

LITTER Rhode Island has a fine of up to $500 for littering.

MUSEUMS Providence, in particular, is rich in museums and libraries with special exhibits on permanent display. Most notable among them are the **Museum of Art, Rhode Island School of Design** (401-454-6500); the **John Hay Library** (401-863-2146), the **Annmary Brown Memorial** (401-863-2429), and the **John Carter Brown Library** (401-863-2725) at Brown University; the **John Brown House** (401-331-8575); the **Governor Henry Lippitt House Museum** (401-453-0688); the **Johnson & Wales Culinary Archives & Museum** (401-598-2805); the **Museum of Rhode Island History** (401-331-8575) at Aldrich House; the **Rhode Island Black Heritage Society** (401-751-3490); and **Roger Williams Park Museum of Natural History** (401-785-9450).

Other major museums include the **Haffenreffer Museum of Anthropology** (401-253-8388) and the **Herreshoff Marine Museum** (401-253-5000) in Bristol; the **South County Museum** (401-783-5400) in Narragansett; the **Newport Art Museum** (401-848-8200), the **Newport Historical Society Museum** (401-846-0813), the **Redwood Library and Atheneum**

(401-847-0292), the **International Tennis Hall of Fame** (401-849-3990), and the **Museum of Yachting** (401-847-1018) in Newport; and the **Providence Children's Museum** (401-331-6588) and the **Slater Mill Historic Site** (401-725-8638) in Pawtucket. The U.S. Naval War College (401-841-4052), part of the Naval Education Training Center in Newport, maintains an excellent **Naval War College Museum,** with many exhibits on the "art and science" of naval warfare, as well as local sea-faring history.

MUSIC SERIES, SUMMER The **Newport Music Festival,** founded in 1969, presents some of the world's finest chamber musicians and introduces important new musical talent each July. More than 50 concerts are held over the course of 2 weeks in Newport's historic mansions. The **JVC Jazz Festival Newport** and the **Newport Folk Festival** are annual outdoor events at Fort Adams State Park in August. The Folk Festival brings such talents as Joan Baez and Arlo Guthrie. The University of Rhode Island in Kingston holds the

Michele Rajotte

Summer Chamber Music Festival in June and July. In July and August there are **Carousel Bayside Concerts** outdoors at Carousel Bayside Park in East Providence, **Summer-Concerts-by-the-Bay** at Blithewold Mansion and Gardens in Bristol, and the 113-year-old **Lafayette Band** plays pop music at both indoor and outdoor concerts in North Kingstown. These are among the summer events listed in the events calendar of the **Rhode Island Tourism Division's** *Rhode Island Visitor's Guide* (401-222-2601; 1-800-556-2484). (Also see *Special Events* listed at the end of each chapter.)

NATURE PRESERVES, COASTAL **Block Island's Scenic Natural Areas** in New Shoreham encompass 175 acres in different locales, offering various activities such as hiking and historical and nature programs. **East Beach/Ninigret Conservation Area** in Charlestown covers 174 acres. Activities include swimming, naturalist programs, fishing and shellfishing, hunting (rabbits, waterfowl), and camping. **Narragansett Bay National Estuarine Research Reserve** in Portsmouth preserves thousands of acres on Hope, Patience, and Prudence Islands. Hope Island is closed during spring and fall because of nesting birds. Naturalist programs are offered in summer at the north and south ends of Prudence, which is accessible by public ferry from Bristol. There is no public transportation to either Patience or Hope. **Norman Bird Sanctuary** in Middletown contains 450 acres; hiking, bird-watching, and naturalist programs are popular activities there. Other nature preserves that are ideal for hiking and birding include **Emilie**

Kim Grant

Ruecker Wildlife Refuge in Tiverton; **Sachuest Point National Wildlife Refuge** in Middletown, with 242 acres of salt marsh, beaches, and grasslands; and the 641-acre **Trustom Pond National Wildlife Refuge** in South Kingstown.

NATURE PRESERVES, INLAND
Fisherville Brook Wildlife Refuge in Exeter contains 70 acres. Hiking is popular here, with wooded trails to a pond with a waterfall. **Great Swamp Wildlife Management Area** in South Kingstown preserves 3,293 acres for hiking, fishing, and hunting. Hikers enjoy 550 acres at **Parker Woodland** in Coventry, and **Powder Mill Ledges Refuge** in Smithfield, headquarters of the Audubon Society of Rhode Island, is open to the public daily for hiking through field and forest. The second largest natural pond in Rhode Island is at **Kimball Wildlife Refuge** in Charlestown.

NEWSPAPERS The *Providence Journal* is the statewide newspaper,

although many communities have their own dailies and/or weeklies. The free *Providence Phoenix,* a cousin of the *Boston Phoenix,* is for the younger crowd and an excellent source of entertainment (concerts, bar bands, literary events) listings.

OBSERVATORIES **Frosty Drew** (401-364-9508), Ninigret Park, off RI 1A, Charlestown. Open on clear Friday nights, year-round. **Ladd Observatory** (401-863-2323), 210 Doyle Avenue, corner of Hope Street in Providence. Open 1 or 2 nights weekly for viewing. Located on the highest point in Providence and with a powerful refractor telescope, Ladd Observatory, which is affiliated with Brown University, is an excellent facility for viewing planets. **Seagrave Observatory** (401-726-1328), 47 Peep Toad Road, North Scituate, off RI 116. Open Saturday 7–10 PM year-round. All observatories are free.

PARKS AND FORESTS Rhode Island has a number of state parks open to the public for hiking, swimming, boating, fishing, picnicking, and skating. Many offer naturalist and recreational programs. Hunting is possible at **Arcadia Management Area** in West Greenwich, Exeter, and Hopkinton, which also provides forestry demonstrations. **Goddard Memorial State Park** in Warwick contains 472 acres, and saltwater fishing is among the activities available there. Other state parks include: **Beavertail State Park** in Jamestown, 153 acres; **Brenton Point State Park** in Newport, 89 acres; **Burlingame State Park** in Charlestown, 2,100 wooded acres; **Colt State Park** in Bristol, 466 acres; and **Lincoln Woods State Park** in Lincoln, 627 acres.

POPULATION According to the latest census information, Rhode Island's population stands at just under 1 million, down slightly from the 1990 census but considerably more than in 1790, when 68,825 souls were counted. Rhode Island is the country's smallest and most densely populated state, with 900 people per square mile. Because most of the population is centered on Providence, however, the state seems predominantly rural.

QUAHOG The quahog is the official shellfish of Rhode Island. This large, hard-shell clam (pronounced *co-hog*) is used in chowder, or mixed with bread, spices, and sometimes chourico, the Portuguese sausage, to make stuffed clams, or "stuffies" as they're known. Stuffies are available at clam shacks everywhere. An annual festival devoted to the quahog is held in Wickford in early October.

RATES, LODGING AND DINING Prices change frequently, and the value of your dollar will vary significantly from one part of the state to another (expect to pay more for a meal or a bed in Newport, for example). Dollar-sign symbols are provided throughout the guide to give you a general sense of what you can expect to pay. Please refer to "Explore with Us" on page 5. Such a rating method, though commonly used, is imprecise, and we always recommend calling ahead to check rates and reservations. We have highlighted inns and restaurants that offer unusual value with the symbol "🏅."

SAILING LESSONS Newport is the sailing center, and there are many sailing schools and programs to choose from: **Fort Adams Sailing Association** (401-849-8385) is a non-profit group offering lessons for juniors and adults; **J World Sailing School** (401-849-5492) provides cruising and racing instruction by the makers of J-boats; **Newport Sailing School** (401-848-2266) offers 2- and 3-day learn-to-sail programs; **Shake-a-Leg Sailing Center** (401-847-3630) has special 20-foot sloops equipped for the physically challenged.

SCENIC DRIVES With 400 miles of coastline and a rural interior, Rhode Island offers many scenic routes. Among those officially designated as scenic routes are **RI 1A,** which runs from Narragansett to Wickford along the coast; **RI 3,** leading from the coast in East Greenwich inland to Hope Valley; **RI 77,** following the Sakonnet River through Tiverton to Little Compton; and **RI 138,** which takes you over the Jamestown Bridge to the island of Conanicut.

SKIING, CROSS-COUNTRY Cross-country skiing can be found at **Goddard State Park** (401-884-0088) in Warwick; **Norman Bird Sanctuary** (401-846-2577) in Middletown; **Pulaski State Park** (401-568-2013) in Burrillville; and

Kim Grant

Slater Memorial Park (401-728-0500) in Pawtucket.

SKIING, DOWNHILL **Yawgoo Valley** (401-295-5366) in Exeter is the state's only remaining downhill ski area. It is quite small, with basic services.

SNOWMOBILING Many of the state parks allow snowmobiling: **Colt State Park** in Bristol; **Pulaski State Park** in Burrillville; **Burlingame State Park** in Charlestown; **Arcadia State Park** and **Beach Pond State Park** in Exeter; and **Lincoln Woods State Park** in Lincoln. For state parks information, call 401-277-2632.

STEAMERS These clams form the basis of the Rhode Island clamboil, or are just served steamed on a platter with clarified butter or clam broth (or both) for dipping. You'll get an occasional argument about exactly what a steamer is—small quahog, littleneck, cherrystone—but most natives agree that it is simply a small, soft-shell clam normally found in tidal flats. Littlenecks are, in fact, small quahogs (steamers have long necks), cherrystones larger (older) members of the family, followed by the largest quahogs, called "chowders."

TAXES Rhode Island has a sales tax of 7 percent, which does not apply to clothes, food, or drugs. Lodgers are subject to a state room tax of 12 percent.

THEATER, SUMMER As this book went to press, the future of Matunuck's **Theatre-by-the-Sea** was still uncertain.

THEATER, YEAR-ROUND The **Colonial Theatre** (401-596-0810) in Westerly serves up tried-and-true Broadway shows (*Evita, Fiddler on the Roof*) in a beautifully restored 19th-century church. The Tony Award–winning **Trinity Repertory Theater** (401-351-4242) in downtown Providence is widely regarded as one of the best regional theaters in the country. There is plenty of theater at area colleges, some of it quite good, and touring companies performing Broadway shows (*Phantom of the Opera, Les Misérables*) make regular stops at the **Providence Performing Arts Center** (401-421-2997). Smaller Providence theaters, presenting less mainstream, sometimes original works, include **Newgate Theatre** (401-454-0454), **Perishable Theatre** (401-331-2695), **Providence Black Repertory Company** (401-621-7122), and **Brown University Theater** (401-863-2838). Two popular dinner theaters are the **Newport Playhouse & Cabaret** (401-848-7529) and **Mill River Dinner Theater** (401-721-0909) in Central Falls. It's worth calling ahead for schedules and special performances if you know you'll be in the area.

TRAIN SERVICE **Amtrak** (1-800-USA-RAIL) makes stops at Westerly, Kingston, and Providence on its Boston–New York runs. The Kingston stop is convenient for those traveling to Newport or South County.

VINEYARDS **Sakonnet Vineyards** in Little Compton (401-635-8486) lets you sample some of its award-winning vintages during guided tours Wednesday through Sunday noon–4 in-season. **Newport Vineyards** (401-848-5161) operates a retail store in Middletown and also offers tours of its nearby vineyard. **Diamond Hill**

Vineyards (401-333-2751) offers tours in Cumberland.

WHALE-WATCHING The best whale-watching is out of Galilee in Narragansett. Contact either the **Frances Fleet** (401-783-4988; 1-800-662-2824) or **Seven B's** (401-789-9250).

WINDJAMMERS Newport is the premier port for windjammer-type sailing cruises. Boats 70 feet and longer make regular half-day, day, and evening sails: the *Adirondack* (401-848-5293; 401-846-1600), a 78-foot schooner departing from the Newport Yachting Center; the *Madeleine* (401-849-3033), a 70-foot schooner sailing four times a day from Bannister's Wharf; and **Windjammer Cruises of Newport** (401-848-5883; 1-800-490-7245).

YACHTING The popularity of yachting in Rhode Island is well known—the America's Cup was traditionally held in Newport until the American loss in 1983. In addition to weekly local and statewide events, Newport, in particular, plays host to a number of national and international regattas and ocean races, including the annual **National Offshore One-Design (N.O.O.D.) Regatta,** the biennial **Rolex International Women's Keelboat Championship,** the **Annapolis to Newport Race,** the biennial **Newport to Bermuda Race,** and the **Classic Yacht Regatta.** For information, call Sail Newport (401-846-1983). Not surprisingly, Rhode Island has several excellent museums devoted to yachting, including the **Museum of Yachting** in Newport (401-847-1018) and the **Herreshoff Marine Museum** in Bristol (401-253-5000), both well worth visiting.

ZOO **Roger Williams Park Zoo** (401-785-3510), 950 Elmwood Avenue, off US 195 in Providence, is the only zoo in Rhode Island. A serious attempt is made to create natural habitats for its various critters, including the most popular attraction, the polar bears.

Kim Grant

Providence

Kim Grant

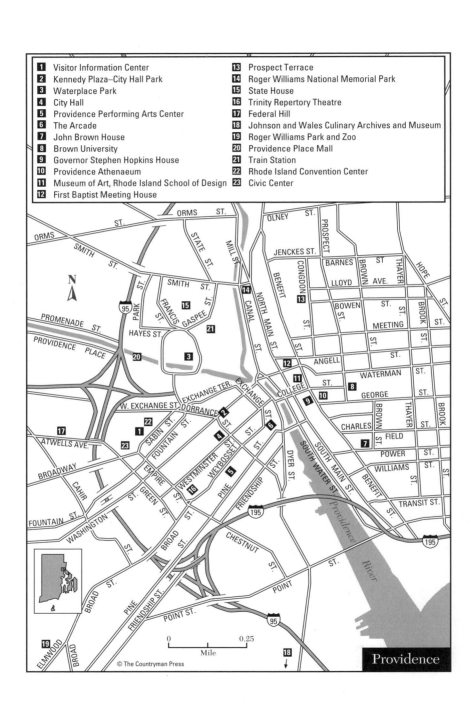

1 Visitor Information Center
2 Kennedy Plaza–City Hall Park
3 Waterplace Park
4 City Hall
5 Providence Performing Arts Center
6 The Arcade
7 John Brown House
8 Brown University
9 Governor Stephen Hopkins House
10 Providence Athenaeum
11 Museum of Art, Rhode Island School of Design
12 First Baptist Meeting House
13 Prospect Terrace
14 Roger Williams National Memorial Park
15 State House
16 Trinity Repertory Theatre
17 Federal Hill
18 Johnson and Wales Culinary Archives and Museum
19 Roger Williams Park and Zoo
20 Providence Place Mall
21 Train Station
22 Rhode Island Convention Center
23 Civic Center

N

0   0.25
Mile
© The Countryman Press

Providence

PROVIDENCE

It was January 1636, and colonial officials of the Puritan Massachusetts Bay Colony were eager to be rid of the reformer-clergyman Roger Williams. He believed in the separation of church and state and loudly criticized civil authorities of the colony, who were decreeing punishments for infractions of church rules. Williams associated enthusiastically with the Native Americans most colonists feared and, indeed, he insisted that the king of England had no right to give away Native American lands. When a vessel was readying for departure to England, the officials made secret arrangements to deport the independent-spirited clergyman. But word of the plot reached Williams just before the vessel was to sail, and with only one companion, Thomas Angell, he fled.

That winter was stormy, and snows were heavy. For 14 weeks the two refugees wandered the woods, seeking a place outside the Massachusetts Bay Colony to settle.

As spring came, their wandering brought them to the banks of the Seekonk River. The land bordering the river looked fertile, and the men felt sure that they were outside Massachusetts's jurisdiction. The Native Americans they met seemed friendly. As the two men prepared to settle down, they sent word back to their Massachusetts Bay friends that they would welcome any who chose to join them. More refugees began to arrive. Building was under way when suddenly a warning came from the governor of the Plymouth Bay Colony: Williams's site, which today is East Providence, was on Plymouth lands, and Williams's presence would not be tolerated.

Grimly, the settlers packed up their belongings, piled them into their one canoe, and launched it on the river, heading toward what they hoped would be friendlier territory on the opposite shore. Fortunately for the settlers, it belonged to the Narragansett chief Canonicus. Williams had known Canonicus during the time he had spent in Plymouth, and the chief made Williams and his companions welcome.

The settlers wasted no time in clearing the land, which the clergyman named Providence in gratitude for God's providence to him in his distress, and which, Williams declared, would ever afterward be a place of refuge for the oppressed.

By 1675 there were 1,000 residents and some 75 houses. More than two dozen of these were burned to the ground in a Native American attack in 1676, but, determinedly, the settlers rebuilt. In 1680 a wharf was added to facilitate trade, and Providence's days of prosperity began.

Today, with a population of 173,000, Providence is the capital of Rhode Island and New England's second largest city, after Boston. Like so many other New England cities, its downtown suffered noticeably in the era of the suburban mall. In recent years, however, the heart of the city has undergone a near-miraculous renewal.

A walkway has been built along the Providence River. There, on and off in summer and early fall, 97 ritual fires glow in midstream at night, and exotic otherworldly music—sometimes chants, sometimes folk music, sometimes the music of nature—plays, attracting thousands. Gondolas and canoes can be rented for a closer view of the WaterFire spectacle.

Here and there along the river, illustrated signs recount the colorful history of the city. Bright banners mark important sites on a self-guided walking tour. Carriage rides show off downtown architecture. New restaurants and cafés have been springing up along the riverfront area.

Since its construction a decade ago, the convention center has been attracting boat, garden, home, car, and pet shows, among others. Pop concerts, sporting events, and the Ringling Bros. and Barnum & Bailey Circus fill the Dunkin' Donuts Civic Center with viewers year-round.

The state's largest mall—with 150 retail stores including Filene's and Nordstrom's, an IMAX theater, and seven full-service restaurants—now sits below the

THE CRAWFORD STREET BRIDGE CROSSES THE PROVIDENCE RIVER IN THE REVITALIZED DOWNTOWN AREA.

Kim Grant

State House. A stunning view of the city's historic College Hill is offered through one side of the mall's glass atrium.

Meanwhile, in old Providence, Benefit Street is considered by many to have the richest concentration of fine 18th- and 19th-century architecture in America. All along the streets of the city's East Side, tall brick and clapboard mansions proclaim the wealth that the shipping trade brought to the city during those centuries. When the British occupied Newport in Revolutionary War days, many a Newport merchant fled to Providence with his money and goods to establish himself in trade there. Foremost among these was James Brown, who established a distillery and a slaughterhouse and entered the shipping trade and whose sons, John, Nicholas, Joseph, and Moses, brought wealth and fame to the city.

John, merchant and shipbuilder, opened trade with China. Joseph became an architect and built many of the city's most handsome edifices. Nicholas provided land and money to establish the university that bears the family's name. Moses gave land for the establishment of a Quaker school and helped William Slater introduce the first water-powered cotton mill in the nation in neighboring Pawtucket.

GUIDANCE Rhode Island Tourism Division (401-222-2601; 1-800-556-2484), 1 West Exchange Street on the fourth floor of the Westin Hotel. Open Monday through Friday 8:30–4. This central tourist office has booklets and brochures about travel in all parts of the state, including the capital. Parking is limited.

Roger Williams National Memorial Park (401-521-7266), North Main and Smith Streets. Open daily 9–4:30 except major holidays. An interpretation of the life and times of Roger Williams and the city he founded is offered through exhibits, slides, booklets, and brochures and by National Park Service guides. There is parking.

Providence-Warwick Visitor Information Center (401-274-1636; 1-800-233-1636), Rhode Island Convention Center, 1 Sabin Street. In the rotunda on the ground floor. Open Monday through Saturday 9–5. Booklets and brochures about the city area are available at this staffed facility. Parking is limited.

GETTING THERE *By car:* The major roads into the city are I-95 north and south, I-195 east and west, RI 146 north and south, RI 10 north and south, US 1 north and south, US 44 east and west, and US 6 east and west.

By air: **Theodore Francis Green State Airport** (401-737-4000) is located 7 miles south of Providence in Warwick and is served by major airlines.

By rail: **Amtrak** (401-727-7380; 1-800-USA-RAIL) links Boston and New York through Providence, and at peak commuter times there is **MBTA** (617-727-3200) commuter rail service with Boston as well. All trains use the station at 100 Gaspee Street.

By bus: **Bonanza** (401-751-8800), 1 Bonanza Way. **Greyhound** (401-454-0790; 1-800-231-2222), 1 Kennedy Plaza. Bonanza's terminal is on the outskirts of the city, and a 10-minute shuttle bus links it with downtown.

MEDICAL EMERGENCY The statewide emergency number is **911**.

The Miriam Hospital (401-331-8500), 164 Summit Avenue. **Rhode Island Hospital** (401-444-4000), 593 Eddy Street. **Roger Williams Medical Center** (401-456-2000), 825 Chalkstone Avenue. **St. Joseph Hospital** (401-456-3000), 200 High Service Avenue, North Providence. **Women & Infants Hospital** (401-274-1100), 101 Dudley Street.

✳ To See

MUSEUMS **Aldrich House** (401-331-8575), 110 Benevolent Street. Open Tuesday through Friday 9–5. Designed in 1825 by Rhode Island architect John Holden Greene, this balustraded, hip-roofed house became the home in 1902 of U.S. Senator Nelson Aldrich, Rhode Island's most prominent politician in the early years of the 20th century. His daughter Abby became the wife of John D. Rockefeller Jr. and was a prominent patron of the arts. (Her folk art collection is a major attraction of Williamsburg, Virginia.) Aldrich House now displays the watercolor portrait citations of Rhode Island Hall of Famers such as entertainers Nelson Eddy and George M. Cohan, Narragansett princess Redwing, and painter Gilbert Stuart.

Johnson & Wales Culinary Archives and Museum (401-598-2805), 315 Harborside Boulevard. Open Monday through Saturday 9–5, with the last guided tour at 4. Call for driving directions. There are half a million items of interest in this little museum, the world's largest culinary collection. On display are cooking utensils from the third millennium BC to the present; favorite recipes of American presidents; presidential china; letters of potentates, writers, artists, and composers on culinary matters; hotel and restaurant silver through the centuries; and pictures of the world's great chefs.

⚘ **Providence Children's Museum** (401-273-5437), 100 South Street. Open Tuesday through Sunday 9–5. Admission is free the first Sunday and the third Friday of each month. This is a hands-on museum for children 2 to 11 years old, with emphasis on both fun and learning. Young visitors can create their own plays with puppets, props, and costumes; pretend to cook in a 1640 kitchen; sit on a giant's lap; and climb through sewer pipes and a manhole to discover life under the city's streets.

Rhode Island Black Heritage Society (401-751-3490), second floor, Arcade Building, 65 Weybosset Street. Open Monday through Friday 10–3 and by appointment. A museum of 19th-century black life in Providence.

The RISD Museum (Museum of Art, Rhode Island School of Design) (401-454-6500), 224 Benefit Street. Open Tuesday through Sunday 10–5; until 9 the third Thursday of each month. Free admission on Sunday and the last Saturday of each month. Sometimes referred to as "the jewel box of Providence," the RISD (*Riz-dee*, as it's known colloquially throughout the state) Museum is exceptionally rich in Newport silver and cabinetwork, French impressionist painting, and ancient Egyptian and Asian art. There is also a modern wing. The adjoining Pendleton House was built in the Georgian style, according to the stipulations of lawyer-collector Charles Pendleton as a condition for housing his collection there. The collection includes Chinese export ware, English and European porcelain and glassware, rugs, and antique furniture.

LIBRARIES John Carter Brown Library (401-863-2725), Brown University campus, corner of George and Brown Streets. Open Monday through Friday 8:30–5, Saturday 9–noon. The first printed accounts of Columbus's arrival in the New World are among the library's collection of 40,000 books and pamphlets describing the development of the New World.

John Hay Library (401-863-2146), Prospect and College Streets. Open Monday through Friday 9–5. Brown University's special collections are kept here. Among them is the third largest collection of Lincoln material in the world (after those at the Illinois Historical Society and the Lincoln National Life Insurance Company of Fort Wayne, Indiana), including some 900 Lincoln manuscripts. Also among the library's treasures are more than 400,000 pieces of American sheet music, thousands of miniature soldiers (including a 20th-century Indian army with elephants, and 1930s Nazi motorcyclists), and letters written by Rhode Island Gothic writer H. P. Lovecraft, who stalked Benefit Street in the dark for inspiration for his eerie stories.

Library of Rhode Island History (401-331-8575), 121 Hope Street. Open Tuesday through Friday 9–5, Saturday 9–4:45. The second largest genealogical collection in New England (after Boston), it includes such materials as birth, death, and marriage records from 1636 to 1850 and 1853 to 1900; maps; census records; books; and historical documents.

Providence Athenaeum (401-421-6970), 251 Benefit Street. Open Monday through Thursday 9–7, Friday and Saturday 9–5; also winter Sundays 1–5 and summer Saturdays 9–1. This 1850 Doric Greek granite building houses one of the oldest libraries in the nation—it began as a subscription library in 1851. Among its treasures is an 1801 ivory miniature by Newport native Edward Malbone that is generally considered the most valuable miniature in the United States. It is in the alcoves here that Edgar Allan Poe courted a fellow poet, the widow Sarah Helen Whitman. The couple met when Poe came to Providence to lecture at Brown University. It's said that Mrs. Whitman was his inspiration for "To Helen" and "Annabel Lee." They became engaged, but the engagement was broken because of Poe's penchant for drink. Broken engagement notwithstanding, she remained the poet's staunch supporter, writing a notable defense of him. Next to the library, the five brick houses of Athenaeum Row, from 257 to 276 Benefit Street, are of some interest. Built in 1845, they are among the city's first row houses.

HISTORIC HOMES AND SITES The Arcade, 65 Weybosset Street. In 1850 *Guyot's Geography* listed this shopping arcade as one of the Seven Wonders of the United States. Much overhauled and refurbished since then, it is today filled with attractive boutiques, small businesses, and fast-food restaurants. Architecturally, the Arcade remains a memorable building. In 1827 Providence banker and investor Cyrus Butler conceived the idea of a covered shopping arcade with colonnaded facades that would recall l'Église de la Madeleine in Paris. Wealthy man though he was, Butler faced problems with its construction. Although he owned half the land on which the proposed arcade was to be built, Benjamin and Charles Dyer owned the other half. They were interested in such a building, but they wanted a say in its design. Butler hired architect Russell Warren to design his half, and the Dyers hired James C. Bucklin to design theirs. Fortunately both architects admired Greek Revival, so there was no altercation—until it came to the facade. Bucklin wanted a series of stone panels to decorate the pediment; Warren favored a simple triangle. The problem was solved by placing Warren's pediment on the Westminster Street end and Bucklin's panels on the Weybosset Street end. They agreed on 22-foot-tall granite monoliths to support the pediments on both sides. At the time of construction, these 12- to 15-ton pillars were the largest monoliths in the country. Hauling them from the quarry in Johnston, Rhode Island, required 12 to 18 oxen. In addition to the pillars, architectural high points of the Arcade are the ironwork on the upper stories of the three-tiered edifice and the cantilevered stairs between the street and the second floor.

Beneficent Congregational Meeting House (401-331-9844), 300 Weybosset Street. For years the large gilded dome of this church was a landmark on the Providence skyline. Built in 1809, its dome is unusual for a Congregational church of its day. It was the choice of the congregation's second pastor, the Reverend James Wilson, who came to Providence from Ireland in 1791. Classical Revival was popular in Dublin at that time, and to some extent the church imitates the Customs House in Dublin. In 1836 architect James C. Bucklin supervised renovations.

THE ARCADE, WITH ITS GRANITE PILLARS, CANTILEVERED STAIRS, AND FANCY IRONWORK, IS A UNIQUE SHOPPING AND SNACKING CENTER.

ANGELL STREET BY THOMAS H. COCROFT

© Thomas H. Cocroft/Collection of Madeleine Standish

John Brown House (401-331-8575), 52 Power Street (at the corner of Benefit Street). Open March through December, Tuesday through Saturday 10–5, Sunday noon–4; in January and February, Saturday and Sunday only. Admission fee. Joseph Brown designed this three-story brick house with brownstone trim for his shipowner brother, John, but died before it was completed in 1788. John Quincy Adams called it "the most magnificent and elegant private house I have seen on this continent." At the time of its construction, it had an uninterrupted view of the harbor below and John Brown's vessels arriving from the Orient laden with tea, silk, and china. Brown's fortuitous decision to trade in the Orient came as a result of failures in the slave trade. After one vessel carrying slaves was lost and half the slaves on a second died of scurvy, Brown's abolitionist Quaker mates encouraged him to substitute canisters of tea and bolts of silk for human cargo. Before long, Brown was the city's wealthiest merchant.

George Washington was among the guests here, for Brown was devoted to the rebel cause, providing ships from his shipyard and cannon from the family

Kim Grant

THE HILLTOP CAMPUS OF BROWN UNIVERSITY ABOVE THE CITY OF PROVIDENCE.

foundry for the Revolutionary army. Furnishings include Hepplewhite, Sheraton, Townsend, and Goddard pieces. There is Chinese export ware, Sandwich glass, Staffordshire earthenware, and, in the coach house, a chariot made in Philadelphia in 1782 that is reputedly the earliest "fancy" vehicle made in America.

Brown University, Prospect and Waterman Streets. Turn right on Benevolent Street and left at the first corner to begin exploring this extensive campus. The privately owned redbrick **Candace Allen House,** where you turn, was built by Providence industrialist Zachariah Allen to soften the heartache his daughter suffered when her fiancé was killed in the War of 1812. **University Hall,** off Prospect Street, is the university's oldest building, constructed in 1770 when the college was moved from Warren. During the Revolution, University Hall became a barracks for the colonial troops and their French allies. The seventh oldest college in the nation, Brown was founded in 1764 and took its name, after its move to Providence, from Nicholas Brown, who gave it extensive funds and land.

General Ambrose Burnside House, 314 Benefit Street. When it was completed in 1867 for General Burnside (for whom sideburns were named), this privately owned, sprawling redbrick house with stone, wood, and cast-iron trim, plus a curved corner and a wraparound porch, was lauded as one of the finest modern houses in Providence. At the time of its construction, Burnside, just back from the Civil War, had been elected governor of Rhode Island. Later he became a U.S. senator.

Edward Carrington House, 66 Williams Street. This three-story Federal-style brick mansion was built as a two-story house in 1810 by John Corliss. Edward Carrington, one of the city's wealthiest merchants and American consul in China from 1808 to 1811, purchased it and added the third story and the richly decorated entrance porch. The house is considered one of the city's great architectural monuments, but it is not open to the public.

Cathedral of St. John (401-331-4662), 271 North Main Street. Under the inspiration of Charles Bulfinch, Providence architect John Holden Greene designed this white-and-brown 1810 cathedral, combining a basically Georgian-style structure with a Gothic Revival tower and Gothic decoration.

Captain Edward Dexter House, 72 Waterman Street. Built in 1799, this is one of the most elaborate Federal-style houses in the city. It was once the home of Charles Pendleton, and its original interior has been re-created at Pendleton House, adjoining the RISD Museum.

Sullivan Dorr House, 109 Benefit Street. This imposing house was built in 1810 for a China trade merchant. One of Providence's finest examples of Federal architecture, its facade is supposedly a copy of Alexander Pope's villa at Twickenham, England. It was Thomas Wilson Dorr, Sullivan's son, who instigated the Dorr Rebellion of 1842, seeking suffrage for all freemen, not only property owners. The house, now privately owned, is built on the lot that originally belonged to Roger Williams. He was first buried behind where the house stands, but his remains were later removed to the city's North Burial Ground and after that to Prospect Terrace.

East Providence. Both East Providence and the **Fox Point** section of Providence are largely Portuguese enclaves, with ethnic bakeries, other food shops, and—especially in East Providence—a number of Portuguese restaurants.

IN DOWNTOWN PROVIDENCE

Kim Grant

Federal Hill. The entrance to the Italian section of Providence, located on Federal Hill just above the heart of the city, is marked by a cement arch topped with a pinecone expressing hospitality. Restaurants, bakeries, cafés, and food shops line the main thoroughfare—Atwells Avenue—and many of its side streets. As in downtown Providence, the last dozen years have marked a revival on Federal Hill. New restaurants, boutiques, and upscale food markets now line the avenue, attracting a younger clientele from all over the city. At De Pasquale Square, once the place where older men of the neighborhood gathered around the fountain on sunny afternoons, there are now outdoor cafés and restaurants. As this book went to press, construction on a boutique hotel was under way. For the visitor

OUTSIDE THE RHODE ISLAND
SCHOOL OF DESIGN ON COLLEGE STREET

Kim Grant

interested in architecture, there are a number of large and interesting turn-of-the-century and early-20th-century structures on the Hill.

First Baptist Meeting House (401-454-3418), 75 North Main Street. This graceful, simple structure was designed by Joseph Brown and is topped with a steeple inspired by St. Martin's-in-the-Fields in London. This 1775 church succeeded two earlier ones that had been used for the Baptist worship introduced by Roger Williams in 1638. Ships' carpenters from Boston, out of work because Parliament had closed the port after the Boston Tea Party, constructed it. With their knowledge of masts and rigging, the builders knew to allow the steeple sufficient give; it swayed just enough not to topple in either the gale of 1815 or the hurricane of 1938. This was the first Baptist church in America and is the mother church for Baptists in this country. Notable in its pale gray interior barely touched with gold are the Ionic columns and the Waterford glass chandelier, first lit in 1792 for the wedding of the architect's niece, Hope. Guided tours are offered from June through the Columbus Day weekend, 10–noon and 1–3.

First Unitarian Church (401-421-4970), Benefit and Benevolent Streets. John Holden Greene, who built this tall stone church in 1816 to replace a two-towered wooden structure that had burned, considered it his masterpiece. Its steeple holds the largest bell ever struck in the Paul Revere and Sons Foundry.

Grace Church (401-331-3225), corner of Mathewson and Westminster Streets. This Victorian Gothic brownstone church was built in 1846. Designed by Richard Upjohn of New York, it is notable for its chimes.

Handicraft Club, 42 College Street. Banker and cotton merchant Thomas Beckwith commissioned John Holden Greene to build this Federal-style brick mansion in 1826, much to the horror of Beckwith's family, who felt that the site selected was much too "far out in the sticks" for respectable city people. Today it's open to club members and occasionally to the public.

Governor Stephen Hopkins House (401-331-2134), 15 Hopkins Street. Open April through November, Wednesday and Saturday 1–4, and by appointment. Stephen Hopkins, one of Rhode Island's two signers of the Declaration of Independence, lived in this house from 1742 to 1785. Long outspoken against royal oppression in the colonies, he reportedly said, his hand shaken by palsy as he prepared to sign the Declaration, "My hand trembles, but my heart does not." Hopkins was governor of the colony of Rhode Island 10 times, chief justice of the

Superior Court, and the first chancellor of Brown University. He is attributed with moving Brown (then Rhode Island College) from Warren, where it was founded.

Thomas Poynton Ives House, 66 Power Street. Built in 1805 for Thomas Poynton Ives and his wife, Hope Brown (for whose marriage the chandelier in the First Baptist Meeting House was first lit), this privately owned Federal house is similar in design to the John Brown House.

Governor Henry Lippitt House (401-453-0688), 199 Hope Street. Open May through October, Friday 11–3 or by appointment. From its construction in 1863 until 1981, this brownstone-trimmed brick Italianate dwelling remained in the Lippitt family. Henry Lippitt, for whom it was built, was Rhode Island's governor from 1876 to 1877. Its interior boasts the finest mid-19th-century Renaissance Revival decorations by local craftsmen in the city. Most notable is the marbleized center hall and the faux-bois ceilings and paneling in both the hall and the billiard room, as well as the stenciling. The house is furnished with Victorian antiques that largely belonged to the family.

Market House, Market Square. This square redbrick building with its fanlights is a design of Joseph Brown's. In 1771 when its construction began, it was carefully sited on a bank of the Providence River so that produce could be brought directly to and from it by ship. In the years immediately preceding the Revolution, this was a center of much intrigue, and in March 1775 tea was angrily burned nearby in response to the tea tax. A plaque marks the spot. Another plaque marks the height reached by the floodwaters of the terrible hurricane of 1938. From 1832 until 1878, this was the seat of Providence city government.

Nightingale-Brown House (401-272-0357; John Nicholas Brown Center for the Study of American Civilization), 357 Benefit Street. Open Thursday and Friday 1–4. One of the largest colonial frame houses in existence, this three-and-a-half-story clapboard home, half hidden behind a wall, was built for Providence merchant Colonel Joseph Nightingale in 1792. He died soon after its completion, and his widow sold it to Nicholas Brown, for whom Brown University, previously Rhode Island College, was named. (Legend has it that Nicholas Brown, on the board of Rhode Island College, and seeking funds for it, proposed that it be named for the donor of a substantial gift. He subsequently became that donor.) Until the 1980s the house remained the residence of succeeding generations of the Brown family. The last family member to occupy it was Anne Kinsolving Brown, widow of John Nicholas Brown, who, when he was born in 1900, was described by the *New York Post* as "the world's richest baby." In the 1930s, after the Lindbergh kidnapping and when John Nicholas's children were growing up, a curious cagelike structure was constructed on top of the house so that the children could play outdoors in safety. The ground-floor dining room, parlor, sitting room, and library, open to visitors, are furnished largely as they were in John Nicholas Brown's lifetime. The upper stories of the house contain Brown family archives and study rooms for scholars.

The Old Arsenal, 176 Benefit Street. James Bucklin designed this Gothic Revival, fortresslike stone structure in 1840 for the Providence Marine Corps of Artillery, the first volunteer artillery battery in the country.

The Old State House (401-222-2678), 150 Benefit Street. Open Monday through Friday 8:30–4:30. From 1762 until 1900 this was the meeting place of the General Assembly, where on May 4, 1776, the act was passed "constituting Rhode Island the first free and independent republic in America and asserting her absolute independence of England." Two months later the Declaration of Independence was signed in Philadelphia.

State House (401-222-2357), 90 Smith Street. Open Monday through Friday 8:30–4:30. The white marble dome of this imposing early-1900s capitol is said to be one of the largest unsupported domes in the world. The statehouse holds two notable works of art: in the Governor's Reception Room, a full-length portrait of George Washington painted by Saunderstown native Gilbert Stuart; and on the first floor, a portrait of Civil War general Ambrose Burnside by Emanuel Leutze, the artist noted for his painting *Washington Crossing the Delaware.* Also of interest is the original parchment charter granted by Charles II to the colony of Rhode Island in 1663, and the sword, epaulets, field desk, locket, and signets of Warwick-born Nathanael Greene, Washington's second-in-command.

South Main Street. Two fine old mansions along this street may be viewed from the outside: the Federal-style Benoni Cooke House at no. 110, with its side entrance, and the Joseph Brown House at no. 50, with its gracefully curved white pediment. A tale is told of how in the 18th century, when the entrance to the Brown House was on the second floor, an officer of the French army billeted there gaily rode his horse up the stairs and into the front hall. The horse refused to walk back down the stairs and had to be led out a direct exit into the garden.

South Water Street. Once the site of the Providence Steam Engine Company, a mid-19th-century complex of stone and brick buildings, today this area is filled with trendy restaurants, bars, galleries, and nightclubs. From many of them, and from walkways in front of them, there is an incomparable view of the river and cityscape.

Thomas Street. The redbrick Providence Art Club, built in 1791 for Seril Dodge, Providence's first jewelry maker, is at no. 11 on this steep little street. His brother Nehemiah, also a Providence jeweler, developed the gold-plating process that made Rhode Island a major jewelry center. The half-timbered Fleur-de-Lys Building at no. 7 was constructed as a studio for Rhode Island artist Sidney R. Burleigh in 1886. Much of the molded, painted, and carved exterior studio decoration is of his design and was executed by Burleigh and fellow artists. The building continues to house studios.

Wickenden Street. Boutiques, art galleries, coffee shops, ethnic restaurants, antiques and collectibles stores, all in old buildings—some restored and some not-so-restored—make this an attractive, lively street by day or night for young singles and couples.

Betsey Williams Cottage (401-785-9457), Roger Williams Park, near the Elmwood Avenue entrance. This little gambrel-roofed house, built in 1785, belonged to a descendant of Roger Williams who gave the first 100 acres for the establishment of the park. It is closed to the public.

BICYCLING ✔ **East Bay Bicycle Path** (401-253-7482). Starting in Providence near India Point Park, this bicycle path runs on reclaimed railroad lines and edges the shore of Narragansett Bay on much of its way to Bristol. More than 14 miles long, it has stopping places for snacks, two picnic areas (at Haines State Park in East Providence and Colt Park in Bristol), restrooms, and telephones along the route, which sometimes passes through towns, sometimes through untrammeled countryside.

BOAT EXCURSIONS ✔ **Newport Fast Ferry** (401-751-9400). Beginning in spring and continuing until the end of October, the Newport Fast Ferry leaves the Point Street Bridge for the 1.5-hour trip to Newport. Call for rates and schedules.

Capt. Joe Dempsey Water Taxi and Charter Service (401-458-BOAT). Forty-five-minute harbor tours aboard a 28-foot, 12-passenger motor launch leave Waterplace Park or the Hot Club dock on South Water Street from June through September. Call for reservations.

La Gondola (401-421-8877; 508-984-8264). Forty-minute excursions from May through October on the Woonasquatucket and Providence Rivers aboard 36-foot, six-person gondolas—one made in America from a 19th-century Venetian design, the other made in Venice. Both are decorated with hand-sculpted wooden carvings. Reservations suggested.

FOR FAMILIES ✔ **All Children's Theater** (401-435-5300), Vartan Gregorian School, 455 Wickenden Street. Performances by children, for children, through-out the school year.

✔ **The Banner Trail Trolley** (401-658-3400), 10 Nate Whipple Highway, Cumberland. Hour-long driver-narrated tours of the city's historic and cultural highlights leave from all downtown hotels Wednesday and Friday 9:30–3 from mid-May until the end of October. Passengers can leave the vehicle at any spot and then board a later trolley.

✔ **Charles I. D. Looff Carousel** (401-435-7518), Bullocks Point Avenue, Riverside, East Providence. The largest and most elaborate of Looff's 62 hand-carved early-1900s figures spin weekend afternoons and evenings noon–9 from Memorial Day to mid-June, and Wednesday through Sunday until Labor Day. Carousel hours then revert to weekends plus Mondays and holidays noon–9 until Columbus Day.

✔ **Fleet Skating Center Providence** (401-331-5544), 2 Kennedy Plaza. Open 10–10. Modeled after New York City's Rockefeller Center outdoor ice rink, this facility in the heart of downtown offers skating opportunities for everyone in the family. In winter the skating is on ice; in summer, in-line skating is offered. Both in-line and ice skate rentals are available.

Also see the Providence Children's Museum under *Museums* and Roger Williams Park and Zoo under *Green Space*.

GOLF **Triggs Golf Course** (401-521-8460), 1533 Chalkstone Avenue. This 18-hole par-72 course was laid out in 1930 in links style, on rolling terrain with many ponds. There is a restaurant and bar, and golf carts and clubs can be rented.

STARGAZING **Ladd Observatory** (401-863-2323), 210 Doyle Avenue, corner of Hope Street in Providence. Open 1 or 2 nights a week fo viewing; call for information. Located on the highest point in Providence and with a powerful refractor telescope, Ladd Observatory, which is affiliated with Brown University, is an excellent facility for viewing planets.

TENNIS **Roger Williams Park** (401-785-9450), Elmwood Avenue. There are eight outdoor tennis courts in the park.

TOURS **Art Gallery Trolley Tours** (401-274-9120; 401-751-2628). On the third Thursday of each month, a trolley leaves the Rhode Island Historical Society on Benevolent Street or 1 Citizens Plaza for a free tour of the city's art galleries, antiques shops, and special art events. Tour takers can get on and off as they please and reboard later trolleys.

Carriage Rides of Providence (401-377-2426; 401-751-1177), Side Hill Farm, 60 Clark's Falls Road, Hopkinton. Half-hour carriage rides through downtown Providence from Easter through October.

✂ **Splash Duck Tours** (401-421-DUCK), corner of Fountain and Eddy Streets beside the Biltmore Hotel. You ride the streets of the city and splash into its waters on these hour-long tours of historic Providence in an amphibious vehicle.

WALKING A **river walk pathway** edges the east embankment of the Providence River between Water Place and the Point Street Bridge. Here and there, placards recount the history of the city, and benches provide resting places. In the warm seasons, picnic tables are set out where the pathway passes the Rhode Island School of Design. On the river itself, on most summer weekends, bonfires burn from sunset to midnight and music plays.

Summer Walks (401-438-0463; 401-331-8575). From June into early October, Summer Walks offers guided walking tours of various parts of the city.

✳ Green Space

Blackstone Boulevard and **Blackstone Park.** Handsome late-19th- and early-20th-century mansions in varying styles and a few intriguing, more modern homes edge this boulevard, which has a wide green center strip for strollers and joggers. Pretty plantings brighten the strip in spring. The 1.6-mile divide of greenery is actually a part of the Blackstone Park that extends below it down to the Seekonk River, where the Narragansett Boat Club has its boathouses. Crews are often seen rowing their shells on the river early in the morning and during the evening.

City Hall Park, Kennedy Plaza. An equestrian statue of General Ambrose

Burnside is one of the centers of attention in this little city park edged by the post office, Kennedy Plaza, and the gold-brick former railroad station.

College Green (Front campus), Brown University, Prospect Street. The wrought-iron Van Wickle Memorial Gates that mark the entrance and exit to the university grounds are opened outward each spring, and the graduating seniors march through to their commencement ceremonies held in the First Baptist Meeting House. In fall, in time-honored tradition, the gates are opened inward to welcome incoming freshmen. The green itself, though small, is a pleasant place for sunning on spring and summer days.

Collier Point Park, Allens Avenue and Henderson Street. This little park with a small boat landing offers a fine view of Providence Harbor. The property was formerly owned by the Narragansett Electric Company, and the old hoppers for the coal that used to fire the plant have been restored as a historic attraction.

Haines Park (401-433-3001; 401-253-7482), Route 103, East Providence. Boating, hiking, and saltwater fishing are among the attractions of this more-than-100-acre park.

India Point Park, George M. Cohan Boulevard, India Point. Though it could do with better upkeep, this little park—with a few trees, a little grass, and paved paths for cyclists and walkers—affords a fine view of Narragansett Bay. This is the start of the East Bay Bicycle Path.

Memorial Park, South Main Street. Shaded by oak trees in front of the Providence County Courthouse, this little park is dedicated to the memory of courthouse designer F. Ellis Jackson and World War II naval officer Henry B. Gardner Jr.

Prospect Terrace, Congdon Street. From this little park, a statue of city founder Roger Williams looks down over his town and the gleaming white dome of the capitol. It is here that Williams is buried.

Swan Point Cemetery, Blackstone Boulevard. There are 210 acres of land here overlooking the Seekonk River, filled with winding lanes, 18th- and 19th-century monuments, and trees, which have made it a prime place for birders. It is indeed perhaps the best spot in the state from which to watch the spring bird migration.

Waterplace Park, Exchange Street. This award-winning 4-acre urban park is set around a tidal basin fed by the Woonasquatucket River. It includes landscaped terraces, an amphitheater for outdoor entertainment, and boat landings for water taxis that carry summer visitors downriver to dining and shopping areas in the South Main Street part of the city. A terraced restaurant overlooks the basin.

Roger Williams National Memorial Park, North Main Street. Open daily year-round 9–4:30. According to legend, a spring that bubbled on this site in 1636 prompted Roger Williams to establish his settlement of Providence here. This informal 4-acre park is a National Park Service property with a visitors center and exhibits.

✔ **Roger Williams Park** (401-785-9450) and **Zoo** (401-785-3510), Elmwood Avenue. For driving through, the park is open daily 7 AM–9 PM. Betsey Williams, great-great-granddaughter of Providence's founder, gave the first 100-acre tract from what was the Williams family farm to the city in 1871, for the establishment of a public recreation area. Today the 430-acre Victorian park has a zoo (open 9–4) with almost 1,000 animals—polar bears, bison, elephants, and giraffes among them—a new Australasian collection, including rare mynah birds, wallabies, and tree kangaroos; a museum of natural history; a small planetarium; a carousel; a Japanese garden; two rose gardens; greenhouses; and lakes for boating.

✳ Lodging

HOTELS Courtyard by Marriott (401-272-1191; 1-888-887-7955; www.courtyard.com), 32 Exchange Terrace 02903. ($$$$) This centrally located hotel overlooks Waterplace Park.

&. **Holiday Inn** (401-831-3900; 1-800-465-4329; www.basshotels .com/holiday-inn), 21 Atwells Avenue 02903. ($$$) Standard Holiday Inn with a central downtown location.

&. **Providence Biltmore** (401-421-0770; 1-800-294-7709; www.providence biltmore.com). ($$$–$$$$) Built in 1922 and now renovated, its situation in the heart of downtown is ideal, but the renovation lacks charm.

&. **Providence Marriott** (401-272-2400; 1-800-228-9290; www.marriott .com), Charles and Orms Streets. ($$$–$$$$) Located near the State House. This hotel was considered the liveliest in town until the opening of the Westin. Top-40 bands frequently play in the lounge, and there is better-than-average hotel fare in its **Stacy's Grill.**

&. **Radisson Hotel** (401-272-5577; 1-800-325-2525; www.radisson.com), 220 India Street 02903. ($$–$$$) Plain but moderately priced. Overlooks India Point Park and has a small pleasant restaurant, the **India Point Cafe.**

&. **Westin Hotel Providence** (401-598-8000; 1-800-228-3000; www .westin.com), 1 West Exchange Street 02903. ($$$–$$$$) This slender, soaring hotel catering to business travelers has 363 rooms and suites, a health club, two bars and a cocktail lounge, a breakfast café, and Agora, a highly rated restaurant (see *Dining Out*).

BED & BREAKFASTS Annie Brownell House (401-454-2934; www.anniebrownellhouse.com), 400 Angell Street 02906. ($$–$$$) This 1899 Colonial Revival house is tastefully furnished with period pieces. There are three rooms with baths, along with a downstairs suite with bath. A full breakfast is served.

The Cady House (401-273-5398; www.cadyhouse.com), 127 Power Street 02903. ($–$$) This circa-1839 house on a quiet street in the College Hill area has three double rooms and two apartments, all with private bath, Victorian-style furnishings with folk art touches, and a garden to swoon over. Expanded continental breakfast included.

Christopher Dodge House (401-351-6111; www.providence-inn.com), 11 West Park Street 02908. ($$$–$$$$) An 1858, 15-room Federal-style house furnished with early American reproductions and marble fireplaces. A 10-minute walk to the city center, 5-minute walk to the Providence Place Mall.

C.C. Ledbetter (401-351-4699), 326 Benefit Street 02903. ($–$$) This mansard-roofed house, whose wide-pine floorboards suggest that it had its beginnings in the late 18th century, is an art lover's delight: There are paintings and reproductions everywhere. Three to four rooms, some with a shared bath, are available to guests, as is a separate living room. Expanded continental breakfast with cheese and crusty French bread included.

Mowry-Nicholson House Bed & Breakfast (401-351-6111; www .providence-inn.com), 57 Brownell Street 02908. ($$$–$$$$) There's a wraparound porch to sit on at this 12-room Victorian house close to both downtown and the Providence Place Mall.

Old Court Bed & Breakfast (401-751-2002; www.oldcourt.com), 144 Benefit Street 02903. ($$–$$$, depending on the season) This 10-room, 10-bath bed & breakfast in an 1863 redbrick house near the Rhode Island School of Design has been charmingly decorated in Victorian style.

The State House Inn (401-351-6111; www.providence-inn.com), 43 Jewett Street 02908. ($$–$$$, depending on the season) This 10-room, 10-bath former tenement house is situated conveniently near the capitol and the Providence Place Mall, though not in a particularly fashionable area.

What Cheer Bed & Breakfast (401-351-6111; www.providence-suites.com), 73 Holden Street 02908. ($$$–$$$$) This five-bedroom Victorian house near the capitol building is near both the Providence Place Mall and the center of town.

DINING OUT ⅼ **Adesso** (401-521-0770), 161 Cushing Street. ($$) Lunch Monday through Friday, dinner daily. The pasta is always a good bet at this casual, California-style restaurant. Salads are made with the freshest of greens, pizzas are imaginative, and desserts are too rich to think about.

ⅼ **Agora** (401-598-8011), 1 West Exchange Street. ($$–$$$) Open Monday through Saturday for breakfast, lunch, and dinner; Sunday for breakfast and brunch. This sumptuous Westin Hotel restaurant specializes in seafood prepared in unusual ways.

Al Forno (401-273-9760), 577 South Main Street. ($$$) Open Tuesday through Saturday for dinner. No reservations are accepted, so be prepared to wait. Wood-grilled pizzas, crisp and thin, are a favorite appetizer at this ever-popular, award-winning restaurant where wood grilling is the specialty. Desserts, which you order as you start your meal so they can be prepared to perfection, are another hallmark.

ⅼ **AquaViva** (401-273-8664), 286 Atwells Avenue. ($$–$$$) Open Tuesday through Saturday for dinner only. Regional Italian cuisine.

✍ ⅼ **Bluefin Grille** (401-272-5852), at the Providence Marriott, Charles and Orms Streets. ($$–$$$) Open for lunch and dinner daily. As its name suggests, fresh seafood is the specialty here, but the grilled T-bone steaks and pork chops will satisfy any carnivore.

Blue Grotto (401-272-9030), 210 Atwells Avenue. ($–$$) Lunch and dinner daily; Saturday, dinner only. Very romantic, with thoughtfully prepared Italian dishes, graciously served.

Cafe Nuovo (401-421-2525), 1 Citizens Plaza. ($$$–$$$$) Open for lunch and dinner Monday through Friday; Saturday, dinner only. Closed Sunday. A handsome—though small—restaurant in an equally handsome riverfront building. In fine weather you can eat outdoors and watch the river. The portions of the trendy Italian cuisine are enormous.

&. **Capital Grille** (401-521-5600), 1 Cookson Place. ($$$–$$$$) Open Monday through Friday for lunch and dinner; weekends, dinner only. The Capital Grille is expensive, but the enormous, dry-aged steak is excellent, as are the creamed spinach and mashed potatoes. There is also seafood and a long (but expensive) wine list. A businessperson's paradise.

Capriccio (401-421-1320), 2 Pine Street. ($$$–$$$$) Open Monday through Friday for lunch and dinner; weekends, dinner only. An elegant and somewhat pretentious Italian restaurant of the old school, serving carefully prepared fare with style. Definitely not for a casual family night out.

Casa Christine (401-453-6255), 145 Spruce Street. ($–$$) Open Tuesday through Friday for lunch and dinner, Saturday for dinner only. Closing time, however, is 7. A cozy, informal family restaurant offering such old favorites as chicken with artichokes, olives, and lemon; veal Parmesan; seafood soup; and baked codfish.

♣ **CAV** (401-751-9164), 14 Imperial Place. ($–$$) Open Monday through Saturday for lunch and dinner; on Sunday, brunch, lunch, and dinner are all served. An innovative, imaginative restaurant decorated with African masks and American antiques, which are also for sale, as part of the decor. The menu is eclectic, including Middle Eastern, Greek, Italian, French, and Oriental dishes. A wide selection of coffees and teas.

Chez Pascal (401-421-4422), 960 Hope Street. ($$$) Open Tuesday through Saturday for dinner. Cassoulet and frogs' legs are the sorts of French dishes on which you can dine at Chez Pascal. Tuesday through Thursday there's a three-course bistro menu offered with a glass of house wine for under $30.

Constantino's Ristorante (401-528-1100), 265 Atwells Avenue. ($$$) Open for dinner Tuesday through Sunday. Northern and southern Italian fare, prepared with care, is offered in elegant surroundings. In spring, summer, and fall you can dine outdoors on dishes like filet mignon rubbed with black truffle butter, or simply have a light antipasto of baby littleneck clams in a spicy pomodoro sauce with garlic, white wine, and herbs, topped with grilled Tuscan bread.

♣ **Downcity** (401-331-9217), 151 Weybosset Street. ($$–$$$) Open Monday through Friday for lunch and dinner, Saturday and Sunday for brunch and dinner. Though the owners have created something of a 1940s diner setting, the food far surpasses standard '40s diner fare. There are appetizers like goat cheese and sausage crostini, and main courses such as warm duck salad.

Eclectic Grille (401-831-8010), 245 Atwells Avenue. ($$–$$$) Open Monday through Saturday for dinner, Sunday for brunch and dinner. This

Federal Hill restaurant favors Italian cuisine, but, as its name suggests, it's eclectic enough to also serve French and Spanish dishes in a downtown setting.

♿ **Gatehouse** (401-521-9229), 4 Richmond Square. ($$$) Open nightly for dinner; Sunday for Brunch. Wood-grilling is a specialty at this stunningly situated restaurant overlooking the Seekonk River. A grand place for a night out.

Gracie's Bar and Grille (401-272-7811), 409 Atwells Avenue. ($$$) Open Tuesday through Sunday for dinner. Comfortable and low-key, Gracie's emphasizes contemporary American fare.

Hemenway's Sea Food Grill and Oyster Bar (401-351-8570), 1 Old Stone Square. ($$–$$$) Open Monday through Saturday for lunch and dinner, Sunday for dinner only. Fresh fish, a spacious, attractive decor, and a view of the Providence River attract diners to this casual restaurant.

Il Piccolo (401-421-9843), 1450 Atwood Avenue, Johnston. ($$) Open Monday through Friday for lunch and dinner, Saturday for dinner only. This small restaurant offers fine food, wine, and service. Grilled chicken breast with arugula, sweet onions, and peppers, and fresh vegetables al dente are highlights.

✐ **India** (401-278-2000), 123 Dorrance Street. ($–$$) Open daily for lunch and dinner. Northern Indian fare that is light and delectable. Lamb biryani—with tender lamb, basmati rice, raisins, almonds, and cashews, all flavored with coriander and cardamom—is especially delicious. The handsome, dark-wood setting contributes to the overall experience.

Julian's (401-861-1770), 318 Broadway. ($–$$) Open Monday through Friday for breakfast, lunch, and dinner; Saturday for brunch and dinner; Sunday for brunch. The freshest of fresh seasonal ingredients, wood grilling, and a patio are what make this casual BYOB restaurant a particularly popular spot among locals.

L'Epicureo (401-454-8430), 311 Westminster Street. ($$$) Dinner Tuesday through Sunday. Wood-grilled veal, lobster, and scallops in a garlic cream sauce are among the main courses on the menu. Everything sounds wonderful and tastes delicious at this splendid Italian restaurant, which began life as a Federal Hill meat market.

✐ ♿ **Lucky Garden** (401-231-5626), 1852 Smith Street, North Providence. ($–$$) Open for lunch and dinner Tuesday through Saturday; Sunday, for dinner only. Cantonese chefs prepare a remarkable Hong Kong menu with such special items as sea cucumber with duck feet. There is also a regular Chinese menu.

Madeira (401-431-1322), 288 Warren Avenue, East Providence. ($–$$) Lunch and dinner daily. Portuguese fare including an all-beef shish kebab that is a specialty of Madeira; bacalhau (dried codfish) that is fried, boiled, or broiled; and Portuguese steak topped with eggs and ham.

Mediterraneo (401-331-7760), 134 Atwells Avenue. ($$–$$$) Open Monday through Friday for lunch and dinner, Saturday and Sunday for dinner. Luncheon offerings of pizza, pasta, Italian deli sandwiches, and salads, as well as grilled chicken, fish, and steak, are very reasonable in this spacious Federal Hill restaurant. At dinnertime the prices go up considerably, but the fare is genuinely Italian.

&. **Mill's Tavern** (401-272-3311), 101 North Main Street. ($$$) Open daily for dinner. *Elegant, hip, New York trendy*—all these adjectives are applied to Mill's Tavern by its patrons, but what it really is, is a fine restaurant that specializes in wood-fired cooking and thoughtful service.

&. **Neath's** (401-751-3700), 262 South Water Street. ($$$$) Open for dinner Tuesday through Saturday. This bistro's Cambodian-born chef offers some of the finest dining in Providence—or any city—combining his Southeast Asian background with French training and fresh New England ingredients. Elegant entrées include native lobster with coconut milk, shiitake mushrooms, and Chow Foon rice. And the setting is just right, too, with a view of the Providence riverfront skyline.

New Japan (401-351-0300), 145 Washington Street. ($$–$$$) Tuesday through Friday for lunch and dinner, Saturday and Sunday for dinner only. This little downtown Japanese restaurant looks as if it belongs in Tokyo and is just fine for teriyaki.

New Rivers (401-751-0350), 7 Steeple Street. ($$–$$$) Dinner Monday through Saturday. Eclectic cooking at this American bistro with an attractive ambience.

Old Canteen (401-751-5544), 120 Atwells Avenue. ($$–$$$) Open for lunch and dinner daily except Tuesday. A fine, old-fashioned Italian restaurant with meticulous service and a loyal following.

Pane e Vino (401-223-2230), 365 Atwells Avenue. ($$–$$$) Open daily for dinner. Veal, in its many forms, is

one of the favorites of the clientele here.

&. **Paragon** (401-331-6200), 234 Thayer Street. ($$) Open daily for lunch and dinner. Lobster, crab-cakes, and octopus are among the more exotic appetizers, and cheese-cake with strawberries flambé is one of the exotic desserts, at this popular, lively, reasonably priced Thayer Street restaurant. You can also have just a simple burger or a fresh salad for lunch.

Parkside (401-331-0003), 76 North Main Street. ($$–$$$) Open Monday through Friday for lunch and dinner, Saturday and Sunday for dinner. There are crisp white tablecloths and waiters in crisp starched shirts at this historic-building restaurant that specializes in rotisserie- and grill-prepared foods.

Restaurant Pizzico (401-421-4114), 762 Hope Street. ($$–$$$) Open Monday through Friday for lunch and dinner, weekends for dinner only. Its devotees describe the northern Italian cuisine at this pleasant East Side restaurant as "elegant" and "fabulous." There might be chicken breasts stuffed with prosciutto and roasted peppers, for example, or tortelloni filled with ricotta and asparagus.

Ran Zan (401-276-7574), 1084 Hope Street. ($$) Open for lunch and dinner Tuesday through Friday; for dinner only Saturday and Sunday. Rhode Island aficionados of Japanese food put Ran Zan high on their list.

Pot au Feu (401-273-8953), 44 Custom House Street. ($$$–$$$$) The dining is elegant on the second floor of this authentic French restaurant serving lunch and dinner Tuesday through Friday and dinner Saturday.

In the downstairs bistro it's more casual and less expensive, but the food is equally well prepared. The bistro serves lunch and dinner Monday through Friday and dinner Saturday. Pot au Feu is the place to go for fine French food.

♿ **Providence Oyster Bar** (401-272-8866), 283 Atwells Avenue. ($$$) Open Monday through Friday for lunch and dinner, Saturday and Sunday for dinner only. You can get Maine oysters, British Columbian oysters, Prince Edward Island oysters, or plain Rhode Island oysters at this welcoming, laid-back raw bar; there's fine fish cookery, too, in the dining room.

♿ **Providence Prime** (401-454-8881), 279 Atwells Avenue. ($$$) Open for lunch and dinner Tuesday through Friday; for dinner only Monday and Saturday. Filet mignon, porterhouse, roast prime rib of beef—Providence Prime is, of course, a beef eater's delight, but there are grilled lamb chops and pork chops, too, and fish and lobster for those who are so inclined.

♿ **Raphael Bar Risto** (401-421-4646), 1 Cookson Place. ($$$–$$$$) Open for dinner only Monday through Saturday. This stylish modern restaurant offers dishes influenced by upscale Italian cuisine.

♿ **Red Fez** (401-272-1212), 49 Peck Street. ($$) Open for dinner Tuesday through Saturday. An eclectic bistro menu that might feature a dish like lamb tagine with couscous or something much simpler. The menu changes regularly.

Restaurant Tokyo (401-331-5330), 231 Wickenden Street. ($$) Open daily for lunch and dinner. There's plenty of ginger and teriyaki sauce at this inviting Japanese restaurant, where seafood dishes are especially favored.

Rue de l'Espoir (401-751-8890), 99 Hope Street. ($$$) Open for breakfast Tuesday through Sunday, for lunch and dinner Tuesday through Friday, for brunch Saturday and Sunday. There's variety aplenty here—comfort food like French toast made with honey-oat bread or sophisticated seafood dishes. Its location near Brown University and the Rhode Island School of Design gives it a slightly avant-garde air.

Sawaddee (401-831-1122), 93 Hope Street. ($$) Open Tuesday through Friday for lunch and dinner, weekends for dinner only. Spicy, exciting Thai cuisine at reasonable prices is what you'll find in this pleasant East Side restaurant.

♿ **Taste of India** (401-453-2288), 421 Wickenden Street. ($) Open daily for lunch and dinner. Fine curry and tandoori cooking in an unpretentious atmosphere.

10 Steak & Sushi (401-453-2333), 55 Pine Street. ($$$–$$$$) Nigiri and sashimi and sushi rolls featuring such delights as scallops and cilantro in a spicy peanut sauce are on the inviting menu at this hip, loud downtown restauramt. For meat eaters there is bacon-wrapped filet mignon or a veal chop with portobello mushrooms and truffle oil.

Trinity Brewhouse (401-453-2337), 186 Fountain Street. ($$–$$$) Lunch and dinner daily. This brewpub offers great food like bratwurst and sauerkraut and fat hamburgers as well as grander fare in a sprawling room located between the Providence Civic Center and Trinity Repertory Company.

Union Station Brewery (401-274-2739), 36 Exchange Terrace. ($$) Open daily for lunch and dinner. Along with the home-brewed beers and ales served at this brewpub, there is a tempting menu—including pizza dough flavored with the leftover ingredients of the brewing process.

XO Cafe (401-273-9090), 125 North Main Street. ($$–$$$) Open 7 nights a week for dinner only. Inventive, sophisticated fare served in an arty, stylish setting. A summer dish might be seared coriander tuna with ginger vinaigrette and serrano mango sorbet; in winter, wood-oven-baked pizza with grilled fresh vegetables followed by a rosemary-garlic crème brûlée would warm the cockles of your heart.

EATING OUT **Andrea's** (401-331-7879), 268 Thayer Street. ($$) This East Side institution has been serving excellent Greek food for decades. The outdoor tables provide a front-row seat to the Thayer Street parade.

Angelo's (401-621-8171), 141 Atwells Avenue. ($–$$) Open Monday through Sunday for lunch and dinner. This is a longtime favorite for home-style, unpretentious Italian cooking.

Bob & Timmy's Pizza (401-453-2221), 32 Spruce Street. ($–$$) Open daily for lunch and dinner. Pizza, pasta, and salad are offered here. The pizza has flair, with up-to-date gourmet toppings.

&. **Butcher Shop** (401-861-4627), 157 Elmgrove Avenue. ($$) Open Monday through Friday for lunch and dinner; Saturday until 6, Sunday until 3. Delicious deli sandwiches and salads, good hamburgers and coffee, though no ambience.

Cactus Grille (401-941-0004), 800 Allens Avenue. ($) Open daily for lunch and dinner. Giant margaritas and many kinds of beer served with enchiladas and burritos, chili and stuffed peppers.

Caserta's Pizzeria (401-272-3618), 121 Spruce Street. ($) Open weekdays from morning until 10:30 PM; weekends until 11:30 PM. Closed Monday. Old-fashioned pizzas with the best of old-fashioned toppings.

East Side Pockets (401-453-1100), 276 Thayer Street. ($) Open daily 9 AM–1 AM. Primarily eat-on-the-street falafel, gyros, chicken kefta, and the like. The college crowd swears by them.

Estrela do Mar (401-434-5130), 736 North Broadway, East Providence. ($$) Portuguese American fare ranging from plain grilled chicken to marinated pork dishes, octopus, little-necks, and cod.

✍ **Fire + Ice** (401-270-1000), Francis Street in the Providence Place Mall. ($$) Open for lunch and dinner 7 days a week. A new concept in dining: Choose your own raw vegetables, meat, and seafood, and take them to be cooked at the 10-foot circular grill overseen by seven chefs. Eat among free-form and soaring spiral sculptures.

🍲 **4 Seasons** (401-461-5651), Ocean State Job Lot, 361 Reservoir Avenue. ($) Lunch and dinner daily. A family restaurant featuring Chinese, Thai, and Vietnamese dishes at low prices.

Kebab 'n' Curry (401-273-8844), 261–263 Thayer Street. ($–$$) Open 7 days a week for lunch and dinner. A casual and inexpensive eatery for—as its name suggests—kebabs and curries. Popular with the college crowds.

Little Chopsticks (401-351-4290), 495 Smith Street. ($) Lunch and dinner daily. Simple Chinese fare for families in a casual setting.

Meeting Street Café (401-273-1066), 273 Meeting Street. ($$) Open 8 AM–11 PM daily. Big, fat deli sandwiches and soups are the specialty here.

Mexico Garibaldi (401-331-4985), 948 Atwells Avenue. ($) Open daily except Monday for lunch and dinner. You could almost be in Mexico City in this little restaurant frequented by Mexican residents of Providence. It's just a hole-in-the-wall, but the tamales, burritos, and enchiladas are splendid.

Nick's on Broadway (401-421-0286), 259 Broadway. ($–$$$) Open for breakfast and lunch Wednesday through Saturday, Sunday for brunch. You can have chowder and half of a delectable sandwich such as honey-barbecued chicken breast for under $10, or steak and eggs with home-fried potatoes and toast at this bargain restaurant.

Olga's Cup and Saucer (401-831-6666), 103 Point Street. ($–$$) Open Monday through Saturday for breakfast and lunch. There is outdoor dining in a little garden during the warm months. Healthy, imaginative light fare. Tantalizing home-baked breads and pastries.

Ribs and Company (401-944-5432), 1383 Atwood Avenue, Johnston. ($–$$) Open daily for lunch and dinner. Baby back ribs, barbecued chicken, and steaks are served in an informal, down-home atmosphere

Solmar (401-431-1122), 497 Warren Avenue, East Providence. ($$) Dinner daily. Delectable Portuguese

dishes like littlenecks with pork and dried salt codfish—in easygoing surroundings.

Spike's Junkyard Dogs (401-454-1459), 273 Thayer Street. ($) Open daily from 11 AM to 1 or 2 AM. The hot dogs here are something special—baked, not grilled, and served in fresh hot rolls topped with spicy mustard, tomato, pickle, and hot peppers.

Stickyfingers (401-272-7427), 133 Douglas Avenue. ($–$$) Lunch and dinner Monday through Friday. Dinner Saturday and Sunday. Colorado-style Mexican fare and barbecue featuring ribs.

Tortilla Flats (401-751-6777), 355 Hope Street. ($–$$) Open for lunch and dinner daily. Popular East Side spot that serves Mexican food,

ALONG ATWELLS AVENUE ON FEDERAL HILL

Kim Grant

naturally, along with crawfish and such specialties as Louisiana alligator.

Venda Ravioli (401-421-9105), 275 Atwells Avenue. ($–$$) Open daily 8:30–3:30. On a summer weekend there may be lines outside waiting for a table at this stylish market and eatery, where the pasta has been homemade for generations and may be simply prepared in a tomato-basil sauce or done in more complicated ways. A local favorite is linguine with hot pepper seeds and fresh calamari. But there are also veal cutlets and grilled shrimp on the menu. After you've finished eating, you can just stroll about and admire the shelves of fresh Italian breads, plus the cases of sausages and cheeses and take-home items. The market itself remains open until 6, except on Sunday when it closes at 2.

Wes' Rib House (401-421-9090), 38 Dike Street. ($–$$) Lunch and dinner daily. Missouri-style barbecue, with corn bread, baked beans, and slaw, is the specialty.

Z-Bar & Grill (401-831-1566), 244 Wickenden Street. ($–$$) Open for lunch and dinner daily. An unpretentious restaurant that locals applaud for its atmosphere. Wood grilling is a specialty, and there is a pleasant garden for summer dining.

ICE CREAM ✐ ♿ **Maximilian's Ice Cream Café** (401-273-7230), 1074 Hope Street. ($) Open 11 AM–10 PM. All the imaginative flavors are invented and created right here at Maximilian's. Try green tea or Baileys Irish cream on a warm night.

CAFÉS Cable Car Cinema Cafe (401-272-3970), 204 South Main Street. ($) Open daily for breakfast, lunch, and supper. A café-and-cinema combo that's distinctly for the young at heart. Much frequented by Rhode Island School of Design and Brown University students, its fare is basic sandwiches, coffee, and brownies.

Coffee Exchange (401-273-1198), 297 Wickenden Street. ($) Open 6:30 AM–11 PM daily. Coffee lovers swear by the Coffee Exchange and like to sit out on its porch in summer. Sandwiches, soups, ice cream, and pastries. A real coffeehouse atmosphere (except for the booming music and the paper cups).

l'Elizabeth (401-861-1974), 285 South Main Street. ($) Open daily afternoon and evening. Subdued elegance is the mark of this lovely little café sporting needlework on its chair seats and pretty round tables. Irish coffee, specialty spirits, sherries and cognacs (or nonspirited drinks), and pound cake and cheesecake are served in a most civilized way.

Jessie's Dessert Bar (401-351-5377), 230 Atwells Avenue. ($–$$) Open daily from noon until 11 or 12. In this stylish dessert bar, there's Italian sorbet and gelato when the weather is hot; espresso, cappuccino, or a fine Italian liqueur with wine biscuits or cake when it's cold outside.

Pastiche (401-861-5190), 92 Spruce Street. ($) Open Tuesday through Thursday 8 AM–11 PM; Saturday until 11:30; Sunday 10–10. Pastry aficionados insist that this is where you find the best pastries in Providence.

✳ **Entertainment**

FILM Avon Cinema (401-421-3315), 260 Thayer Street. A typical college-town movie house, featuring art films and offbeat movies on double bills that change often.

Cable Car Cinema (401-272-3970), 204 South Main Street. Another art house popular with students from nearby Brown and RISD.

IMAX (401-453-5629), Providence Place Mall. In this enormous theater with its realistic effects, you feel you are part of the film you are seeing

MUSIC AND DANCE Festival Ballet Providence (401-353-1129), 825 Hope Street. One of the largest ballet companies in New England, the Festival Ballet dances at the Rhode Island School of Design Auditorium, the Providence Performing Arts Center, and Veterans Memorial Auditorium.

Ocean State Chamber Orchestra (401-434-0068), 127 Valley Street. Some of the area's finest freelance musicians offer three or four adventuresome, eclectic programs each year

Opera Providence (401-331-6069), 83 Park Street. It might be *The Marriage of Figaro.* It might be a cheery musical. It could be a Valentine's Day or Christmas season event. Opera Providence sometimes performs at Veterans Memorial Auditorium, and sometimes in the Nazarian Center at Rhode Island College.

Providence Singers (401-683-1932). A 100-voice choral group that has been giving concerts in church and college venues for more than 30 years.

Rhode Island Chamber Music Concerts (401-863-2416), Alumnae Hall, Brown University. Four or five chamber music programs are presented annually.

Rhode Island Civic Chorale and Orchestra (401-521-5670). Three programs a year in various downtown churches.

Rhode Island Philharmonic Orchestra (401-831-3123), Veterans Memorial Auditorium, 69 Brownell Street. This 54-year-old symphony orchestra, which ranks among the best in New England, offers seven classical programs from October through May, occasional summer pops and family concerts, and chamber music programs.

THEATER Brown University Theater (401-863-2838), Catherine Bryan Dill Center for the Performing Arts, Waterman Street. A variety of performances are offered throughout the year.

Newgate Theater (401-454-0454), 134 Mathewson Street. In the Mathewson Street United Methodist Church, this small, intimate company likes to perform exciting off-off-Broadway-style plays.

Perishable Theatre (401-331-2695), 95 Empire Street. Productions at this little theater are alternative and experimental.

Providence Black Repertory Company (401-621-7122), 274 Westminster Street. Several productions annually of contemporary plays by black writers.

Providence Performing Arts Center (401-421-2997), 220 Weybosset Street. Touring companies bring Broadway shows to this handsomely renovated onetime movie theater.

Rhode Island College Performing Arts Series (401-456-8000), Roberts Hall, Rhode Island College, Mount Pleasant Avenue. This group presents programs of theater, dance, and pops and classical music.

Trinity Repertory Company (401-351-4242), 201 Weybosset Street. This Tony Award–winning repertory company is among the outstanding theaters of its kind in the country.

SPECTATOR SPORTS Providence Bruins (401-273-5000), Dunkin' Donuts Center, West Exchange Street. From September through April this top development affiliate for the Boston Bruins plays at the "Dunk."

NIGHTLIFE The Call (401-421-7170), 15 Elbow Street. Rock, blues, and alternative rock.

THE TRINITY REPERTORY HAS A NATIONAL REPUTATION.

Kim Grant

Club Oxygen (401-521-7110), 235 Promenade Street. Oxygen has something for everyone, offering top-40 dance music and hard rock, plus a quiet bar.

The Complex (401-751-4263), 180 Pine Street. Four clubs in one: top 40, swing, disco, and dueling pianos.

Fusion (401-621-8888), 99 Chestnut Street. This nightclub in a historic building offers local deejays creating techno sound.

The Green Room (401-351-7665), 145 Clifford Street. A good place to escape the crowds and enjoy food and music. Call for live-music dates.

Hell (401-731-4122), 73 Richmond Street. Thursday-night deejay hip-hop music; Sunday Gothic Night, with black or medieval garb required; Friday and Saturday techno dancing.

Hi-Hat (401-453-6500), 3 Davol Square. This is an inviting jazz club serving sophisticated light meals.

Hot Club (401-861-9007), 575 South Water Street. This funky waterfront bar has an award-winning jukebox.

Living Room (401-521-5200), 23 Rathbone Street. Dance parties.

Lupo's Heartbreak Hotel (401-272-LUPO), 239 Westminster Street. Live rock, blues, and country music are all offered here. At the adjoining Met Cafe, up-and-coming local bands play in a cozy, friendly space. Blues are a specialty.

Olive's (401-751-1200), 108 North Main Street. James Bond martinis, blue martinis, burgers, pizzas, and big-band swing.

Pulse (401-272-2133), 86 Crary Street. New York– and Boston-based deejays remix techno.

Strand Theater (401-272-8900), 79 Washington Street. Heavy metal, rock, and dancing are what bring the crowds here.

✴ Selective Shopping

ANTIQUES SHOPS **Benefit Street Antiques** (401-751-9109), 140 Wickenden Street. A wide selection of antique furniture, china, and glass.

Tilden Thurber (401-272-3200), 292 Westminster Street. Floor upon floor of fine antique furniture, china, glass, silver, and paintings in a spacious, showroomlike setting.

ART GALLERIES **AS 220** (401-831-9327), 95–115 Empire Street. A gallery for alternative art that also offers performances and has its own café.

Bannister Gallery (401-456-9765), 600 Mount Pleasant Street. This Rhode Island College gallery exhibits works largely by Rhode Island artists, some by students.

Bell Gallery (401-863-2932), List Art Center, Brown University, 64 College Street. Cutting-edge works by national and international artists.

Bert Gallery (401-751-2628), 540 South Water Street. Works of 19th- and 20th-century New England artists.

Sarah Doyle Gallery (401-863-2189), 185 Meeting Street. Rotating shows of high caliber and generally with a feminist slant.

C. Francis Gallery (401-831-3546), 141 Wayland Avenue. Contemporary photography, painting, and sculpture, Oriental antiques.

Lenore Gray Gallery, Inc. (401-274-3900), 25 Meeting Street. Painting and sculpture by Rhode Island artists.

JRS Fine Art (401-331-4380), 218 Wickenden Street. Lithographs, paintings, pottery, and baskets by local artists.

Krause Gallery at the Moses Brown School (401-831-7350), 250 Lloyd Avenue. Exhibits of jury-selected work. Closed weekends.

Martina & Company (401-351-0968), 120 North Main Street. Sculptural jewelry.

Providence Art Club, 11 Thomas Street. Painting and sculpture, primarily by Rhode Island artists, is exhibited.

VanNoppen Glass Gallery (401-272-3104), 18 Imperial Place. Glassblowing, viewing, and sales. Call for appointment.

Woods-Gerry Mansion (401-454-6142). When the Rhode Island School of Design acquired this redbrick Italianate mansion some years ago and sought to demolish it, the Rhode Island Historic Preservation Commission intervened. An outstanding example of the architectural work of Rhode Island architect Richard Upjohn, it was constructed in 1860. It now serves as a gallery for student and faculty work.

BOOKSTORES **Books on the Square, Inc.** (401-331-9097), 471 Angell Street. General fiction and nonfiction, hardcover and paperback.

Books on the Square at Trinity (401-521-3111), 201 Washington Street in Trinity Playhouse. Open Tuesday through Sunday noon–8. Carries principally biographies of theater personalities, plays, books about theater.

Brown Bookstore (401-863-3168), 244 Thayer Street. The Brown

University bookstore. A full-service college bookstore selling remainders, used books, professional books, and textbooks.

Cellar Stories (401-521-2665), 111 Mathewson Street. Used, hard-to-find, out-of-print, old, and rare books; much Rhode Island history. There is also a search service.

College Hill Bookstore, Inc. (401-751-6404), 252 Thayer Street. A general bookstore. Art, music, and bargain books are found here as well as books on tape.

Johnson & Wales University Downtown Campus Bookstore (401-598-1105), 1 Cookson Place. Open Monday through Thursday 9–6, until 4 on Friday during the academic year; open Monday through Thursday 9–4:30, until 4 on Friday in summer. Best sellers, children's books, coffee table books, T-shirts, mugs—souvenirs of Johnson & Wales.

Johnson & Wales Harborside Bookstore (401-598-1445), 265 Harborside Boulevard. Books on culinary arts. College and book supplies.

Map Center (401-421-2184), 671 North Main Street. Maps, atlases, travel books.

Myopic Books (401-521-5533), 5 South Angell Street. On a warm day you can browse outside in the garden or browse inside this comfortable little store dealing in used, out-of-print, first-edition, and rare books.

Rhode Island College Bookstore (401-456-8025), 600 Mount Pleasant Avenue. Open Monday through Thursday 8:45–7, until 4:15 on Friday, during the academic year; open Monday through Friday 8:15–3:45 in summer. Hardcovers, paperbacks,

remainders, gifts, greeting cards, jewelry, and stationery.

RISD Store (401-454-6465), 30 North Main Street. Open Monday through Thursday 8:30–7, Friday until 5:30, Saturday 10–6, and Sunday noon–5 during the academic year; open Monday through Friday 8:30–5:30 in summer. Photography, architecture, graphic arts, fine arts. School supplies.

Second Thoughts Bookstore (401-331-9140), 1281 North Main Street. Used, rare, and out-of-print books of all sorts.

Tyson's Old and Rare Books (401-431-2111), 178 Taunton Avenue, East Providence. Americana is the specialty in this well-appointed and well-organized collection of rare and used books.

✒ **Wayland Toy & Stationery** (401-421-6623), 13 South Angell Street. This is a very small toy and bookshop. Hardcover juvenile books, greeting cards, stationery, puzzles, and toys.

SPECIAL SHOPS Belleau Art Glass (401-456-0011), 424 Wickenden Street. When the daffodils and lilies are no longer in bloom in your garden, this is the place to come for a handblown substitute. And there are handblown vases and Christmas tree ornaments, too.

Comina (401-273-4522), 201 Wayland Avenue. Jewelry and gifts, teak, oak, and rosewood furniture from Pakistan and Azerbaijan.

Field & Rose (401-331-LEAF), 139 Elmgrove Avenue. Engagement rings can be fashioned to order here, and after the wedding ring has joined the engagement ring, look for hand-painted Hungarian china or French

Limoges china to give as a wedding gift. Estate jewelry and Chinese tea are also sold.

Frog and Toad (401-831-3434), 795 Hope Street. You can buy catttail slippers from China, jewelry from the Philippines, paper from India, and straw articles from Zambia in this understated gift shop.

Garrison Confections (401-279-2462), 17 Washington Street. Hand-made "artisanal" chocolates are sold by the piece or pound at this little shop next door to the Providence Biltmore Hotel.

Mignonette (401-272-4422), 301 Wickenden Street. The fragrance of English lavender mingles here with perfume from the French flower fields of Grasse. For the discerning, there are also Italian lingerie and jewelry from the Czech Republic.

On Paper (401-272-2984), 405 Wickenden Street. Antique frames are the specialty at On Paper, but there is art and antiques to be had, too.

OOP (1-800-281-4147), 297 Thayer Street; a second shop is in the Providence Place Mall. Vintage jewelry and local handmade jewelry, art glass, pottery and stationery, stuffed animals, games, puppets and whirligigs, toffee crisps from England, hand-painted folk furniture.

The Peaceable Kingdom and Black Crow (401-351-3472), 116 Ives Street. Native American art and folk art from around the world. Textiles, masks, dolls, clothing, jewelry, rugs, and much more.

Providence Cheese (401-421-5653), 178 Atwells Avenue. Every Italian cheese you could possibly want, plus Italian breads, homemade pasta, and pickles.

Providence Place Mall (401-270-1000), Providence Place. Department stores, specialty shops, jewelers, restaurants, a food court—all in one place in the state's largest mall.

Roma Cafe and Gourmet (401-331-8620), 310 Atwells Avenue. Italian cheese and fresh breads and pasta, olive oils and salami and espresso makers—anything and everything for the Italian American kitchen. You can eat here, too.

Simple Pleasures (401-331-4120), 6 Richmond Square. In 1895 this red-brick building was Mahoney's Blacksmith Shop on the banks of the Seekonk River. Today it houses tastefully selected eclectic gifts from all over the world. There are tooled-leather bags from Paraguay, vintage English furniture, silk scarves and Japanese ties, and handcrafted jewelry.

Uncle Sig's (401-453-5334), 808 Hope Street. All manner of old-fashioned toys are for sale in this unpretentious neighborhood shop.

✳ Special Events

February: **Rhode Island Spring Flower and Garden Show** (401-458-6000), Rhode Island Convention Center.

April: **Taste of Elmwood** (401-273-2330), Roger Williams Park Casino. Indoor ethnic food festival offering specialties from Vietnam, the Dominican Republic, Guatemala, Cambodia, Colombia, and El Salvador, among others. **Conservation Week** (401-785-3510), Roger Williams Park Zoo. A behind-the-scenes look at the zookeepers.

May–October: **WaterFire** (401-272-3111), Waterplace Park. Two

Saturdays a month in summer and fall, and occasionally midweek. Floating bonfires are lit in the Providence River accompanied by taped music.

June: **Festival of Historic Houses** (401-831-7440).

June–August: **Carousel Bayside Concert** (401-434-3311, ext. 289), Carousel Bayside Park, Bullocks Point Avenue, East Providence. Outdoor concerts.

July: **Sail Rhode Island** (1-800-233-1636). Tall sailing ships anchor off India Point Park, and a Waterfront Festival welcomes them. **Annual Algonquin Indian School Pow Wow** (401-941-5640), Roger Williams Park, 1000 Elmwood Avenue. Demonstrations of Native crafts, dancing, and drumming. Native American food and crafts booths. **Annual East Providence Heritage Festival** (401-434-3311, ext. 289; 401-434-9057), Pierce Memorial Field, Mercer Street, East Providence. Ethnic foods, music, children's activities, concerts, crafts, and public awareness exhibits. **Puerto Rican Festival** (401-421-0495), Temple of Music, Roger Williams Park, 1000 Elmwood Avenue. A family festival of food, music, and other entertainment.

August: **Cityarts Festival** (401-434-3311, ext. 289), Carousel Bayside Park, Bullocks Point Avenue, East Providence. From 11 to dusk, rain or shine. Exhibits by area artists plus live concerts.

September: **Dominican Festival** (401-941-0536), Temple of Music,

Roger Williams Park, 1000 Elmwood Avenue. A family festival of food, music, and other entertainment. **Annual Heritage Day Festival** (401-277-2669), State House lawn, Smith Street. Ethnic subcommittees celebrate their heritages and cultures with song, dance, food, and ethnic entertainment. **Autumn Festival** (401-435-7596), East Providence Senior Citizen Center grounds, Waterman Street, East Providence.

October: **Federal Hill Festival** (401-861-9870). Parade and street festival with vendors selling Italian specialties. **Great Northeast International Beer Festival** (401-458-6000), Rhode Island Convention Center. More than 250 local breweries offer their beer to test. **Jack-O'Lantern Spectacular** (401-785-3510), Roger Williams Park Zoo. Some 5,000 lighted jack o'lanterns brighten 3 acres of parkland.

December: **Festival of Trees,** Rhode Island Convention Center. **Annual Latin Christmas Carol Celebration** (401-863-2123), Sayles Hall, Brown University campus. Christmas carols sung in Latin, readings from Latin texts, music from the university organist on the restored Sayles Hall organ. **Annual Tree Lighting** (401-434-3311, ext. 289), East Providence City Hall, 145 Taunton Avenue. Santa Claus arrives by fire engine. Holiday carols and refreshments. **Annual Holiday Ballet *Coppelia*** (401-334-2560), Roberts Hall Theater, Rhode Island College, 600 Mount Pleasant Avenue.

North of Providence

BLACKSTONE RIVER VALLEY,

FOSTER AND SCITUATE

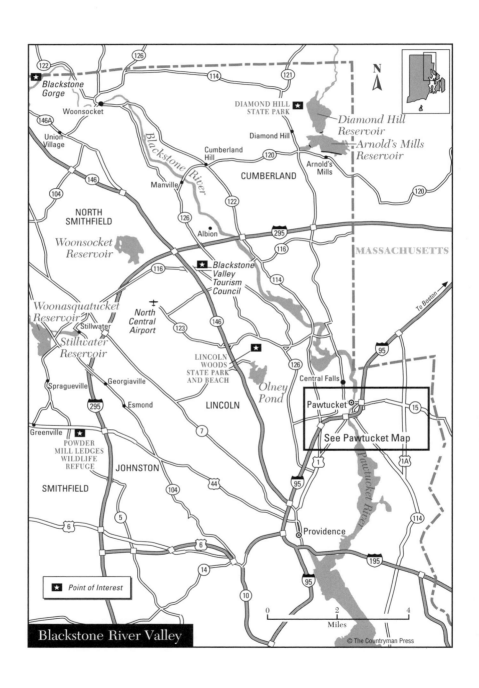

Blackstone River Valley

BLACKSTONE RIVER VALLEY, FOSTER, AND SCITUATE

Thirty-five miles south of Boston, on a spot overlooking a bend in the river that today bears his name, the Reverend William Blackstone erected a cottage in 1635. He was a Church of England clergyman who came to the New World for greater religious freedom, and his cottage began the settlement of the Blackstone River Valley.

This "Sage of the Wilderness," as Blackstone was called, was the first white settler in the area. He had made his journey from Boston on the white bull that he always rode, carrying with him nearly 200 books—probably the largest library in the New World at that time. A stone monument marks the spot across from the Ann & Hope Specialty Shops in Cumberland where, presumably, Blackstone lived.

There are now three cities in the Blackstone River Valley—Pawtucket, Woonsocket, and Central Falls—as well as several towns, many mill villages, and some rural areas. Pawtucket, "Place by the Waterfall," is the oldest of the three cities and was the birthplace, in the 1790s, of America's industrial revolution.

When Roger Williams was negotiating with the Narragansetts for land to settle in the 1630s, he was uninterested in the wooded, stony terrain of what is now Pawtucket; it was not deemed suitable for farming. But in 1655 blacksmith Joseph Jenks Jr. took advantage of the wood in Pawtucket's forests to fire his forge, establishing a smithy where the Blackstone River tumbles over Pawtucket Falls and becomes the Pawtucket River.

Soon Jenks was producing plows, harrows, and scythes for the farmers of Providence, and business was good enough to attract other blacksmiths. Though Native Americans destroyed the settlement of Pawtucket in King Philip's War, it was rebuilt, and the replacement forges, like their predecessors, flourished.

Samuel Slater began producing cotton yarn in his Pawtucket mill in 1793, with Blackstone River–powered machinery. At about the same time, a mile above Pawtucket Falls a chocolate mill was established—also using Blackstone waterpower—at what today is Central Falls.

Woonsocket, the third of the Blackstone Valley cities and the northernmost city in Rhode Island, had its beginning in 1666 with a sawmill built at a spot that Native Americans called Miswoosakit—"At the Very Steep Hill." The earliest settlers of Woonsocket chose farming as their livelihood, but after Slater proved so successful with his water-powered cotton mill, Woonsocket residents decided to build their own mill. The first Woonsocket cotton mill was established in 1810, and more followed. Spinning and weaving woolens became the city's specialty.

By the second half of the 19th century Woonsocket's mill industry had gained considerable renown, and many Eastern European and Russian immigrants found their way to Woonsocket's mills. French Canadian immigrants also came in great numbers, and by the 1930s nearly three-quarters of the city's population was first- or second-generation French Canadian. French was heard on the city's streets, and the radio station and newspapers were French. Even today the French influence remains widespread.

Mill villages sprang up all along the river's length, also nourished by the Blackstone's waterpower. As a result, much of the Blackstone River Valley is heavily populated today, even though the mills are largely gone. To some extent factory outlets have replaced the mills, and these provide some interest to the tourist, but until recently there was little to lure the visitor. Indeed, the Blackstone River and the Pawtucket and Seekonk Rivers that it flows into were long victims of industrial pollution. But in recent years these rivers have been cleansed and revived, and waterfront parks provide public access to the rivers where anglers now find sunfish, trout, pickerel, catfish, and bass. On weekends during the warmer months an open vessel, the *Blackstone Valley Explorer,* travels the waterways, offering glimpses of the flora and fauna that are flourishing again.

And then there are those parts of the valley that have always remained rural—where hills rise and fall and apple blossoms perfume the air in spring. (According to legend, William Blackstone developed the first purely American apple: the Yellow Sweeting.)

The Pawtucket Red Sox—a Triple-A farm team of the Boston Red Sox—play their games in Pawtucket's McCoy Stadium. In Lincoln there is greyhound racing. Roast chicken dinners at poultry farms entice travelers on weekend outings.

Though the glory days of the valley's cities have largely come and gone, architectural structures that testify to this bygone era still stand. Of all Rhode Island, it is the Blackstone River Valley that is experiencing the greatest revival of tourism. The traveler must bear in mind, however, that the process is just beginning. Sites of interest to tourists are often unmarked by signs. Obtaining maps and detailed information from the local tourist office is essential.

Rural western Rhode Island lies between Connecticut and the Blackstone River Valley watershed area of Glocester. Forests of white pine, oak, and birch edge its miles of winding, hilly roads. Every now and then the traveler will come upon a cluster of old houses or a farmhouse set far back from the road. There are beautiful fieldstone walls along some stretches, and in spring apple blossoms bloom in old orchards. One of the state's two covered bridges is on Central Pike in Foster. It was rebuilt in authentic 19th-century style after its predecessor had been destroyed by fire.

Two Foster villages worth a visit are Foster Center and Moosup Valley. The white spire of the 1882 Greek Revival Second Baptist Church rises above Foster Center, reached by Foster Center Road (RI 94). Annual town meetings are still

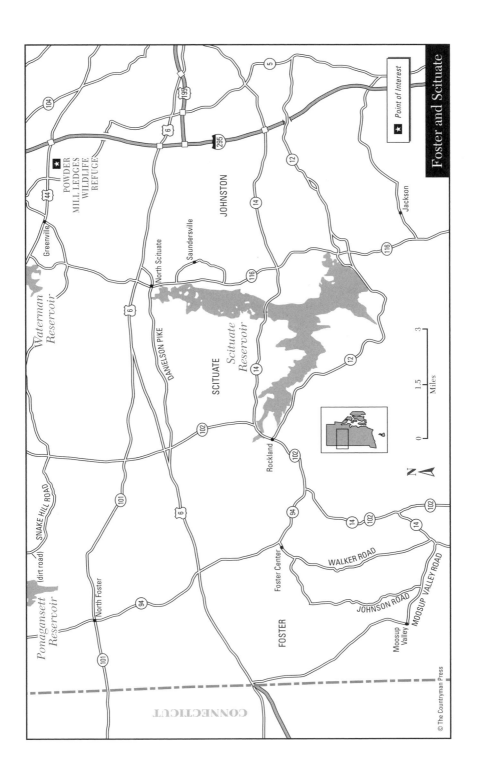

Foster and Scituate

★ Point of Interest

CONNECTICUT

Ponaganset Reservoir

Waterman Reservoir

Scituate Reservoir

POWDER MILL LEDGES WILDLIFE REFUGE

JOHNSTON

SCITUATE

FOSTER

Greenville

North Scituate

Saundersville

Jackson

Rockland

Foster Center

North Foster

Moosup Valley

SNAKE HILL ROAD

(dirt road)

DANIELSON PIKE

WALKER ROAD

JOHNSON ROAD

MOOSUP VALLEY ROAD

44

104

195

6

295

5

12

14

116

116

12

6

102

101

94

102

102

14

14

94

101

6

N

0   1.5   3
Miles

© The Countryman Press

held in the white-clapboard 1796 Town Meeting House that has been the site of this New England form of local government since 1822, and the oxblood-red library was originally a one-room schoolhouse. In the village of Moosup Valley, the white Congregational church, the Grange, the library, and the Valley Store form a picturesque scene near Green Acres Pond, notable for its trout.

Scituate, along with its administrative center of North Scituate, lies on the 6-mile-long Scituate Reservoir on RI 116. With its bandstand-graced green, 1831 Baptist church, a few shops, and yellow and white 18th-century clapboard houses, North Scituate presents a traditional New England picture. On the outskirts of the village are apple orchards where picking your own in fall is always a treat and finishing with a cup of coffee and hot apple pie at the orchard shop is possible.

Western Rhode Island is for lackadaisical rambling on a pretty summer's day or in crisp, colorful autumn. Though the area lacks spectacular sights, it does offer beautiful scenery and some good examples of 18th-century New England villages.

GUIDANCE Blackstone Valley Tourism Council and Visitors' Center (401-724-2200; 1-800-454-2882), 175 Main Street, Pawtucket 02860. Open daily 9–5. Not only are booklets and brochures about the Blackstone Valley available here, but you can also browse in an exhibition gallery with changing displays on the history and crafts of the region and see an orientation film on the Blackstone Valley shown in a new movie theater with art deco touches—velvet seats and stained-glass decor—that come from the 1920s LeRoy Theater, which was demolished a few years ago.

GETTING THERE *By car:* Automobile is by far the best way to explore the Blackstone River Valley and western Rhode Island, but travelers should bear in mind that tourism is just getting established here. From Providence take I-95 north to Pawtucket and Central Falls. To reach Woonsocket, take RI 146 north from Providence.

By bus: **Bonanza** (617-720-4110), from Boston, serves Pawtucket. **Rhode Island Public Transit Authority** (RIPTA; 401-781-9400) has minimal service to most of the communities of the Blackstone River Valley.

MEDICAL EMERGENCY The statewide emergency number is **911.**

Pawtucket Memorial Hospital (401-729-2000), 111 Brewster Street, Pawtucket.

✳ Villages

Albion, RI 146, Lincoln. Though the English settled this little town in the early 1800s, French Canadian immigration transformed it into a predominantly French-speaking area after the Civil War. Several imposing mansard-roofed tenements for mill workers still stand, as does a curious World War I memorial statue of a doughboy, with the inscription in both French and English.

Harrisville, RI 107, Burrillville. The worsted mill, around which this picturesque village grew, was built about 1857, utilizing the waterpower from Mill

Pond for its dam in the center of the community. Now on the National Historic Register, Harrisville owes its charm to Austin T. Levy, a New Yorker who became the owner of the Stillwater Worsted Mill in the 1930s. Levy planned to settle in Harrisville and wanted to make the hamlet more his idea of a "typical" New England village. To do so, he renovated Harrisville's two churches, the Berean Baptist Church on Chapel Street and the white-spired Universalist church in the village center on Main Street. He hired the architectural firm that had built the Providence County Courthouse to design a redbrick assembly hall in pseudo-Colonial style as well as a town hall and a library. A post office was later built in the same style (and presented with much fanfare to the federal government, which had never had a post office building donated to it before). Exceedingly proud of his village creation, Levy, a winter resident of the Bahamas, invited his neighbor there, the duke of Windsor, to come see his New England mill village.

Manville, Lincoln. A handful of old brick mill houses remain here on Old River Road (RI 126).

Quinnville, Lincoln. Six early-19th-century clapboard mill houses and an old farmhouse still stand here along the Blackstone River on River Road.

Slatersville, RI 102, North Smithfield. Fifteen years after the construction of the cotton mill that bears his name in Pawtucket (see *Museums*), Samuel Slater, his brother John, William Almy, and Smith Brown bought water rights and established two mills here. They built houses, churches, and schools for their workers in what was to become an example of paternalistic industry. Thanks to a 20th-century preservationist, Henry P. Kendall, the pretty little white-clapboard houses of Slatersville still stand under leafy trees. There is a pleasant village green with a Greek Revival Congregational church at its head. On both sides of Greene Street stand the mill workers' and mill owners' houses, all with the Greek Revival decoration that Kendall added. He made this addition both to bring more charm to the little village and, in the 20th century, to erase the visible difference between workers' and owners' homes.

Union Village, RI 146, North Smithfield. This village was once known as the Cross Roads. The white-clapboard Friends Meeting House here dates only from 1881, but it stands on the site of an earlier meetinghouse where the mothers of two Rhode Island heroes—Declaration of Independence signatory Stephen Hopkins and Continental army general Nathanael Greene—both worshipped.

✳ To See

MUSEUMS

In Central Falls

Lysander and Susan Flagg Museum and Cultural Center (401-727-7440), 209 Central Street, next to the public library, Central Falls. Open Wednesday 10–noon, Thursday 10–noon and 2–4. In the Ballou Room, named for Civil War Union major Sullivan Ballou, killed at the battle of Bull Run, is memorabilia of many U.S. wars—the Civil War, World Wars I and II, the Korean and Vietnam conflicts, the engagements in Panama. Elsewhere in the museum is a full-figure autographed painting of baseball great Ted Williams by Central Falls painter Lorenzo Denevers. Small admission fee.

✧ **Slater Mill Historic Site** (401-725-8638), Roosevelt Avenue, Pawtucket. Open May through October, Tuesday through Sunday 10–5; closed November through April. It was in the old mill here in 1793 that Samuel Slater, a manufacturer's apprentice from Derbyshire, England, used water-powered machines to produce the first cotton yarn made in America. Slater, it is said, carried the plans in his head when he emigrated across the ocean. (Because of English fears that the secrets of their machinery would leave the country, Slater had to disguise himself as an agricultural laborer to obtain passage.) Once in the New World, he elected to settle in Pawtucket after learning that businessman Moses Brown (see the introduction to "Providence") was interested in improving some machinery he had purchased. Brown was impressed with Slater's ability and hired him. With Brown's son-in-law William Almy and nephew Smith Brown, Slater built the mill that stands today to house that improved machinery. The mill now displays a replica of an original carding engine and drawings of the other machines (the originals are in the Smithsonian Institution in Washington, DC) as well as a series of textile machines—some very rare—that date from 1838 to 1960. Also open to visitors is the 1758 **Sylvanus Brown House.** Once the home of a millwright and carpenter who worked at the mill, it is furnished with his early-19th-century belongings. On guided tours, costumed docents demonstrate spinning and weaving, and guests are invited to try their hand at this work, too. In the adjoining **Wilkinson Mill** of 1810, a 19th-century machine shop operates, powered by a 16,000-pound waterwheel.

In Woonsocket
Museum of Work and Culture and Woonsocket Visitors Center (401-769-9675), 42 South Main Street at Market Square. Open Monday through Friday 9:30–4, Saturday 10–5:30, and Sunday 1–5. Small admission fee. From 1915 to 1925 this redbrick building housed the Barnai Worsted Company, manufacturing woolen goods for military uniforms and men's fashions. Re-created in the museum are the shop floor of the mill itself, part of a three-family tenement replica such as Quebecois immigrant workers would have occupied in the early years of the 20th century, a church interior, a 1914 union hall, and the classroom of a parochial school.

WINERY **Diamond Hill Vineyards** (401-333-2751), 3145 Diamond Hill Road, Cumberland. Call for hours. The "new tradition" wines of this 34-acre vineyard are made from the apples, pears, peaches, and blueberries grown on the property. Traditional grape wines are Pinot Noir, Chardonnay, and blush. The wines, with an alcohol content reaching up to 11 percent, are sold only at the vineyard, and buyers can have their own names affixed to their bottles.

HISTORIC HOMES AND SITES

In Glocester
Job Armstrong Store (401-568-1866), 1181 Main Street (part of a village commercial block), Chepachet Village. Open Saturday 11–3 in summer and early fall.

Exhibits of artifacts from the Glocester of yesteryear. Antique postcards and history-related items are for sale for the benefit of the historical society. This circa-1800 building is the headquarters of the Glocester Heritage Society.

In the Pawtucket area

Eleazer Arnold House (617-227-3956), 449 Great Road, Lincoln. Open only by appointment. Of principal interest to those with a bent for architecture, this late-17th-century, stone-ended house with its huge chimney is the best example of its period in Rhode Island. Now owned by the Society for the Preservation of New England Antiquities, the house was considered a mansion and served as a tavern in its early days. Travelers on the Great Road that extended from Providence to Mendon, Massachusetts, one of the earliest colonial roads, recognized it from a distance by its chimney.

Daggett House (401-722-6931; 401-724-5748), Slater Park off US 1A, Pawtucket. Open June through September, Saturday and Sunday 2–5, and by appointment. This gable-roofed house, built by farmer John Daggett in 1685, replaced a smaller one destroyed by Native Americans in King Philip's War. The Daggetts were slaveholders, and the cellar still has the rings from which a slave would swing his hammock. The house is notable for its 17th-century antiques, colonial pewter, the china that belonged to General Nathanael Greene, and two bedspreads that belonged to Samuel Slater's family. This is a DAR-operated property.

Friends Meeting House (401-245-5860), Great Road, Lincoln. Call for hours. This gray-clapboard meetinghouse, part of which dates from 1703, was one of the earliest gathering places of Friends in New England.

✑ **Hannaway Blacksmith Shop** (401-333-1100, ext. 289), 671 Great Road, Lincoln. Call for hours. One Sunday each month between April and November, this reconstructed, 19th-century barnlike structure is open for blacksmithing demonstrations.

Hearthside, Great Road, Lincoln. In 1810, using money won in a Louisiana lottery, mill owner Stephen Hopkins Smith built this Federal-style stone house in the hope it would win over a young Providence woman he wished to wed. Unfortunately, it didn't. She found the house too remote, and Smith lived on in it alone. Today, although the house is owned by the town, it can only be viewed from the outside.

✑ **Kelly House** (401-333-0295), Quinnville, on the bikeway of the Blackstone River Park, Lincoln. Open April through November, daily 9–4:30. Audios, videos, and photographic displays recount the story of the Blackstone Canal, which lasted barely 20 years in the early 19th century. Then the railroad took over the transportation of goods from Worcester to Providence. Built in 1835, the Kelly House was the home of the superintendent of the Kelly Cotton Mill whose owner, Captain Wilbur Kelly, was a leader in the plans for the canal construction.

✑ **Looff Carousel** (401-728-0500, ext. 251), Slater Park, Pawtucket. Open 11–5 weekends and holidays from April through June and Labor Day through November 1. Open daily 11–5 from July through Labor Day. Also open the first three

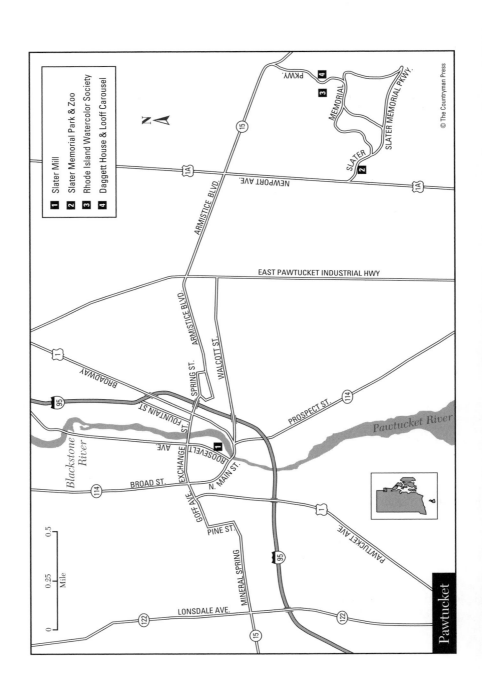

Pawtucket

Legend:
1 Slater Mill
2 Slater Memorial Park & Zoo
3 Rhode Island Watercolor Society
4 Daggett House & Looff Carousel

N

© The Countryman Press

0   0.25   0.5
Mile

weekends in December. It is wise, however, to call in advance to verify hours. Soon after his arrival in America in the 1870s, Danish-born furniture maker Charles Looff carved the figures of this carousel from pieces of leftover wood in his free time. These are the earliest examples of Looff work extant and include 42 horses, three dogs, a lion, a camel, and a giraffe. Looff went on to achieve fame as the carver of the carousel on New York's Coney Island. One of the last examples of his work is at Crescent Park in Riverside.

Moffitt Mill, Great Road, Lincoln. This pretty little stone-and-clapboard mill on the Mosshasuck River was built in 1812 as a machine shop. Later it was used for the manufacture of shoelaces and braid. Though not open to the public, it's one of the most attractive old mill buildings still standing in Rhode Island.

In Woonsocket

Church of the Precious Blood (401-766-0326), Park and Carrington Avenues. This redbrick gable-roofed Victorian Gothic church was erected in 1880.

Congregation B'nai Israel (401-762-3651), 224 Prospect Street. Founded in 1893, this is the oldest Conservative synagogue in Rhode Island. The present striking building was designed by synagogue architect Samuel Glazer and is brightened by stained-glass windows depicting biblical events. They are the work of Israeli Avigdor Arikha, who learned his art in the workshop of Marc Chagall.

Globe Mill Tenements, 810–816 Front Street. Built about 1830, this Federal-style four-family structure is the city's largest remaining collection of old mill houses.

Harris Block and City Hall (401-762-6400), 169 Main Street. Open Monday through Friday 8:30–4. Edward Harris arrived in the 1830s and found a collection of six mill villages here that he eventually turned into the town of Woonsocket. He built one factory to make cashmeres, and another, completed during the Civil War, was considered the finest woolen mill in the country. He built the Harris Block, initially known as the Harris Institute, in 1856. On the lower level were shops whose rents went to finance the free school that he established on the second floor for his mill workers, where on Sundays they learned to read and write. On the third floor was an assembly hall, where, in 1860, Abraham Lincoln gave a campaign address. Eventually a public library, one of the first of its kind in the state, took the place of the second-floor school. The city now owns the Harris Block, and city council meetings are held there.

St. Ann's Church (Dominique Doiron, 401-767-3777), 82 Cumberland Street. Inside this buff-colored stone church, completed in 1918 for the rapidly growing French Canadian population of the city, are religious frescoes painted by Italian-born artist Guido Nanchieri. Nanchieri had studied in Florence, then moved to Montreal in 1914 to open a stained-glass business. After he had contracted with the pastor of St. Ann's, the Reverend Ernest Morin, to do the frescoes, it was discovered in Canada that Nanchieri had once painted the figure of Mussolini astride his horse. It was 1940, and anti-Mussolini sentiment was strong in Canada and the United States. Because he had done such a work, Nanchieri was arrested and sent to an Ontario concentration camp. It was only with the help of Father Morin that he was released. He used pre–World War I members of the community as models for such scenes as *The Temptation of Adam and Eve* and *The Life of St. Anne.*

St. Charles Church (401-766-0176), North Main and Daniel Streets. This square-towered granite Gothic church, erected in 1868, is another of Woonsocket's early Catholic churches.

Train Station (401-762-0440), 1 Depot Square. Open Monday through Friday 8–5. Now National Park Service headquarters, this brick and terra-cotta building was built in 1882 as a depot for the Providence & Worcester Railroad. It replaced an 1847 structure that Edward Harris had erected when he brought in the first railroad. For many years its clock tower was renowned for the copper locomotive weather vane on top. The original vane was sold—and its replacement stolen. Discussions continue about the possibility of another replacement.

Union Saint–Jean Baptiste d'Amerique Building (401-769-0520), 1 Social Street. This Indiana-limestone structure was designed in 1926 by Woonsocket's leading early-20th-century architect, Walter F. Fontaine, to house the nation's largest Franco-American insurance society. The insurance company, and its outstanding collection of books and papers on the subject of French Canadians in the United States, is now at 68 Cumberland Street. The collection is open to the public, but it's wise to make an appointment.

An **outdoor mural** of old Woonsocket's mills and churches by Ron Deziel is found at 547 Clinton Street, behind the Kennedy Manor Senior Housing complex.

SCENIC DRIVES *In Burrillville:* **East Avenue** (RI 107) winds through the pretty little mill village of Harrisville, and Sherman Farm Road unfolds along the rolling fields of northern Rhode Island farm country.

In Foster: **Johnson Road** offers fine vistas over Moosup Valley.

In Glocester: **Reynolds Road** (RI 94) meanders through rich, hilly farmland; **Wallum Lake Road** (RI 100) goes up hill and down dale past reservoirs and lakes; and **Cucumber Hill Road** dives down into Moosup Valley past horse farms.

In Lincoln: **Breakneck Hill Road** affords vistas of horse farms and fields edged with stone walls; **Great Road** passes through rolling, wooded countryside, including the extensive Chase Farm acreage; **Limerock Road,** narrow and wooded, is a fine route for viewing the Blackstone Valley's fall foliage; and **I-295,** passing through Cumberland, Lincoln, and Smithfield, offers long vistas over the Blackstone River Valley.

In Smithfield: **Snake Hill Road** winds through woods and fields, past farms and orchards bright with apple blossoms in spring. **Swan Road** runs through fragrant apple-orchard country.

✳ To Do

AIRPLANE RIDES **Boston-Providence Skydiving** (401-333-3663), North Central Airport, RI 123, Lincoln. Skydiving from April to November.

Skylanes Flight School (401-333-1440), North Central Airport, RI 123, Lincoln. Flights in three-passenger planes offered to view spring and fall foliage.

ANIMAL FARMS ♪ **Daggett Farm** (401-728-0500, ext. 251), Slater Park off US 1A, Pawtucket. Open 8:30–4. On this 6-acre working farm there are cows and horses, chicken and sheep, rabbits and donkeys to view.

♪ **Homestead Gardens** (401-765-4847), 200 Industrial Drive, Slatersville. Open April through December, daily 10–5. On this 65-acre farm, sheep and llamas graze. There is fishing for youngsters in the springs and ponds. In the barn, bulbs and crafts are sold.

APPLE PICKING AND FARM STANDS You'll find good apple picking in late summer and fall at the following farms: **Snowhurst Farm** (401-568-8900), 421 Chopmist Hill Road, Chepachet; **Knight's Farm** (401-949-1694), Snake Hill Road, Glocester; **Barden Orchards** (401-934-1413), 56 Elmdale Road, North Scituate (also pumpkins and blueberries in-season); **Sunset Orchards** (401-934-1900), Gleaner Chapel Road, North Scituate; and **White Oak Farm** (401-934-0749), 74 White Oak Lane, North Scituate.

Appleland Orchard (401-949-3690), 135 Smith Avenue, Greenville. Open daily 9–5 summer and fall, selling apples, peaches, and pears.

Harmony Farms (401-934-0950), 359 Sawmill Road, Harmony. Call for hours. Pick-your-own blueberries.

Jaswell's Farm (401-231-9043), 50 Swan Road, Smithfield. Open daily 10–5 from June through December. Pick-your-own apples, strawberries, and raspberries in-season. The stand sells homemade cider, honey, and seasonal vegetables.

♪ **Phantom Farms** (401-333-2240), Diamond Hill Road, Cumberland. Open daily year-round 6:30 AM–6 PM. Pumpkins, apples, and chrysanthemums brighten this roadside stand in fall, when you can pick your own apples, too. Inside, the treats include such apple confections as pies and muffins. Sometimes there are hayrides for visitors. Honey from farm hives is for sale, and in spring and summer fresh vegetables abound.

♪ **Wright's Dairy Farm** (401-767-3014), Woonsocket Hill Road (off RI 146A), North Smithfield. Open Monday through Saturday 8–7, Sunday 8–4. Dairy-fresh milk, cream, eggs, and whipped cream pastries are sold in the farm bakery; tours of the dairy are offered in summer.

BOATING *Blackstone Valley Explorer* and *Spirit of the Blackstone Valley* (401-724-1500; 1-800-619-BOAT), Blackstone Valley Tourism Council, 175 Main Street, Pawtucket. The 34-foot-long, 49-passenger open riverboat *Blackstone Valley Explorer* tours Pawtucket Harbor in April and plies the Blackstone River and Canal on Sundays from May through October. The 10-passenger, 20-foot pontoon boat *Spirit of the Blackstone Valley* visits secluded valley water sites not accessible to the larger *Explorer.*

CANOEING AND KAYAKING Now that the **Blackstone River** is clearer, it's becoming an increasingly attractive waterway for canoeists. The stretch from Albion to Lonsdale is particularly accessible and pretty. Wildlife that can be seen in the environs of Manville include sandpipers, herons, and snapping turtles.

Friends of the Blackstone Valley (401-334-2153), 6 Valley Stream Drive, Cumberland. Canoe trips on the Blackstone River and Canal between Valley Falls Marsh and Lincoln.

FISHING *In Burrillville:* The **Clear River** access is north of Pascoag on RI 100 in White Mill Park. Offers good trout fishing. Access **Roundtop Pond** off RI 96. Stocked with trout. **Spring Lake** (also called Herring Pond) is full of largemouth bass. Access by Black Hut Road. The **Wakefield Pond** access is by the state boat ramp and parking area. Panfish and largemouth bass are plentiful there.

In Cumberland: The **Blackstone River** is accessible in many places, where you can fish for trout. **Howard Pond** is known for panfish and largemouth bass. The access is from Howard Road.

In Glocester: The **Chepachet River** is accessible from behind the Chepachet Fire Station, on US 44. Trout fishing is most popular here. **Bowdish Reservoir** is full of panfish, largemouth bass, and pickerel. Access is through the George Washington Management Area off US 44, where there is a state boat ramp and parking. **Pascoag Reservoir** borders Burrillville as well as Glocester. It is accessible by the state boat ramp off Jackson Schoolhouse Road. Panfish, largemouth bass, and pickerel are likely catches. **Smith** and **Sayles Reservoir** access is by a state launching ramp and parking area off Sand Dam Road. There is a 10-horsepower limit on outboards. Fish for yellow perch, largemouth bass, and pickerel. Access **Waterman Reservoir** along US 44 for shore fishing of largemouth bass and northern pike.

In Lincoln: **Butterfly Pond** access is from Great Road. Fish for panfish and

CANOEING THE BLACKSTONE RIVER

Blackstone Valley Tourism Council

largemouth bass. **Olney Pond** offers a state boat ramp, a parking area, and shore-fishing facilities. Go for the trout and largemouth bass.

In North Smithfield: **Round Top Brook** is a good trout-fishing spot. Access to the Round Top Fishing Area is from RI 96. **Upper Slatersville Reservoir** is accessible from the state boat ramp and parking area off RI 102. Largemouth bass and panfish are found here. **Woonasquatucket Reservoir** (Stump Pond) is off RI 5 and RI 116. Fish for largemouth bass, northern pike, and pickerel.

In Pawtucket: **Slater Park Pond** is stocked with pickerel, trout, and sunfish.

GOLF **Country View Golf Club** (401-568-7157), 49 Club Lane, Burrillville. An 18-hole par-70 course with hilly terrain, two ponds, and a restaurant.

Foster Country Club (401-397-7750), 67 Johnson Road, Foster. The club offers an 18-hole course, with a restaurant and golf shop.

HAY- AND SLEIGH RIDES ✍ **Chepachet Farms** (401-568-9996), 226 Tourtellot Hill Road, Chepachet Village. Hay- and sleigh rides, plus a petting corral.

John W. Cole (401-568-9303), Chepachet Village. Hay- and sleigh rides as well as carriage rides. By appointment.

HORSEBACK RIDING **Sunset Stables** (401-722-3033), 1 Twin River Road, Lincoln. Guided trail rides through Lincoln Woods Park.

ICE SKATING **Lynch Arena** (401-728-7420), Dexter and Beatty Streets, Pawtucket. Open Monday through Friday 11:30–1, Saturday and Sunday 2–3:30. This is a municipal ice-skating rink open to the public.

Rhode Island Sports Center (401-767-2200), 1186 Eddie Dowling Highway, North Smithfield. Open to the public for ice skating weekday mornings and, briefly, Sunday afternoons.

STARGAZING **Seagrave Observatory** (401-726-1328), 47 Peep Toad Road, North Scituate, off RI 116. Open Saturday evenings 7–10 year-round (later in summer). Free. Built by Frank Evans Seagrave in 1914, this rural observatory's main telescope dates from 1878, but there is more modern equipment available for use as well.

SWIMMING **Bowdish Reservoir** (401-277-1415), George Washington Management Area off US 44, Glocester. Lifeguard and fee.

Frank Moody State Beach (401-277-1415), Lincoln Woods off RI 146, Lincoln. A pretty beach in a pretty park setting, but on summer weekends it's wise to arrive early.

Casimir Pulaski Memorial State Park (401-277-1415), George Washington Management Area, Pulaski Road off US 44, Glocester. Swimming in Peck's Pond, Burrillville. Bathhouses and lifeguard.

Spring Lake, Spring Lake Road, Burrillville. There is a fee for swimming in this pleasant lake. Lifeguard.

World War II Memorial State Park, Social Street, Woonsocket. Pond in an urban setting. Bathhouses and toilets.

TENNIS Courts open to the public are available at the following locations:

In Burrillville (401-548-9470), **Burrillville School,** East Avenue, Harrisville; **Middle School,** RI 102, Glendale.

In Cumberland (401-728-2400), **Currier Play Area,** Broad Street; Tucker Field Athletic Complex, Mendon Road; Windsor Park, Snake Hill Road.

In Lincoln (401-333-1100), **Lime Acres,** Jenckes Hill Road, Limerock.

In North Smithfield (401-767-2200), **North Smithfield High School,** RI 104; **Pacheco Park,** off Main Street, Slatersville.

In Pawtucket (401-728-0500), **Slater Park,** RI 1A.

In Smithfield (233-1000), **Smithfield High School,** Pleasantview Avenue; Willow Field, Tucker Road.

✳ Green Space

Arboretum at Riverside (401-724-8733), 724 Pleasant Street, Pawtucket. Five miles of wooded trails and paths edge the Seekonk River and abut Riverside Cemetery, laid out in 1874 and inspired by the work of renowned landscape architect Frederick Law Olmsted. In May, Azalea Day celebrates these colorful flowers. At other times it's pleasant simply to stroll in the shade of the trees brought here from all parts of the world. There is a small admission fee.

William Blackstone Park, Broad and Blackstone Streets, Cumberland (across from the Ann & Hope Specialty Shops). A granite monument to the first Blackstone River Valley settler, the Reverend William Blackstone, is the centerpiece of this 1-acre park.

Blackstone Gorge State Park, North Smithfield. This is an impressive wooded and rock-ledge park overlooking the Blackstone River Gorge, which is the only spot in Rhode Island for white-water canoeing. The park can be difficult to find because there is no marked access point. Take RI 146 north from North Smithfield to RI 146A north, turning right onto St. Paul's Street, then left onto RI 122. Continue to County Street, where you turn left and go to the dead end. It's then a short walk (don't be discouraged—it's through backyards, but access is allowed) to the woods above the river. Take any one of the three paths to the left (one is decorated with modern sculptures fashioned of wood and twigs). After about 5 minutes you'll arrive at the spectacular gorge overlook.

Blackstone River State Park, Old Lower River Road, Lincoln. Off RI 146, take the RI 116 north exit to the second set of lights. Go right and immediately left onto River Road; then take the first left downhill. Go left again and park. As this book went to press, this little park between the Blackstone River and the Blackstone Canal was unmarked. Set beneath an underpass in urban Rhode Island, it's not easy to find, although once discovered it's a peaceful retreat from the city bustle. Though the park is only a stone's throw from the highway, the rush of a waterfall masks vehicle sounds. The canal was constructed by Irish

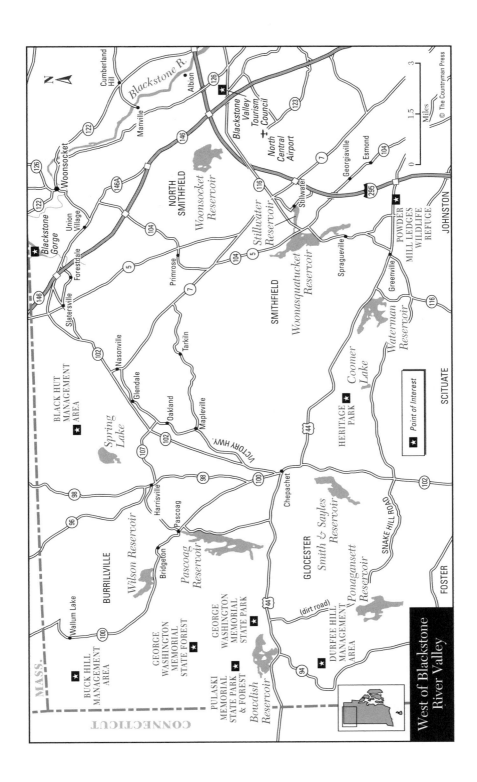

West of Blackstone
River Valley

immigrants in the 1820s to transport manufactured products the 45 miles between Worcester, Massachusetts, and Providence. Although sections of the canal have washed away, it has been restored in this park, and you can amble the towpath between river and canal for about 2 miles, seeing the occasional blue heron. An extension of the bike path (see *To Do* in "Providence") to the park is in the works.

Buck Hill Wildlife Management Area, Buck Hill Road, Burrillville. There are blazed trails past ponds and old stone walls, through woods rich in song- and game birds. During hunting season, fluorescent orange clothing is required.

Chase Farm (401-333-1100), Great Road, Lincoln. The 100 acres of this former dairy farm are open to the public for hiking, picnicking, kite flying, sledding, and horsehoe pitching. There's also a butterfly garden.

Diamond Hill Park, Cumberland. This wooded, rocky park, which takes its name from the abundant quartz crystals, has unmarked trails and fields and a pond and picnic area.

☌ **Heritage Park,** Glocester (between the villages of Harmony and Chepachet). There are rock ledges, ski and hiking trails, picnic tables, brooks, and pine woods in this 127-acre town park that is ideal for Sunday-afternoon excursions with children.

Lincoln Woods State Park, RI 123, Lincoln. In this 627-acre park of woods, kettle holes, and rock outcroppings, you can idle away many a summer afternoon. There is a pond for fishing and swimming, and trails for walking and riding. This is a great spot for cross-country skiing during winter.

The Monastery, Diamond Hill Road, Cumberland. In 1900 a Cistercian monastery was established on a 500-acre site here and was, at that time, one of only three Cistercian monasteries in the United States. Today the hilly, forested terrain is the property of the town of Cumberland, and a rugged walking trail winds through trees and fields, past a marsh and a monument called *Nine Men's Misery.* This marks the spot where the bodies of nine colonial soldiers killed in King Philip's War were found.

Powder Mill Ledges Wildlife Refuge, Putnam Pike (RI 44) and Cedar Swamp Road, Smithfield. Two miles of hiking trails thread through this area, the headquarters of the Audubon Society of Rhode Island.

Casimir Pulaski Memorial Recreation Area, Pulaski Road, Glocester. The attractions of this state park include a beach, covered bridge, pond, picnic area, and four ski trails that, in the off-season, are fine for walking.

☌ **Slater Park,** RI 1A, Pawtucket. This is a pretty, manicured park that has a particular appeal for children with its Looff Carousel, picnic sites, playground, barnyard, and duck-feeding pond. Adults will enjoy walks along the Ten-Mile River Canal, lawn bowling, and tennis.

Valley Falls Heritage Park, Broad Street, Cumberland. A ruined mill stands on this 2-acre site beside a waterfall; interpretive signs explain how it once worked. There is a picnic area and historic footbridges over sluiceways.

George Washington Management Area, Burrillville and Glocester. Access is north of US 44 along a gravel roadway. This 3,489-acre area contains ponds and wetlands; evergreen, oak, and maple forests; many trails; and fine spots for winter birding. Among the evergreens there may be ovenbirds, northern waterthrushes and hermit thrushes, pine warblers, and occasionally tufted titmice. In the deciduous forest, many warblers pass through during spring and fall migrations. Animals of the area include white-tailed deer, cottontail rabbits and snowshoe hares, foxes, coyotes, and raccoons. During hunting season, which runs from October through March, all visitors and hunters must wear 200 square inches of fluorescent orange.

Also see Frank Moody State Beach, Spring Lake, and World War II Memorial State Park under *Swimming*.

✳ Lodging

Since the Blackstone River Valley is largely a rural area, the number of accommodations is limited.

BED & BREAKFASTS Pillsbury House (401-766-7983; 1-800-205-4112), 341 Prospect Street, Woonsocket 02895. ($) An 1875 mansard-roofed Victorian house with a wrap-around porch in the city's tree-shaded North End. Four air-conditioned rooms, all with private bath, in a former mill superintendent's house. Apple pancakes are among the items on the breakfast menu.

Samuel Slater Canal Boat (401-724-2200; 1-800-454-2882), Cumberland Landing, Cumberland. ($$$–$$$$) One large double cabin and two single cabins, with breakfast, are available for a family or a party of four friends from August through November.

Whipple-Cullen Farmstead Bed & Breakfast (401-333-1899), 99 Old River Road, Lincoln 02865. ($$) A 1736 farmhouse with two rooms (each containing double beds), a shared bath, some fireplaces, a common keeping room for guests, and a Victorian porch overlooking 5 acres of fields and woods. Adequate but nothing fancy.

CAMPGROUNDS Bowdish Lake Camping Area (401-568-8890), Bowdish Lake. Write: P.O. Box 25, Chepachet 02814. Off US 44, 5 miles west of Chepachet Village. Open May 1 through October 15. The 450 sites near Lake Bowdish are suitable for tents or for RVs up to 35 feet in length. Water, electricity, dumping stations, toilets, hot showers, hiking trails, boat and canoe rentals, fishing, playgrounds, and recreation halls are available. Entertainment, sports, and crafts activities are offered in July and August.

George Washington Management Area (401-568-2013), 2185 Putnam Pike, Chepachet 02814. This area is located off US 44, 2 miles east of the Connecticut line and 5 miles west of the junction of US 44 with RI 102. Open mid-April through mid-October. Overlooking Bowdish Reservoir in a wooded area, 45 primitive tent and trailer campsites plus two shelters provide splendid spots to spend the night after a day of swimming and hiking.

✳ Where to Eat

DINING OUT ♪ ♿ **Chan's Fine Oriental Dining** (401-765-1900), 267 Main Street, Woonsocket. ($) Open daily for lunch and dinner. Live jazz and comedy shows are the highlights of Chan's weekends. As for the food, it's largely Cantonese and Mandarin, with an occasional Polynesian or spicy Szechuan dish.

Gian Carlo's Ristorante (401-765-3711), 153 Hamlet Avenue, Woonsocket. ($$–$$$) Open Tuesday through Saturday for lunch and dinner. A sophisticated Tuscan-influenced restaurant specializing in wood-grilled steaks and chops.

Parente's Restaurant (401-231-7600), 153 Douglas Pike, Smithfield. ($–$$) Open daily for lunch and dinner. Prime rib and lobster are two of the favorites at this unpretentious restaurant with very reasonable prices.

✐ ♿ **Stage Coach Tavern Restaurant** (401-568-2275), Putnam Pike, Chepachet Village. ($$) Open Wednesday through Sunday for lunch and dinner. It was in this tavern in 1842 that Thomas Wilson Dorr, instigator of the Dorr Rebellion, established his headquarters. He had been elected the People's Governor to seek universal white male suffrage in Rhode Island, rather than suffrage based on property rights. Troops of the governor elected by the property owners attacked him here with his supporters, and shots were fired through the tavern door. Today this is a tavern-restaurant, paneled and picturesque, with an extensive menu (the specialty is prime rib) and wine list.

EATING OUT The Blue Onion (401-769-4646), 65 Founder's Drive, behind the Holiday Inn Express. ($) Open Wednesday through Saturday 6 AM–9:30 PM, Sunday and Monday 6–2. Even though it's off the road, it's

hard to miss this shiny bright blue diner.

Bocce Club (401-762-0155), 226 St. Louis Avenue, Woonsocket. ($) Open Wednesday through Saturday for dinner, Sunday noon–8:30. You can dine here on an old bocce court if you like. The family-style chicken dinner includes an antipasto rather than a salad.

Box Seats (401-762-0900), 350 River Street, Woonsocket. ($–$$) Open daily for lunch and dinner. The fried clams here win awards as the best in the state. Scallops and fish-and-chips are also skillfully deep-fried.

Garden Grille (401-726-2826), 727 East Avenue, Pawtucket. ($$–$$) Open Monday through Thursday 10–9, Sunday 8:30–3 and 5:30–8. Tabbouleh, mixed green salads, wood-grilled vegetables and pizza, tofu specials.

✐ **Greenville Inn** (401-949-4020), 36 Smith Avenue, Smithfield. ($) Open Monday through Saturday for dinner, Sunday for lunch and dinner. Prime rib on the bone and family-style chicken (in this case, soup, salad, chicken, and macaroni for well under $10).

Kountry Kitchen (401-949-0840), 10 Smith Avenue, Smithfield. ($) Open Sunday through Wednesday 6:30–2, Thursday through Saturday 6:30–8. It's the weekday country breakfast of home fries, two eggs, and toast for under $2 up to 9 AM that makes this a favorite stopping place for locals. Lunch and early supper (until 6 PM) are offered, too.

✐ **Modern Diner** (401-726-8390), 364 East Avenue, Pawtucket. ($) Open Monday through Saturday 7–2:30, Sunday 7–2. This meticulously cared-for 1940s-style diner has old-time favorites like liver and onions and fish-and-chips. A Pawtucket classic.

Moon's Landing (401-658-0449), 4077 Mendon Road, Cumberland. ($) Open Monday through Wednesday for lunch, Thursday through Saturday for lunch and dinner until 8:30, Sunday 8–noon. A casual little restaurant that is popular with senior citizens for its early hours (the last orders are taken at 7 PM). The menu ranges from clam cakes to sirloin steaks. Home-baked goods and Grape-Nut pudding are specialties.

✋ ♿ **The New England Fish Company** (401-729-9600), 271 Newport Avenue, Pawtucket. ($–$$) Open Tuesday through Saturday for lunch and dinner; Sunday for dinner. Fish chowder, lobster rolls, fresh Maine clams, and fish-and-chips are favorites.

Purple Cat (401-568-7161), US 44 and RI 100, Glocester. ($$) Open Tuesday through Sunday for lunch and dinner. This is a cozy roadside restaurant popular with local residents, offering meat, fish, and pasta dishes.

✋ **Wright's Farm** (401-769-2856), 84 Inman Road, Nasonville. ($) Thursday through Saturday 4–9 and Sunday noon–8. Chicken family-style is a northern Rhode Island tradition, and nowhere is it better presented than at this hillside chicken farm. You can get half a roast chicken, shells, salad, and rolls for well under $10.

Ye Olde English Fish & Chips Shop (401-762-3637), Market Square, Woonsocket. ($) Tuesday through Saturday 10–6. Aficionados insist that this little shop sells the best fish-and-chips in the state—crisp-fried and fresh.

SNACKS **Hartley's Pork Pies** (401-726-1295), 871 Smithfield Avenue, Lincoln. Open Wednesday through Saturday 7–2, or as long as the supply lasts. You have to arrive well before 1 to get a taste of this old-English dish of beef or pork with potatoes under piecrust. Take-out only.

🐾 ✋ **Ice Cream Machine** (401-333-5053), 4288 Diamond Hill Road, Cumberland. Open April through October, daily 11–8. There are 35 ice cream and three sherbet flavors to choose from at this ice cream stand opposite Diamond Hill Park. For the family pet, try the sugar-free, nondairy Frosty Paws ice cream.

✋ **Scoops at the Falls** (401-229-0033), Central Falls above the *Blackstone Valley Explorer* landing. The setting for this little summertime ice cream establishment over Valley Falls couldn't be nicer.

✳ Entertainment

THEATER/FILM **Blackstone River Theater** (401-725-9272), 549 Broad Street, Cumberland. The Pendragon Celtic Band offers its own weekend music and dance performances as well as sponsoring visits from leading musical groups from the United States, Canada, and Europe in this renovated former Masonic temple.

Community College of Rhode Island Theater (401-333-7000), Flanagan campus, 1762 Louisquisset Pike, Lincoln. Occasional performances.

Community Players (401-725-6860), Jenks Junior High School, Division Street, Pawtucket. This community theater group that has been in existence more than 75 years performs comedies, mysteries, and Broadway musicals four times annually.

Mill River Dinner Theater (401-721-0909), 409 High Street, Central Falls. Popular light fare is performed by a local theater company.

Rustic Drive-In (401-769-7601), RI 146, North Smithfield. This is the last drive-in movie theater still in operation in Rhode Island.

The Sandra Feinstein-Gamm Theatre (401-723-4226), 172 Exchange Street, Pawtucket. Plays like William Shakespeare's *Julius Caesar* and Arthur Miller's *The Crucible* are the sort of serious theatrical fare this Trinity Repertory Company–like theater offers in a handsomely renovated space adjoining Pawtucket's historic Armory Building.

Stadium Theater (401-762-4545), Monument Square, Woonsocket. Restoration is now complete on this elaborate 1920s theater, with its ceiling mural of muses and its fountains of cherubs, its impressive theater pipe organ and fine acoustics. Touring companies offer concerts, dance, musicals, and drama.

Stone Soup Coffee House (401-457-7147), 210 Main Street, Pawtucket. For more than 20 years musicians have been entertaining the public with folk music on Saturday nights at the Stone Soup Coffee House.

SPECTATOR SPORTS **Lincoln Park** (401-723-3200), RI 146, Lincoln. Open daily for dog races year-round except on Christmas and Easter.

McCoy Stadium (401-724-7300), 1 Columbus Avenue, Pawtucket. The Pawtucket Red Sox, the Triple-A farm team of the Boston Red Sox, play here.

✳ Selective Shopping

ANTIQUES SHOPS **Brown & Hopkins Country Store** (401-568-4830), Main Street, Chepachet Village. Open Thursday through Saturday 11–4, Sunday noon–5. This is said to be America's longest-operating country store. It opened in 1809 and still sells sour lemon drops, black licorice, and root beer barrels in its penny-candy case by the potbellied stove on the ground floor. The two top floors are for browsers, containing a clutter of antiques of varying quality and sorts.

Chestnut Hill Antiques (401-568-4365), Victory Highway, Chepachet Village. Open on and off during spring, summer, and fall, so call for an appointment. Old watches and old postcards are the specialty here.

Country Cupboards (401-568-0606), 1503 Putnam Pike (US 44), Chepachet. Open Wednesday through Saturday 11–5, Sunday 1–5. Early-19th-century painted country furniture.

Harold's (401-568-6030), 1191 Main Street, Chepachet Village. Open weekends 11–5 (more or less, but call before you go). Old lamps of all kinds are sold at Harold's, where chairs are caned and rush seats made, too.

The Hope Chest (401-949-2333), 2953 Hartford Avenue, Johnston. Open daily 10–5. An antiques and collectibles store with thousands of items and a second location in Narragansett.

The Old Post Office (401-568-1795), 1178 Putnam Pike (US 44), Chepachet. Open Monday and Thursday through Saturday 11–5, Sunday noon–5. Here some 10 to a dozen dealers offer collectible toys, books, glass, jewelry, china, furniture, and handcrafts.

Stone Mill Antiques (401-568-6662), Main Street, Chepachet Village. Open 10–5 Saturday and Sunday year-round. Carriages sit outside this antiques shop, where the specialty is European imports.

The Town Trader (401-568-8800), 1177 Putnam Pike (US 44), Chepachet. Open year-round Wednesday through Sunday.

ART GALLERIES Pawtucket Arts Collaborative Gallery (401-273-5367), Blackstone Valley Visitors' Center, 175 Main Street, Pawtucket. Call for hours. This is a small gallery of changing exhibits by local artists.

Rhode Island Watercolor Society (401-725-1876), Slater Park Boathouse, off US 1A, Pawtucket. Open Tuesday through Saturday 10–4, Sunday 1–5. Exhibitions of watercolors by painters from Rhode Island and neighboring Massachusetts.

J. H. Rowbottom Fine Arts (401-333-1109), 150 Meadow Road, Cumberland. Open Thursday 3–6, Friday 7–9. Exhibitions by Rhode Island artists.

BOOKSTORES Bryant College Bookstore (401-232-6240), Bryant Center, John Mowry Road, Smithfield. Open Monday through Thursday 8:30–6:30, Friday 8:30–4, and Saturday 10–2 during the academic year; Monday through Friday 9–4 in summer. General titles.

Waldenbooks at Lincoln Mall (401-333-2120), 622 George Washington Highway (RI 116), Lincoln. Open Monday through Saturday 10–9:30, Sunday 10–6. General titles and local travel.

CRAFTS SHOP J&M Hobbies (401-647-7778), 180 Danielson Pike, Scituate. If you like to make model railroads, do puzzles, play with or collect die-cast toy cars, J&M Hobbies is the place to come.

FACTORY OUTLETS Ann & Hope Specialty Shops (401-722-1000; 401-722-1001), 1 Ann & Hope Way, off RI 122, Cumberland. Open Monday through Saturday 9:30–8, Sunday 11–5. There's a fashion outlet here for stylish men's and women's clothes, along with a children's outlet, a bed and bath shop, a garden, pet, and patio shop, and a shoe shop. Everything is a markdown from the original.

Colonial Mills, Inc. (401-724-6840), 560 Mineral Spring Avenue, Pawtucket. Open Monday through Saturday 9–5. Colonial Mills produces braided rugs for Old Sturbridge Village and Yield House, among others, but prices here are much, much lower.

Lorraine Mill Fabrics (401-722-9500), 593 Mineral Spring Avenue, Pawtucket. Open Monday through Wednesday and Friday 10–6; Thursday 10–8; Sunday noon–5. This is one of the largest fabric stores in the country, including bridal, fashion, and an extensive home decorating department—and with good savings. Rhode Island School of Design students buy here, so you'll find some interesting, more bizarre fabrics. To get here from I-95 north, take exit 27. Turn right onto Pine Avenue, left onto Main Street, then right onto Mineral Spring Avenue. From I-95 south, take exit 25, turn right onto Smithfield Avenue, then right onto Mineral Spring Avenue.

Slater Fabrics Store (401-727-9068), 5 Industrial Drive, Cumberland. Open Monday through Friday 10–5, Saturday 10–2. High-quality fabrics for home furnishings and clothing are usually available in large quantities, at about $1.25 a yard. To reach the store, take exit 11 off I-295 south. Go right onto RI 114, then right onto Industrial Road. From I-295 north, take exit 11, go left onto RI 114, then right onto Industrial Road.

SPECIAL SHOPS **Cherry Valley Herb Farm** (401-568-8585; 401-568-3901), 969 Snake Hill Road, Glocester. Open Thursday through Saturday 10–4, Sunday 1–4. Herbs from the Cherry Valley garden are used to make wreaths, herb vinegars, fragrant oils, potpourris, and similar items. Cookbooks and garden books are sold as well.

Pentimento (401-334-1838), 322 Sneech Pond Road, Cumberland. Open daily 11–7 in summer, Wednesday through Sunday 11–6 in fall and winter. Once a grain mill operated here, powered by the water in Abbott Run Stream; today only this granary building remains. In it, antiques, collectibles, and crafts are sold; in summer, espresso, pastry, and sherbet are served on the deck above the stream.

Slater Mill Museum Shop (401-725-8638), 67 Roosevelt Avenue, Pawtucket. Open most weekdays and some weekends in summer and in the pre-Christmas season, but call for hours. Jellies and jams and honey, books on weaving and spinning and the industrial revolution, replicas of children's toys of the past, and gift cards are among the offerings in this gift shop.

The Slater Mill Store and Café (401-725-8918; 401-725-8919), in the Blackstone Valley Visitors' Center, 175 Main Street, Pawtucket. Call for hours. This is an upscale gift shop carrying handwoven fabrics, handmade hats, jewelry, metal sculpture, and glass items designed by Rhode Island artists.

Also see *To Do* for apple-picking farms and farm stands.

✳ **Special Events**

March: **Rhode Island Whitewater Championships** (401-568-8605), Mapleville, Burrillville.

April: **Pawtucket Red Sox Opening Day** (401-724-7300), McCoy Stadium, Pawtucket.

May: **May Breakfast** (401-949-4441), Smith-Appleby House, 220 Stillwater Road, Smithfield. Reservations must be made in advance for this festive salute to spring. The **Limerock Baptist Church May Breakfast** (401-334-2999), 1075 Great Road, Lincoln, also welcomes the month of May.

June: It's **Strawberry Social** time (401-949-4441) at the Smith-Appleby House, 220 Stillwater Road, Smithfield.

July: **Fourth of July Ancient and Horribles Parade,** Chepachet Village, brings marchers and bands together from all across the state. **Cumberland Fourth of July Parade,** Nate Whipple Highway, Cumberland. Road race, parade, band concert. **Annual chicken barbecue** at the Foster Center Volunteer Fire Department, RI 94. **Smithfield Independence Fireworks and Concert** (401-949-4590). **Arnold Mills July 4 Parade** (401-334-9996).

July–August: **City of Central Falls Summer Concert Series** (401-727-7474), Jenks Park, Broad Street, Central Falls. **Jazz and Blues Concert** (401-765-1900), Chan's Restaurant, Woonsocket.

August: **Cumberland Fest,** with booths, entertainment, and fireworks. There's a **Blueberry Social** at the Smith-Appleby House in Smithfield.

September: During the gala **Pawtucket Arts Festival** (401-724-2200; 1-800-454-2882), dragon boats race on the river, artists display their paintings and sculpture in Slater Park, and the Rhode Island Philharmonic plays out of doors to make it a grand time for all at this 2-week-long event. The **Central Falls Antique & Custom Car Show** (401-727-7474) features more than 300 vehicles on display at the Higginson Avenue Sports Complex. **French Farmer's Market and Heritage Days** (401-769-9846), River Island Park, Market Square, Woonsocket. Open-air farmer's market, trolley tours of the city, arts and crafts, apple pie contest. At **Manville Settlers Day Festival,** costumed interpreters demonstrate colonial-era crafts and skills.

October: **Autumnfest** (401-762-8072) is a 3-day celebration featuring ethnic foods, parades, and fireworks at World War II Memorial Park on Social Street in Woonsocket. **Scituate Art Festival** (401-647-0057), on the village green, RI 116, North Scituate.

November: **Annual Harvest Supper** (401-949-4441) at the Smith-Appleby House in Smithfield has meals offered by servers in colonial costume. Reservations are required. **Christmas in the Village Bazaar** (401-333-0139) is a seasonal highlight at St. Joseph's Parish Center, 1303 Mendon Road, Cumberland.

December: The **Looff Carousel** (401-728-0500, ext. 251), Slater Park, Pawtucket, whirls merrily to celebrate the season, and there are strolling clowns, hayrides, face painting, and Christmas carols. **Christmas Shopping by Candlelight and Open House Tours** (401-568-1800) brighten the holidays in Chepachet Village, Glocester. There's a **Christmas Open House** (401-333-1100, ext. 289) at the Valentine Whitman House, 1147 Great Road, Lincoln. **Christmas at Smith-Appleby House** (401-231-7363) in Smithfield includes a gaily decorated 17th-century house and barn. Pawtucket has a **Winter Wonderland** in Slater Park (401-724-2200), and a **Christmas Lights Trolley Tour** takes visitors (who must make reservations by calling 401-724-2200) from Cumberland to Lincoln to see the festive decorations. **Candlelight Shopping** (401-568-5140), Chepachet Village.

South of 3
Providence

WARWICK, CRANSTON, AND

SURROUNDING TOWNS

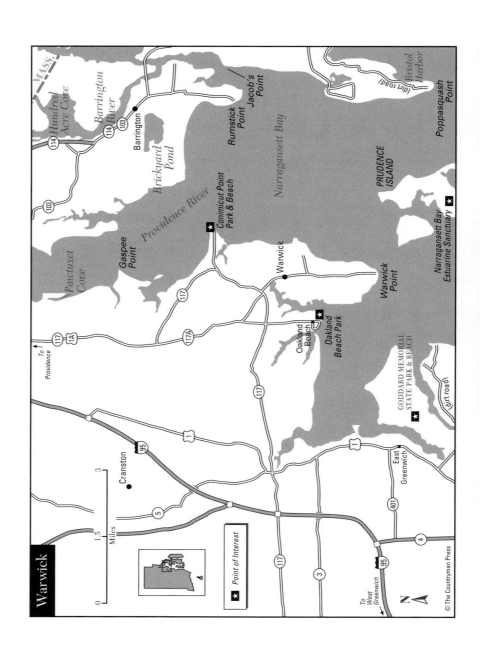

Warwick

Miles
0   1.5   3

Cranston

To Providence

To West Greenwich

PRUDENCE ISLAND

Narragansett Bay

Providence River

Pawtuxet Cove

Gaspee Point

Conimicut Point Park & Beach

Rumstick Point

Jacob's Point

Brickyard Pond

Barrington River

Hundred Acre Cove

Barrington

MASS.

Bristol Harbor

(dirt road)

Poppasquash Point

Narragansett Bay Estuarine Sanctuary

Warwick Point

Warwick

Oakland Beach

Oakland Beach Park

GODDARD MEMORIAL STATE PARK & BEACH

(dirt road)

East Greenwich

★ Point of Interest

© The Countryman Press

N

WARWICK, CRANSTON, AND SURROUNDING TOWNS

Outh of Providence, edging Narragansett Bay, sprawl the bedroom communities of Cranston and Warwick. They are riddled with superhighways and speckled with malls and housing developments, but here and there a visitor will find sites and pockets of interest.

Indeed, early in Rhode Island's history these towns were supremely important. Gaspee Point in Warwick was the site of Rhode Island military defiance of the British in 1772, when Warwick men set fire to the grounded British revenue cutter *Gaspée*. Revolutionary War hero General Nathanael Greene lived just over the Warwick line in Coventry, in the village of Anthony, where his house still stands.

In Cranston the 19th-century mansion of two Rhode Island governor Spragues—uncle and nephew—has recently been restored and may be seen by appointment.

Although urban sprawl has left little green space and often overwhelms historic and architectural attractions, the determined visitor can bypass the traffic jams and shopping malls to find good restaurants, special historic areas of interest, beaches for walking, and spectacular views over Narragansett Bay. On elegant Warwick Neck, hidden estates with a Newportish air overlook the bay. Comfortable little Pawtuxet Cove showcases colonial and Victorian homes on tree-lined streets. To the south of Warwick and Cranston lies a gem of a Rhode Island town: East Greenwich. Many of its handsome houses were built during its heyday as an agricultural and seafaring community just before the Revolutionary War. Boats bob at anchor at the yacht club, and old-fashioned shops still edge the historic Main Street.

GUIDANCE **Providence-Warwick Convention and Visitors Bureau** (401-274-1636; 1-800-233-1636), American Express Way, Waterplace Park.

Warwick Tourism Office (401-738-2000, ext. 6402; 1-800-4-WARWICK; www.warwickri.com), 3275 Post Road.

Cranston Chamber of Commerce (401-785-3780; www.cranstonchamber .com), 48 Rolfe Square.

Coventry Town Hall (401-821-6400), 1610 Flat River Road.

East Greenwich Chamber of Commerce (401-885-0020; www.eastgreen wichchamber.com), 591 Main Street.

GETTING THERE *By car:* From Providence, to avoid the traffic on I-95, take US 1 (sometimes Scenic RI 1A). From time to time this follows the shore of Narragansett Bay.

By bus: The **Rhode Island Public Transport Authority** (RIPTA; 401-781-9400) has frequent bus service throughout the day.

By air: Warwick is the site of Rhode Island's main airport, the **Theodore Francis Green State Airport** (401-737-4000). There are connections with various cities around the country from this spiffy modernized airport that puts many a larger city's airport to shame. Controversial modern artworks decorate it inside and out.

MEDICAL EMERGENCY The statewide emergency number is **911.**

Kent County Hospital (401-737-7000), 455 Tollgate Road, Warwick.

✳ To See

HISTORIC SITES John Waterman Arnold House (401-467-7647), 11 Roger Williams Avenue, off Warwick Avenue, Warwick. Headquarters of the Warwick Historical Society, this pleasant, late-1700s farmhouse is notable for its beehive oven, paneled dining room, and 18th-century furniture. As this book went to press, however, the house was temporarily closed for restoration; call for opening hours.

General Nathanael Greene Homestead (401-821-8630), 50 Taft Street, Anthony, Coventry. Open April through October, Wednesday and Saturday 10–5,

LIFE AS A DOG ON NARRAGANSETT BAY

Michael Salerno

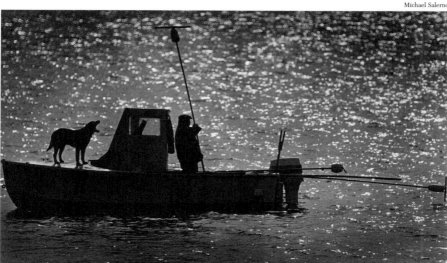

SETTLING IN FOR THE NIGHT

Michael Salerno

Sunday 1–5. Small admission fee. This handsome gray-clapboard house on a cleared hill was the home of the Rhode Island–born general who was Washington's second-in-command during the Revolution. Its study is furnished with pieces that actually belonged to the general and his wife. The Victorian parlor contains items belonging to General Greene's grandson. Below the house, in a pretty country setting, the general's brother Jacob, his wife, Margaret, and their children are buried. The general himself is buried in Savannah, where he died.

Kent County Courthouse/East Greenwich Town Hall (401-886-8607), 125 Main Street, East Greenwich. Open Monday through Friday 8:30–4:30. This square-towered yellow- and white-clapboard structure set back above Main Street was built in 1804 as the Kent County Courthouse and continued to serve in that capacity until 1978. Then, vacant and in disrepair, it was scheduled for demolition until concerned citizens saw to its preservation and restoration. The building was reopened as the town hall in 1996, and its handsome interior merits a visit. It was in the original courthouse on the site that, in 1775, the Rhode Island Colony's General Assembly enacted a resolution that ultimately resulted in the creation of the U.S. Navy.

Paine House (401-397-5135), 7 Station Street, Coventry. Open June through September, Saturday 1–4, and by appointment. This 17th-century colonial home is attractively furnished with period pieces.

⚓ **Governor Sprague Mansion** (401-944-9226), 1351 Cranston Street, Cranston. Open by appointment. Two Rhode Island governors lived in this recently restored, 28-room 1790s house with an 1864 addition. They were uncle and nephew, and both were named William Sprague. The Sprague family, originally farmers, acquired their wealth from nine textile mills. In addition to the house itself, there is a carriage house containing sleighs, carriages, a pony cart, a Conestoga wagon, and a gypsy wagon.

General James Mitchell Varnum House (401-884-1776), 57 Peirce Street, East Greenwich. Open June through August, Thursday through Saturday; otherwise, by appointment. George Washington, Lafayette, and Thomas Paine were all guests in this handsome house that was started in 1773 by Continental Army general Varnun. But it took seven years to finish because its owner was so eager to plan and construct it himself. Some of its walls are paneled, while others are covered with hand-painted 19th-century Chinese wallpaper. Period furnishings fill the house, and its unusual bric-a-brac includes Chinese temple vases from the sultan of Muscat, which were given as a reward to an East Greenwich sea captain for delivering Arabian vases to Queen Victoria. There is Sheffield silver, a Lowestoft tea set, and General Nathanael Greene memorabilia.

✳ To Do

BICYCLING Cranston–Warwick Bike Path (401-222-4203, ext. 4042). Five miles of what will one day be a 25-mile bike path from Providence to Connecticut follows an abandoned rail line. You can get on at the Cranston–Warwick border below I-295.

Coventry Greenway (401-822-9174). A 5-mile-long trail through villages and greenery from Quidnick Village at the West Warwick town line to Coventry Center.

Goddard Memorial State Park (401-884-2010). Eight miles of woodland trails wind through this pretty park.

FOR FAMILIES ✐ Impossible Dream Park (401-823-5566), 575 Centerville Road, Warwick. Open April to mid-October. A life-sized dollhouse, fort, garage, castle, and miniature golf are among the highlights of this playground, which—although created for physically challenged youngsters—is open to all.

GOLF Coventry Pines Golf Course (401-397-9482), 1065 Harkney Hill Road, Coventry. A nine-hole course in a wooded setting.

Cranston Country Club (401-826-1683), 69 Burlingame Road, Cranston. This 18-hole course offers both flat and hilly terrain plus several ponds. There is a bar and a place for snacks.

East Greenwich Golf and Country Club (401-884-5656), 1646 Division Road. A nine-hole golf course with a snack bar and lounge.

Midville Country Club (401-828-9215), 100 Lombardi Lane, West Warwick. Slightly hilly with a pond. In summer there is a hot dog concession stand and a bar.

Seaview Golf Course (401-739-6311), 150 Gray Street, Warwick. A short, narrow nine-hole course with two ponds overlooking Greenwich Bay.

CROSS-COUNTRY SKIING Goddard Memorial State Park (401-884-2010), Warwick. This park of 400 acres is ever-popular with cross-country skiers after snowstorms.

SPORTS CENTER Mickey Stevens Sports Complex (401-738-2000, ext. 6809 or 6811), 975 Sandy Lane, Warwick. Tennis courts, a swimming pool, and a winter ice rink are all operated by the city. Call for information on hours and fees.

SWIMMING Briar Point Beach (401-833-9170), Briar Point Avenue off Arnold Road, Coventry. At this little beach on 600-acre Lake Tiogue, there is supervised swimming from mid-June through Labor Day; you'll also find picnic facilities, a playground, and parking.

TENNIS Tennis Rhode Island (401-828-4450), 636 Centerville Road, Warwick. Six indoor courts open to the public.

✳ Green Space

BEACHES ✷ Conimicut Point Park, Point Avenue off RI 117, Warwick. There is a shallow-water beach and a playground for children and—in summer—a lemonade stand near the Conimicut Light.

✷ **Gaspee Point,** Warwick. This is a quiet beach for youngsters to enjoy with their pails and shovels. To reach it from Pawtuxet Village, take the Narragansett Parkway south for 1 mile, then turn left onto Spring Green. At the first rotary, go left to the beach.

Oakland Beach Park, Oakland Beach Avenue, Warwick. This extensive beach on Greenwich Bay has a pleasant seafood restaurant. This is where, 60 years ago, the trolley from Providence brought day-trippers. In winter it's an ideal place for a waterfront stroll.

Merrill S. Whipple Conservation Area, RI 117 and Sandy Bottom Road, Coventry. In this 57-acre wooded area along the south branch of the Pawtuxet River are hiking trails, vernal pools, waterfowl observation posts, and trout-fishing sites.

PARKS Goddard Memorial State Park (401-884-2010), Warwick. This was an area of sand dunes along Greenwich Bay until the 1870s, when property owner Henry Russell began planting acorns. The oak, and other tree varieties, thrived. When Russell died, Colonel William Goddard continued his work, and the trees did so well that in the early 1900s the USDA Forest Service called it "the finest example of private forestry in America." The forest of some 400 acres was given to the state in 1927. Today the park offers bridle and walking paths, a sandy swimming beach, outdoor concerts in summer, and cross-country skiing in winter.

Pawtuxet Park. The little bayfront park in Pawtuxet Village is a perfect place for a stroll along Pawtuxet Cove. To get here, drive south from Providence on Broad Street, through Cranston, into Pawtuxet Village.

Salter's Grove Park, Narragansett Parkway at Landon Road, Pawtuxet Cove. Wildflowers dot this small but pleasant wooded park on the waterfront. There is a marsh frequented by waterfowl, a boat ramp, a jetty for fishing and walking, and duck hunting for licensed hunters in-season.

Warwick City Park, Asylum Road, Warwick. A wooded park with a pretty beach, bicycle paths, and ball fields.

✳ Lodging

HOTELS AND MOTELS ♿ **Crowne Plaza Hotel at the Crossings** (401-732-6000; 1-800-2-CROWNE; www.crowneplaza.com), 801 Greenwich Avenue, Warwick 02887. ($$$$) Warwick's largest and grandest hostelry, with 266 rooms, a pool, a resturant, and an attractive garden.

🍸 ♿🐾 **Motel 6** (401-467-9800, 1-800-4-MOTEL-6; www.motel6 .com), 20 Jefferson Boulevard, Warwick 02888. ($) This 118-room three-story, two-building motel is 2 miles from Green Airport. It has no elevator. There is an outdoor pool and a restaurant next door.

♿ **Radisson Airport Hotel** (401-739-3000; 1-800-333-3333; www.radisson.com), 2081 Post Road, Warwick 02886. ($$$$) Operated in conjunction with Johnson & Wales University, this 111-room hotel is staffed by university students. Food is also prepared and served by students in the bistro.

Sheraton Providence Airport Hotel (401-738-4000; 1-800-325-3535; www.sheraton.com), 1850 Post Road, Warwick 02886. ($$$$) The Sheraton is situated just beside the T. F. Green Airport, and a shuttle bus links the two. A pool and workout facilities are available.

BED & BREAKFASTS **Allen House** (401-885-7979), 71 Verndale Drive, East Greenwich 02818. ($–$$) A ranch house with a pretty garden and a miniature waterfall on a quiet residential street offers two rooms, private baths, deck, and screened porch. Continental breakfast.

🐾 **The 1873 House** (401-884-9955), 162 Peirce Street, East Greenwich 02818. ($$) Victorian antiques add their charm to a second-floor three-room suite that can accommodate a family of five (children under 12 free). The suite has its own kitchen and private bath and is in the heart of the town's historic district. Continental breakfast.

CAMPGROUNDS 🐾 🐾 **Colwell's Campground** (401-397-4614; 401-397-5818), Peckham Lane off RI 117, Coventry 02896. Open May through September. Sites for 69 trailers and six tents. Electric hook-ups, telephone, pets allowed.

🐾 🐾 **Hickory Ridge Family Campground** (401-397-7474), Route 102, Greene 02827. Open May through October 10. Sites for 200 trailers. Varying hook-ups, hot showers, pets allowed.

🐾 **Westwood Family Campground** (401-397-7779), 2093 Harkney Hill Road, Coventry 02896. Open May 15 through October 15. Sites for 64 trailers and 10 tents. Varying hook-ups, a freshwater beach, hot showers, and a playground are among the ameneties.

✳ Where to Eat

DINING OUT **Café Fresco** (401-398-0027), 301 Main Street, East Greenwich. ($$–$$$) This isn't a restaurant for intimate tête-à-têtes. It's brash and big and noisy, but the seafood and steaks and pasta in this Italianish restaurant are uniformly well prepared, and the service is friendly.

Han Palace (401-738-2238), 2470 West Shore Road, Warwick. ($–$$) Open Sunday through Thursday 11:30–10, Friday and Saturday until 11. Chinese food, attractively presented.

&. **Harbourside Lobstermania** (401-884-6363), Water Street, East Greenwich. ($$) Open daily for lunch and dinner. Right in the lap of shellfish country, you can have lobster virtually any way you choose.

India Restaurant (401-663-3324), 5000 Post Road, East Greenwich. ($$) This Benny's Mall restaurant specializing in northern Indian dishes is open daily for lunch and dinner and serves a 17-dish buffet on Sunday 11–3.

&. **The Indian Club** (401-884-7100), 455 Main Street, East Greenwich. ($$) Open daily for lunch and dinner. Burnished copper pots, pointed arches in the Mughal tradition, and statues of Indian deities lend atmosphere to this attractive restaurant that serves both northern and southern Indian dishes. You can have such full meals as a tandoori (clay-oven-baked) mixed grill, a curry, or a simple but satisfying aloo naan (flatbread filled with potatoes, peas, and spices).

Jefferson Grille (401-737-1110), 137 Kilvert Street, Warwick. ($$) Open for lunch and dinner daily except Sunday. Wood-grilled meats, vegetables, and pizzas are all nicely seasoned. For those with a sweet tooth, delicious homemade desserts are offered at this near-the-airport restaurant.

&. **L'attitude** (401-780-8700), 2190 Broad Street, Pawtuxet Village, Cranston. ($$) Open for lunch and dinner daily, and for brunch on Sunday. The specialty here is the bistro meal served family-style. It always includes a bowl of salad and might be followed by a whole roast chicken with potatoes and baby carrots, or a shellfish risotto with mussels and shrimp, calamari, scallops, chicken,

and andouille sausage. It's enough for two or three and the price is right— about $25. There is also always good fresh-grilled fish and, for the sweet-toothed, delectable bananas Foster with spiced rum and homemade vanilla ice cream.

&. **Legal Seafoods Oyster Bar and Grille** (401-732-3663), 2081 Post Road, Warwick. ($$) Open for lunch and dinner daily. A few university students from Johnson & Wales assist in serving at this restaurant next door to the Radisson Airport Hotel, where they also assist. Fresh fish, as at all restaurants in the Legal Seafoods chain, has priority on the menu.

&. **Portofino** (401-461-8920), 897 Post Road, Warwick. ($$) Open for dinner nightly except Sunday. The strip-mall location leaves something to be desired, but the Italian fare is some of the best around. Once inside, you'll find a romantic setting. Portions are sizable, but try to leave room for the desserts.

&. **Post Office Cafe** (401-885-4444), 11 Main Street, East Greenwich. ($$–$$$) Open for dinner daily except Sunday and Monday. Open for Sunday brunch 10–2:30. A few years ago patrons stood in line in the lobby of this handsome redbrick former post office to buy their stamps. Now they sit on lounges waiting to be ushered to their tables in the old mailroom. There's charm aplenty in this creative transformation of a fine historic building. The fare is Italian, with elegant chicken and veal dishes as well as plenty of inviting pasta.

&. **Shogun Seafood Steakhouse** (401-738-8336), 75 Jefferson Boulevard, Warwick. ($$) Open daily for dinner. Formerly Soli's, this is a typical Japanese steak house where the filet mignon and the lobster and shrimp are grilled on a hibachi right at your table. There's sushi as well.

✦ **Spain** (401-946-8686), 1073 Reservoir Avenue, Cranston. ($$–$$$) Open daily for dinner except Tuesday. Paella for two, sirloin steak in roasted garlic and red wine sauce, a seafood combination in white wine, garlic, and parsley sauce—all are among the specialties at this Spanish restaurant.

Temptations (401-823-3009), 289 Cowesett Avenue, West Warwick. ($$) Open for lunch and dinner daily except Monday. The waiters are tuxedo-clad, the Italian menu is extensive, the pasta is fresh, and the three-colored linguine topped with lobster and shrimp is just garlicky enough.

✦ ✦ **Tomato Vine Restaurant** (401-732-2569), 545 Greenwich Avenue, Warwick. ($–$$) Monday through Saturday for lunch and dinner, Sunday for dinner 1–8. A homey, hospitable Italian restaurant that specializes in pasta and wood-oven pizza.

Twenty Water Street (401-885-3700; 401-885-3703), Water Street, East Greenwich. ($$–$$$) Open for dinner Monday through Saturday. It would be hard to beat the view of East Greenwich Harbor from this waterfront restaurant. Favorite dishes from the eclectic menu include rack of lamb and chicken tarragon. And, of course, there is fresh fish on the menu!

✦ ✦ **Twin Oaks** (401-781-9693), 100 Sabra Street, Cranston. ($$–$$$) Open daily for lunch and dinner except Monday. This is an unpretentious perennial Rhode Island family favorite, especially for its roast beef, veal, and steaks.

EATING OUT ✦ ✦ **Bugaboo Creek Steak House** (401-781-1400), 30 Jefferson Boulevard, Warwick. ($$) Open daily for lunch and dinner. Hearty ribs, burgers, chicken, and steak dinners are served with 22 kinds of beer and well-mixed drinks. The Canadian-ski-lodge setting includes fishing rods and talking moose heads.

✦ ✦ **Café Luna** (401-944-1438), 22 Midway Road, Garden City, Cranson. ($$–$$$) Open for lunch and dinner daily except Monday. Nothing fancy, but always fresh. Good salads like roasted pepper or chickpea for lunch; salmon with a honey glaze for dinner.

✦ ✦ **Caffe Itri** (401-942-1970), 1686 Cranston Street, Cranston. ($–$$) Open for lunch and dinner Monday through Friday, for dinner only Saturday; closed Sunday. Homemade pasta is very popular here, but there is also a wide variety of Italian dishes at reasonable prices.

✦ ✦ **Cherrystone's** (401-732-2532), 898 Oakland Beach Avenue, Warwick. ($) Open Sunday through Thursday 11:30–9, Friday and Saturday until 10. This establishment is an old-time favorite for watching the sun set over Narragansett Bay. The unpretentious food—pasta and seafood—can be enjoyed on the deck.

✦ ✦ **The Crow's Nest** (401-732-6575), 288 Arnold's Neck Drive, Apponaug, Warwick. ($) Open daily for lunch and dinner. The filling, inexpensive fare here includes chowder, fish-and-chips, and clam cakes.

✦ ✦ **Efendi's Mediterranean Grill** (401-943-8800), 1255 Reservoir Avenue, Cranston. ($$) Open Monday through Saturday for lunch and dinner, Sunday for brunch. Greek,

Turkish, Italian dishes are all on the menu.

♿ **Greenwich Bay Gourmet** (401-541-9190), 50 Cliff Street, East Greenwich. ($) Open from 8 AM to 5 or 6 PM daily except Sunday. There are entrées like grilled chicken with artichokes and lemon, grilled salmon with a citrus basil glaze, roasted vegetable wraps, and roast turkey on homemade focaccia. It's bright and cheery, and the food is to eat in or take out.

✍ ♿ **The Grille on Main Street** (401-885-2200), 50 Main Street, East Greenwich. ($–$$) Open daily for lunch and dinner. Salads, burgers, grilled pizzas, fried calamari—casual fare in a big, dark-walled setting with an upscale saloon look.

🍴 ✍ ♿ **Haruki** (401-463-8338), 1210 Oaklawn Avenue, Cranston. ($$) Open daily for dinner, Monday through Saturday for lunch and dinner. Authentic Japanese food—sushi, sashimi, teriyaki, tempura, maki (fish rolled up with rice in seaweed)—are all on the menu of this simple, casual restaurant that the whole family can enjoy.

Jigger's Diner (401-884-5388), 145 Main Street, East Greenwich. ($) Open 6–1. This is an old-fashioned diner, circa 1917, that prides itself on its jonny cakes, meat loaf, and croquettes as well as its homemade pies and cakes. Service tends to be laid back.

✍ ♿ **Meritage** (401-884-1255), 5454 Post Road, East Greenwich. ($$) Open daily for lunch and dinner. Wood grilling is the specialty of this bistro—wood grilling of chicken and steak, pork chops, vegetables, and pizzas. Among the pastas, a particularly popular one is the pasta jambalaya of chicken and shrimp in a Cajun-spiced cream sauce.

✍ ♿ **Mike's Kitchen–VFW Tabor Franchi** (401-946-5320), 170 Randall Street, Cranston. ($$) Open for lunch and dinner daily, except Tuesday and Saturday when no dinner is served, and Sunday when no meals are served. A Rhode Island phenomenon: a casual, down-home Italian restaurant in a Veterans of Foreign Wars hall. The fried squid is a local favorite.

Nonna Cherubina (401-738-5221), 2317 West Shore Road, Warwick. ($) Open daily except Monday dinner. Northern Italian food is served in this cozy house-turned-restaurant. Homemade pasta entrées are under $15.

✍ **Olerio's** (401-943-1980), 1099 Park Avenue, Cranston. ($–$$) Open daily except Sunday for lunch and dinner. Generous portions of both northern and southern Italian cooking are served in this busy, informal setting.

♿ **ReBar Grill** (401-732-9533), 2299 Post Road, Warwick. ($–$$) Open daily for lunch and dinner. If you're a beer drinker, you have a choice of nearly three dozen varieties on tap at this lively, casual eatery where nachos, salads, burgers, pizza, and seafood accompany the brew.

♿ **Restaurant Tokyo** (401-826-7538), 1134 Bald Hill Road, Warwick. ($$) Open daily for lunch and dinner. Dine on hibachi-grilled steak in a tatami room, or try tempura dishes or sushi in this traditional Japanese restaurant.

✍ ♿ **Rocky Point Chowder House** (401-739-4222), 1759 Post Road, Warwick. ($) Open daily for lunch and dinner. For decades the enormous

Rocky Point Shore Dinner Hall was a favorite spot for Rhode Island family dining. This little eatery is what remains of it. There are the same clam cakes and clam chowder (red or white). Fish-and-chips and deep-fried shrimp are also on the menu.

Sunflower Cafe (463-6444), 162 Mayflower Avenue, Cranston. ($$) Open Sunday through Friday for lunch and dinner; Saturday for dinner only. Clay cookery from the time of the Romans is featured in this northern Italian restaurant that serves polenta and risotto as often as pasta.

Warehouse Tavern (401-885-3703), 20 Water Street, East Greenwich. ($) Open daily for lunch and dinner. Grilled fish and meat are wise choices at this informal, harbor-view restaurant.

CAFÉS **Felicia's Cafe** (401-886-4141), 5763 Post Road, Warwick. ($) Open Monday through Thursday 6 AM–8 PM, Friday and Saturday until 11 PM, Sunday 7–6. It's hardly a Viennese café where you can browse among the newspapers all day, but Felicia's has something in common with that: There are computers for browsing while you sip your coffee and eat your breakfast pastries.

Little Falls Bakery and Café (401-781-8010), 2166 Broad Street, Pawtuxet Cove, Cranston. This warm, friendly little café with paintings by local artists on the walls is where Pawtuxet Villagers spend their spare time. They enjoy the art and conversation along with the muffins and scones.

Ursula's European Bakery (401-941-4122), Broad Street and Park Avenue, Edgewood. Open Tuesday noon–6, Wednesday through Saturday 10–6. The coffee is as full bodied as

the blend that Austrians took from the Turks centuries ago, the pastries are flaky and rich, and the cakes are fit for a king in this tiny little bakery-café that unfortunately has very limited space.

✳ Entertainment

THEATER **Greenwich Odeum** (401-885-9119), 59 Main Street, East Greenwich. In this restored 1926 vaudeville theater, folk, jazz, and classical concerts are held, and touring theater companies perform.

✳ Selective Shopping

ANTIQUES AND COLLECTIBLES
Country Squire Fine Antiques (401-885-1044), 86 Main Street, East Greenwich. Open principally on Sunday or by appointment. American furniture and silver, largely 19th and 20th century, is the specialty here.

Harbour Galleries (401-884-6221), 253 Main Street, East Greenwich. Estate jewelry, with an emphasis on cameos and antique engagement rings, is what's sold in this little corner shop that has been in business for more than 20 years.

Stevens Oriental Rugs (401-885-6066), 88 Main Street, East Greenwich. Antique Persian and Turkish rugs and modern Indian and Pakistani rugs are among those that this shop's Iranian-born rug dealer–owner sells.

ART GALLERIES **A&C Fine Arts** (401-884-1575), 1575 South County Trail, East Greenwich. Open Monday through Friday 10–6, Saturday 9–5, Sunday noon–5. In this handsome museumlike gallery, the work of more than 30 American and Canadian painters, in all media and varied styles, is shown. An outdoor sculpture garden was under construction as this book went to press.

BOOKSTORES **Borders Bookshop** (401-944-9160), 81 Hillside Road, Garden City Center, Cranston. Hardcovers and paperbacks, fiction and nonfiction of general interest.

Heritage Book Store (401-732-5038), Theodore Francis Green State Airport. Paperbacks, hardcovers, and newspapers for travelers.

Murder by the Book (401-739-7224), 1645 Warwick Avenue, Warwick. Call for hours. Espionage, true crime, mystery, and detective.

Twice Told Tales (401-785-9599), 2210 Broad Street, Pawtuxet Village, Cranston. Used paperbacks and some new books along with handknit baby sweaters, handmade jewelry, cards.

SPECIAL SHOPS **Apponaug Color & Hobby Shop** (401-737-5506), 1364 Greenwich Avenue, Apponaug, Warwick. Back in the 1950s this was a paint store (hence its name), but its owner, Charles Moore Sr., was having a hard time making ends meet. "If you sold toy trains, you might be able to pay the light bill," a friend said to him one day. The idea struck his fancy, and now, a generation later, Charles Moore Jr. is selling electric trains and model boats, ships, and planes plus all the accessories.

The Chocolate Delicacy (401-884-4949), 219 Main Street, East Greenwich. Two Vassar graduates have gotten together to make chocolates at this tantalizing shop, where it's hard to choose among the truffles and the fudge and the red lobster lollipops.

Clock Shop International (401-826-1212), 667 Bald Hill Road, Warwick. Grandfather and grandmother clocks, wall and mantel clocks—clocks of all eras for all tastes fill this shop.

Gracefully Yours (401-885-1010), 442 Main Street, East Greenwich. North Carolina country furniture decorated with hand-painted scenes is the major attraction of this home furnishings and gift store.

The Green Door (401-885-0510), 130 Main Street, East Greenwich. Hand-painted glass and wooden bowls, silk flower arrangements, miniature Chinese tea sets and miniature Limoges boxes, Raku pottery from South Africa, vintage linens and quilts are all among the offerings in this charming little gift shop.

Healy Flute Company (401-885-2502), 1776 Revolution Street, East Greenwich. In this town where George Washington was an overnight guest of Continental army general James Mitchell Varnum, it's only appropriate that there be a maker of fifes—the instrument whose melodies accompanied the Continental army soldiers. Flutes are also handmade here behind the general's house.

Historic Pontiac Mills (401-737-2700), 334 Knight Street, Warwick. A wide variety of shops are upstairs and down in this old mill complex that once was the site of the Fruit of the Loom manufacturing company. Hand-painted furniture, antiques, collectibles, vintage clothing—all are to be found in this rabbit-warren-like complex.

Juggles (401-885-4578), 5600 Post Road (in Benny's Mall), East Greenwich. Teddy bears and baby dolls, imported wooden toys, hand puppets and playhouses—nothing naughty but everything nice that a child craves seems to be part of Juggles's stock.

Scrumptions (401-884-0844), 5600 Post Road (in Benny's Mall), East Greenwich. Scruptious, indeed, are the scrumptions—maple walnut creams and truffles and chocolate-covered cherries and the like—that are sold by the piece or the pound at this attractive little chocolate and pastry shop.

Tailored Crafts (401-885-1756), 232 Main Street, East Greenwich. Navajo, Hopi, and Zuni jewelry from the Southwest may have come a long way to Rhode Island, but the selection here is first-rate. There's some pottery, too.

Wild Birds Unlimited (401-826-0606), 1000 Bald Hill Road, Warwick. There's everything for the bird lover here: binoculars, birdhouses, bird feeders, birdseed, clocks that sing birdsongs, decorative ceramic birds, bird books, and bird-themed greeting cards.

FARM STANDS **Briarbrook Farm** (401-884-2066), 2693 South County Trail, East Greenwich. Open daily 9–5 from Easter until the day before Christmas.

✳ Special Events

May: **Gaspée Days** (401-781-1772). A crafts fair and other events at various points in Cranston and Warwick commemorate the June 9, 1772, burning of the British revenue schooner *Gaspée* by Rhode Island patriots. Events begin in mid-May and continue into June. **Memorial Day Parade,** East Greenwich.

June: **East Greenwich Chamber of Commerce Golf Classic** (401-885-0020). **Quonset Air Show,** Quonset State Airport, North Kingstown. **Blessing of the Fleet** (401-738-2000), East Greenwich Cove, Warwick.

July: **Fireworks Display** (401-738-2000), Oakland Beach Seawall. **Canoe Race,** East Greenwich Cove, Warwick. **Trinity Rep Performs Shakespeare** (401-738-2000, ext. 6404), Goddard Park, Warwick.

July–August: **Concert series** (401-738-2000, ext. 6404), Tuesday and Thursday in Warwick parks.

August: **Oakland Beach Festival** (401-738-2000). Crafts, music, and a flea market. **Trinity Rep Performs Shakespeare** (401-738-2000, ext. 6404), Goddard Park, Warwick.

September: **Apponaug Village Festival** (401-738-2000), City Hall, Post Road, Warwick. Flea market, pony rides, crafts, and entertainment. **Summer's End Concert** (401-885-0020). **Rhode Island Philharmonic Orchestra Pops Concert** at Eldridge Field, East Greenwich.

November: **Veterans Day Parade,** East Greenwich (401-885-0020). **Heritage Festival** (401-738-2000), Warwick.

December: **Holidays in East Greenwich** (401-885-0020) includes the tree-lighting and carol ceremony, strolling carolers, breakfast with Santa, candlelight luminaria along Main Street, and candlelight tours of historic buildings and selected private homes. **Tree lighting** in Apponaug. **Carol singing** (401-738-2000, ext. 6404), Warwick Mall.

East Bay

BARRINGTON, WARREN, AND

BRISTOL

Kim Grant

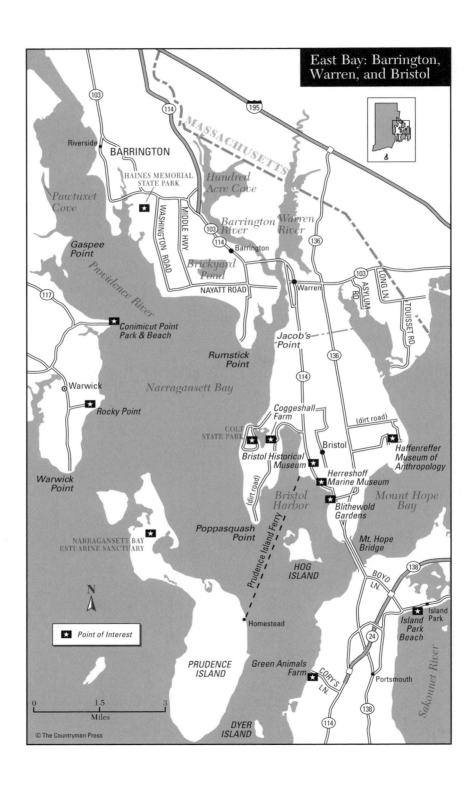

East Bay: Barrington,
Warren, and Bristol

103

114   195

MASSACHUSETTS

Riverside   BARRINGTON

HAINES MEMORIAL
STATE PARK

Hundred
Acre Cove

Pawtuxet
Cove

103   *Barrington* *Warren*
       River   *River*

114   Barrington   136

Gaspee
Point

WASHINGTON ROAD

MIDDLE HWY.

Brickyard
Pond

103   LONG LN.

ASYLUM RD.

TOUISSET RD.

Providence River

NAYATT ROAD   Warren

117

Conimicut Point
Park & Beach

Jacob's
Point

136

Rumstick
Point

114

Warwick

Narragansett Bay

Rocky Point

Coggeshall
Farm   (dirt road)

COLT
STATE PARK   Bristol

Warwick
Point

Bristol Historical
Museum

Haffenreffer
Museum of
Anthropology

Herreshoff
Marine Museum

Bristol
Harbor   Blithewold
Gardens   *Mount Hope*
Bay

(dirt road)

Poppasquash
Point

NARRAGANSETT BAY
ESTUARINE SANCTUARY

Mt. Hope
Bridge

138

Prudence Island Ferry

HOG
ISLAND

BOYD
LN.

N

Point of Interest

Homestead

24

Island
Park Beach

Island
Park

Portsmouth

PRUDENCE
ISLAND

Green Animals
Farm

CORY'S LN.

138

0   1.5   3
Miles

© The Countryman Press

DYER
ISLAND

Sakonnet River

BARRINGTON, WARREN, AND BRISTOL

Until the 17th century Native Americans of the Wampanoag tribe happily inhabited what are now sites of the three towns of Bristol County: Barrington, Warren, and Bristol. They hunted on the wooded, abundant land and fished its rivers and Narragansett Bay. In 1621 two Pilgrim Fathers from the Plymouth Bay Colony approached the Wampanoag chief, Massasoit, to talk about buying land from him. They succeeded, and before long a trading post was established where Massasoit lived, in what is now Warren.

Relations were amicable between the white settlers and the Wampanoags during Massasoit's lifetime. Indeed, there was genuine respect and affection between the Pilgrim Fathers and the old sachem. But everything changed when he died in 1661. One of his sons, Wamsutta, died mysteriously when problems arose over hunting rights on lands the settlers claimed. His incensed brother, Metacom, also known as King Philip, vowed revenge and set out to get rid of the Pilgrims. King Philip's War began in Bristol in 1675, uniting the Wampanoags from the east side of Narragansett Bay with the Narragansetts from the west side against the settlers. Before the war ended, tribes from central Massachusetts and Maine were also involved, and their joint determination to oust the settlers resulted in New England's bloodiest Indian war.

King Philip's War ended in 1676 with a horrible massacre of the Narragansett. King Philip was killed at the hands of a fellow Wampanoag, and the lands he had sought to save for his people fell forever to the colonists.

As the Wampanoags had prospered on the fertile land and rich surrounding waters, so did the colonists. They farmed in Barrington, and they built boats and entered the shipping trade in Warren and Bristol. The captains' and shipowners' tall white houses still line the streets of these two communities—their prosperity born of the slave trade and whaling. In Warren most of the old houses remain in private hands; in Bristol the public is invited to visit Linden Place, one of the grandest of the shipowners' houses and offering a most engaging history.

GUIDANCE **Bristol County Chamber of Commerce** (401-245-0750), 654 Metacom Avenue, Warren. Open Monday through Friday 9–4:30.

GETTING THERE *By train or bus:* Take **Amtrak** (1-800-USA-RAIL) to Providence and a **Rhode Island Public Transport Authority** (RIPTA; 401-781-9400) bus from Providence to any of the three Bristol County communities.

GETTING AROUND Local taxi service is provided by **A Taxi** (401-245-6684), Warren.

MEDICAL EMERGENCY The statewide emergency number is **911.**

Barrington Emergency Room (401-247-2870), 310 Maple Avenue, Barrington. Open Monday through Friday 8–8, Saturday and Sunday 9–5.

Bristol County Medical Center (401-253-8900), 1180 Hope Street, Bristol. Open Monday through Friday 8–8, Saturday 9–5, Sunday and holidays 10–4.

Metacom Medical Center (401-247-1500), 629 Metacom Avenue, Warren. Open Monday through Friday 8–5, Saturday and Sunday 9–1.

Warren Medical Center (401-247-1000), 851 Main Street, Warren. Open Monday through Friday 8–5, Saturday 8–noon.

✳ Villages

Barrington. Nowadays this pretty little area set between the Barrington River and Barrington Harbor is largely a bedroom community for neighboring Providence only 12 miles away, but its setting is singularly attractive. Welcoming the visitor arriving from Providence is the white-steepled 1710 **Barrington Congregational Church** (401-246-0111), which replaced a meetinghouse destroyed in King Philip's War. The nearby half-timbered and fieldstone, English Tudor–style **town hall** was built in 1887–88, largely of stones contributed by local farmers. **Belton Court** (Middle Highway), an early-19th-century gray stone manor house, is now the headquarters of the Zion Bible Institute. Its grounds are open to the public. **Tyler Point Cemetery,** between the Barrington and Warren Rivers, has picturesque gravestones, some dating back to 1702. During the Revolutionary War a Hessian soldier was killed by a farmer in Barrington—the only incident of that war that took place in this town.

Warren was once known as the Town of Ten Churches; three of historic importance still stand. The gray stone **Warren Baptist Church** (401-245-3669) on Main Street replaces a meetinghouse burned by the British in 1778; it was in its parsonage, also burned, that Rhode Island College (later renamed Brown University) was founded in 1764. The white-clapboard **St. Mark's Episcopal Church** (401-245-3161) on Lyndon and Broad Streets, with the lions of St. Mark guarding the doors flanked by fluted columns, almost has the look of an Egyptian tomb. Both the 1844 Gothic-style Baptist church and the 1830 Greek Revival St. Mark's were designed by Russell Warren. Surely the most spectacular church in Warren is the enormous **First Methodist Church** (401-245-8474) on Church Street, whose tiered clock steeple rises 130 feet. Built in 1845 after a Christopher Wren design, it's one of the oldest Methodist churches in New England. Unfortunately, except for Sunday services and by appointment, these churches are all closed to the public.

Warren's other architectural attractions include the gray stone turn-of-the-20th-century **George Hail Free Library** (401-245-7686) on Main Street, with its stained-glass windows, sweeping staircase, and second-floor museum filled with memorabilia of both Native American times and Warren's seafaring days. The Federal-style **Masonic Temple** (401-245-3293) at Baker and Narragansett Way, built in 1796, has exterior carving and an interior made of timbers salvaged from sunken British ships. Handsome old houses line the streets of Warren, with some of the finest on Main, Miller, Union, Liberty, and Water Streets. Only the red-clapboard 1753 Samuel Maxwell House on Church Street (see *Historic Homes*) is open to the public, however. Locals like to direct visitors to the tablet that marks the site of **Massasoit's Spring** and campsite and to the Firemen's Museum (see *Museums*).

Bristol. Of the three Bristol County communities, Bristol is the richest in attractions for the visitor, with museums, parks, gardens, grand mansions, and fine examples of New England architecture. Handsome Federal and Greek Revival houses possess columns and semicircular windows, doorway fanlights, and fine carving. There are Italianate houses with brackets under the roof, mansard-roofed Second Empire houses, and gingerbread-decorated Gothic Revival and shingle houses. Most of what stands in town today was built between 1825 and 1920. Some houses date from Bristol's prosperous years as a shipping port, when its families grew wealthy from privateering and the slave trade as well as through more legitimate businesses (one-fifth of all slaves coming to America were brought in Rhode Island ships, and most of these hailed from Bristol). Other elegant homes were built during Bristol's industrial and boatbuilding years.

HARBOR VIEWS

Kim Grant

Imposing clapboard structures like the Russell Warren–designed Federal houses at 82, 86, and 92 State Street, his Greek Revival house at 647 Hope Street, and **Linden Place,** used in the filming of *The Great Gatsby,* are architectural highlights. At Hope and Court Streets the heavy stone Romanesque Revival **Burnside Memorial Building** honors General Ambrose Burnside, who commanded Union troops at the battle of Bull Run and returned from the Civil War to become Rhode Island's governor. At the corner of Walley and Hope Streets is **Seven Oaks,** which was designed by James Renwick, architect of St. Patrick's Cathedral in New York.

Bristol's oldest house, and the oldest three-story wooden building in New England, is the 1698 **Joseph Reynolds House** at 956 Hope Street. The young marquis de Lafayette had his headquarters there in 1778. (According to local legend, Mrs. Reynolds did not recognize the marquis, who was one of the first in the French party to arrive, as Lafayette and took him to task for eating too much and not leaving enough for his commander.) Among civic buildings of architectural note is the **Bristol County Courthouse** on High Street, one of the five meeting places of the General Assembly until 1814. With its octagonal belfry, this structure is believed to be the work of either Russell Warren or John Holden Greene. The Bristol County Jail at 48 Court Street, now the Bristol Historical and Preservation Society (see *Museums*), was built in 1828 of ships' ballast. Bristol's 1814 **First Baptist Church,** also on High Street, bears a resemblance to the First Baptist Meeting House in Providence. **St. Michael's Episcopal Church** (401-253-7717), at 399 Hope Street, is a brownstone Gothic Revival church that replaces two earlier churches on the site. The first of these was burned by the British in 1778, when they mistakenly took it for the Congregational church and thought its tombs were powder magazines.

✳ To See

MUSEUMS ✐ **Bristol Historical and Preservation Society Museum and Library** (401-253-7223), 48 Court Street, Bristol. Call for museum hours, as they change occasionally. Built in 1828 out of ballast from Bristol sailing ships, this museum and library is quite interesting. Originally the county jail, the building still contains a windowless cell. Also on exhibit are a writing desk and table that belonged to Benjamin Franklin, General Burnside's saddle and sword, a candlestand that Charles Dickens is said to have used on a visit to Newport, ship models and children's toys, and portraits by an early itinerant painter, Cephus Thompson.

✐ **Coggeshall Farm Museum** (401-253-9062), Colt State Park, Route 114, Bristol. Open daily October through February 10–5, March through September 10–6. This little farm museum shows what agricultural life was like in Rhode Island in the late 18th century. Wiltshire sheep graze, and Dominique chickens, the oldest strain in America, peck at their feed. Visitors may watch red Devon cattle being milked as well as planting and lumbering operations. All farm animals are types known to have been on area farms in the late 1700s.

✐ **Firemen's Museum** (401-245-7600), 42 Baker Street, Warren. Open by appointment. This restored headquarters of the Narragansett Steam Fire Company Number 3 displays memorabilia of the early days of firefighting, such as Little Hero, the town's first fire engine, dating from 1802.

✍ **Haffenreffer Museum of Anthropology** (401-253-8388), Tower Street off Metacom Avenue, Bristol. Open June through August, Tuesday through Sunday 11–5; September through May, Saturday and Sunday 11–5. In the 17th century this 500-acre site was the summer encampment of the Wampanoag tribe. It's now a Brown University museum for thousands of Native American artifacts of North, Central, and South America. King Philip was shot here while seeking refuge at a spring. Trails through the woods and fields of the preserve are open to the public.

✍ **Herreshoff Marine Museum** (401-253-5000), 7 Burnside Street, Bristol. Open May through October, 7 days a week 10–4; ship model room open Friday 1–4. This museum is set on Narragansett Bay, on the site of the Herreshoff Manufacturing Company. From 1863 to 1945 thousands of yachts and schooners and eight America's Cup defenders came off the ways there. Today the museum houses 46 Herreshoff boats as well as photographs, models, and building plans of many others. The company's founders, among the most notable of all American yacht builders, were John Brown Herreshoff, who went blind at the age of 18, and his brother, Captain Nathanael (Nat) Greene Herreshoff. Despite his blindness, John was able to dictate boat specifications to Nat, who would then make a model. John would judge the design by feeling the model and suggest alterations. Among the boats on display is the catboat *Sprite*, which the pair built as teenagers; it has been called "the first yacht in America." On the bay below the museum is anchored the 56-foot yawl *Belisarius*, which was Captain Nat's last design.

A **Young Mariner's Discovery Center** where youngsters can learn to hoist sails, crank winches, and steer boats is also part of the museum, as is the America's Cup Hall of Fame, which recounts the history of that international sailing race.

HISTORIC HOMES AND SITES **Blithewold Mansion, Gardens & Arboretum** (401-253-2707), 101 Ferry Road, Bristol. Grounds open year-round 10–5; mansion open mid-April through October, 11–3:30 Wednesday through Sunday except holidays. Brown University graduate Augustus Van Wickle built the original Blithewold—"Happy Wood"—as a summer "trinket" for his wife, Bessie, in 1895. Earlier he had presented her with a 72-foot $100,000 Herreshoff yacht, which she adored, but it couldn't be moored where they lived in Hazelton, Pennsylvania. The Blithewold property, with 32 acres and possible moorings in either Bristol Harbor or Narragansett Bay, seemed the perfect place. A 45-room mansion was duly constructed with Van Wickle coal-mining money. Unfortunately Augustus had relatively little time to enjoy his mansion, for he was soon killed in a hunting accident. Bessie remarried, but tragedy struck again when in 1907 the original Blithewold burned to the ground. The stone-and-stucco mansion that stands today was built a year later in the style of a 17th-century English manor house. Bessie, who enjoyed travel immensely, filled the house with mementos of her journeys. The grounds and gardens were laid out by New York City architect

John DeWolf and contain unusual trees and plants, including a giant sequoia nearly a century old that is the largest of its kind east of the Rockies and a chestnut rose that bears pink blossoms in June. Spring daffodil gardens and summer rose gardens are also especially noteworthy.

Linden Place (401-253-0390), 500 Hope Street, Bristol. Open May through September, Saturday and Sunday 1–4, Wednesday 2–4. This wedding-cake-like Federal mansion, notable in this century as the summer residence of actress Ethel Barrymore (Colt), was built in 1810 by shipowner and slave trader General George DeWolf to be "the most beautiful and the best" residence in Bristol. Russell Warren of Tiverton, who was to become known as one of Rhode Island's finest architects, designed the home. High-living General DeWolf spared no expense, either in the building of his house or in the entertaining of his guests. (He is said to have bought a solid silver pitcher and bowl for President James Monroe when he visited once.) Much of DeWolf's money, however, came from convincing others to invest in his schemes, and in 1825 they failed. His Caribbean sugar plantations didn't flourish, and he also lost shiploads of slaves. So on a snowy December night, he and his family slipped away by coach to flee to Cuba.

The day after his departure, his Bristol creditors realized that their money would never be repaid, and they descended on his house to lay claim to the equivalent in goods. Emptied, the house fell first to DeWolf's brother and later to his nephew, William Henley. In 1840 Henley rehired the then-established Russell Warren to add onto the house. But Henley, too, had financial problems and went

THE GARDENS AT BRISTOL'S BLITHEWOLD MANSION ARE SPECTACULAR YEAR-ROUND

Kim Grant

bankrupt. On his death his widow moved into a third-floor bedroom and turned the rest of the mansion into a boardinghouse. When she died in 1865, Linden Place went on the auction block. Edward Colt, a mysterious young man from Connecticut, bought it. All of Bristol was curious about the young stranger, until it was revealed that he was purchasing the house on behalf of his mother, Theodora DeWolf Colt, daughter of the original builder, General George DeWolf. Theodora was only 5 on the snowy December night when her family fled, but Linden Place had remained a beloved misty memory. By 1865 she was a wealthy widow (she married into the Colt firearms family) and was able, at last, to return to the house in which she had been born.

Maxwell House (401-245-0392), 59 Church Street, Warren. Open 10–2 Saturday and by appointment. This sparsely furnished 1755 brick house, the oldest house near the Warren waterfront, is of some interest. It is still being brought back to the look it had in its earliest days. Notable are its beehive oven, steep gable, and handsome old bricks of varying shades.

SCENIC DRIVES **Long Lane,** Warren. Few winding country roads remain in Warren, but Long Lane, turning into Touisset Road around Touisset Point, has views of both Mount Hope Bay with Fall River across it and the Kickemuit River with Bristol on the other side.

Mathewson Road, Barrington. Elegant houses line this attractive road along the Warren and Barrington Rivers. In summer you'll see sailing yachts skimming the waters.

Nayatt Road, Barrington. There are beautiful homes along this road above Narragansett Bay.

Poppasquash Road, Bristol. This tree-shaded winding road edging Bristol Harbor in Colt State Park is a short but charming drive.

Rumstick Road, Barrington. Barrington thrived as a summer community at the turn of the 20th century, and many of the Tudor estates with river views are reminders of this period.

✳ To Do

BICYCLING **Colt Park Bike Trail.** A 3-mile bike loop through the grounds of the former Colt estate offers views of Narragansett Bay, coves, and marshes and is linked with the East Bay Bike Path.

East Bay Bicycle Path (401-245-0750). Beginning in Providence at India Point Park, 14.5 miles of paths for cyclists make their way along Narragansett Bay, over saltwater rivers, and through woods and brush in Barrington, Warren, and Bristol. Maps are included in the *Rhode Island Visitor's Guide,* which can be obtained by calling the above number.

BOAT EXCURSIONS **Bay Queen Cruises** (401-245-1350), 461 Water Street, Warren. Spring, summer, and fall cruises of Narragansett Bay, aboard the 114-foot *Vista Jubilee.*

THE EAST BAY BICYCLE PATH

Rhode Island Tourism Division

BOAT LAUNCHES Barrington Town Beach, Bay Road, Barrington. **Bristol Narrows,** Narrows Road, off RI 136, Bristol. Access to Mount Hope Bay. **Colt State Park,** Colt Drive, Bristol. Access to upper Narragansett Bay. **Haines Memorial State Park,** Metropolitan Park Drive, East Providence. Access to Bullocks Cove and the lower Providence River. **Independence Park,** Thames Street, Bristol. Access to Bristol Harbor. **Mount Hope Bay,** Annawamscott Drive off RI 136, Bristol. Access to Mount Hope Bay. **Striper Marina,** Tyler Point Road, Barrington. Access to the Warren River and upper Narragansett Bay. **Thames Street,** at the foot of State Street, Bristol. Access to Bristol Harbor. **Walker Farm,** County Road, Barrington. Access to Hundred Acre Cove.

CANOEING AND KAYAKING Northwind Sports (401-254-4295), Thames Street Landing, Bristol. Sales and rentals of all kinds of adventure sports equipment, as well as lessons and tours. Kayaks, sailboards, ice boating.

Ocean State Adventures (401-254-4000), 99 Poppasquash Point, Bristol. Sea kayaking tours.

DIVING East Bay Dive Center Inc. (401-247-2420), 8 Church Street, Warren. Diving instruction and rental of diving equipment.

FISHING Brickyard Pond (401-277-3576), Barrington, and the **Kickemuit River** (401-277-3576), Warren, offer good freshwater fishing. You must have a license.

Narragansett Bay and **Mount Hope Bay** (401-277-3075). For blues, snappers, tautog, scup, and summer flounder. No license required.

GOLF Bristol Golf Club (401-253-9844), 95 Tupelo Street, Bristol. Carts are available at this nine-hole par-71 course. Restaurant.

SAILING Barrington-Newport Sailing School (401-246-1595), 5 Beaver Road, Barrington. Beginner, intermediate, and advanced 10- and 14-hour courses are offered in summer.

✔ **Barrington YMCA** (401-245-2444), 70 West Street, Barrington. Summer sailing instruction for children and adults.

✔ **Bristol Yacht Club** (401-253-2922), Poppasquash Road, Bristol. Summer instruction for children and adults.

SWIMMING **Barrington Town Beach,** Bay Road, Barrington. Open daily 9–6 June through September. Narragansett Bay swimming with lifeguards on duty but no parking for out-of-town cars.

✿ **Bristol Town Beach,** Colt Drive off RI 114, Bristol. Open Memorial Day through Labor Day. The calmer waters of upper Narragansett Bay here are ideally suited for families with kids, and the beach fronts on 455 acres of Colt State Park land. Swimming with lifeguards. Parking fee for nonresidents.

TENNIS The following have outdoor courts open to the public: **Barrington High School,** 120 Lincoln Avenue, Barrington. **Barrington YMCA** (401-245-2444), 70 West Street, Barrington. Two outdoor tennis courts. **Bristol Town Common,** corner of Church and Wood Streets, Bristol. **Burr's Hill Park,** South Water Street, Warren. Parking is limited to town residents. **Jamiel's Park,** Market Street, Warren. **Kent Street Tennis Courts,** Kent Street, Barrington.

✳ Green Space

Audubon Society of Rhode Island Environmental Education Center (401-245-7500), 1401 Hope Street (RI 114), Bristol. Open daily 9–5; admission $5 for adults, $3 for children. Walking trails wind through 28 acres of woodlands, and a boardwalk meanders over marshes to the edge of Narragansett Bay. The center is on the Warren–Bristol town line and is bisected by the East Bay Bicycle Path. The sleekly modern main building has exhibits of interest to both adults and children.

Hugh Cole Nature Trail and Park, Asylum Road, Warren. This town-maintained trail leads to the Hugh Cole Well and spring near the Kickemuit River.

Colt State Park (401-253-7482), RI 114, Bristol. Open dawn to dusk. Two bronze bulls mark the main entrance to the 455 acres of this state park that once was part of the Colt estate. Today azaleas brighten the grounds in spring, and roses perfume the air in summer. There are picnicking and fishing spots, boat-launching facilities, and hiking trails.

Green Acres Heritage Park, off Child Street, Warren. Trails ramble through 80 acres of woods and fields. The abutting Warren Reservoir provides many fishing opportunities.

Mount Hope Farm (401-254-1745), 250 Metacom Avenue (RI 136), Bristol. Two hundred acres of fields and woodlands laced with walking paths overlook Mount Hope Bay at this onetime gentleman's farm that has been preserved for the public to enjoy. The Governor Bradford House (see *Bed & Breakfasts*) is on the National Register of Historic Places and dates from the 1680s.

Osamequin River Nature Trail and Walker Farm, Hundred Acre Cove, RI 114, Barrington. There are 30 acres of field, farmland, and riverbank to explore here as well as boating and fishing. Winter presents fine opportunities to look for waterfowl; summer brings sharp-tailed and seaside sparrows. Parking is only available for town residents.

Touisset Marsh, Touisset Road, Warren. This 67-acre Rhode Island Audubon Society area offers walkways through fields and marshland where great blue herons, ospreys, snowy egrets, and even the occasional bald eagle may be seen.

✳ Lodging

INNS Bristol Harbor Inn (401-254-1444; 1-866-254-1444), 259 Thames Street, Bristol 02809. ($$$) This 40-room boutique-style inn-hotel has a prime location on the waterfront at Thames Street Landing, an area that has in the past decade become an attractive harborfront destination with shops, restaurants, and Bristol's first real hotel.

Nathaniel Porter Inn (401-245-6622), 125 Water Street, Warren 02885. ($$) Built by a sea captain in 1795, this three-bedroom inn (with private baths and canopy beds) has the pleasantly creaky feel of colonial days, but for modern summer visitors there is air-conditioning. Guests share

THE NATHANIEL PORTER INN IN BRISTOL

Kim Grant

an upstairs parlor that has an attractive tile fireplace (that cannot, however, be used for fires). Continental breakfast is included, and guests should have at least one main meal in one of the pretty dining rooms (see *Dining Out*).

Rockwell House Inn (401-253-0040), 610 Hope Street, Bristol 02809. ($$) A full, hearty breakfast that includes homemade granola as well as tea or sherry in the afternoon are among the attractions at this spacious four-bedroom, four-bath inn near the Bristol waterfront and on the Fourth of July parade route. Built in 1809 in the Federal style, the inn also reflects later architectural styles. A fieldstone "courting fireplace" can heat the porch, where breakfast is served in summer, spring, and fall. The courting fireplace was built in 1910 by then-owner Charles Rockwell to cheer up a jilted daughter who later became happily and firmly engaged beside it. In winter breakfast is served in the large candlelit dining room. Like the style of this enormous house, furnishings are eclectic.

William's Grant Inn (401-253-4222), 154 High Street, Bristol 02809. ($$) An early-19th-century Federal house, this deep blue inn offers five rooms cooled by ceiling fans and with either private or shared baths. Family and friends have done much interior mural painting and decoration, and although the decor is a trifle heavy-handed, the William's Grant Inn is cozy and friendly. Breakfasts include egg dishes, Belgian waffles, and blueberry pancakes.

BED & BREAKFASTS Bradford-Dimond-Norris House (401-253-6338), 474 Hope Street, Bristol 02809.

($$) Familiarly known as the Wedding Cake House, this imposing white-clapboard mansion was started in 1792 by Rhode Island deputy governor William Bradford. It replaced his earlier home, which the British had destroyed in their raid on Bristol in 1778. In the 1840s Governor Francis Dimond was the owner, and when his daughter, Isabella, and her husband, Samuel Norris, moved in, they asked architect Russell Warren to add his touches to it. He contributed the north wing, an Ionic-style porch, and Chinese Chippendale balustrades. Later the third story that gives it its wedding-cake aspect was added. Today there are four spacious antiques-furnished rooms for guests, all with private bath. Breakfast is served overlooking the garden. The house is on the Fourth of July parade route.

Governor Bradford House at Mount Hope Farm (401-254-9300; 1-877-254-9300), 250 Metacom Avenue (RI 136), Bristol. ($$) Staying in one of the charming guest rooms in this colonial-era homestead that once belonged to the Haffenreffer family is like entering another era. The house sits on 200 acres of preserved waterfront land that had been part of a farm since the 1600s.

Hearth House (401-253-2084), 736 Hope Street, Bristol 02809. ($–$$) Three pleasant rooms are available in this 1798 brick-red-fronted captain's house, also called the Parker-Borden House, with a view of Bristol Harbor and a garden to enjoy. Its owners provide genuine Irish porridge for cold-weather breakfasts as well as their homemade muffins. Noisy Hope Street is, however, a factor to consider.

The Swanson House (401-254-5056), 150 Ferry Road, Bristol 02809.

($$) A suite consisting of two bedrooms, a sitting room, bath, and half bath occupies the entire second floor of this spacious 1930s house set on tree-shaded grounds across from Blithewold and near the Roger Williams University campus. A family of three or four can be comfortably accommodated. The morning breakfast basket left in the hall consists of fruit and juice, a thermos of coffee, and fresh baked goods.

✳ Where to Eat

DINING OUT & **Hot Point** (401-254-7474), 31 State Street, Bristol. ($$$) Open nightly, except Monday, for dinner; Saturday for lunch and dinner; Sunday for champagne brunch. Such inventive gourmet dishes as molasses-marinated pork tenderloin and saffron-steamed mussels are offered in small and cozy surroundings.

& **The Lobster Pot** (401-253-9100), 121 Hope Street, Bristol. ($$$) Open daily, except Monday, for lunch and dinner. The view of Narragansett Bay is spectacular, and this seafood restaurant has been an area mainstay since the 1920s. The quality of its cooking, however, tends to vary.

Nathaniel Porter Inn (401-245-6622), 125 Water Street, Warren. ($$$) Open Tuesday through Saturday 5–9, Sunday 10:30–2 and 4–8. Diners at the Nathaniel Porter Inn may pay a little more than at other Bristol County restaurants, but for those extra dollars they will get seductive, old-fashioned surroundings—candlelight and fireplaces in cozy dining rooms—and thoughtfully prepared Continental cuisine. Dishes include smoked filet mignon in plum tomato sauce; sautéed chicken breast stuffed with apricots and basil, served with Grand Marnier and cream sauce; and baked trout encrusted with pecans, peanuts, and sesame seeds. Desserts are equally creative.

♦ ♂ ♿ **Redlefsen's** (401-254-1188), 444 Thames Street, Bristol. ($$) Open for dinner only, daily from 5 PM. It's not just anywhere in Rhode Island that those with a hearty appetite will find schnitzel with anchovies and capers.

♿ **S.S. Dion** (401-253-2884), 520 Thames Street, Bristol. ($$) Open daily, except Sunday, for dinner. Arrive in time to see the sun set over Bristol Harbor if you can, and corner a table with a water view. Unfortunately there will be a parking lot between you and the water, but there's still the colorful sky to see. There's nothing fancy, just straightforward fish dishes—devotees insist that the best-prepared swordfish in Rhode Island is served here.

Tav-Vino/The Blue Collar (401-245-0231), 267 Water Street, Warren. ($$) Open for dinner Tuesday through Sunday. The more formal Tav-Vino is upstairs, and the Blue Collar is downstairs. This comfortable, cozy waterfront restaurant can be hard to find because its sign is hidden behind a tree. Once there, however, you'll enjoy good seafood, veal, and chicken dishes, hot Portuguese bread, incomparable mud pie, and an extensive wine list. Try to get a table with a harbor view.

♿ **Tyler Point Grille** (401-247-0017), 32 Barton Avenue, Barrington. ($$) Open nightly for dinner. The bobbing masts of boats in Barrington Harbor surround this restaurant, which offers a wide assortment of Italian appetizers

LOBSTER IS THE SPECIALTY AT WARREN'S WHARF TAVERN.

Kim Grant

and pasta plus wood-grilled and oven-roasted meats and fish.

 & **The Wharf Tavern** (401-245-5043), 215 Water Street, Warren. ($$) Open daily for lunch and dinner. The specialty at this Warren River tavern is lobster, prepared in multitudinous ways: thermidor, Newburg, sautéed in sherry butter, in salad, stuffed with scallops and shrimp, or simply baked or boiled. There are other fine fish dishes, too, at reasonable prices as well as charcoal-broiled steak of many cuts and chicken and pasta dishes. On the lunch menu, in addition to the fish dishes, there are low-calorie salad plates, sandwiches, and soups.

EATING OUT

In Bristol

& **Aidan's Pub** (401-254-1940), 5 John Street. ($) Open daily, except Monday, for lunch and dinner. A good Irish pub serving such simple Irish fare as fish-and-chips, bangers and mash (sausages and mashed potatoes), and Irish breakfasts with Irish brown bread. It's set almost on the water, across from where the Prudence Island ferry docks.

 Bristol Bagel Works (401-254-1390), 420 Hope Street. ($–$$) Open 6:30 AM–3 PM (until 1 on Sunday). Made-on-the-premises coffee and bagels of all varieties are available here. In warm weather you can enjoy them outside. Soup and sandwiches are also on the menu.

 & **Quito's Seafood Restaurant** (401-253-9042), 411 Thames Street. ($) Open March through late November daily, except Tuesday, for lunch and dinner. Fresh fish fare is offered outdoors or indoors in a casual waterfront setting.

 & **The Sandbar** (401-253-5485), 775 Hope Street. ($) Open daily, except Monday, for lunch and dinner. Portuguese touches add to this little restaurant that serves low-priced, plentiful meals in a casual setting. Blade meat and kale soup, scrod Portuguese-style with tomato and onion, and Italian pasta dishes with seafood are what attract the clientele here. Wine comes by the tumbler.

In Warren

Bullocks (401-245-6502), 50 Miller Street. ($) Open Tuesday through Saturday for lunch in summer, daily for dinner year-round. On a pretty day you can dine outdoors on a crisp, cool salad, a sandwich, a bowl of chowder, or seafood. You can order something light to eat as late as 10 PM.

 & **The Center Cafe** (401-245-0540), 5 Miller Street. ($) Open 7–3 daily. Sharing space with the Warren Antique Center, this coffee bar (with headquarters and bakery in Bristol) is the place to go in Warren for muffins and bagels and conversation with the locals. If you tire of the chatter, you can amble into the adjoining antiques shop to browse for a while. Both share the space of what was once the Lyric Theatre.

& **Crossroads Restaurant** (401-245-9305), 133 Market Street. ($–$$) Open daily, except Monday, for lunch and dinner. Fabulous sandwiches and chicken and lobster salads are favorites at this simple little pub. Dine in a garden room with plants and skylights or in a dark and cozy nook.

 & **Tuscan Tavern** (401-247-9200), 632 Metacom Avenue. ($$) Open daily, except Monday, for dinner. Here, from the largest wood-burning oven in the state, come crusty pizzas and bruschettas with a Tuscan flavor as well as plenty of pasta dishes, steaks, chicken, and fresh fish. Half and family-style portions are also offered.

SNACKS

In Warren
Coffee Depot (401-247-9890), 501 Main Street, Warren. Great, fresh-roasted coffee drinks such as lattes and espressos are served from a copper-topped bar. Customers sip at their leisure while ensconced in deep leather chairs and surrounded by works by local artists. Live folk-style music adds to the mix on Saturdays. Sandwich wraps and pastries, too.

✍ ♿ **Delekta Pharmacy** (401-245-6767), 496 Main Street. ($) Open weekdays 8–8, Saturday 8–5, Sunday 8–1. For generations, Rhode Islanders have been frequenting this old-fashioned drugstore on hot summer days for cool, thick coffee cabinets—the coffee syrup is made on the premises and blended with ice cream and milk. Of course, there are sundaes and sodas, too.

Parvenue Bakery (401-247-9900), 40 Market Street. Parisian-chic bakery sells whole tortes and tarts, as well as pastries and cookies.

✳ Entertainment

2nd Story Theater (401-247-4200), 28 Market Street, Warren. This highly regarded troupe puts on full-length plays with ticket costs of around $10—a real bargain for theater buffs.

✳ Selective Shopping

ANTIQUES AND COLLECTIBLES
Alfred's Antiques (401-245-3465),

331 Hope Street, Bristol. It's Christmas in Alfred's windows year-round. Inside, mahogany furniture, china, and crystal are charmingly displayed.

Alfred's Annex (401-253-2339), 297 Hope Street, Bristol. More of Alfred's but mostly on consignment.

The Center Chimney (401-253-8010), 39 State Street, Bristol. Estate jewelry and country furniture, glass and porcelain of quality.

D'Antiques (401-253-1122), 676 Hope Street, Bristol. Largely collectibles.

Jesse James Antiques (401-253-2240), 44 State Street, Bristol. Quality collectibles, 1920s furniture.

Robin Jenkins Antiques (401-254-8958), 278 Hope Street, Bristol. A small shop with an eclectic assortment of collectibles and a few antiques.

Marie King Antiques (401-245-1020), 382 Main Street, Warren. Furniture, art, and china are attractively arranged in a colonial house in the heart of Warren.

The Meeting House (401-247-7043), 47 Water Street, Warren. Eighteenth-, 19th-, and 20th-century painted farmhouse furniture and reproductions of 18th-century tinware sconces, 19th-century chamber lights, and hogscraper candlesticks are on sale on the ground floor of the 1790 Jabez Bowen House.

The Square Peg (no phone), 51 Miller Street, Warren. A crowded jumble of junk with, perhaps—for the discerning searcher—a few items of interest. It is the Square Peg's eclectic collection that is said to have started the antiques craze in Warren.

The Stock Exchange (401-245-4170), 57 Maple Avenue, Barrington.

Everything from African masks to ship models, golf clubs, dolls, beach pails, and furniture in this multistory consignment shop.

Wren & Thistle (401-247-0631), 19 Market Street, Warren. There's a nice selection of quality antiques in this small shop.

BOOKSTORES **Barrington Books** (401-245-7925), Barrington Shopping Center, 180 County Road, Barrington. Greeting cards, books, and book-related toys are sold in this customer-friendly independent bookstore.

Good Books of Bristol (401-254-0390), 495 Hope Street, Bristol. Books of all kinds fill this welcoming shop just across from Linden Place.

Roger Williams University Bookstore, Barnes & Noble (401-254-3036), 1 Old Ferry Road, Bristol. Books of general interest as well as textbooks are available in this on-campus store.

FACTORY OUTLETS **Jamiel's Shoe World** (401-245-4389), 471 Main Street, Warren. A great collection of first-rate shoes (not seconds) at bargain prices.

Samsonite Factory Outlet (401-245-7098), 91 Main Street, Warren. Luggage and travel accessories of all kinds.

SPECIAL SHOPS **Basically British** (401-253-5722), 54 State Street, Bristol. A British-Irish food and specialty shop that carries some 50 kinds of tea, the pots to pour it from, the cozies to keep it warm, biscuits, Devon clotted cream, Marmite, jam sets, and even Union Jacks.

Blithewold Gift Shop (401-253-4130), 101 Ferry Road, Bristol. In this gift store at the Blithewold Mansion and Gardens, the gifts understandably reflect the environment. There are attractive garden decorations, cards designed with floral patterns, and garden books.

Boo Bracken & Co. (401-253-8614), 361 Hope Street, Bristol. An attractive, eclectic shop filled with artsy hand-painted items for the home, as well as interesting craft jewelry and gifts.

chatelaine (401-254-2002), Thames Street Landing, Bristol. A New York attitude characterizes this chic little boutique, right on the harbor, that carries *Sex and the City*–style clothes for women.

European Kitchen (401-254-2305), 11 State Street, Bristol. A bright, small shop close to Thames Street Landing that specializes in colorful plates, kitchenware, and linens from Provence to Portugal.

Grasmere (401-247-2789), 40 Maple Avenue, Barrington. Dried floral arrangements and prettily presented plants and fresh flowers are augmented by English country-style vases and garden accessories.

Herreshoff Marine Museum Nautical Shop (401-253-5000), 7 Burnside Street, Bristol. This gift shop in the Herreshoff Marine Museum has such items for the yachtsman or the want-to-be yachtsman as heavy-weather gear, compasses and ship's clocks, marine books, bookends, and paperweights with a nautical touch.

Imago (401-245-3348), 16 Cutler Street, Warren. Open Thursday through Sunday 11–5. A group of artists with studio space nearby grabbed at the chance to renovate this mill space and turn it into a gallery space for high-quality contemporary works including paintings, pottery, and sculpture.

Kate & Company (401-253-3117), 301 Hope Street, Bristol. There's a little bit of this and a little bit of that—baskets, gourmet foods, hand-painted furniture, decorative wooden boxes, dried wreaths, and picture frames—in this attractive little gift shop.

Linden Place Gift Shop (401-253-0309), 500 Hope Street, Bristol. Well-selected gifts—pewter, crystal, paper, china—are in keeping with the tradition of historic Linden Place.

Teapots & Tassels (401-247-0980), 280 County Road (RI 114), Barrington. Lushly displayed housewares, gifts, pantry items, and women's clothing (upstairs, at Panache) are inside this homey-looking brick building across from Barrington's imposing town hall.

❅ **Woof** (401-253-5755), 54 State Street, Bristol. This dog boutique has a nice selection of canine accoutrements, along with "gourmet" dog biscuits and other goodies.

FARM STAND **Frerich's Farm** (401-245-8245), Kinnicutt Avenue, Warren. Open late April through December, Tuesday through Sunday 9–5.

✳ **Special Events**

March: **Maple Sugaring** (401-253-9062), Coggeshall Farm Museum, Colt State Park, Bristol. Tree tapping, sugar on snow. First weekend in March.

April: **Daffodil Week** (401-253-2707), Blithewold Gardens, Ferry Road, Bristol. First week in April.

Mid-April through mid-May: **Blithewold Mansion and Gardens Annual**

Spring Bulb Display (401-253-2707), Blithewold Gardens, Ferry Road, Bristol. More than 50,000 flowering bulbs herald the arrival of spring.

Late April: **All Manner of Good Work Crafts and Skills Display** (401-253-9062), Coggeshall Farm Museum, Colt State Park, Bristol. Such traditional 18th-century crafts and skills as blacksmithing, coopering, and rake making are demonstrated.

May: **May Breakfasts** (401-222-2601), churches, schools, veterans posts. Jonny cakes and other traditional breakfast dishes. **Sheepshearing** (401-253-9062), Coggeshall Farm Museum, Colt State Park, Bristol. Usually the third weekend of May.

Early June: **Bristol County Striped Bass Tournament** (401-245-6121), Striper Marina, Tyler Point Road, Barrington.

Late June: **Children's Day** (401-253-9062), Coggeshall Farm Museum, Colt State Park, Bristol. Such 18th-century children's games as ninepins, sticks and hoops, top spinning. Usually the last Sunday in June.

June–August: **Concerts-by-the-Bay** (401-253-2707), Blithewold Gardens, Ferry Road, Bristol. Usually every other Sunday afternoon.

July: **Bristol Fourth of July Parade** (401-245-0750). The nation's oldest (1785) parade of civic, military, and firefighters' contingents marches through the streets of Bristol. **Firemen's Memorial Parade,** Barrington–Warren. **Barrington–Warren Rotary Club Quahog Festival** (401-245-3725), Burr's Hill Park, Warren. Live entertainment and clambake, open to the public.

July–August: **Fire Company Clambakes,** Warren. Individual fire companies have clambakes on weekends either at their fire stations or at the Rod and Gun Club in Warren. Individual town fire companies can provide information.

August: **Blessing of the Animals** (401-251-9062), Coggeshall Farm Museum, Colt State Park, Bristol. **Bristol Rotary Club Waterfront Festival** (401-254-0354), Guiteras School grounds. Two days of food, games, crafts, and music.

Late September: **Harvest Fair** (401-253-9062), Coggeshall Farm Museum, Colt State Park, Bristol. Music, pony rides, hayrides, jonny cakes and chowder, crafts, pumpkin painting.

October: **Pumpkin and Indian Corn Sale** (401-253-9062), Coggeshall Farm Museum, Colt State Park, Bristol. Pumpkin and corn sale, with cider making.

November: **Warren Holiday Festival** (401-245-7340), Water and Main Streets, Warren. The day after Thanksgiving, holiday lights are lit along both streets. The festival continues through the post-Thanksgiving weekend with a visit from Santa Claus, gingerbread cookie workshops, hayrides, and music.

December: **Christmas Tree Sale and Father Christmas Visits** (401-253-9062), Coggeshall Farm Museum, Colt State Park, Bristol. **Christmas at Blithewold** (401-253-2707), Blithewold Mansion, Ferry Road, Bristol. Period decor, vignettes of Christmas past, and a 20-foot Christmas tree in the turn-of-the-20th-century mansion. **Bristol Festival of Lights** (401-245-0750). Downtown concert, lighting ceremony, refreshments.

Sakonnet 5

TIVERTON

LITTLE COMPTON

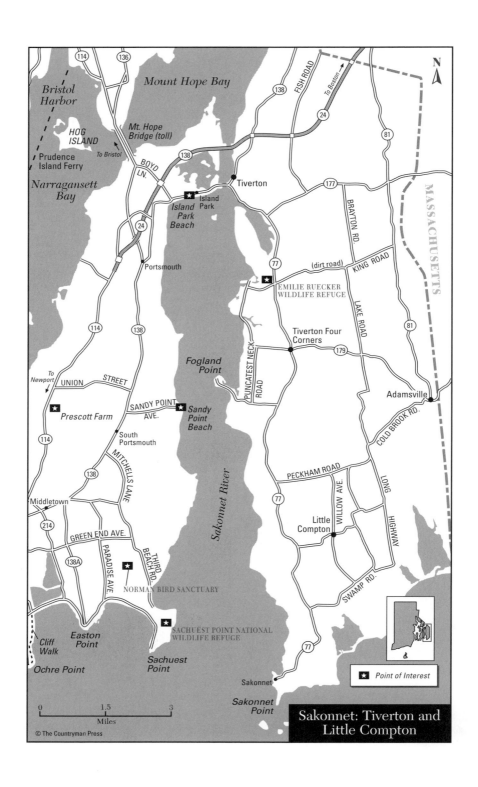

Sakonnet: Tiverton and
Little Compton

© The Countryman Press

TIVERTON

Sakonnet consists of two towns, Tiverton and Little Compton, which once were part of the Massachusetts Bay Colony and now make up the southeastern-most part of Rhode Island. Meaning "Place of the Black Geese" to members of the Wampanoag tribe, Sakonnet is the rural part of Newport County, lightly populated except for a few pockets, and filled with pastures and woods.

Once a popular waterfront resort centered on the area known as Stone Bridge, Tiverton is a sleepy rural community that has been around about as long as Plymouth Colony. The town was included within Rhode Island's borders by royal decree in 1746, although it took several skirmishes with Massachusetts to settle the issue. While officially Rhode Island, Tiverton nevertheless retains its Bay State mentality; its accents, culture, and most of its residents have roots in Massachusetts. Tiverton, like its neighbor Little Compton, was not occupied by the British during the Revolution (although it suffered periodic raids) and served as a haven for rebels and a staging point for sorties across the Sakonnet River.

GETTING THERE *By car:* From Aquidneck Island on RI 24, take the first or second exit off the Sakonnet River Bridge; from points north on RI 24 south, take the Tiverton exit, and turn left onto Main Road (RI 77).

MEDICAL EMERGENCY The statewide emergency number is **911.**
Tiverton Rescue is 401-625-6744.

✳ To See

HISTORIC SITE Fort Barton, Highland Avenue, across from town hall. Highland Avenue can be reached from Main Road by taking any left up the hill before the remains of the Stone Bridge—Lawton Avenue in particular. Park your car (free) and walk up the blacktop path to the heights above. Fort Barton was hastily erected in 1777 in response to the British capture of Newport. Named for Colonel William Barton, who kidnapped General Prescott, the fort was really an earthworks with some timber support. However, from its height 110 feet above the Sakonnet River, its guns held a sweeping command of the north end of Aquidneck. The fort was the jumping-off place for the attack on Aquidneck in

1778, a move that, but for the defection of the French fleet at a crucial moment, might have ended the war in its second year. Today the fort has been partially restored, and there are 3 miles of hiking trails and a lookout that will give you a good view of the northern end of Aquidneck Island and surrounding waters.

SCENIC DRIVES **Main Road** (RI 77) is a nice country road, surrounded by pastures and running between inland woods and the Sakonnet River. It remains a favorite Sunday ride for area families. Driving south from Stone Bridge, you will pass Nanaquaket Pond and a settled area before reaching a more rural setting. At 3119 Main Road, on the left, you'll notice a two-chimney house set back a bit. This is the **Abraham Brown House,** also known as the Adoniram Brown House. Lafayette stayed here during a stopover in Tiverton in 1778.

At 3622 West Main Road, on your right, is the **Captain Robert Gray House,** birthplace in 1755 of the man who skippered the first American ship to sail around the world (1780–90). Captain Gray also discovered the entrance to the Columbia River, giving the United States a convincing claim to the Pacific Northwest. He died at sea of yellow fever in 1806. The house is privately owned, but a small plaque near the street recalls its historical connection.

Half a mile up the road is Tiverton Four Corners, where there are several notable structures. The stately yellow house on the near left is the **Soule-Seabury House,** built in 1760 by Abner Soule, whaler, blacksmith, and soldier. His son, Cornelius Soule, enlarged the house in 1809 but in 1816 was forced to deed it to Cornelius Seabury, merchant and farmer, for payment of a debt. Once open as a museum, the building, unfortunately, was sold some years ago, along with all of its original furnishings. But don't be surprised if you see an ancient mariner comfortably seated on the stone wall outside—some local residents swear they've seen the spirit of Abner Soule return to his former homestead.

VIEW OF AQUIDNECK ISLAND FROM SAKONNET

Kim Grant

The building across the street, on the northwest corner of the intersection, was for years the **A. P. White Store,** built as a country general store in 1875. It now houses Provender, an upscale (and excellent) gourmet food store (see *Where to Eat*). The late-Victorian structure has a high mansard roof and cupola. Original proprietor Andrew Peregrine White was postmaster, ice cutter, dry-goods supplier, and social director for this section of Tiverton for many years.

Also at Four Corners (next to Gray's Ice Cream and general store) is the **Chase-Cory House,** a simple gambrel-roofed house that dates to at least 1730 and contains a 7-foot fireplace with beaded chimney. Owned by the Tiverton Historical Society, it is open to the public June through September on Sundays 2–4:30.

From Four Corners, you may continue straight on RI 77 to Little Compton, or take a left onto East Road (RI 179). Bear right at the fork onto Stone Church Road, pass the **Old Stone Church** (built back to front so the congregation could keep watch for hostile Native Americans), and continue down the long grade into the village of Adamsville, part of Little Compton. The large white private house across the street from Simmons' Variety was home to Rudolf, a son of the Von Trapp family who fled the Nazis in Austria. From Adamsville, you can wind your way via several routes to Little Compton center, or return to the Four Corners and turn left to continue on Main Road.

✳ To Do

BOAT TOURS **Sakonnet Boathouse** (401-624-1440), 169 Riverside Drive, under the Sakonnet Bridge. Weekdays 10–6, Saturday 9–5, Sunday noon–5. Kayak tours and instructions. Also offers kayaks and assorted outdoor gear.

FOR FAMILIES ✔ **Alpacas of Henseforth Farm** (401-624-4184), 460 East Road, about 1 mile east of Tiverton Four Corners. Call for an appointment. The Hensle family raises alpacas, gentle fiber-bearing animals similar to llamas, on this private farm in south Tiverton. "We like to show our alpacas to people who are interested in alpacas," says Mrs. Hensle, adding that the animals are "friendly but shy." There also are guinea hens, ducks, and a pack of enthusiastic but friendly dogs roaming the place.

HORSEBACK RIDING **Roseland Acres** (401-624-8866), 594 East Road (left at Tiverton Four Corners). Hourly trail rides, indoor ring, and lessons in Western and hunt-style riding.

SWIMMING **Fogland Beach,** Fogland Road, off Main Road (RI 77) via Neck Road. The drive to this rocky little beach takes you through some beautiful rural countryside. The 0.5-mile beach itself is on a peninsula reaching into the Sakonnet River, whose calm, salty waters make for ideal family bathing. *Fogland* is not just a random name—this area frequently is wreathed in fog while the rest of the state basks in sunshine.

Grinnell's Beach, Main Road at Stone Bridge. A 0.25-mile crescent of sand, framed by a seawall that's been a teen hangout for generations. That oval of tree and rock you see offshore is called Gould Island and is a private bird sanctuary, off-limits to human visitors.

✳ Green Space

Emilie Ruecker Wildlife Refuge (401-624-2759), 137 Sapowet Avenue, about 0.3 mile from Main Road. Open dawn to dusk year-round. Free entry and parking. Operated by the Audubon Society of Rhode Island, this 1.5-mile walk on the shores of the Sakonnet River is a bird lover's paradise. Once a farm, donated to the Audubon Society in 1965, the property contains salt marshes, wooded areas, rocky outcroppings, and thick underbrush—a variety of terrain and foliage that attracts a variety of birds: herons, snowy egrets, pheasants, and sandpipers. The refuge offers something during any season. Trails are marked by color and are easy to follow.

Weetamoo Woods, between East Road and Lafayette Road, both off Main Road (RI 77). Lafayette Road is almost opposite the Sapowet Avenue route to the Ruecker refuge; the park entrance is less than 0.5 mile up Lafayette. Open all year and free. Four hundred acres of woods named for Weetamoo, or Weetamo, sachem of the Pocasset tribe of the Wampanoags, who wintered here until the time of King Philip's War. You can follow several trails—a walk around the perimeter is under 5 miles—that are all easygoing. Sites include an abandoned sawmill and some impressive rock outcroppings. Snakes and quicksand abound in Tiverton folklore, but there haven't been any reported incidents since the refuge was developed by the town Open Space Committee several years ago and opened to the public.

✳ Where to Eat

Evelyn's Drive-In (401-624-3100), 2335 Main Road (RI 77), Nanaquaket. ($) Open daily until 8 PM. Hamburger-and-clam stand overlooking peaceful Nanaquaket Pond. Order an overstuffed lobster roll with fries and take a seat at one of Evelyn's picnic tables.

🍴 ♿ **Four Corners Grille** (401-624-1510), 3841 Main Road, just before Tiverton Four Corners. ($) Open daily 7–9. Very nice country-pub atmosphere, with breakfast dishes, imaginative (and tasty) sandwiches—lemon tarragon chicken, the Wampanoag (smoked turkey and cucumbers)—and excellent dinners, from fried clams or scallops to shepherd's pie or meat loaf. Try the lobster bisque and crabcakes. Outdoor court in summer.

Moulin Rouge (401-624-4320), 1403 Main Road, just south of Sakonnet River Bridge (second exit). ($$) Open daily, except Tuesday, for dinner. You've got to love a place in Tiverton, Rhode Island, that has a model of the Eiffel Tower in its front yard. Nothing especially fancy—steak, seafood, and French-inspired dishes with a variety of sauces.

Provender (401-624-8096), 3883 Main Road, at Tiverton Four Corners. ($) Open 9–5 daily except Tuesday. Housed in the former A. P. White Store, which also served as the local post office, this gourmet food shop and deli offers fancy sandwiches, picnics, and lots of homemade desserts.

SNACKS Coastal Coffee Roasters (401-624-2343), 1791 Main Road at

Stone Bridge. Donald and Lisa Machado roast their own beans and serve espressos, lattes, and other coffee drinks, as well as snacks and pastries, at this waterfront coffeehouse with outdoor seating in summer.

Gray's Ice Cream (401-624-4500), junction of RI 77 and 179 (Tiverton Four Corners). Open daily in summer 6:30 AM–10 PM. One of the few independent ice cream makers left in the state, Gray's has been attracting hordes of summer weekend customers since 1922. The ice cream is so rich that plain old vanilla, chocolate, and strawberry will do. Or you can go native and order a coffee cabinet (frappe or milk shake to the rest of North America).

Homegrown Marketplace (401-625-2400), 1759 Main Road at Stone Bridge. Vivacious Kate Dobbrow is locally famous for her hot homemade salsas, made with Rhode Island–grown tomatoes and other fresh ingredients. She also has burritos and other take-out lunch foods, most homemade.

✳ Selective Shopping

Cottage at Four Corners (401-625-5814), 3847 Main Road. Upscale, country-style furniture, ceramics, glassware, cookbooks, and bath items are beautifully displayed on two floors.

Courtyards (401-624-8682), 3980 Main Road. Great place filled with chiseled stone birdbaths, concrete lawn and garden decorations, outdoor furniture, sundials, pottery, and a nice selection of jewelry. One of a number of interesting shops in the Mill Pond Shops complex, just past Four Corners.

Donovan Gallery (401-624-4000), Main Road, near Tiverton Four Corners. Mostly paintings, but also glassware, sculpture, and ceramics, much of it by local artists and quite good. Exhibitors include sculptor Mika Seeger and painter-fisherman Tom Sullivan.

Helger's Produce (401-625-5169), 2474 Main Road. This farm stand offers fruits, vegetables, plants, and shrubs at reasonable prices. Also a take-out restaurant in-season, featuring burgers, fried clams, and the like, which you can enjoy at picnic tables.

Virginia Lynch Gallery (401-624-3392), 3883 Main Road, at Tiverton Four Corners. Open Wednesday through Saturday 10–4, Sunday 1–4. Upstairs from Provender, this country gallery produces quality exhibits, showing such artists as *New Yorker* contributor Edward Koren and Massachusetts seascape painter Roger Kizik. The gallery also shows work by the late Harry Nadler, former chairman of the art department at the

LITTLE COLONIALS AT THE INDEPENDENCE DAY PARADE

Tom Gannon

University of New Mexico, and by his wife, Helen Nadler.

Stone Bridge Dishes (401-625-1599), 3879 Main Road. A Sakonnet institution, Stone Bridge Dishes has been around for decades, although at several locations. A wide selection of everyday pottery and glassware, as well as an encyclopedic selection of kitchen gadgets.

✳ Special Events

Fourth of July weekend: **Tiverton Waterfront Festival.** Games, crafts, music, pizza cook-off at Grinnell's Beach near Stone Bridge.

Mid-July: **Arts & Artisans Festival** (1-800-677-7150), Tiverton Four Corners. Nice weekend outdoor show of art and crafted items.

August: **Concert series** (401-624-2600), Tiverton Four Corners. Mostly folk music, every Sunday in August.

Early September: **Union Library Association book sale** (401-625-6799), 3832 Main Road, at Tiverton Four Corners. Annual book sale to benefit this one-room lending library, believed by some to be the second oldest in Rhode Island (after the Redwood in Newport).

LITTLE COMPTON

Little Compton, directly south of Tiverton, is a picture-perfect New England town, one of the few in Rhode Island to boast a classic village green anchored by church, municipal buildings, and commercial enterprises. The rarity of church-centered greens in Rhode Island lies in its roots as a renegade colony founded upon absolute separation of church and state (while still tolerating all forms of religious expression). Little Compton is an exception because it began its existence as a creature of Plymouth Colony. Covering 21.6 square miles and with a population of less than 4,000, this is one of the more rural towns in the state, with rolling farmlands and thick woods. To the west and south, it is bordered by the bright blue Atlantic Ocean; fishing, as well as farming, is a longtime occupation. Year-round and summer residents are proud of the town's character and setting (KEEP LITTLE COMPTON LITTLE was a popular bumper sticker some years ago), and so far they have succeeded in preserving things the way they've been for centuries.

GETTING THERE *By car:* RI 77 (Main Road) south from Tiverton.

MEDICAL EMERGENCY The statewide emergency number is **911.**

Little Compton Rescue is 401-635-2323.

✳ To See and Do

HISTORIC HOME **Wilbur House** (401-635-4035), West Main Road (RI 77). Open mid-June through mid-September, Tuesday through Saturday 2–4. Small admission charged. The original two-story, two-room section of this house dates from 1680. You can distinguish it from rooms added by succeeding generations of the Wilburs during the 18th and 19th centuries by its low ceilings and exposed beams. Restored in 1956 by the Little Compton Historical Society, the house contains furniture from the 17th and 18th centuries. There's also a display of antique farming and household equipment in the neighboring barn. Early settler Samuel Wilbor, who came over from Portsmouth in search of larger pastures, gave birth to the Wilbor clan that has split in several directions over the years and given rise to at least four spellings of the surname, including *Wilber,* *Wilbur,* and *Wilbour.* Adherents of the latter were considered to be putting on airs by adding the *u* to the venerable name.

PARTS OF THE WILBUR HOUSE DATE FROM 1680.

HISTORIC SITES **Commons Burial Ground,** Little Compton Commons. This plot, extending down from behind the graceful United Congregational Church, was laid out in 1675. It is the final resting place for many early settlers, including Elizabeth Pabodie, who was the first infant born in the New World and the daughter of John ("Speak for yourself") and Priscilla Alden. Buried here also is Benjamin Church, the "Indian fighter" who in 1676 put an end to King Philip's War, which had ravaged the colony. Anyone familiar with colonial churchyards knows our ancestors' predilection for plain talk, even on their tombstones. Next to the grave of LYDIA, WIFE OF MR. SIMEON PALMER is another stone, with the 1776 inscription ELIZABETH, WHO SHOULD HAVE BEEN THE WIFE OF MR. SIMEON PALMER. Now that's having the last word.

Gray's Grist Mill (508-636-6075), Adamsville Road (RI 179). Open Tuesday through Sunday noon–4, but call ahead to be sure. The easiest way to get here is to take a left at Tiverton Four Corners on RI 179, bear right at Stone Church Road, and follow down the hill to Adamsville. The mill uses the engine from a 1946 Dodge truck instead of wind or water for power, but grinds out the real stuff our ancestors ate—corn, rye, and the special white flint cornmeal that's an essential ingredient in real jonny cakes.

FISHING *Oceaneer* (401-635-4292), Sakonnet Point Marina. Inshore fishing for blues and bass, offshore for bonito, tuna, and sharks. Parties of up to six on this 38-foot Oceans sportfisherman run by Captain Bud Phillips.

SWIMMING **Goosewing Beach,** South Shore Road. This beautiful beach, at the easternmost point of the Rhode Island coast, is owned by The Nature Conservancy. Thanks to one of those ongoing disputes that keep local politics exciting, access is tricky. Park in the town lot, if there's room, and cross over to

Goosewing. The beach faces open water that sometimes kicks up.

Little Compton Town Beach (South Shore Beach), South Shore Road. Fairly stiff entrance fees here could be construed as another attempt to keep Little Compton "little." Four hundred yards of sand in a setting that offers the same beauty as Goosewing.

WINERY **Sakonnet Vineyards** (401-635-8486), 162 West Main Road, 4 miles south of Tiverton Four Corners. Guided tours and wine tastings May through October, Wednesday through Sunday noon–4. Free. Built in the 1970s and cultivated on farmland that the original owners determined enjoys a climate similar to that of Burgundy, Sakonnet Vineyards is more than a local winery. Its vintages (Vidal Blanc, America's Cup White) have won national prizes. There's also a guest house on the premises; see *Lodging*.

✳ Green Space

Wilbur Woods (Indian Valley), Swamp Road, off West Main Road. A maze of paths (some drivable) and trails through natural woodlands. There's at least one brook flowing through the area (crossable by several wooden bridges and by stone steps), a pool, and a waterfall. Visitors will find tables and benches made from large stones as well as various inscriptions on rocks—all the work of 19th-century farmer Isaac Wilbour, who intended to fashion a memorial of sorts to the Native Americans who made Sakonnet their summer campground. This is a great natural habitat as well as a nice place to picnic. The woods are dotted with fireplaces for grilling.

Also see *Swimming*.

✳ Lodging

The Roost (401-635-8486), Sakonnet Vineyards, 162 West Main Road 02837. ($$) Three guest rooms, all with private bath, in the original farmhouse at this working vineyard (see *Winery*). Room rates include continental breakfast. This is a nice rural setting, and you can imbibe freely during the winery tour, then hit the sack instead of the road.

The Stone House Club (401-635-2222), 122 Sakonnet Point Road 02837. ($–$$) This private club rents out simply furnished rooms in a big stone farmhouse (the granite walls are 2 feet thick) that dates from 1836. There are 11 rooms on the two floors above the restaurant and pub here; the 4 on the third floor share two baths. Two new rooms (Loft 1 and Loft 2) have been installed out in the barn. Continental breakfast comes with your room. The Stone House offers a beautiful rural setting above a field overlooking the ocean.

✳ Where to Eat

DINING OUT **The Stone House Club** (401-635-2222), 122 Sakonnet Point Road. ($$–$$$) Open for dinner Tuesday through Sunday in-season; open Friday through Sunday from September to June. Private club that also welcomes nonmembers for dinner. Varied cuisine from American to French (seafood, grilled tournedos) as well as some vegetarian dishes, all served in the publike Tap Room of this rugged 1836 edifice.

EATING OUT & **The Barn** (401-635-2985), Adamsville Road. ($) Open 6–11:30 AM weekdays; until 12:30 PM weekends. Housed in a real barn, this place serves breakfast only—omelets, French toast, and such—which you can take outdoors on the patio or upstairs in the loft.

Common's Restaurant (401-635-4388), east side of the Commons. ($) Open daily for breakfast, lunch, and dinner. This diner-*cum*-restaurant *is* Little Compton, the kind of place where summer people, tourists, and fifth-generation quahoggers rub shoulders at breakfast and lunch. Varied menu includes jonny cakes, fresh seafood pie, bulging lobster rolls, and just plain ham steak or a cheeseburger.

✳ Selective Shopping

C. R. Wilbur, General Merchandise (401-635-2356), the Commons. Next door to the Commons restaurant, this meandering emporium is your classic general store, offering everything from nails to postcards, books to beach towels. It's a grocery store as well.

FARM STANDS **The Country Stand,** 374 West Main Road. Fresh produce, some organically grown, plus sandwiches and baked goods. Outdoor dining in the shade.

Delucia's Berry Farm (401-635-2698), 96 Willow Avenue. Fresh berries in-season, jams and jellies.

Walker's Roadside Stand (401-635-4719), 261 West Main Road. Very good selection of locally grown fruits and vegetables. This is a busy place on a summer afternoon; take care when parking.

GARDEN CENTER **Peckham's Greenhouse** (401-635-4775), West Main Road. The Peckhams are a knowledgeable group and they sell healthy plants at a good price: perennials, herbs, and some exotic plants, including several varieties of orchids.

✳ Special Events

Fourth of July: **Chicken barbecue and fair** on the town green; fireworks.

Kim Grant

Newport 6

Kim Grant

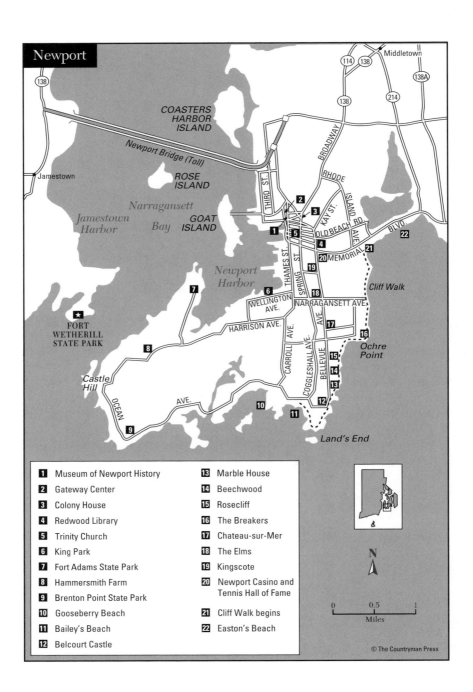

Newport

Middletown

Jamestown

COASTERS HARBOR ISLAND

Newport Bridge (Toll)

ROSE ISLAND

Narragansett Bay

Jamestown Harbor

GOAT ISLAND

Newport Harbor

★ FORT WETHERILL STATE PARK

Castle Hill

THIRD ST.

BROADWAY

RHODE ISLAND AVE.

KAY ST.

OLD BEACH RD.

BLVD.

MEMORIAL

THAMES ST.

SPRING ST.

Cliff Walk

WELLINGTON AVE.

NARRAGANSETT AVE.

HARRISON AVE.

Ochre Point

CARROLL AVE.

COGGLESHALL AVE.

BELLEVUE AVE.

OCEAN AVE.

Land's End

1	Museum of Newport History	**13**	Marble House
2	Gateway Center	**14**	Beechwood
3	Colony House	**15**	Rosecliff
4	Redwood Library	**16**	The Breakers
5	Trinity Church	**17**	Chateau-sur-Mer
6	King Park	**18**	The Elms
7	Fort Adams State Park	**19**	Kingscote
8	Hammersmith Farm	**20**	Newport Casino and Tennis Hall of Fame
9	Brenton Point State Park		
10	Gooseberry Beach	**21**	Cliff Walk begins
11	Bailey's Beach	**22**	Easton's Beach
12	Belcourt Castle		

N

0   0.5   1
Miles

© The Countryman Press

NEWPORT

Newport, sometimes called America's First Resort, owes its existence to the sea. Situated at the mouth of Narragansett Bay and blessed with a fine deepwater harbor, Newport quickly grew from a small settlement founded by Massachusetts refugees in 1639 to a bustling seaport. As early as 1646 residents were busy building ships, and by the middle of the next century the town was a major port in the New World, rivaling New York and Boston in size and importance. The local fleet was heavily involved in the slave trade, and the city was a haven for privateers—often indistinguishable from outright pirates—who'd as soon plunder a British ship as one flying the French or Dutch flag.

It was the sea and the natural beauty of the promontory on which the city stands that attracted wealthy visitors beginning in the early 18th century, culminating with the influx of wealthy New York society families toward the turn of the 19th century. Their presence helped make the city the country's "first" resort, and the extravagant mansions, or "summer cottages," as they were called, draw many of today's visitors.

Newport's nickname also can be traced to the impressive number of "firsts" it lays claim to. Among them: the first U.S. post office and first free public school (1640); the first synagogue in the United States (1789); the first gaslit street (1803); the first open golf tournament (1895); the first national grass-court tennis championships (1881); and, in the field of vehicle control, the first traffic ordinance (1687), as well as the first motorized traffic arrest (1904—the offense: doing 15 miles per hour).

Aside from its natural attributes, which include a mild summer climate softened by a prevailing southwest sea breeze, Newport is an important treasury of colonial homes—thanks in part to a 3-year occupation by British and Hessian troops at the start of the Revolution. During the occupation, the city lost much of its population, all of its commerce, and many of its buildings. By war's end the city was deeply in debt and no longer a port of consequence. As a result, Newporters were too poor to tear down their humble (now prized) dwellings in the name of progress.

The city today retains traces of its past, with the somewhat muted rough-and-tumble of the waterfront coexisting with the splendor of the Bellevue Avenue marble palaces and the timeless character of its many colonial buildings and cobbled byways. Newport, especially in summer, can be serene and raucous, often simultaneously. But it is never dull.

GUIDANCE The one-stop information center for Newport and environs is the **Gateway Center** (401-849-8098; 1-800-326-6030), 23 America's Cup Avenue, run by the Newport County Convention & Visitors Bureau. Besides brochures and a helpful staff, the center offers room reservation services, tickets to many attractions, informational displays, and a narrated slide show. Visitors receive a free half hour of parking in the adjoining Gateway parking garage.

GETTING THERE *By car:* Newport is on the southern tip of an island, accessible from the south and west by US 95 (via RI 138) and the Newport (Claiborne Pell) Bridge; from the north, US 24 or US 195 lead to Newport, via either RI 138 or RI 114.

By bus: **Bonanaza Bus Lines** (401-846-1820), 23 America's Cup Avenue, at the Gateway Center, has direct connections from Boston and Providence. **Rhode Island Public Transportation Authority** (RIPTA; 401-781-9400) buses also provide direct service from Providence and the **Amtrak** (1-800-USA-RAIL) railroad station in South Kingstown, 19 miles away.

THE NEWPORT HARBOR AND BRIDGE AT DUSK

Kim Grant

By shuttle: **Cozy Cab** (401-846-2500), 129 Connell Highway, provides shuttle service to and from T. F. Green State Airport in Warwick.

By ferry: **Rhode Island Public Transit Authority** (RIPTA; 401-781-9400) runs high-speed ferry service between Providence and Newport from May through October. The trip takes about an hour. For reservations, 401-453-6800, ext. 1263 (Providence) or 1264 (Newport), or visit www.nefastferry.com.

GETTING AROUND *By car:* Most visitors to Newport arrive by car—and promptly get snagged in a summer-long traffic jam that virtually paralyzes the city's many colonial-era streets. When and if you find a place to park (more on that later), the best way to negotiate the city is on foot. This is a very walkable city, with most of the main attractions close together.

Parking is an ongoing problem in the City by the Sea, whose 300-year-old streets were designed for horse-powered transportation. Parking meters in the downtown area provide a stingy 15 minutes per quarter, and be warned: The city has a 2-hour limit in any one space; beyond that, you may (and probably will) be ticketed whether there is money in the meter or not. Nor do the meters shut down at 6 PM—Newport meters run until 9 PM.

Other parking options include private and several (quickly filled) municipal parking lots as well as rare on-street spaces in outlying neighborhoods. Once again, the visitor must be wary. Between Memorial Day and October 1, resident parking is in effect after 6 PM on many side streets, and cars without Newport stickers will be ticketed. Look for small RESIDENT PARKING signs on telephone poles, or ask a resident for guidance. Those staying at a neighborhood B&B or guest house often can obtain a temporary resident parking permit from the proprietor.

By guided tour: Guided tours are an excellent means of quickly getting acquainted with the city, its points of interest, and some of its history. Do-it-yourselfers can rent a cassette tour of Newport at the Gateway Center and follow the narration as they take a drive by the mansions and along Ocean Avenue. A helpful map is included in the service.

By bus: **Viking Tours** (401-847-6921), 23 America's Cup Avenue, at the Gateway Center. Daily May through Columbus Day. Bus tours of varying length, including admission to one, two, or more mansions.

By foot: **Newport on Foot** (401-846-5391). In summer Anita Rafael conducts at least one historical walking tour per day, with an emphasis on Newport history to be found within a 10-block area of Historic Hill and Washington Square. Tours normally last 90 minutes. She also offers topical tours, including one on the history of drinking in Newport, which concludes with a tour of White Horse Tavern, the country's oldest taproom.

By rail: **Old Colony & Newport Railway** (401-849-0546), 19 America's Cup Avenue, beside the Gateway Center. Saturday, Sunday, and holidays from July 1 to early September. This 90-minute rail trip runs along the West Shore of Aquidneck to Portsmouth, where the train makes a stop at Green Animals, a topiary garden.

By taxi: **Cozy Cab** (401-846-2500), 129 Connell Highway; **Rainbow Cab** (401-839-1333), 326 Coddington Highway; **Yellow Cab** (401-846-1500), 129 Connell Highway. Good places to find taxicabs are in Washington Square or at the Gateway Center.

MEDICAL EMERGENCY The statewide number for emergencies is **911.**

Newport Hospital (401-846-6400) is located at Broadway and Friendship Street.

✳ To See

Much of what there is to see in Newport is connected with its history. In some cities if you want to see history, you have to go to a museum. In Newport you just take a right or left out of your hotel, and start walking. A handful of museums can be found in Newport, and the mansions technically could be considered museums. But most of the city's history has been incorporated into contemporary life—in the 18th-century dwellings that serve as homes, shops, or restaurants, and in the narrow, gaslit lanes.

Out in the open air you'll also have a chance to enjoy Newport's natural beauty—an attribute even the natives never seem to tire of. There's Ocean Avenue, the Cliff Walk, and a number of conveniently located seaside parks. Beyond it all is the sea; you can experience the magnificent waves breaking over the rocks at the southern tip, the vista of First Beach from the heights of Memorial Boulevard, or the quiet of the inner harbor. Be sure to catch as many sunsets as you can—Newport Harbor looks to the west.

MUSEUMS International Tennis Hall of Fame (401-849-3990), in the Newport Casino, 194 Bellevue Avenue. Open daily 9–5. Adults $8, seniors $6, children $4 ($20 per family). Newport has good reason to call itself the home of American tennis: One year after the Newport Casino was built in 1880, it became the site of the first National Men's Championship and all subsequent lawn tennis nationals until 1915. The National Grass Court Championships are held here each year, as are professional men's and women's tournaments.

Designed by Stanford White, the casino complex is a wonderful example of period architecture surrounding green grass courts that predate those at Wimbledon. The stately atmosphere belies the fact that the casino was founded by two Newport society delinquents. Visiting British polo player Captain Henry Candy, acting on a dare from publisher and yachtsman James Gordon Bennett, rode his horse onto the front porch of the ultrastaid Newport Reading Room club on Bellevue Avenue. The members were not amused; Candy was barred from the club, and Bennett was reprimanded. Bennett's response was to build

THE INTERNATIONAL TENNIS HALL OF FAME

Kim Grant

his own club, which soon became a gathering spot for Newport's best, especially during Tennis Week each August. The casino was designated a National Historic Landmark in 1987.

Today the front portion of the complex houses the Hall of Fame and museum, billed as the largest tennis museum in the world. Filling two floors, the museum contains at least a dozen rooms filled with every kind of tennis memorabilia, including equipment, trophies, period costumes, paintings, and photographs. There is a Davis Cup Room and Davis Cup Theater, where old tennis films are shown.

International Yacht Restoration School (401-848-5777), 449 Thames Street. Open daily 10–5; closed January through March. Free admission. Visitors can watch shipwrights and students restore classic wooden vessels and take a tour of the 1885 schooner *Coronet*.

The Museum of Newport History (401-841-8770), Brick Market, at the foot of Washington Square. Open daily 10–5, Sunday noon–5; closed Tuesday. Adults $5, seniors $4; children under 12 cost $3. Validated free parking at Long Wharf Mall North and the Gateway Center. If you've never been to Newport before, this is a good place to start. The museum is a quick means of getting acquainted with 300 years of local history in as little as half an hour. Lots of interactive exhibits and interesting artifacts, photographs, and oral histories. The building itself, designed by Peter Harrison and completed in 1762, is of historical importance and has been designated a National Historical Landmark. Built as a market and warehouse by Long Wharf merchants, Brick Market anchored the west end of busy Washington Square, the center of early Newport civic and commercial activity.

Also offered are walking tours of Newport historical areas ($7, including admission to the museum) and/or a tour of Colony House ($6) on Thursday, Friday, and Saturday.

Museum of Yachting (401-847-1018), Fort Adams State Park, off Ocean Avenue. Open June through October, daily 10–5. Admission $4 adults, $3 seniors and children. Housed in a 19th-century brick building that looks out over the waterfront, this museum offers a tour of the history of yachting through its displays of photos, paintings, boating gear, and various kinds of vessels. The America's Cup Gallery traces the history of this prestigious event, which took place off Newport from the glorious J-boat days of the 1930s, when Harold S. Vanderbilt manned the helm, to the era of the 12-meter boats, when the Cup was lost to Australia in 1983. The 12-meter *Courageous*, two-time Cup defender, is part of the museum collection. There is also a Singlehanded Hall of Fame that honors intrepid sailors from around the world who have taken to sea alone, many of whom have Newport ties. Outside, you may see the museum's own J-class sloop, *Shamrock*, or its sister ship, *Endeavour*, lying at anchor nearby.

Looming beside the museum is Fort Adams, a sturdy granite structure that is one of the largest seacoast fortifications built in the United States. During the Revolution, patriots began fortifying this strategic point overlooking the entrance to Narragansett Bay, but the occupying British destroyed their work. In 1799 the fort was rededicated and named for President John Adams. It fell into disrepair until the War of 1812 put a scare into Congress, and work began in earnest to build a fort that could withstand attack from land or sea. Begun in 1824, the fort took 33 years to complete and, in fact, never was attacked. It served briefly as the U.S. Naval Academy during the early years of the Civil War when Annapolis was threatened. An ongoing restoration effort has opened parts of the fort to the public for the first time in decades; call 401-841-0707 for current hours. The surrounding park, which offers a superb spot to fish, swim, or watch yachts come and go, is open daily 6 AM–11 PM. Rangers collect a nominal fee for each passenger car from Memorial Day to Labor Day; free the rest of the year.

Naval War College Museum (401-841-4052), Coasters Harbor Island, through Gate 1 at the southern end of the Naval Education and Training Center. Open June through September, Monday through Friday 10–4, weekends noon–4. Free admission. The War College is where navy officers get their advanced training. The museum, located in Founders Hall, offers exhibits on the history of the "art and science" of naval warfare as well as local seafaring history.

The Newport Art Museum (401-848-8200), 76 Bellevue Avenue. Open daily 10–5 Memorial Day through Labor Day; 10–4 Tuesday through Saturday and noon–4 Sunday the rest of the year. Adults $6, seniors and students $4, children under 5 free. Designed by Richard Morris Hunt, the J. N. A. Griswold house that now serves as the art museum's main building is a prime example of mid-Victorian stick-style architecture, in which vertical and diagonal "sticks" on the exterior suggest the underlying structure. The museum has regular exhibits by internationally known artists in four galleries, including the adjacent, mausoleumlike Cushing Gallery. There's also a permanent collection of 19th- and 20th-century American artwork.

The Newport Artillery Company (401-846-8488), 23 Clarke Street, just off Washington Square. Open May through October, Saturday 10–4. Small admis-

THE MUSEUM OF YACHTING IN NEWPORT'S FORT ADAMS STATE PARK

Kim Grant

sion fee. Chartered in 1741 by King George, the company is the oldest militia in continuous service in America. Its headquarters, built in 1836 in solid Greek Revival style, houses military uniforms and weapons from colonial times to the present as well as artifacts from more than 100 countries.

Newport Historical Society (401-846-0813), 82 Touro Street, just up from Washington Square. Open Tuesday through Friday 9:30–4:30, Saturday 9:30–noon. Free admission. The historical society building incorporates the Sabbatarian Meeting House built in 1729. The meetinghouse is the oldest of its faith in the United States and contains a beautiful wineglass pulpit. The society's collection contains rare and valuable paintings and fine period furniture, especially that made by the local Goddard and Townsend families.

The reference collection contains many manuscripts and historical documents that recall the flavor and tempo of early colonial life in Newport, back when the city was an active center of trade, politics, and intrigue. The first floor has changing exhibits. Upstairs, the library contains the second largest genealogical collection in Rhode Island and will conduct research for a small fee. The society also conducts walking tours of colonial Newport from June 15 through September on Friday and Saturday mornings at 10. The 2-hour tour is $6 for adults; children under 12 are free.

HISTORIC SITES AND BUILDINGS Colony House (401-846-2980), at the head of Washington Square. Free tours daily July through Labor Day 9:30–4 and by appointment in the off-season. This handsome building, designed by Richard Munday and built in 1739–41, is the second oldest capitol in the United States. It served as the seat of government for both the colony and the state of Rhode Island when Newport was the capital city. Colony House once was the site of public whippings and pillorying of colonial lawbreakers. (Law in the colonies was harsh; for example, children who struck their parents could be put to death.) It also played a central role in the Revolution. It was from here that Governor Stephen Hopkins issued the order in July 1764 to open fire on the British warship *St. John*—possibly the first shots fired in what was to become the Revolutionary War. And it was from here that Rhode Island declared its independence from Britain on May 4, 1776, anticipating the Declaration of Independence by 2 months. During the war George Washington met here with French general Rochambeau to plan the final defeat of Cornwallis at Yorktown. (Other notables who have been entertained at the Colony House include Lafayette and Presidents Jefferson, Jackson, and Eisenhower.) Upstairs, in the Governor's Council Chamber, hangs a full-length portrait of Washington by Gilbert Stuart.

Common Burial Ground, Farewell Street. Once well beyond the city limits, the burial ground started as several distinct cemeteries, the south side for freemen, the north for slaves. Of the 3,000 or so stones here, about 800 date from the 1600s to before 1800. Among them are some excellent examples of colonial gravestone carving. The adjacent Island Cemetery, with an entrance on Warner Street, is notable for its monuments to the Perry brothers and *Standing Angel,* by Augustus Saint-Gaudens, a major sculptor of the late 19th century.

The Old Stone Mill, Touro Park at the corner of Mill Street and Bellevue Avenue. One of the real architectural oddities in America, the stone mill has been attributed to Vikings, Native Americans, and Portuguese or English colonists, which would mean it dates from somewhere between 1100 and 1650. Recent thinking holds it was built as a windmill by Governor Benedict Arnold, fifth great-grandfather of the notorious Arnold. But the peculiar architecture, along with the suit of armor found farther up the coast and immortalized in Longfellow's "The Skeleton in Armor," has convinced many locals that the Vikings were responsible. Some say it may have served as a lighthouse, while others maintain it was simply Arnold's mill-granary, fortified because of the ongoing Indian wars. At any rate, situated as it is amid one of Newport's prettiest parks, it is well worth a visit. If you hang around long enough, you'll probably hear a new theory about it.

Redwood Library (401-847-0292), 50 Bellevue Avenue, at the corner of Redwood Street. Open Monday through Saturday 10–5. Built in 1748, this National Historic Landmark was designed by Peter Harrison and is the oldest library building in America in continuous service. The structure, which has been enlarged four times, is Palladian in style. Although built of wood like most early buildings in Newport, the siding has been blasted to resemble stone. The library's lending service is private, but the building is open to the public. Writers Henry James and Edith Wharton visited often, and it's easy to see why: Inside and out on the grounds, the library is one of the most pleasant and peaceful sites in the city. The Redwood has an excellent collection of early American paintings and rare books.

NO ONE REALLY KNOWS WHO BUILT THE OLD STONE MILL IN TOURO PARK—OR WHY.

Tom Gannon

the Point. The house and garden are open mid-June to mid-September, daily
10–5, with tours on the hour. Admission $9 for adults, $3.50 for children. A
National Historic Landmark, the Hunter House is considered by architectural
historians to be one of the finest examples of a mid-18th-century dwelling in the
country. Aside from its pure lines and stately proportions, the house is rich in
history. More accurately called the Nichols-Wanton-Hunter House, it had its
modest beginnings in 1748 when Jonathan Nichols bought the property on what
was then called Water Street. Nichols was heavily engaged in the sea trade; he
owned several ships, and there was probably a wharf and warehouse buildings on
the site. According to a city map of 1758, a one-chimney dwelling also stood
there.

Upon Nichols's death in 1757, the house was bought by Colonel Joseph Wanton Jr.,
a politically active merchant who added a south portion to the dwelling, giving it
very much the appearance it has today. Both Wanton, a colonial deputy, and his
father, governor of the colony, were staunch Tories and were forced into exile
across the bay in 1775 as the rebellion heated up. With the arrival of British
forces in 1776, Wanton came back to Newport, where he served as superintendent of police. But when the British withdrew three years later, the Wantons were
again forced to flee. They died in exile, but Wanton Jr.'s Tory politics probably
saved the house from destruction—an estimated 300 others on the Point and
elsewhere in town were destroyed by the British.

When the French allies reached Newport in 1780, the house became headquarters for Admiral de Ternay, whose fleet delivered French commander Rochambeau and his troops to America. De Ternay's stay was brief; contracting a fever,
he died on December 15, 1780, on his warship *Duc de Bourgogne*, anchored
near the house. After several years of neglect, the house was purchased by
William Hunter, a lawyer, U.S. senator, and ambassador, who landscaped the
grounds and, mainly through 44 years of ownership, gave the house its name.

Today the house has been meticulously restored by the Preservation Society of
Newport County. Although many of the original furnishings were lost, the house
has been refurnished with authentic Queen Anne, Chippendale, and Hepplewhite pieces made by the Townsend and Goddard families and other colonial
craftsmen.

Wanton-Lyman-Hazard House (401-846-0813), 17 Broadway, just up from
Washington Square. Open Thursday through Saturday 10–4. Admission $4. Now
situated somewhat incongruously in a commercial district, this restored house is
one of the oldest in the city. Built between 1650 and 1700, its steeply pitched
roof and central chimney are typical of the homes built by the early settlers. The
interior walls are still covered with the original plaster—made, in some cases,
from ground shells and molasses. There's also a fine early colonial fireplace.

A number of notable residents lived at this address, including Martin Howard Jr.,
a Tory who had to flee for his life during the Stamp Act riot of August 26, 1765.
During the French occupation, the house was frequented by French officers
courting Polly Lawton, a Quaker teenager considered one of the most charming

NEWPORT'S COLONIAL-ERA WASHINGTON STREET

young women on either side of the Atlantic. "A nymph rather than a woman . . . so much beauty, so much modesty," a count confided to his diary. Their attentions were to no avail—Polly married an American soldier, Major Daniel Lyman. A National Historic Landmark, the house has been furnished by the Newport Historical Society. There is a restored colonial garden out back.

Samuel Whitehorne House (401-847-2448; 401-849-7300), 416 Thames Street. Open May through October, Friday 1–4 and Saturday through Monday 10–4. Adults $8, children $3. Now operated by Doris Duke's Newport Restoration Foundation, the Whitehorne House was built in 1811 and is a fine example of Federal-period architecture, when brick was being introduced into the construction of residences. Captain Samuel Whitehorne Jr., a prosperous merchant, was the original owner, but shipping losses bankrupted him, and he lost the home at auction in 1844. The house contains many fine period furniture pieces, including works by Goddard and Townsend, and silver and pewter made by Newport silversmiths between 1740 and 1840. Outside, there's a garden typical of the Federal period with early varieties of plants rarely seen now.

THE MANSIONS AND THE GILDED AGE Henry James called them "white elephants" and "grotesque." A former French ambassador, perhaps forgetting Versailles, once referred to them as "horrors." Others have described them as the perfect symbols of the Gilded Age, a time when America's newly rich sought ways to flaunt their tax-free wealth. Architectural monstrosities or gracious reminders of a past glory, the mansions that line Bellevue Avenue and Ocean Avenue are without a doubt the single most popular attraction in the City by the Sea. They are visited by more than 1 million people each year, and to come to Newport without seeing at least one would be like missing the ocean.

Newport was always a favorite summer place for the wealthy, beginning well before the Revolution, but it wasn't until the 1880s, when New York society began arriving in force, that the city entered its heyday. Much of the opulence—some would say extravagance—of the time was due to a new definition of *wealth*. Where once the accumulation of a million dollars defined wealth, the new fortunes, built on coal, railroads, oil, and finance, were measured in tens and hundreds of millions. Lacking hereditary titles or long family tradition, the members of this new elite attempted to create an instant American aristocracy by doing what they did best: spending money.

The Golden Era was ushered in with lavish balls and dinners, set in equally lavish surroundings. No matter that a family might spend no more than a month here in summer—each "summer cottage" had to be more opulent than the one next door. And opulent they were. The Marble House, including furnishings, cost a total of $11 million when it was built in 1892, about a tenth of what it would cost today. Not so much, really, when you consider that families spent as much as $200,000 for a single party. For her Fête des Roses in 1902, Grace Vanderbilt provided $10,000 worth of "favors" for her guests and brought in the entire company of the hit play *The Wild Rose*, a feat that involved closing the theater in New York for 2 days.

MARBLE HOUSE WAS MODELED AFTER THE PETIT TRIANON AT VERSAILLES.

Kim Grant

The summer colonists spent so much and so freely that a newspaper correspondent was prompted to report that Newport's rich "devoted themselves to pleasure regardless of expense." Not so, corrected Colonel George Waring, a prominent resident, who explained that the rich were actually devoting themselves to expense regardless of pleasure. A disapproving Henry James wrote that the summer visitors "danced and they drove and they rode, they dined and wined and dressed and flirted and yachted and Casino'd." It couldn't last, of course, and the advent of the income tax and, finally, the Depression put an end to these excesses of America's richest families. For most, the great summer homes became too expensive to own, and by 1950 only a handful were left in private hands.

Fortunately for posterity, the Preservation Society of Newport County—formed in 1945 to preserve the historic, colonial-era Hunter House—

began acquiring the mansions as they closed up. It now owns six of the best, including Rosecliff, the Elms, and the Breakers.

A word about the architecture of the mansions and Richard Morris Hunt, who designed some of them: Most of the architecture is derivative, modeled after the great houses and palaces of Europe. The European tradition came naturally to Hunt, who was the first American to receive a degree from the École des Beaux-Arts in Paris, where he became familiar with the neoclassical and neobaroque design elements regarded as the height of artistic expression. His training came in handy for an America that after the Civil War had no defined style of its own and was compelled to look back to Europe for direction.

All the mansions open to the public are either on or directly off Bellevue Avenue between Bowery Street and the beginning of Ocean Avenue. The Preservation Society houses are well marked with green-and-white signs, and free parking is provided at each estate. Tours generally last about 45 minutes. Admission varies: $15 for the Breakers, $10 for the other houses, $4 for children; combination tickets for two or more mansions are available at discounts.

Beechwood (401-846-3772), Bellevue Avenue, just south of Rosecliff. Open mid-May through November 1, daily 9–4. Adults $15, children and seniors $10. This stucco mansion was designed by Calvert Vaux and Andrew Jackson Downing and built in 1851–52. (Vaux was the less famous partner of Frederick Law Olmsted, who designed Central and Prospect Parks in New York City.) With its high-ceilinged piazzas on three sides, Beechwood was a summer showcase for years. But it wasn't until the 1880s, when Mrs. William Backhouse Astor— "Queen of the Four Hundred"— took up residence, that Beechwood came into its own.

ROSECLIFF HAS SEEN ITS SHARE OF TRAGEDY.

Kim Grant

Caroline Astor, who had married the grandson of John Jacob Astor I, was the ruling grande dame of New York's Fifth Avenue society. The term *Four Hundred* referred to the number of people who could fit comfortably into her city ballroom. By her own definition, the family she married into was "old money," unlike the Vanderbilts, who had made their money in "trade" and whom, for a time, she was able to bar from the inner circles of society.

House tours are conducted by costumed guides who greet you as one of Mrs. Astor's personal guests and provide lively and humorous sketches of life at the time. Special tours, which require reservations, include a tea dance/tour and a murder mystery tour.

Belcourt Castle (401-846-0669), Bellevue Avenue at Lakeview Avenue. Open daily year-round except January. Summer hours between late May and November 1 are 9–5; winter hours are 10–4. Adults $10, seniors $8, students $7, and children $5. Now owned by the Howard B. Tinney family, Belcourt was designed by Richard Hunt for Oliver Hazard Perry Belmont in 1891. The medieval-style museum-castle, based on plans for a Louis XIII hunting lodge that Hunt saw in France, is a departure from Hunt's usual grandiose palaces.

The castle contains 60 rooms, each done in a different period of French, Italian, or English design. Notable features include the hand-carved Grand Stair—a reproduction of the Francis I stair in the Musée de Cluny in Paris—and the elegant Versailles dining room. Within the many rooms is the family collection of antiques and art treasures from 32 countries. The castle contains many fine Oriental rugs and what is said to be the largest collection of stained glass in the country. Also on display is a 23-karat-gold Royal Coronation coach, decorated with oil paintings and gold lead and weighing 4 tons.

One of the nicest features of the castle is the center courtyard, where Mr. Belmont had his horses exercised daily (the stables are built into the house). Belmont was kind to his horses: They slept in a Hunt-designed stable on white linen sheets embroidered with the Belmont crest. After a tour, visitors are invited to have tea or coffee. Besides the regular tour, Belcourt hosts a weekly Thursday "ghost tour" at 5 PM (reservations required), which consists of a slide show, a tour of the castle, and a chance to meet Belcourt's own ghost, believed to be a monk who hangs out in the medieval chapel.

The Breakers (401-847-6543), Ochre Point Avenue. Open April through October, daily 10–5, and for special hours during the Christmas season. The Breakers is the largest, most opulent, and best known of the Newport mansions and a National Historic Landmark. To reach it, turn off Bellevue Avenue at either Victoria, Shepard, or Ruggles Avenue. The estate is enclosed by a beautiful, ornamental wrought-iron fence. From the back, the grounds command an awe-inspiring view of the Atlantic Ocean. The grounds also feature an original parterre garden and many unusual imported trees and shrubs.

Covering nearly an acre of Cornelius Vanderbilt's 11-acre oceanfront property, the four-story limestone palace contains 70 rooms, including a two-story ballroom that epitomizes the Gilded Age. It took a force of hundreds of workers just 2 years to complete the building. Entire rooms were built overseas by European craftsmen and shipped to Newport. Crystal chandeliers were equipped for gas as well as electricity in case the power failed. Bathroom taps supplied either fresh rainwater or salt water, hot and cold. The house contains all the original furnishings.

The Breakers was opened with a coming-out party for 20-year-old Gertrude Vanderbilt on an August evening in 1895. Missing was architect Richard Hunt, who had died on July 31. Cornelius Vanderbilt, who inherited $70 million of the Vanderbilt family's railroad empire fortune, was not able to enjoy his summer home for long: He suffered a stroke in 1896 and died 3 years later at the age of 56. The Countess Laszlo Scechenyi (née Gladys Vanderbilt) sold the house to the Preservation Society in 1972. Countess Szapary, her daughter, still resides in the family quarters on the third floor.

The tour includes admission to the Breakers Stable and Carriage House on nearby Coggeshall Avenue. Built in 1895, the stable contains a central carriage room on the ground floor and 28 stalls at the rear. The horses are gone, but some period carriages and coaches are on display.

Chateau-sur-Mer (401-847-0037), Bellevue Avenue, corner of Shepard Avenue. Open April through October, daily 10–5. Another of the Preservation Society's houses, and one of the older mansions in Newport and a fine example of mid-Victorian architecture, this house is actually a blending of two structures. The first was built in 1852 by a local contractor for William Shepard Wetmore, another China trader who settled in Newport. Twenty years later it was enlarged by Richard Morris Hunt, who added a French ballroom and so altered the house that what you see today is largely his design. Some critics felt that he converted a charming Victorian villa into a somewhat severe pile of granite, but the imposing result was a hint of grander summer palaces to come.

The neighborhood surrounding Chateau-sur-Mer is built up now, but once the 35-acre estate offered a clear view of the sea, hence its name. Note the many exotic plants on the grounds and the Chinese moon gate on the south side, which once framed an ocean vista.

The first room on the tour is the elegantly paneled library, originally the kitchen. For a time it served as a billiard parlor for the second owner, George Peabody Wetmore, governor and senator; but when he died, his spinster daughters had the pool table removed and the cue racks converted to coatracks. The whole house is notable for its extensive wood paneling done in the "honest" style—all the mistakes were left to be seen—and large ornate mirrors. Many of the original furnishings are displayed, including a fine collection of Rose Medallion and Rose Mandarin china sets acquired by Wetmore. On the second floor is a special treat for children: a charming collection of Victorian toys and dollhouses. Each Christmas the Preservation Society decorates the house in Victorian holiday style and opens it to the public.

The Elms (401-847-0478), Bellevue Avenue, corner of Dixon Street. Open April through October, daily 10–5. Built in 1901 for Philadelphia coal baron Edward J. Berwind, the French-style château is the best furnished of the Preservation Society's houses. As striking as the house is—in a coolly classical manner—the biggest attraction is the 14 acres of grounds and sunken French gardens complete with terraces, fountains, statues, and teahouses. There's a wide variety of exotic trees and shrubs, all labeled. This is a perfect place to stroll on a sunny afternoon.

Designed by Horace Trumbauer of Philadelphia after the 18th-century Château d'Asnières near Paris, the Elms offers more than meets the eye. Although from the ground it appears to be a two-story structure topped with a sculpture-bearing parapet, in reality there is a hidden third story that contains the servants' quarters—16 rooms and three baths. In the same way, kitchen and laundry facilities are discreetly concealed in the basement. A secret underground railroad, which surfaced a block away on Dixon Street, transported the coal to fuel the huge burners that kept the house and furnishings warm during winter.

Kingscote (401-847-0366), Bellevue Avenue at the corner of Bowery Street. Open April through October, daily 10–5. Heading south down the avenue, this is the first mansion you come to, but perhaps it should be saved until after you've viewed several of the other Preservation Society mansions. With its wooden exterior and charming early-Victorian design, Kingscote comes as a welcome change of pace after you've viewed the huge granite and marble structures farther along. Among the oldest summer residences in the city, Kingscote was built in 1839 by Richard Upjohn for George Noble Jones of Savannah, Georgia, who continued the tradition of southern families summering in Newport. On what was, at the time, 2 acres surrounded mostly by farmland, Upjohn designed a Gothic Revival house that was picturesque without being overly quaint. A dining room was added in 1881 by Stanford White of McKim, Mead, and White, who later designed Rosecliff.

The least well known of the society's houses, Kingscote is well worth a visit to see its early Rhode Island furniture and art. There is also a priceless collection of porcelain and paintings courtesy of later owner William Henry King, who made his fortune in the China trade. The interior of the house is rich with parquet floors, a Tiffany glass wall in the dining room, and mahogany paneling.

Marble House (401-847-2445), Bellevue Avenue, just south of Beechwood. Open daily 10–5 April through October. Another Preservation Society house. Designed by Richard Hunt for William K. Vanderbilt in 1892, Marble House looks like a mansion should, with a white marble driveway curving up to an arch under a porte cochere, pilasters and capitals, and 10 tons of bronzed entrance grille. Hunt's model was the Petit Trianon at Versailles, Marie Antoinette's private hideaway, and the result epitomizes the architect's notion of the Beaux-Arts neoclassical style. Like the Breakers, the house retains its original furnishings, which cost $9 million in early-1900s dollars. Out on the grounds, near Cliff Walk, Alva Vanderbilt oversaw construction of a red-and-gold-lacquered teahouse; when she realized there was no means of making tea in it, she ordered a tiny railroad to be built from the main house, which carried her footmen back and forth with a silver tea service.

The Gold Ballroom—the gold is real—was the scene of many extravagant entertainments. It was here that Alva (as Mrs. Oliver Hazard Belmont—she had divorced William Vanderbilt and married her cross-avenue neighbor) held one of her most famous dinners, 10 courses at which her 100 "guests" were dogs in various forms of fancy dress. The newly divorced Alva had given a more serious party earlier, in 1895, to present her (reluctant) daughter Consuelo to the titled but poor duke of Marlborough, who dutifully proposed. After an unhappy marriage, Consuelo divorced the duke in 1921 to marry again—for love.

Ochre Court (401-847-6650), 100 Ochre Point Avenue, off Narragansett Avenue. Open daily 9–4. Free, although donations are welcome. Now the administration building for Salve Regina University, Ochre Court is a 50-room medieval-style mansion designed in 1891 by Richard Hunt for Ogden Goelet, a wealthy New York real estate developer. Although much of the building is taken up by college offices, visitors can see the great hall, which rises three stories. In keeping with the medieval atmosphere, the walls are finished with heraldic designs carved in Caen stone. Many of the original furnishings have been removed, but the hall still has its huge marble Atlas table, so called because of the carved Atlas figures that support it. Other rooms open to the public contain many fine period paintings, and there is a stained-glass window dating from the Middle Ages above the landing on the grand staircase. Outside, the grounds sweep down to the Cliff Walk and an unobstructed view of the Atlantic Ocean.

Rosecliff (401-847-5793), Bellevue Avenue. Open daily 10–5 April through October. With its white terra-cotta finish, heart-shaped grand staircase, and beautiful rose garden, Rosecliff is the most romantic of the Newport mansions. Designed in 1900 by Stanford White for the Hermann Oelrichses, the house boasted the largest ballroom in the summer colony and was the scene of many notable entertainments during the Gilded Age. For one of these, the White Ball, Tessie Oelrichs decreed that all the women guests wear white and powder their hair. The men, for contrast, dressed in black. The ballroom was filled with white roses, orchids, and lilies of the valley, and Mrs. Oelrichs even had a fleet of full-sized white artificial ships constructed, which was anchored out in the Atlantic and illuminated for full effect.

Like many romantic settings, Rosecliff saw its share of tragedy. A later owner had the mansion renovated for his family without ever being able to see it. While on his way to view the finished work, he was killed in a car accident. The family immediately sold the house. The flower gardens and decorative pools make strolling the grounds a must.

Rough Point (401-849-7300), Bellevue Avenue. Open for tours mid-April to early November, Tuesday through Saturday. Tickets ($25 for all visitors) are sold at the Gateway Center, and reservations are recommended. A shuttle bus brings visitors from the center to the mansion, as there is no on-site parking. The last house on the left, before Bellevue makes a sharp right and becomes Ocean Avenue, is concealed from street view by a high gate, but is visible from the ocean side from the Cliff Walk. The gates are testimony to the desire for privacy by the late owner, tobacco heiress Doris Duke, who founded the Newport Restoration Foundation responsible for rehabbing many of Newport's finer colonial homes. The house, built in 1888–91 for Frederick Vanderbilt, is just as Duke left it before her death in 1993, filled with her personal effects, furnishings, and an impressive collection of museum-quality artwork. Despite its undeniable grandeur, this is one mansion that also looks like a home. And the setting, right on the wild Atlantic, is spectacular.

HISTORIC HOUSES OF WORSHIP **Channing Memorial Church** (401-846-0643), Pelham Street across from Touro Park. Open by appointment. Built in the mid-19th century, the church contains two beautiful stained-glass windows by John La Farge and a bronze plaque by Augustus Saint-Gaudens. The church is dedicated to William Ellery Channing, a Newporter credited with founding the Unitarian Church in America. Channing (his statue stands across the street in the park) was a philosopher, writer, and friend to many Newport literary figures. He did most of his preaching at the Union Church in Boston and in the Boston area but summered in Newport. Julia Ward Howe, early feminist and author of "Battle Hymn of the Republic," had a pew here.

Newport Congregational Church (401-849-2238), corner of Spring and Pelham Streets. Open Memorial Day through Labor Day, Tuesday and Thursday 10–noon, and by appointment. It has been called Church of the Patriots because its members refused to side with Mother England during the Revolution. As a result, the original church building on Mill Street was converted to a barracks for British troops and later a hospital for French forces. The church was heavily damaged; all that exists today is the cornerstone, bearing the legend FOR CHRIST AND PEACE, now at the parish house. The existing church, built in 1857, contains an interior designed by artist John La Farge and well worth seeing. The walls have a distinct Byzantine flavor, and the opalescent stained-glass windows were made using a technique devised by La Farge.

Quaker Meeting House (401-846-0813), corner of Marlborough and Farewell Streets, one block north of Washington Square. Open by appointment. Recently restored, the Friends Great Meeting House was built in 1699 and is the oldest in the country. An outstanding example of 17th-century architecture, the meeting-house contains models and architectural exhibits, as well as changing exhibits on Quaker life and dress. The Quakers, persecuted in Massachusetts, found a welcome home in Newport. There they rose to political and commercial power, building many of the fine captains' homes in the neighboring Point section. (The Friends, however, did incur resentment on occasion, especially during the Revolution, for what was considered to be an overly pacifist attitude toward the British. In several instances windows in Quaker homes were broken by angry "patriots.")

St. Mary's Church (401-847-0475), corner of Spring Street and Memorial Boulevard. Open Monday through Friday 7–11:30 AM, except holidays. Built between 1848 and 1852, this English Gothic church was designed by Patrick Keeley of New York. Jacqueline Bouvier and Senator John F. Kennedy, later the 34th president, were married here on September 12, 1953. St. Mary's is the seat of the oldest Catholic parish in the state and was designated a National Shrine in 1968.

Touro Synagogue (401-847-4794), 72 Touro Street. Open June through Labor Day, Sunday through Friday 10–5; spring and fall, Friday and Sunday 1–3. Saturday services at 9 AM, Friday services at 7:30 PM in summer, 6 PM the rest of the year. The oldest house of Jewish worship in North America and a National Historic Site, Touro Synagogue is one of the most handsome buildings in the city. Jews, like Quakers, were early settlers in the colony, which was noted for its religious tolerance. It was designed in 1759 by renowned colonial master builder Peter Harrison, who modeled it after Sephardic Jewish temples in Portugal and Holland. The result was a simple but elegant classical building, whose lines may have influenced Thomas Jefferson's plans for Monticello.

Jefferson, George Washington, and other prominent men of the time were visitors to the synagogue, and it was to the Jewish community here that President Washington pledged religious freedom in the newly independent nation. His proclamation, containing the stirring words "To bigotry no sanction, to persecution no assistance," is read each year at Touro. After the Revolution, the building served as a temporary home for the General Assembly and the state Supreme Court while Colony House was repaired. The synagogue's interior, one of the most beautiful in any colonial house of worship, has been restored to its original glory.

At the corner of Bellevue Avenue and Kay Street, a short walk up the street, is Touro Cemetery, which is open daily. Here you will find headstones dating from the 1640s and inscribed in Hebrew, Spanish, Portuguese, and English.

Trinity Church (401-846-0660), a National Historic Landmark on the corner of Church and Spring Streets at the head of Queen Anne Square. Open June 15 through Labor Day, Monday through Saturday 10–5, and afternoons in spring and fall. Sunday services are at 8 and 10 AM in July and August, and at 8 and 11 AM the rest of the year. Considered by many the finest church building in Newport and possibly all of America, Trinity Church was built in 1725–26 by Richard Munday after designs by Christopher Wren, the great 17th-century English architect. What's especially remarkable is that Munday chose to interpret English baroque principles using wood rather than masonry.

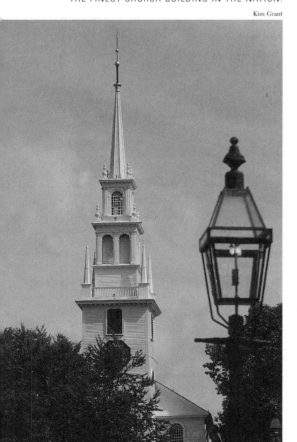

MANY CONSIDER NEWPORT'S TRINITY CHURCH THE FINEST CHURCH BUILDING IN THE NATION.

Kim Grant

The church was spared British depredation during the Revolution because of its Church of England ties. Today it is notable for its tall, graceful spire, its Tiffany stained-glass windows (the first two on the left), and its triple-deck wineglass pulpit, the only one in America. Distinguished visitors have included George Washington (his pew was no. 81) and Dean George Berkeley, later bishop of Cloyne, who often preached here during his 3-year stay. More recently the Archbishop of Canterbury and Queen Elizabeth II visited in 1976 as part of the Bicentennial celebration. The gallery holds the original organ case given to the church in 1733 by Berkeley; it was made by Richard Bridge of London, is believed to have been played by Handel, and is the second oldest organ in the country.

In the small graveyard beside the church lies Lucia, the infant daughter of Berkeley, as well as Admiral d'Arsac de Ternay, whose fleet arrived with Rochambeau during the Revolution and who died here of fever. A monument to de Ternay, given by King Louis XVI, is in the church vestibule.

United Baptist Church (401-847-3210), 30 Spring Street, behind Colony House. Open daily 9–4. Dr. John Clarke was the founder and first pastor (1638) of this church. In 1663 Clarke obtained a royal charter for Rhode Island from King Charles II, which set a precedent for the colonies by guaranteeing full freedom of religious pursuits. The church contains a room displaying items of historical interest.

SCENIC DRIVE **Ocean Avenue** is one of the great coastal drives in the country, taking you past the mansions of the Gilded Age and some breathtaking vistas of sea and breaking waves. Ocean Avenue, which skirts the southern rim of Aquidneck, can be approached from two directions: From the east it begins where Bellevue Avenue ends; from the west you can pick it up at the end of Wellington Avenue, which runs along the south end of the harbor.

Most of the large houses along Bellevue and Ocean Avenue have their stories. One is **Clarendon Court,** on the east side of Bellevue a few houses beyond Marble House, opposite Rovensky Park. This is where Claus von Bülow either did (first trial) or did not (second trial) attempt to murder his wife, heiress Sunny von Bülow, with a lethal injection of insulin. The house was designed in 1904 by Horace Trumbauer, architect of the Elms, and is patterned after an 18th-century English house. The quiet park across the street was given to the city by John Rovensky, who owned Clarendon Court at one time.

Crossways, on Ocean Avenue, straight ahead after you make the turn past Bailey's Beach, was built by McKim, Mead, and White, and is notable for its four-column Colonial-style portico. During the heyday of Newport society, it was noted more for being the summer residence of the imposing Mrs. Stuyvesant Fish, who reigned over Newport with the Vanderbilts and Astors. Mrs. Fish was a sort of Don Rickles of her set, abruptly cutting short her dinner parties and insulting her guests, who couldn't wait to be asked back for more abuse. "Make yourself at home," she told one group. "Certainly there is no one who wishes you were there more than I." Crossways, alas, now belongs to the condo set.

✳ To Do

BOAT EXCURSIONS Several firms offer 1- or 2-hour narrated tours of Newport Harbor and Narragansett Bay. These are a bargain and a great way to get out on the water. ***Amazing Grace*** (401-849-2111) departs Sayer's Wharf, next to the Moorings restaurant. ***Spirit of Newport*** (401-849-3575) departs Newport Harbor Motel & Marina, America's Cup Avenue. ***Viking Queen*** (401-847-6921), Goat Island, offers 1- and 2.5-hour cruises of Newport Harbor and Narragansett Bay. The longer tour includes a stop at the Hammersmith Farm dock and a tour of the house.

You can sail out of Newport in anything from a 20-foot sloop to 80-foot-and-up schooners. Among the sailing vessels giving tours: *Adirondack* (401-846-1600), Newport Yachting Center. This 78-foot schooner makes day and evening trips from the Yachting Center on America's Cup Avenue. *Madeleine* (401-849-3033), a 70-foot schooner departing Bannister's Wharf four times daily. *Flying Sailor Tours* (401-848-2100), a 57-foot catamaran sailing from Long Wharf. *Rumrunner II* (401-847-0298), Bannister's Wharf, offers high-speed bay and harbor tours, some with historical society guides. **The Schooner** *Aurora* (401-849-6999) is the harbor's largest charter schooner at 101 feet. (Also see *Sailing/Rentals*.)

FISHING There's some good saltwater fishing in the Newport area. Bass, bluefish, and blackfish all run fairly steadily from spring to late fall. Try Ocean Avenue—at Agassiz Beach near Castle Hill, off the rocks at Brenton Point, or at state-run King's Beach near Price's Cove. Beavertail on the southern tip of Jamestown is also good. Good sources of information are **Edwards Fishing Tackle** (401-846-4521), 36 Aquidneck Avenue, Middletown, and in Jamestown, Gregory Zeek of **Zeek's Creek Bait & Tackle** (401-423-1170), 194 North Road. If you're in town on a Friday, check the weekly fishing report in the *Newport Daily News*, the city's daily newspaper.

Charter fishing is surprisingly limited in Newport, given its ocean location, but several boats offer inshore and offshore trips. (Also see *Fishing* in "Narragansett" for more charter boats.) For information about area charters, write to the R.I. Party & Charter Boat Association, P.O. Box 3198, Narragansett 02882. The cost for adults is usually $30–40 per person, or $300 and up for a half-day charter, $700 and up for a full day.

Fishin' Off (401-683-5557), Goat Island. Full- or half-day charters for up to six people aboard a 36-foot Trojan sportfisherman. Mostly inshore fishing for striped bass or bluefish but also the occasional offshore jaunt for tuna. Captain Jim Korney.

The Saltwater Edge (401-842-0062), 561 Thames Street, supplies guides to take you fly-fishing in the surf or out on a boat. Hour lessons in fly-fishing. Outings include gear and flies.

FOR FAMILIES ✍ **Accidental Artist** (401-841-8809), 516 Thames Street. Children get to paint, then fire their own pots and other ceramic pieces.

✍ **Ryan Family Amusement Center** (401-846-5774), 266 Thames Street. Video games galore—a virtual arcade—in a Victorian-style building downtown. Great break from all the historical and cultural activities in Newport.

KAYAK/BICYCLE RENTALS **Ten Speed Spokes** (401-847-5609), 18 Elm Street, just north of the Gateway Center. You can rent a kayak (training held) for half-day and full-day tours, or combine a kayak/bicycle rental. Must be over 16.

Adventure Sports (401-849-4820), Long Wharf. Sea kayak rentals.

SAILING/RENTALS Sailing instruction is offered in sessions of several days up to a week and generally costs a minimum of $300–500 per person. Call around to see what a particular school specializes in (racing or cruising skills, small or larger boats).

Fort Adams Sailing Association (Sail Newport; 401-849-8385), Fort Adams State Park. Offers sailing instruction as well as half-day and day charters. Those renting boats are asked to demonstrate competency, of course.

J World Sailing School (401-849-5492), 1 Commercial Wharf. Hands-on instructions in sailing and/or racing by certified instructors.

Newport Sailing School (401-848-2266), Goat Island, provides instruction for beginning and intermediate sailors.

&. **Shake-A-Leg Sailing Center** (401-847-3630), Fort Adams, has specially equipped 20-foot sloops for the physically challenged.

Sightsailing of Newport (401-849-3333), Bowen's Wharf, offers small-boat sailing tours for two to six people as well as rentals and instruction.

Also see *Boat Excursions*.

SWIMMING See *Green Space—Beaches*.

TENNIS/RACQUET SPORTS There are free City of Newport courts at five locations in the city. **Pop Flack,** behind Almac's shopping center on Bellevue, has four courts with lights. **Hunter,** off Third Street, in the north end of the city, has two courts. **Vernon,** on Caswell Avenue off Vernon Avenue in the north end, near the Middletown line, has four courts. In the south end there are the three courts at **Murphy Field** on Carroll Avenue. Nearby at **Rogers High School** on Old Fort Road there are six courts.

Newport Casino (401-846-4567), Bellevue Avenue. The same grass courts that Ashe, Evert, McEnroe, and Navratilova have played on are open to the public, from May through October, except during tournaments. Open daily 10–7. The fee is $25 per person per hour or $35 per person for 90 minutes of court time.

Newport Squash Racquets (401-846-1011), 8 Freebody Street. Four singles courts just off Memorial Boulevard, one block from Bellevue Avenue. Open 9–7 weekdays, 9–2 weekends. The fee is $10 per person for 45 minutes, racquet and ball included.

Tennis Indoor Club (401-849-4777), Memorial Boulevard, one block down from Bellevue. Open daily 6 AM–11 PM. The fee for these indoor courts is $32 per hour in the morning, $36 per hour in the afternoon.

✳ Green Space

BEACHES Newport and its neighboring towns have been blessed with a plentiful supply of good bathing beaches. And because the Gulf Stream lies relatively close offshore, the waters are warm by New England standards—certainly warmer than on much of Cape Cod, for example. Although some of the better spots along the southern tip of the island have been staked out by private clubs, most of the sandy stretches remain in the public domain. On the hottest summer days, especially on weekends, parking can be a problem. To be assured of a spot, arrive well before noon or wait until 4 or 5 PM, when the crowds have gone and the water and air are still warm from the day's sun.

Bailey's Beach (East), or "People's Beach," as it's sometimes called, is at the junction of Bellevue Avenue and Ocean Avenues. This is as close as most of us will get to Bailey's Beach proper, the most exclusive bathing in Newport. You'll also have to come by foot or by bike since there's no parking area. But the swimming is excellent, and there's often good surf.

Easton's Beach (401-848-6491), 175 Memorial Boulevard. Also known as First Beach and Newport Beach, this popular bathing spot is a 0.75-mile stretch from the northern edge of the Cliff Walk in Newport to the Middletown line. Access is easy—just follow Memorial Boulevard down the hill to the entrance. During Victorian times the water at Easton's was considered an elixir, and the infirm were carted down for a dip. Bathing was a much more modest activity at that time; the sexes were strictly segregated, women getting the first turn at 10 AM. "At noon all this changed," recalled George C. Mason in his chronicle, *Newport and Its Cottages.* "The white flag is hauled down; a red bunting takes its place; the ladies retire, and for a few hours the beach is given up exclusively to gentlemen." Newport's largest public beach, it has three parking lots accommodating around 700 cars. There's limited on-street parking, but don't park in a restricted zone—you'll be ticketed and towed. On weekends and many evenings, a carousel and bumper boat operation is open. Surfing is permitted in a restricted area at the east end of the beach.

𝄞 **Fort Adams State Park,** off Harrison Avenue on the way to Ocean Avenue. This modest beach on the south side of Brenton Cove is the perfect place for family swimming. There's a roped-off area for budding swimmers and plenty of picnic tables and charcoal grills. Lifeguards are on duty 10 AM–6 PM between Memorial Day and Labor Day. Small entrance fee for out-of-state vehicles other than bicycles.

𝄞 **Gooseberry Beach** (401-847-3958), off Ocean Avenue, shares a cove with private Hazard's Beach on the west and is one cove over from exclusive Bailey's Beach to the east. As well as an attractive setting, Gooseberry offers safe ocean bathing for families. The parking lot has room for 150 cars, but there is a parking fee. Restrooms and a concession stand are available.

𝄞 **King Park** on Wellington Avenue in Newport is close to town, looking north across the harbor, and parking along Wellington is free. Lifeguards are on duty Memorial Day through Labor Day 9–6, and on most hot days the beach will be crowded with families. Charcoal grills and picnic tables are available, and you can sit on the grass under the trees or down on the sand. The shallow portion of the water is marked off with buoys for kids; there's a raft with a slide for the more daring swimmers. On land, there are free bathhouses, swings, and slides. Because of its proximity to the city, the water quality here is questionable following heavy rains, and swimming is sometimes banned for short periods.

PARK Brenton Point State Park, Ocean Avenue. Free parking. This 89-acre park, on the site of a former estate, offers broad lawns for lounging or kite flying, picnic tables, toilets, and scenic overlooks, including an observation tower. This is a great place for viewing the waves or parking for a stroll along the seawall.

WALK **Cliff Walk** is a 3.5-mile path that runs from Easton's (or First) Beach off Memorial Boulevard on the north to Bailey's Beach on Ocean Avenue. You can enter at various points, but a good starting point is at the end of Narragansett Avenue, where you can scramble down the Forty Steps for a look at the crashing surf. From there, the sometimes treacherous path twists, winds, and even tunnels between the ocean many feet below and the backyards of the Bellevue Avenue mansions. Storm damage has been repaired by the Army Corps of Engineers, but it's still wise to stick close to the path rather than risk a (very long) drop to the rocks.

✳ Lodging

Note: Unless otherwise indicated, the zip code for Newport is 02840.

HOTELS ⟋ **Best Western Mainstay Inn** (401-849-9880; 1-800-528-1234), 151 Admiral Kalbfus Road, at the exit ramp of Newport Bridge. ($$–$$$) Rates vary almost weekly at this inn, which has 165 rooms and a full-service restaurant, although it remains a bargain by Newport standards.

Hotel Viking (401-847-3300; 1-800-556-7126), 1 Bellevue Avenue, at the top of Touro Street and Historic Hill. ($$$–$$$$) Slightly outside the city's center, in one of the more pleasant sections of town, the Viking is still within reasonable walking distance of downtown and the waterfront. It was once the queen of Newport hotels, the largest in the city until the newer buildings on the waterfront were built; the original Colonial-style building is on the National Historic Register. Some of the waterside rooms have spectacular harbor panoramas, similar

GOOSEBERRY BEACH

Kim Grant

to the view you can enjoy from the hotel's **Top of Newport** lounge. There's an outside patio and a small jazz bar where Ella Fitzgerald sang. Thornton Wilder stayed here while he wrote his Newport book, *Theophilus North*.

& **Hyatt Regency Hotel** (401-851-1234), Goat Island. ($$$$) The second largest of Newport's hotels, with 253 rooms, the Hyatt is a bit removed from the hustle of the city, which is the way many guests prefer it. Excellent views of the harbor and bay. The Hyatt is a short, pleasant walk across the causeway from the Point section, or you can make use of the hotel's shuttle van. But perhaps the best thing about being at the hotel is that you don't have to look at it: The hulking brick structure is considered by many to be an eyesore on an island in the middle of an otherwise beautiful harbor. Several restaurants and lounges.

Newport Harbor Hotel & Marina (401-847-9000; 1-800-955-2558), 49 America's Cup Avenue. ($$$–$$$$) In a city where names can sometimes be deceptive, the Harbor Hotel is indeed right on the harbor. It's also downtown and close to the wharf action. Restaurant and nightclub offering live entertainment.

& **Newport Marriott** (401-849-1000; 1-800-228-9290), Long Wharf, America's Cup Avenue, adjacent to the Gateway Center. ($$$$) The Marriott, opened in 1988, is the city's largest hotel, with more than 300 rooms. The hotel has an impressive five-story atrium as you enter, two restaurants, several lounges with live entertainment or deejay, an indoor pool, and a health club with sauna for guests' use. Racquetball courts are available for a

small fee, and in summer there is an oyster bar. The Marriott also has a good central location, on the harbor and close to downtown and the wharf areas.

Vanderbilt Hall (401-846-6200; 1-888-826-4255), 41 Mary Street, off Spring Street. ($$$$) The city's newest luxury hotel (and among its most expensive), in a handsome building on Historic Hill, has 35 rooms including suites; there's a dining room open to the public and specializing in fish dishes, and three smaller themed dining areas (for example, the Monte Cristo, celebrating cigars). All the usual amenities, including indoor pool, exercise room, billiard room, and so on.

INNS Admiral Benbow Inn (401-848-8011; 1-800-343-2863), 93 Pelham Street. ($$$–$$$$) Just up the hill from downtown and around the corner from Bellevue Avenue, the Admiral Benbow offers a measure of tranquillity but is still close to the heart of things. Built not for an admiral but a sea captain (Augustus Littlefield) in 1855, the inn contains 15 nicely done rooms in post-Colonial style. Pineboard floors, four-poster beds, and lofty arched windows reminiscent of Touro Synagogue add to the effect. A "gourmet continental breakfast" is served in the brick-walled common room warmed by a big cast-iron stove. This is one of three Admiral inns in the city owned by the same group, all of them providing above-average accommodations.

Admiral Farragut Inn (401-848-8015), 31 Clarke Street. ($$$–$$$$) Clarke Street, just off Washington Square and one block up from

Thames Street, is one of the oldest byways in the city, with lots of history contained in its short length. For several years now it's been the "street of B&Bs and inns," with many of the colonial homes converted to guest houses. Admiral Farragut is in the circa-1750 Robert Stevens House, which served as quarters for several of General Rochambeau's aides during the Revolution. The three-story building has been restored to reflect colonial authenticity, with 12-over-12-paned windows, hardwood floors, and exposed ceiling beams. You can have breakfast seated at a long pine table or in one of several high-backed booths. The 10 rooms all have private bath but no TV (there's a television in the common room).

Admiral Fitzroy Inn (401-848-8018; 1-800-343-2863), 398 Thames Street. ($$$–$$$$) Grandest of the Admiral operations, the Fitzroy, in a former convent on Thames Street, is more a small hotel than an inn. The 17 rooms on five floors (there is an elevator) are individually decorated and feature brass or European-style sleigh beds. Two have outside decks, and all have a private bath, cable TV, and telephone. A full breakfast is served in a cheery room downstairs. Despite its location in the thick of things, this is a remarkably quiet retreat. It's unlikely that the inn's namesake ever tied up in Newport (he was best known as skipper of the *Beagle*, the ship that transported Charles Darwin to new discoveries), but models of a barometer of his invention are on display (and also for sale) in the lobby.

☙ **Bannister's Wharf** (401-846-4500), Bannister's Wharf. ($$$–$$$$) One of the few places in town that accepts pets. Part of the Clarke Cooke House complex, this inn has five rooms and a suite overlooking the docks, as well as two suites on the second and third floors of a building adjacent to the Clarke Cooke House (see *Dining Out*) restaurant; all have private bath. For those who really want to be in the middle of summer wharf life.

Brinley Victorian Inn (401-849-7645), 23 Brinley Street, off Kay Street. ($$$) Tucked away on a side street but still close to Bellevue Avenue and downtown, the Brinley contains 17 rooms (all but 4 with private bath) in two 19th-century buildings. There are porches to relax on and a great courtyard, where you can have a full breakfast in warm weather. Owners John and Jennifer Sweetman have redone the rooms to brighten what was a slightly worn, if still charming, milieu.

Castle Hill Inn & Resort (401-849-3800), Ocean Avenue. ($$$$) This Shingle-style mansion—small only by Newport standards—was built in 1877 for Professor Alexander Agassiz, naturalist and geologist, who chose the castle-shaped point of land as the ideal place for his marine laboratory. He sited his house on the crest of a hill with a sweeping view of the ocean and his laboratory at the foot, facing the harbor. There are nine rooms in the main house, including the dramatic Turret Room, all recently renovated and with private bath and ocean view. The six Harbor House rooms are close by, all with private bath, but for the ultimate in luxury there's nothing in Newport to rival the beach cottages, which are a short walk from the main inn and right on a private ocean beach. The inn also operates an excellent restaurant, serving a sophisticated menu that changes with the seasons but is always one of the best in the city. This is a special place in an incomparable setting, a longtime favorite of its many returning guests.

The Chanler (401-847-1300), 117 Memorial Boulevard. ($$$$) A brand-new addition to Newport's increasingly crowded field of luxury-level accommodations, the Chanler has a spectacular setting overlooking First Beach at the beginning of the famously scenic Cliff Walk. The French Empire mansion it occupies was built in 1873 by New York congressman John Chanler as his summer home, but the place had seen some less-than-glorious seasons before this most recent overhaul restored it to glory. There are 20 rooms—each decorated in a distinctive theme such as Gothic or Mediterranean—including six villas outside the main building. A restaurant, the **Spiced Pear,** is over-the-top elegant and is overseen by celebrated chef Richard Hamilton.

Cliffside Inn (401-847-1811), 2 Seaview Avenue. ($$$$) Seaview, off Cliff Avenue, is just a few steps from the start of the Cliff Walk above First Beach. A former summer cottage for Governor Thomas Swann of Maryland, this 1880s Victorian contains seven antiques-furnished guest rooms and 10 suites, all with a fireplace and whirlpool bath. A later resident was Newport artist Beatrice Turner, whose lifework consisted of more than 1,000 self-portraits, several of which hang in the inn. There's also a screened porch and lots of shade. The Cliffside is the largest of a trio of "Legendary Inns of Newport" owned by the Baker family and offering some of Newport's most sumptuous accommodations. The others are the **Adele Turner Inn** and the **Abigail Stoneman Inn.** All three serve elegant afternoon teas for their guests, but the Cliffside's is the most elaborate.

Sanford Covell House (401-847-0206), 72 Washington Street. ($$$–$$$$) This inn is a wonderful bright blue Victorian house in a great spot: right on the shore of the upper harbor in the Point section. There is a backyard heated saltwater pool, a Jacuzzi, and a long porch perfect for catching the sunset. Five Victorian-appointed rooms are furnished with original artifacts. All have private bath and include a continental breakfast served downstairs.

Hydrangea House (401-846-4435), 16 Bellevue Avenue. ($$$$) One of the prettier inns in the city, this is a quiet haven in a busy part of town, across from the Hotel Viking at the head of Bellevue Avenue. Eight nicely done rooms, all with original art and all with private bath. The owners recently, and somewhat reluctantly, added TVs and phones to the rooms, responding to the modern taste for remaining hooked up even while trying to get away. From the back porch guests can enjoy the inn's garden, featuring, of course, lots of hydrangea shrubs.

Inn at Old Beach (401-849-3479), 19 Old Beach Road, near Bellevue Avenue. ($$$$) Owners Luke and Cynthia Murray have put a lot of work into transforming this Gothic Revival "cottage" into a comfortable, thoughtfully appointed guest house. Built in 1879 for retired China trader Stephen Powell and his wife, the main house features five rooms, all with private bath, three with working fireplace. Each room has a flower theme picked by Cynthia and is deco-

THE CHANLER OCCUPIES A RESTORED FRENCH EMPIRE MANSION OVERLOOKING CLIFF WALK.

Katherine Imbrie

rated appropriately (the Ivy Room has a more masculine, hunt-club motif). A carved oak staircase leads to the four second-floor rooms; a beautiful stained-glass panel depicting the four seasons highlights the first landing. The inn's only television is in one of two downstairs parlors. A "continental-plus" breakfast is served at separate tables in the dining room or outdoors on the porch or patio. An 1850s carriage house contains two more rooms, for those who prefer extra privacy. The grounds are exceptional, with plantings, benches, a lily pond, and a gazebo. There are nice architectural touches throughout the house—and thoughtful touches by the innkeepers as well, including a second-floor pantry with an ironing board and umbrellas for each room.

Ivy Lodge (401-849-6865), 12 Clay Street, off Bellevue Avenue. ($$$$) This large Victorian—or "small mansion," as the owners describe it—is located on a quiet side street in the heart of the Mansion District. Designed by Stanford White and built as a summerhouse in 1886, Ivy Lodge has a wraparound veranda—the perfect spot to catch a cool summer breeze—and an impressive oak-paneled entryway that rises 33 feet. The regal staircase, with hand-turned balusters, was crafted of English oak by local ship's carpenters. There are eight guest rooms on three floors, all with private bath. A full breakfast, prepared by the host-chef, is served at a long dining room table or out back on the veranda.

Jailhouse Inn (401-847-4638), 13 Marlborough Street, one block from Washington Square. ($$–$$$) Housed in the former county jail (circa 1772) and Newport police station, this unique inn now serves voluntary inmates. Just the same, the front desk and breakfast room retain their cell bars, and the jailhouse motif is carried out in the black-and-white-striped bed linen. The inn has 24 rooms, all with a private bath, cable TV, and telephone. Continental breakfast.

Sarah Kendall House (401-846-3979; 1-800-758-9578), 47 Washington Street. ($$$–$$$$) Built by merchant Isaac Choate Kendall, a Rockefeller partner, in 1871 for his second wife, Sarah, this National Historic Register Victorian structure is one of the more impressive houses on the Point. The front porch overlooks the historic Hunter House across the street and, beyond that, the harbor. Inside, there are lofty ceilings and fine wood floors in the sizable parlor and dining room, where a full breakfast is served each morning (the owners also run a bagel shop). The four guest rooms on the second floor and one on the third all have private bath. The largest, fronting Washington Street, is the former master bedroom and enjoys a sweeping harbor view. Despite the tranquillity, it's just a 2-minute walk to Long Wharf and downtown Newport.

La Farge Perry House (401-847-2223), 24 Kay Street. ($$$) Painter and stained-glass artist John La Farge lived here with his wife in the mid-1800s. The six comfortable and well-appointed rooms in this period inn—part of Newport's Hill neighborhood—put guests within an easy walk of Washington Square and Bellevue Avenue. A full breakfast is served in a lovely dining room that features an original mural of Newport painted around 1900.

La Forge Cottages (401-847-4400), 96 Pelham Street. ($$$–$$$$) Comfortable rather than opulent, La Forge has a great location: close to

the action but in a relatively quiet neighborhood bordering Touro Park. There are no cottages—the name dates from the turn of the 20th century, when Madeline La Forge opened a rooming house and began buying nearby properties to expand the business. The current inn has six rooms and four small suites, one with a balcony. Each room has a private bath, TV, small refrigerator, telephone, and ceiling fan, in addition to air-conditioning. A full breakfast is delivered to your room each morning.

Francis Malbone House (401-846-0392), 392 Thames Street. ($$$$) This is a beautifully restored and furnished Georgian colonial house (circa 1760) in the heart of downtown. Eighteen rooms in two wings, including an adjoining suite that once served as a countinghouse, are furnished with Queen Anne reproductions and queen-sized four-poster beds. All have private bath, and nine have a working fireplace. There is a very nice garden out back and a terrace where breakfast is served in good weather. Three elegant sitting rooms on the first floor provide lots of room to relax or socialize. Although in the center of Newport's busiest street, this solid house offers a calm and quiet atmosphere.

Melville House (401-847-0640), 39 Clarke Street. ($$–$$$) The seven guest rooms (five with private bath) in this 1750s house are small but comfortable; for those who want more space, a fireplace suite is available November through April. One of the inn's best features is its location, on a relatively peaceful byway that is close to Historic Hill and downtown. The street itself is resonant with history:

The Vernon House at the corner of Clarke and Mary Streets was home to the comte de Rochambeau during the Revolution, and the French general met there with George Washington and Lafayette to plan the final victory at Yorktown; the Reverend Ezra Stiles, historian, scientist, and friend to Benjamin Franklin, lived at no. 14, where he planted mulberry bushes in an attempt to introduce silkworms to the colony.

Mill Street Inn (401-849-9500), 75 Mill Street. ($$$$) Halfway between the waterfront and Bellevue Avenue, this inn features contemporary rooms, all suites, in a restored sawmill built in 1815. There are also eight townhouse suites, which are more expensive. Parking is available in an underground garage. Buffet-style breakfast is served, weather permitting, on the rooftop deck. A good, central location.

Pilgrim House (401-846-0040, 1-800-525-8373), 123 Spring Street. ($$–$$$) By Newport standards, this is a modestly priced inn in a great location within easy walking distance of Thames Street. Nothing fancy, but comfortable, with a rooftop deck that provides a view of the harbor. Ten rooms, each with private bath. Continental breakfast.

Stella Maris (401-849-2862), 91 Washington Street. ($$$–$$$$) Built as a summerhouse in 1861 and named Blue Rocks by a New York businessman, this three-story mansion was renamed Stella Maris ("Star of the Sea") by the Sisters of Cluny, who made it their convent until 1989, when the current owners converted it to an inn. Situated near the north end of Washington Street, across from Battery Park, Stella Maris commands excellent views of the harbor and Newport Bridge from its several

THE SARAH KENDALL HOUSE IS ON THE NATIONAL HISTORIC REGISTER.

Kim Grant

porches and waterside rooms. There are good-sized rooms on the second and third floors, the former with working fireplaces, the latter with window seats, and all with private baths. There's also a single cottage out on the grounds that's ideal for a couple with children. Breakfast of granola, homemade breads, cereal, and yogurt is served buffet-style and taken in a sunroom or outside on the patio.

Victorian Ladies (401-849-9960), 63 Memorial Boulevard. ($$$–$$$$) Definitely one of the nicer inns in the city, Victorian Ladies offers 11 rooms, split among the main house—an 1841 Victorian—and two outbuildings. The rooms are done in "subtle Victorian," say the operators, and all come with private bath and air-conditioning. Despite its location on a busy thoroughfare—en route to the beaches—the inn is sufficiently insulated from traffic noises. You won't have much driving to do if you stay here—the Cliff Walk and First Beach are just steps away.

Wayside Guest House (401-847-0302), 406 Bellevue Avenue. ($$$) This handsome, Georgian-style brick building was added onto an existing Victorian structure in 1896 to serve as a home for Elisha Dyer, dance master for society cotillions from Palm Beach to Maine. Dorothy Post rents out 10 of the 22 rooms in what is one of the oldest continuously run inns in the city. Most of the rooms are large and airy—the "library" guest room on the first floor has a 15-foot ceiling. Many are furnished with four-poster canopy beds, and all come with ceiling fan and a private bath. Continental breakfast is served in the large family dining room. Guests get to use the 18-by-36-foot in-ground swimming pool—a rarity for guest houses. Directly across from the Elms, in the heart of the Avenue district.

Yankee Peddlar Inn (401-846-1323; 1-800-427-9444), 113 Touro Street. ($$$$) Busy, central location close to downtown. Nineteen rooms come with continental breakfast. The owner is an experienced hotelier, operating inns from Miami Beach to Martha's Vineyard.

BED & BREAKFASTS Don't expect bargain prices from Newport bed & breakfast operations: Rooms average $150 and up—way up—per night. Rates quoted are for peak season, between April and October; prices drop anywhere from 10 to 30 percent off-season. In most cases it is still cheaper to stay at a B&B than at one of the name-brand hotels, and the atmosphere is almost always cheerier and more personable. By law, a place that calls itself a B&B is required to serve breakfast. Competition has spurred owners to provide ever-more-sumptuous spreads, and even so-called continental breakfasts should provide more than enough fuel to start the day.

Reservations are recommended during the busy season and on weekends during spring and fall. Some B&Bs require a minimum stay of 2 nights— 3 on holiday weekends or during special events—so it's wise to check ahead. An increasing number don't permit smoking on the premises. Reservation services are free and provide the only access to a considerable number of smaller guest houses that don't advertise. **Anna's Victorian Connection** (401-849-2489; 1-800-884-4288), 5 Fowler Avenue, is one of the more established services, with

100 or so listings. Its clients include all kinds of accommodations—the *Victorian* refers to the owners' own homes. **Bed & Breakfast of Newport** (401-846-5408; 1-800-800-8765), 33 Russell Avenue. Cindy Roberts, who operates her own B&B, Bluestone, is one of the reliable reservationists in town, with hundreds of smaller bed & breakfasts that you might not otherwise find. **Bed & Breakfast Society** (401-846-2130; 1-800-227-2130), Halidon Avenue. Helen Burke's service specializes in rooms in the Mansion and Ocean Avenue parts of town. **Taylor-Made Reservations** (401-848-0300; 1-800-848-8848), 39 Touro Street. Karen Taylor has a large network of rooms for hire and is the official reservation maker for the Newport Jazz and Folk Festivals.

Elliott Boss House (401-849-9425), 20 Second Street. ($$$) Two upstairs antiques-furnished rooms in this quiet 1820s house on the Point. Tom and Loretta Goldrick, former booksellers, have a beautifully landscaped garden, a regular feature of the annual Secret Gardens Tour. In summer a full breakfast is served out on the back patio, within sight and scent of the rose garden.

George Champlin Mason House (401-847-7081; 1-888-834-7081), 31 Old Beach Road. ($$–$$$) This beautiful 1873 Swiss-chalet-style Victorian was the home of famed Newport architectural historian George Champlin Mason (he designed it himself). Now it's a B&B with five rooms, all with private bath, three with working fireplace. Just a few blocks from Bellevue Avenue at Touro Park.

The Clarkeston (401-849-7397), 28 Clarke Street. ($$–$$$$) Colonial-style inn on historic Clarke Street near downtown. Nine guest rooms, five with working fireplace, four with Jacuzzi, and all with private bath. The front portion of the house dates from 1705, when it was the home of Joseph Burrill. The house has been nicely restored, and you can see evidence of the original flooring and doors in two third-story rooms. The rooms, furnished with four-posters and thick mattresses, are named for well-known Newporters—Doris Duke, Alva Vanderbilt, and Harry Belmont among them—and come with appropriate reading material. Rooms include full breakfast.

1885 Marshall Slocum Guest House (401-841-5120), 29 Kay Street. ($$–$$$) Just a block and a half from Bellevue Avenue, this pleasant, airy guest house is within reasonable walking distance of Historic Hill and downtown. Joan Wilson operates a friendly, unpretentious B&B, with five guest rooms, all with private bath, on the second and third floors of this former parsonage. Full breakfast is served from 8 to 10 in the dining room or, weather permitting, on the back porch. Wednesday night is lobster night at Marshall Slocum. This is a pleasant neighborhood, with stately houses lining Kay Street, once home to writers and artists (Henry James spent summers farther down the street). A shady front porch with a porch swing and rockers is the place to take it all in.

Rose Island Lighthouse (401-847-4242), 365 Thames Street. ($$$) For those who like to combine romance with roughing it, an overnight stay on Rose Island, 1 mile offshore, between the Point section and the Newport Bridge, might be the ticket. While other innkeepers may boast of their amenities, Charlotte Johnson, director of the Lighthouse Foundation, is happy to tell you what a stay on Rose Island does *not* include: breakfast, running water, electricity, maid service (you're asked to make your own bed), or conventional bath facilities (there's a jury-rigged eco-toilet). Says Johnson, "We give you a bed, basically," in one of two rooms in the lighthouse museum. "You do get to go up in the tower," she adds. And you get the run of a 16-acre island and the use of a rowboat. In warmer weather the brave may choose to take an outside solar shower. The light was first lit in 1870, then relit, with the help of the nonprofit foundation, in 1993. You'll go to Rose Island via boat ($5 per person each way) if the weather is right—otherwise the foundation arranges for you to stay in town; the return trip is equally unpredictable: "Last winter we managed to strand people out there pretty regularly," Johnson says.

The Willows (401-846-5486), 8 Willow Street. ($$$–$$$$) The irrepressible owner, Pattie Murphy, sends up breakfast in bed and will (if you wish) give you a wake-up tour, via intercom, that provides an overview of the history and attractions of the city. Guests also get to enjoy the inn's fragrant garden, filled with white, pink, and blue flowers, which is a regular on the annual Secret Gardens Tour on the Point. The Willows gardens were recently featured in a HG television special on the gardens of Newport. Seven rooms, each with deep feather bed and private bath with Jacuzzi.

✴ Where to Eat

You can dine very well in Newport, thanks to *Homarus americanus* and the French—which shows you how far the tastes of local residents have evolved in the last 200 years.

At one time, difficult as it is to believe, *H. americanus*, the lobster, was shunned by educated palates and considered throwaway food, fit only for bait or for the tables of the poor. Happily, it was discovered somewhere along the line that the lobster ranks with any other food known to humans, and fortunately Rhode Island and nearby ocean waters abound with the creatures.

As for the French, they've made quite an inroad since the days of the British occupation. The British may have been the enemy, but they shared the same language, religion, and culture as the majority of Americans. Before they retreated, they solemnly warned the colonists that the French not only worshiped the pope, but also ate—can you imagine?—such things as frogs' legs and snails. Well, Newporters were famous for their religious tolerance (although the General Assembly had to hastily okay the presence of Roman Catholics in the colony for the arrival of General Rochambeau and his troops), and the first French masses in America were celebrated in 1780–81 at Colony House in Washington Square. It did not take long for French cooking to catch on, and today the best restaurants in the city celebrate French cuisine.

You can eat well here for moderate amounts, or you can spend a lot. Lobster is, of course, the great equalizer, although you will find differences of $10–20 among restaurants. Because lobster prices are in constant flux, many restaurants don't post a fixed price; ask your waiter or waitress for the daily quote. And watch the extras—an appetizer and dessert can double the cost of dinner. Most Newport restaurants post their menu outside the door, so you can compare prices without entering. But don't be fooled by a full house, especially in the waterfront area—the food might be great or the place may simply be packed with unsuspecting tourists.

DINING OUT & **Asterisk** (401-841-8833), 599 Thames Street. ($$–$$$$) Open daily for lunch and dinner. Located in a former mechanic's garage, this is a charming contemporary spot on lower Thames, with soothing burgundy paint over the cinder blocks and art on the high walls. Two garage-bay doors roll up in warm weather, à la Paris, and a smattering of tables and chairs are offered outside. The "fusion" menu—green curry shrimp and scallops with jalapeño peppers is one example—which combines Mediterranean, Oriental, and maybe a few other influences, may not suit everyone's taste, but there's mainstream fare, too; the crabcakes are as good as they get north of the Beltway. Asterix, by the way, is a popular French comic-book character; following a copyright-infringement battle, the restaurant changed the spelling of its name.

Black Pearl (401-846-5264), Bannister's Wharf. ($$–$$$$) Open daily for lunch and dinner. Located in a former sail loft and named for the original owner's hermaphrodite brig, the Pearl is two restaurants in one. On one side is an informal tavern, serving sandwiches, light dinners, and excellent chowder and French onion soup. The other side, the Commodore's Room, is one of Newport's more formal restaurants, with fine cuisine inventively prepared and served in a Colonial-style setting. Regular entrées include a 2.5-pound lobster, grilled or steamed, served with tomato-basil and white butter sauce; salmon fillet with mustard-dill hollandaise sauce; and "21 Club" chicken hash. You can take home the Pearl chowder, hot or frozen, by the quart and half gallon.

Canfield House (401-847-0416), 5 Memorial Boulevard. ($$$–$$$$) Open daily for dinner. Baked stuffed lobster and châteaubriand are the house specialties (and two of the more expensive menu items) in this elegant 1897 building that once hosted a gambling casino. This is a dressy, another-era place; the fireplace lounge is a great place for a hot toddy on a cool day.

& **Christie's** (401-847-5400), 351 Thames Street. ($$–$$$) Open daily for lunch and dinner. A waterfront institution, Christie's has long been as popular with residents as with visitors. Lots of room, lots of tables, upstairs and down. You can order steak and prime rib, but the main attraction is seafood, especially lobster and the house Narragansett Seafood Pie. There's a busy bar with live entertainment and, in summer, an even more popular bar at the end of Christie's dock.

Clarke Cooke House (401-849-2900), Bannister's Wharf. ($$$–$$$$) Open daily for lunch and dinner. This ever-changing restaurant (there's currently a bistro, a middle-ground restaurant, and a formal, high-priced dining room as well as a sushi bar) is housed in a 1790s building moved here from Thames Street in 1973. The Cooke House is a landmark on the waterfront and enjoys a long-standing status as a favorite of celebrity sailors and just plain celebrities. The top-floor restaurant displays fancy French ways with lamb, beef, and seafood. A must-visit for those who enjoy an elegant meal and a taste of ultra-Newport waterfront nightlife.

& **La Forge Casino** (401-847-0418), 186 Bellevue Avenue. ($$–$$$) Open daily for lunch and dinner. A Newport institution, with mainstream meat and seafood dishes (the shrimp stuffed with lobster and baked is a house favorite). The Porch dining room overlooks the greens of the adjoining Newport Casino, offering a breath of spring even in cold weather. The Casino Room, open for lunch and dinner, is an early-1900s restaurant-*cum*-Irish-pub with lots of salads, sandwiches, and moderately priced pub dinners such as Dublin Shrimp. A small but strategically located sidewalk café overlooks the broad Bellevue sidewalk, a perfect spot, the owners point out, for observing the daily parade of "cabbages and kings." Diners can get a discount to visit the adjoining Tennis Hall of Fame.

& **La Petite Auberge** (401-849-6669), 19 Charles Street. ($$$–$$$$) Open daily for dinner. Classic French cuisine; escargots in a French mushroom sauce and lobster bisque are typical appetizers. Entrées include such dishes as roast duckling, lobster tails, and even boeuf Wellington. Authentic French sauces abound. Dinner is served in five intimate dining rooms in this colonial house where naval hero Stephen ("Our country, right or wrong . . .") Decatur once resided. In warm weather grilled dishes are served in a more informal courtyard setting.

Le Bistro (401-849-7778), Bowen's Wharf. ($$–$$$$) Open daily for lunch and dinner. French country food in one of the best restaurants in the city. Entrées include such offerings as 7-hour leg of lamb, roast chicken, and Burgundy sausage with hot potato salad. Game dishes are added to the fare in cooler weather, with such things as grilled antelope steak and duck confit with sweet-and-sour onion relish. Sunday brunch might include baked eggs Provençal, "real" French toast, and what owner John Philcox calls the Great Bistro French Paradox: sausage, pâté, prosciutto, and cheeses. The main dining room is one floor up from the street. There's also a cozy third-floor bar with a harbor view where you can eat as well.

Mamma Luisa (401-848-5257), 673 Thames Street. ($$–$$$) Open daily, except Monday, for dinner. Authentic northern Italian cooking (Mamma was a chef in Bologna) in this lower Thames ristorante. A sampler plate of two or three kinds of pasta (under $20) is an excellent way to start. Spinach-stuffed gnocchi, veal scaloppine in balsamic sauce, and lots of pasta fill out the menu.

The Mooring (401-846-2260), Sayer's Wharf, off America's Cup Avenue. ($$–$$$) Open daily for lunch and dinner. Seafood and meat dishes done up in straightforward style in a Victorian structure that once served as a summer outpost of the New York Yacht Club. If the weather is pleasant, the deck out back offers one of the best views of busy Newport Harbor; if there's a chill, try a table near the great fireplace inside.

Newport Dinner Train (401-841-8700), 19 America's Cup Avenue, next to the Gateway Center. ($$$$) Full-course meals served as you proceed slowly (about 10 miles per hour) aboard the Old Colony railroad train along the west side of Aquidneck Island. Usually several choices of entrée, such as shrimp, prime rib, and the chef's choice of chicken, veal, or lamb. This is a dress-up affair—jackets required—and while it may not be the Orient Express, it's as close as you'll get in these parts.

The Place at Yesterday's (401-847-0116), 38 Washington Square. ($$$–$$$$) Open daily for dinner. While the original Yesterday's (see *Eating Out*) next door serves up burgers, nachos, and light dinners, the Place, alternatively known as the Wine Bar, turns out some of the finest and most imaginative dishes in town. Portobello mushrooms are a fad, but here they are done right—close your eyes and it could be tenderloin you're tasting. Whether you choose crabcakes or soft-shell crabs with garlic mayonnaise, everything here is prepared just right and beautifully presented. In fact, the food is so delicious, you may be tempted to avoid taking off on their multivintage "wine flight" sampler.

Pronto (401-847-5251), 464 Thames Street. ($$–$$$) Open daily for lunch and dinner. Italian cooking with a nouveau twist in a casual setting. Try the fettuccine or ravioli in four-cheese sauce—Asiago, Gorgonzola, Fontina, Parmesan—or grilled quail on a bed of roasted corn risotto. Mozzarella salad or bruschetta—in this case with eggplant and roasted red peppers—is a great way to start your meal.

Puerini's (401-847-5506), 24 Memorial Boulevard. ($$–$$$) Open daily for dinner. Very popular with the locals, the dining rooms here (all smoke-free) fill up quickly on summer nights as long lines gather outside. Homemade pasta (the spinach pasta is excellent) in lots of varieties at reasonable prices account for the family-run restaurant's popularity. Have some gelato for dessert.

The Red Parrot (401-847-3140), 348 Thames Street. ($$–$$$) Open daily for lunch and dinner. Caribbean-influenced dishes (Cayman Cajun shrimp, Jamaican jerk) and, of course, seafood on two floors of dining. The large bar is a popular hangout for racers during the sailing season. At the junction of America's Cup Avenue and Thames Street, this place is as central as it gets.

Restaurant Bouchard (401-846-0123), 505 Thames Street. ($$–$$$) Open daily, except Tuesday, for dinner. One of the city's newer French restaurants, Bouchard offers traditional bistro fare—sautéed veal sweetbreads and breast of duck, along with Dover sole and restuffed lobster. Validated parking on adjacent Waites Wharf.

Rhode Island Quahog Co. (401-848-2330), 250 Thames Street. ($$) Open daily for lunch and dinner. Seafood is the order of the day in this casual but lively place right in the heart of downtown Newport. There's a front porch just off the sidewalk that fills up early when the weather's cooperative.

The Rhumb Line (401-849-6950), 62 Bridge Street. ($$–$$$) Open daily for lunch and dinner. Set in the Colonial Point neighborhood, a block and a half from the Gateway Center, the Rhumb Line (a nautical term for a direct line between two points) is a quiet haven away from the commercial area. Warm, inviting atmosphere. Known among locals for its mussels, fish, and veal dishes as well as sandwiches and daily specials.

Salas' Dining Room (401-846-8772), upstairs at 343 Thames, just around the corner from America's Cup Avenue. ($–$$) Open daily for dinner. A true family dining room, popular with both residents and visitors, Salas' supplies lots of noise, camaraderie, and good food at good prices. Spaghetti is offered by the pound or fraction thereof. Lobster and clambakes, too. Dinner begins at 4 PM, and the place fills quickly. No reservations are accepted, so come early or be prepared to wait. The adjoining bar, which serves excellent piña coladas, makes the wait easier.

🍴 ⛐ **Salvation Café** (401-847-2620), 140 Broadway. ($) Open for dinner Tuesday through Sunday 5–10. This cozy, two-room café is a little off the beaten path, several blocks north of Washington Square in a block that has recently become home to a number of good, moderately priced restaurants. It's well worth a visit for its inventive fusion cuisine and generous vegetarian fare. The common denominator here among the specials posted on a blackboard each evening (the specials *are* the menu) is spicy: Jamaican jerk shrimp, chicken, and beef; pad Thai with shrimp; scallion and caper tempura. The decor is camp (busts of JFK and Elvis, potted palms), the atmosphere relaxed, and the food, well, spicy.

⛐ **Sardella's** (401-849-6312), 30 Memorial Boulevard, next door to Puerini's. ($$–$$$) Open daily for dinner. Italian food, with more of a gourmet touch and a slightly more formal atmosphere than its neighbor.

Extensive menu of northern and southern specialties—Sogliole alla Fiorentina, Cotolette al Griglia. Excellent antipasti, including snail salad (a Rhode Island favorite) and fried mozzarella.

Scales and Shells (401-846-3474), 527 Thames Street. ($$–$$$) Open daily for dinner. For seafood lovers only, but you'll probably love the seafood you get in this bustling informal-but-tony restaurant on lower Thames. Seating is in one big room with the kitchen grills open for all to see. The daily menu is posted on a large blackboard on one wall. Mesquite-grilled shrimp, grilled clam pizza, and fresh fish of all kinds are all good bets. Pasta with red or white sauce and vegetable kebabs are served with meals or available as main courses. No frying here; everything is grilled. No smoking—except for the grills—on the premises. Terms are cash only, no credit cards.

Tucker's Bistro (401-846-3449), 150 Broadway. ($$) Open daily for dinner. Tucker's brings a touch of class to Newport's north end, serving a mix of nouveau California/New York cuisine in comfortable surroundings. Appetizers include that Ocean State standby, calamari; entrées range from red meat to vegetarian lasagna; and desserts are chocolatey and imaginative.

⛐ **Twenty-two Bowens Wine Bar & Grille** (401-841-8884), 22 Bowen's Wharf. ($$–$$$) Open daily for lunch and dinner. A great setting right on cobblestoned Bowen's Wharf and the inner harbor makes this upscale restaurant popular with both tourists and locals. Steaks are a good bet.

Vincent's on the Pier (401-847-3645), West Howard Street, on the harbor. ($$–$$$) Open daily for lunch and dinner. Along with Christie's, this is an original waterfront restaurant and a longtime tourist favorite because of its location. The emphasis is on fresh seafood, especially lobster, and you can choose from three kinds of chowder: lobster bisque, thick and creamy clam chowder, and fish chowder, after a blackfish recipe concocted by pirate Tom Tew before the Revolution. Meat lovers can opt for steak or chops. Family dining in close quarters and live music in the adjoining lounge, where the locals congregate.

West Deck at Waites Wharf (401-847-3610), 1 Waites Wharf. ($$–$$$) Open daily for lunch and dinner; closed January and February. Right on the water toward the south end of the harbor, this restaurant has a small indoor dining room and a bar where those who can't get a table are welcome to dine. The menu changes with the season but always features fresh, inventive fare that's far more sophisticated than the sometimes boisterous outdoor bar-and-grill scene would indicate. This place is an insiders' favorite—a bit off the beaten path and a real find for foodies.

White Horse Tavern (401-849-3600), corner of Marlborough and Farewell Streets. ($$$$) Dinner daily, lunch daily except Tuesday. A Big Splurge by anybody's definition, the White Horse is arguably the most formal, and one of the most expensive, restaurants in town. The setting, in the oldest still-operating tavern in America, is colonial, with candlelit atmosphere. This is fine dining with expert service at its best. Perennial menu favorites are the beef Wellington, rack of lamb, and châteaubriand. Before, after, or in lieu of dinner, you can relax in the comfortable fireplace

bar where patriots once conspired to rebellion (and probably a little piracy) while quaffing tankards of cider.

EATING OUT & **Aidan's Pub** (401-845-9311), 1 Broadway, across from the Colony House. ($) Open daily for lunch and dinner. Fairly authentic Irish pub (the owner's Irish, the bar was shipped over from Eire), serving such standbys as bangers and mash, fish-and-chips, and a quite-good shepherd's pie.

Brick Alley Pub (401-849-6334), 140 Thames Street. ($–$$) Open daily for lunch and dinner. Always crowded, this pub, just around the corner from Washington Square, has its own "ultimate nacho" fans, but you'll also find burgers, fresh fish, homemade pasta, and a big salad bar. The drinks are sizable as well. In warm weather enjoy the outdoor patio at the rear, where you can forget for a time that you're in the middle of a city.

Dry Dock Seafood (401-847-3974), 448 Thames Street. ($) Open daily for lunch and dinner. Seafood—fried clams, shrimp, baked fish—in a very casual setting. Some of the cheapest fish in town.

Fourth Street Diner (401-847-2069), 184 Admiral Kalbfus Road. ($) Open for breakfast, lunch, and dinner. Classic diner food in a classic diner: cheeseburgers, open-faced prime rib sandwiches, Portuguese soup. Desserts—lemon meringue pie, tapioca pudding—fit the setting and the bill.

Franklin Spa (401-847-3540), corner of Spring and Thames Streets. ($) Breakfast and lunch are served at this combination soda fountain/variety store. This is no deli—the hot turkey sandwiches are made from real turkeys. One of the best (and busiest) spots for cheap eats in the heart of downtown.

Handy Lunch (401-847-9480), 462 Thames Street. ($) One of the last of Newport's lunch counters, the Handy serves breakfast all day, and lunch—meat loaf, American chop suey—for under $5, in an atmosphere that is loud, friendly, and decidedly local. Popular with both the New York Yacht Club types and commercial fishermen.

Marina Grille (401-846-2675), Goat Island. ($–$$) Open daily for lunch and dinner. Sailors from yachts docked nearby and Newporters who desire the illusion of leaving town make up much of the clientele here. The Pub serves sandwiches and soups in an airy setting all day, along with some lighter meals. Steak and seafood dinners in the evening. Outside, there's a great view of Newport across the harbor.

Mudville Pub (401-849-1408), 8 West Marlborough Street. ($–$$) Open daily for lunch and dinner. A genuine sports bar (owner Kevin Stacom is a former Boston Celtic), Mudville is also a great place to grab a sandwich or a light meal. The burgers are among the best in town. A bullpen outdoor area overlooks the action at Cardines Field from a right-centerfield perspective. Lively, noisy atmosphere and some interesting sports memorabilia: The dude with the wild hair and mustache battling Stacom for the ball in one photo is coach Pat Riley, in his pre-mousse days.

Newport Creamery (401-846-6332), Bellevue Shopping Center. ($) Open daily for breakfast, lunch, and dinner. Rhode Island's equivalent of Friendly's serves much the same fare: sandwiches and ice cream desserts at reasonable prices in an air-conditioned

setting. Jackie Kennedy Onassis was a customer when visiting her hometown, and you're liable to spot a celebrity or two in town for a shoot or a vacation. No smoking.

& **Portabella** (401-847-8200), 136 Broadway. ($) Open Tuesday through Saturday 8:30–8:30; Sunday 8:30–3; closed Monday. Set back from busy Broadway by a courtyard (parking available), Portabella is a touch of Providence's Federal Hill in colonial Newport. Despite appearances, this is a take-out place, although there are some outside tables. Great breads (nearby restaurants order it) and many Italian specialties, available by the pound or fraction thereof: chicken Marsala, veal and mushrooms, sausage and peppers or rabe. Try a panino ("little bread") sandwich stuffed with prosciutto, mozzarella, and fresh tomato.

Wharf Deli & Pub (401-846-9233), 37 Bowen's Wharf. ($) Open daily for lunch and dinner. Reasonably priced sandwiches and salads in the heart of the high-rent wharf district. The back porch is a great place to people-watch, and there's always plenty of Bass Ale and other brews on tap.

Yesterday's (401-847-0125), 28 Washington Square. ($–$$) Open daily for lunch and dinner. Big menu, strong on sandwiches, burgers, and, a major draw, the locally famous Yesterday's Nachos. Full meals served as well, many with a Mexican flair, in early-1900s saloon decor. In all a good, centrally located place to enjoy a casual meal.

✳ Entertainment

If you can't find entertainment in Newport, you're not looking or listening. Newport's reputation as a rowdy party town has been a matter of much civic debate for several years and the object of an ever-tightening string of regulations and ordinances aimed at quieting down the nightlife and allowing residents and visitors the chance for at least a few hours' sleep per night. There is something going on in virtually every restaurant, hotel, and bar in the city, especially along the waterfront. Entertainment ranges from easy jazz and acoustic to deejays to out-and-out rock-and-roll. Crowds of young and old fill the streets each summer night, and people-watching (and interacting) could be considered a major source of entertainment.

Newport Grand (401-849-5000), Admiral Kalbfus Road. The only slots casino in the area is just off the second exit ramp from the Newport Bridge.

MUSIC **Christie's** (401-847-5400), Christie's Landing, off Thames Street. This outdoor bar/dance scene has become so popular that the restaurant has begun charging separate admission. There's a more sedate band inside for the older crowd.

Newport Blues Cafe (401-841-5110), 286 Thames Street. Dinner with a New Orleans flavor downstairs; live music in the upstairs lounge.

One Pelham East (401-847-9640), corner of Thames and Pelham Streets. This oldie but goodie has been putting on live bands since the 1970s. A popular midtown spot.

THEATER/FILM **Newport Playhouse & Cabaret** (401-848-7529), 102 Connell Highway. Broadway comedies and musicals. Dinner and a play or just the play.

Opera House (401-847-3456), 19 Touro Street, on Washington Square. The old theater has been divided into three screens, showing first-run films.

Jane Pickens (401-846-5252), 49 Touro Street, on Washington Square. Last of the big-screen movie palaces in town, the Pickens presents quality first-run and offbeat flicks. The man in the lobby, greeting patrons and asking people how they liked the movie, is owner Joe Jarvis, who got his start in show business in 1936 as an usher.

SPECTATOR SPORTS 🎭 🎿 **Sunset League Baseball,** Cardines Field, corner of America's Cup Avenue and Marlborough Street, across from the Gateway Center. For just $1 for adults, 50¢ for kids, you can take in a Sunset League baseball game. Started in 1919, the league is reputed to be the oldest surviving amateur circuit, featuring college talent, sometime pros, and prospects. Cardines Field, around since 1908, is even older than Boston's Fenway Park. Where else can you watch a baseball game with colonial houses crowding the outfield fence? Games begin at 7 PM weekdays, 1 or 3 PM on Saturdays.

✳ Selective Shopping

Newport has its share of tourist-trap T-shirt and trinket shops as well as the usual scattering of national outlets—Dansk, Helly Hansen, the Gap, Banana Republic, Rockport Company Store, and so on. It also has locally owned stores, some long in business, some with the paint still drying. It's up to the customer to discern the difference, but that, after all, is part of the fun of shopping.

ANTIQUES SHOPS The best place to begin antiques hunting in Newport is on Franklin Street, which runs between Thames and Spring Streets beside the main post office. There are at least a dozen shops on this short street, catering to just about any taste or budget. More shops, on Spring Street and Thames Street, are within easy walking distance.

A&A Gaines (401-849-6844), 40 Franklin Street. Upscale emporium selling period furniture, clocks, and China trade wares.

The Drawing Room of Newport (401-841-5060), 152–154 Spring Street. Authentic furnishings from Newport's Gilded Age, with a sideline of Zsolnay Hungarian art pottery and fine European porcelains.

JB Antiques (401-849-0450), 33 Franklin Street. Porcelain, silver, paintings, and furniture.

New England Architectural Center (401-845-9233), 22 Franklin Street. Chandeliers, pillars, furniture, and assorted architectural elements.

Newport China Trade Co. (401-841-5267), 8 Franklin Street. Domestic antiques and 18th- through 20th-century export china and porcelain: Rose Medallion plates, temple jars, therapeutic porcelain pillows.

ART STORES AND GALLERIES
Arnold Art Store and Gallery (401-847-2273), 210 Thames Street. Arnold's began life as an art supply store, then blossomed into a full gallery that specializes in marine painting but also shows other local and regional art.

DeBlois Gallery (401-847-9977), 138 Bellevue Avenue. Created by a coalition of local artists, DeBlois has regular shows exhibiting the best work of member and guest artists.

Fisher Gallery (401-849-7446), 136 Bellevue Avenue. A frame shop, Fisher's also sells fine art, with an emphasis on works from the Southwest.

Norton's Oriental Gallery (401-849-4468), 415 Thames Street. Open daily in-season. Conservation framing and sales of contemporary and antique Oriental textiles, rice paper paintings, and prints. Kaye Norton is an expert appraiser of Oriental art for museums and private collectors. The gallery also custom-designs frames for fine art.

Rag and Bone Art (401-848-0005), 6 DeBlois Street, off Bellevue. This tiny frame shop and gallery offers limited-edition prints, original paintings, and works by local artists, including some by Louise Netzband, who runs the place with her husband, Ernie.

Roger King Fine Arts (401-847-4359), 21 Bowen's Wharf. Roger King buys and sells fine art by American and European painters of the 18th, 19th, and 20th centuries. King is an expert in early African American art.

Candida Simmons Gallery (401-848-0339), 223 Spring Street, around the corner from Franklin Street. Antique prints, old views of Newport, and original art by Simmons and other local artists.

Spring Bull Studio (401-849-9166), 55 Bellevue Avenue. Part of this shop is a permanent collection of works by local artists, including Richard Grosvenor (William F. Buckley is a collector). The other section presents shows that change monthly. Mostly representation work, including seascapes, landscapes, and portraits. This is also a working studio, so you might see Grosvenor and other artists at work when you stop in. *Spring Bull* refers to the studio's original location at the corner of Spring and Bull Streets.

Vareika Fine Arts (401-849-6149), 212 Bellevue Avenue. One of the larger galleries in New England dealing in "museum-quality" American art of the 18th, 19th, and early 20th centuries. Vareika's specialty is artists who have some Newport connection, including works by John La Farge, William Trost Richards, John F. Kensett, Childe Hassam, and Edward M. Bannister.

Viewpoint Gallery (401-849-2328), 105 Swinburne Row, Brick Market Place (fronting on Thames). This frame shop also has a good selection of original art and reproductions, including much maritime work.

BOOKSTORES **Armchair Sailor Bookstore** (401-847-4252), 543 Thames Street. Huge selection of nautical and sailing books and materials, including charts for just about anywhere in the world. Geared to the sailor, but owner Ron Barr also offers an excellent, and hard-to-find, line of Penguin classics and classy nonfiction books. A great place to browse on lower Thames.

The Newport Bookstore (401-847-3400), 116 Bellevue Avenue. One of several shops in the city selling fine used and rare books, this one specializing in naval and military history, Americana, and local history. Professor Donald Higgins knows his stuff.

Waldenbooks (401-846-5067), Bellevue Shopping Plaza; there's another

outlet (401-846-7160) at the Newport Mall, 199 Connell Highway. Popular chain with the latest in fiction and nonfiction best sellers. Both outlets have strong sections on books of local and regional interest.

SPECIAL SHOPS **Army and Navy Surplus** (401-847-3073), 262 Thames Street. This crowded shop—part museum, part army-navy store that's gotten way out of hand—has been written up in, of all places, *Vogue* magazine. Besides the usual trenching tools, pea coats, and marine knives, you can buy diving helmets, field radios, gas masks, and regular camping equipment. Also a good place to shop for Levi's, flannel shirts, and some of the cheapest Newport T-shirts in town.

Ball & Claw (401-848-5600), 55 America's Cup Avenue at Bowen's Wharf. Jeffrey Greene's fine hand-crafted furniture in period styles recalls the era when Newport's cabinetmakers were among the best in the world. The shop also sells accessories for the home including paintings, quilts, porcelain, and lamps.

Cadeaux du Monde (401-848-0550), 26 Mary Street. Fine crafts and folk art from around the world—clothing, bags, jewelry, and handwoven rugs are sold in what the owners describe as an "alternative trading organization." The owners are happy to give you the story behind each of the items for sale and expound a little on the culture that produced it.

Carroll Michael & Company (401-849-4488), 115 Bellevue Avenue. Part pharmacy, part parfumerie, Carroll Michael offers fine soaps and cosmetics, potpourris, and gourmet foods along with the antibiotics—all in a reproduced colonial apothecary setting.

Down Under Jewelry (401-849-1078), 479 Thames Street. Jeanine Payer designs and displays an unusually fine collection of handcrafted jewelry in this unpretentious shop at the artsy end of Thames.

Ebenezer Flagg (401-846-1891), 65 Touro Street, corner of Spring Street. Custom and production flags, pennants, yacht ensigns, and wind socks. Ebenezer Flagg was a patriot who died during the Revolution. Company founder Leo Waring, who set his store near the (now underground) spring where Newport's founders first settled, found Flagg's name on a headstone in the Common Burial Ground. Leo, who died in the late 1980s, was a Massachusetts native who passionately believed that Newport was one of the last bastions of democracy in the world.

Flashback—Old Tyme Photos (401-846-1433), Brick Market Place. Dress up in vintage clothes and have a modern-day tintype taken.

Michael Hayes (401-846-3090; 401-849-1888), 204 Bellevue Avenue and 19 Bowen's Wharf. Designer clothing for men, women, and children tops the charts for style (and price), even in fashion-savvy Newport.

J. T.'s Chandlery (401-846-7256), 364 Thames Street, downtown. Close to the waterfront, J. T.'s has been in the marine hardware business since 1909. As much a boutique as a chandlery, the store sells varnish and Vaurnet sunglasses, shackles and fishermen's sweaters.

The Market-Newport Gourmet (401-848-2600), 43 Memorial Boulevard. Specialty sandwiches, baked goods, and entrées-to-go make this small, upscale market a great place to stop to pick up the goods for a picnic. Gourmet pantry items, too.

Onne van der Wal Photography (401-849-5556), Bannister's Wharf. Lushly displayed framed photographs capture the nautical spirit of Newport.

Papers (401-847-1777), 178 Bellevue Avenue. Cards, stationery, and gifts combine elegance with utility at this small shop in the carriage trade block of tony Bellevue.

Karol Richardson (401-849-6612), 24 Washington Square. Natasha, daughter of designer Karol, has her mother's eye for easy, sophisticated styles for women.

Rue de France (401-846-3636), 78 Thames Street, two blocks north of Washington Square. Open daily in summer 10:30–5:30. This is the only retail outlet for a firm that has gained national attention via catalog sales: fine French lace and linens, table accessories, and other decorative items, especially work from artisans in Provence.

Runcible Spoon (401-849-3737), 180 Bellevue Avenue. An appealing kitchen- and tableware emporium features Italian ceramics, French table linens, and lots of other elegant appointments for the fashionable cook.

Thames Street Glass (401-846-0576), 688 Thames Street. Glassblower Matthew Buechner creates beautiful objects—vases, bowls, perfume bottles—in his studio adjacent to a small retail space on lower Thames. His work has been collected by the Corning Museum of Glass in Corning, New York (where his father served as president of Steuben Glass), and the Frauenau Museum of Glass in Germany. Visitors can watch Buechner fire and blow glass at the shop; any object with the slightest of flaws goes onto the seconds table at a bargain price.

Third & Elm Press (401-846-0228), 29 Elm Street, corner of Third Street. Open Wednesday through Saturday 9–5. Ilse Nesbitt makes and sells her own woodblock prints, notepaper, small books, and Christmas cards—many with a Newport theme—in this old-fashioned print shop on the Point.

Karen Vaughan (401-848-2121), 148 Bellevue Avenue. An eclectic selection by designer Vaughan of furniture and accessories for the home. Fun gift items, too.

✳ Special Events

Newport has a full calendar of special events, from its jazz and folk festivals to regattas to the Black Ships Festival that celebrates the city's historic ties to Japan. For a listing of events, contact the **Gateway Center** (401-849-8098).

January 1: **Polar Bear Plunge,** Easton's Beach at noon. Polar Bear members swim throughout the year; each New Year's Day, they are joined by scores of amateurs and hundreds of spectators.

Late January, early February: **Newport Winter Festival** (401-849-8048). Ten days of activities to brighten up the winter—fireworks, concerts, dogsled racing, snow/sand sculpture contest, carriage rides.

March: **Irish Heritage Month** is a monthlong program of Irish drama, music, culture, and cuisine at various venues throughout the city.

June: The **Secret Gardens Tour,** usually held the second weekend of the month, gets you behind the garden gates of more than a dozen homes in Newport's Colonial Point section. Benefactors of the Arts (401-847-0514), 33 Washington Street, Newport 02840. About 2 weeks later, 10 gardens on Historic Hill are opened for a day of public touring. Hill Association (401-847-6519). **Bud Light Pro Volleyball,** early June at Easton's (Newport) Beach (401-848-6491), 175 Memorial Boulevard.

July: The **Newport Music Festival** offers 2 weeks of great classical music in and around the mansions. Morning, afternoon, and evening concerts. Information, 401-846-1133; tickets, 401-849-0700. **Miller Lite Hall of Fame** (401-849-3990), professional tennis tournaments at the Newport Casino and Tennis Hall of Fame. For tickets or information, call 401-849-3990. **Black Ships Festival** (401-846-2720) salutes Newport's historic ties to Japan, dating from 1853, when Newport native son Commodore Matthew Perry, acting at the behest of President Millard Fillmore, pressured the Japanese to open their shores to foreign trade. There are no ships at this festival (*Black Ships* is how the Japanese described Perry's fleet), but there are plenty of events celebrating Japanese culture, including tea ceremonies, origami, sumo wrestling, and dancing. **Newport Rhythm and Blues Festival** (401-847-3700), at Fort Adams. Two days celebrating homegrown music with such performers as Aretha Franklin and the Neville Brothers.

August: **Newport Folk Festival** (401-847-3700) presents two afternoons of top-flight folk music. This is the place where Bob Dylan shocked the audience by plugging in his guitar. Generally the first weekend of the month at Fort Adams State Park, Fort Adams Road. **JVC Jazz Festival** (401-847-3700), the second weekend in August, turned 40 in 1994 and continues to bring the best of the old(er) performers as well as the latest in fusion and modern jazz. Fort Adams State Park, Fort Adams Road. **Weekend of Coaching** (401-847-1000), usually the third weekend of the month. Newport returns to its Gilded Age as society returns to its favorite 19th-century pastime: clopping about in horse-drawn coaches.

Labor Day weekend: The annual **Classic Yacht Regatta** brings together some of the finest old sailing vessels afloat. Much of the racing and the Parade of Sail is visible from various points around the harbor.

Mid-September: The **Newport International Boat Show** (401-846-1600) at the Newport Yachting Center is one of the largest in-water sail- and powerboat shows in the country.

Late September: **Taste of Newport** (401-846-1600), Newport Yachting Center. Newporters love this weekend event, in which area restaurants serve up samples of their trademark dishes. A great way to check out a lot of chefs in an afternoon.

December: **Christmas in Newport** is a monthlong series of events: religious services, madrigals, colonial masques, a reading of "A Visit from St. Nicholas," written by Newport summer resident Clement C. Moore, and a crafts fair (okay, there's a talking Christmas tree, too). December 31 is **Opening Night,** an evening of indoor/outdoor events modeled after Boston's First Night, which brings in the New Year in a joyful but alcohol-free manner. Music, theater, dancing—a full slate of cultural and fun activities at various venues throughout the city.

Aquidneck and Conanicut

MIDDLETOWN

PORTSMOUTH

JAMESTOWN

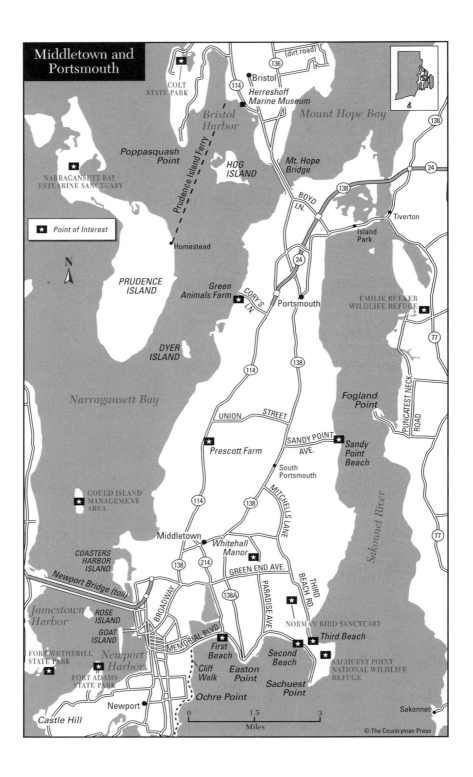

Middletown and Portsmouth

COLT
STATE PARK

(dirt road)

(136)

Bristol

(114)

Herreshoff
Marine Museum

*Bristol
Harbor*

Mount Hope Bay

(138)

*Poppasquash
Point*

HOG
ISLAND

*Mt. Hope
Bridge*

(24)

NARRAGANSETT BAY
ESTUARINE SANCTUARY

BOYD
LN.

(138)

Tiverton

Prudence Island Ferry

Island
Park

★ Point of Interest

Homestead

(24)

PRUDENCE
ISLAND

Green
Animals Farm

CORY'S LN.

Portsmouth

EMILIE RUECKER
WILDLIFE REFUGE

N

DYER
ISLAND

(77)

Narragansett Bay

(138)

Fogland
Point

(114)

PUNCATEST NECK ROAD

UNION STREET

SANDY POINT
AVE.

Sandy
Point
Beach

Prescott Farm

South
Portsmouth

GOULD ISLAND
MANAGEMENT
AREA

(114)

(138)

MITCHELLS LANE

Sakonnet River

(77)

Middletown

*Whitehall
Manor*

(138)

(214)

GREEN END AVE.

COASTERS
HARBOR
ISLAND

Newport Bridge (toll)

(138A)

PARADISE AVE.

THIRD BEACH RD.

*Jamestown
Harbor*

ROSE
ISLAND

BROADWAY

NORMAN BIRD SANCTUARY

GOAT
ISLAND

MEMORIAL BLVD.

Third Beach

FORT WETHERILL
STATE PARK

*Newport
Harbor*

First
Beach

Second
Beach

SACHUEST POINT
NATIONAL WILDLIFE
REFUGE

FORT ADAMS
STATE PARK

Cliff
Walk

Easton
Point

Sachuest
Point

Ochre Point

Newport

0   1.5   3

Miles

Sakonnet

Castle Hill

© The Countryman Press

MIDDLETOWN

Middletown and Portsmouth, the two towns that cover most of Aquidneck Island, and Jamestown, on Conanicut Island to the east, are not nearly as well known as Newport; nonetheless, they offer some worthwhile attractions of their own.

Middletown, all 12.9 square miles of it, derives its name from its location between the first Aquidneck Island settlement, Portsmouth, and its famous neighbor, Newport, to the south. Separated from Newport in 1743, Middletown was heavily garrisoned by British and Hessian troops during the Revolution and was the site of the British Green End Fort, now reduced to a plaque on Vernon Avenue. The great valley that bisects Middletown was the final barrier to American troops, who invaded the island from Tiverton in 1778 and almost succeeded in trapping upward of 7,000 royalist troops between them and the French fleet. Alas, the French sailed off, and the Americans were forced to withdraw. Middletown for years boasted many of the remaining working farms in this once agricultural state. The farms are gone for the most part, but the town still seems like "country" to folks leaving the confinement of Newport.

GUIDANCE Information about Middletown (and all Aquidneck) is available at the **Newport Gateway Center** (401-849-8098), 23 America's Cup Avenue, Newport 02840.

GETTING THERE *By car:* Directly to the north, and also to the east, of Newport, Middletown is accessible via half a dozen or more routes. From Newport, follow Broadway north to One Mile Corner, which becomes Middletown's West Main Road. Or you can follow Memorial Boulevard east, past First Beach, and cross the line at the bottom of the long hill. From the north (Portsmouth), RI 114 and 138 (West Main and East Main Roads, respectively) lead to the town border.

MEDICAL EMERGENCY The statewide emergency number is **911.**
Newport County Medical Treatment Office (401-847-4950), 67 Valley Road,

is a walk-in clinic for minor emergencies and medical complaints. Open Monday through Friday 8–8, Saturday and Sunday 9–5.

✻ To See

HISTORIC HOMES **Prescott Farm** (401-847-6230), West Main Road (RI 114). Open daily 10–4 April through December. Small fee. Shortly before midnight on July 9, 1777, a band of 40 raiding colonists, led by Colonel William Barton, landed their rowboats on the west shore of British-controlled Aquidneck Island. Splitting into five groups, they sneaked up to a farmhouse owned by Mrs. John Overing, captured the guard, and burst inside. When they left minutes later, they took with them (still in his nightclothes) General William Prescott, commander of the British occupying troops and the highest-ranking prisoner taken during the Revolution. Prescott was later exchanged for a captured American general. Barton was awarded a sword by Congress, and the house in Middletown has been known as Prescott Farm ever since. In addition to the house itself, the farm complex (owned by Doris Duke's Restoration Foundation) includes a late-18th-century grain mill moved to the site several years ago. There's also a guardhouse and a country store that offers cornmeal ground at the mill.

Whitehall (401-846-3116), on Berkeley Avenue, off Green End Avenue. Open July 1 through Labor Day, daily 10–5; other times by appointment. Admission is $3. This is a fine colonial farmhouse built in 1729 by the British philosopher and cleric Dean George Berkeley (pronounced *Bark-ley*). Berkeley, later to become bishop of Cloyne, Ireland, arrived in Newport that year accompanied by his bride and with a scheme to open up commerce and bring religion to the "savages" of Bermuda. "The town of Newport," he wrote home, "contains six thousand souls, and is the most thriving place in all America for bigness." While waiting for the king to grant him £20,000 for his mission, Berkeley preached at Trinity Church, helped found the Redwood Library, and made Whitehall a center for religious and philosophical discussion. The dean gave up his dream after three years and returned to Ireland; his house was taken over by a succession of tavernkeepers, served as quarters for British troops during the Revolution, and eventually fell into disrepair. It is now owned by the Rhode Island chapter of the National Society of Colonial Dames of America.

✻ To Do

FOR FAMILIES ✐ **Hi-Way Bowl & Mini Golf** (401-849-9990), 105 Chases Lane. Open daily until 10, later on weekends. Outdoor miniature golf course; indoor bowling and various electronic games.

✐ **Skater Island** (401-848-8078), 1747 West Main Road. Open daily 9–9. This indoor skateboarding facility has enough ramps and platforms to keep any kid happy for several hours. $10–12 per session.

HELICOPTER RIDES **A Bird's Eye View** (401-843-8687; 1-877-914-8687), 211 Airport Access Road, Middletown. Jeff Codman takes up to two people on scenic rides for $95 per couple.

Beach Road. Trail rides.

SAILBOARDING **Island Windsurfing** (401-846-4421), 86 Aquidneck Avenue. Located near the beaches, just down the hill from Newport, Island Windsurfing rents rigs and also offers two levels of lessons: a 2-hour introductory session and an advanced course, 6 hours over 2 days. Lessons are given either at Third Beach in Middletown or at Fort Adams State Park in Newport.

SWIMMING **Sachuest Beach** (Second Beach) in Middletown is the most popular beach in the area, with a long expanse of dunes and sand running between Hanging Rock and a nature preserve on Sachuest Point. To get there, follow Memorial Boulevard or Aquidneck Avenue to Purgatory Road. Public parking on pavement can handle up to 1,000 cars.

✎ **Third Beach,** off Third Beach Road in Middletown. Smaller but less crowded than Second Beach, this beach is ideal for younger swimmers, with little or no surf and warmer waters from the mouth of the Sakonnet River.

✳ Green Space

Norman Bird Sanctuary (401-846-2577), 583 Third Beach Road. Open daily 9–5 (no dogs, please); closed Mondays between Labor Day and Memorial Day. Admission $4 adults, $3 seniors, $1 children. The sanctuary is a 450-acre bird and wildlife habitat with 7 miles of nature trails open to the public. There are usually a few local species in captivity (while on the mend), but everything else you're lucky enough to see will be in the wild. There are guided tours by appointment for groups of 10 or more and regular Sunday-morning bird walks. One of the big attractions here is Hanging Rock, a striking mass of rock 50 feet high that overlooks the Atlantic. Dean Berkeley is said to have written part of his anti-freethinker treatise *Alciphron* here, in a recess now called Bishop Berkeley's Chair.

Purgatory Chasm, Purgatory Road, on the cliff overlooking Second Beach. The chasm is a narrow but deep cleft in the rocky cliff that was created by thousands of years of erosion by the sea below. Or was it? A Narragansett legend says it came about when the devil repeatedly chopped away at the head of an uncooperative Native American maiden. There are countless other stories about lovers who dared each other to hop across the fissure. Don't try it—it's more than 160 feet straight down.

Sachuest Point National Wildlife Refuge (401-364-9124), Sachuest Point Road, past Second Beach. Open daily dawn to dusk. This 242-acre refuge offers a little of everything—salt marsh, beach, grassy woodlands—with 3 miles of hiking trails. Good place for viewing migratory shorebirds. As in any coastal grassy area, dress sensibly to discourage Lyme-disease-bearing deer ticks, which are prevalent here. Also, keep any dogs on a leash or risk a ticket from a ranger.

✳ Lodging

Note: Unless otherwise indicated, the zip code for Middletown is 02842.

HOTELS AND MOTELS 🐾 **Bay Willows Inn** (401-847-8400; 1-800-838-5642), 1225 Aquidneck Avenue. ($–$$) Twenty-one rooms (including one where your dog can sleep), both smoking and nonsmoking.

♿ **Courtyard by Marriott** (401-849-8000; reservations: 1-800-321-2211), 9 Commerce Drive, off West Main Road. ($$–$$$) The Courtyard chain is a no-frills Marriott operation, originally designed to attract the business crowd. The Middletown facility, with 148 rooms, gets its share of families as well. The restaurant serves breakfast only.

🐾 ♿ **Howard Johnson's** (401-849-2000; 1-800-446-4656), 351 West Main Road, near Two Mile Corner. ($$–$$$) Standard HoJo, with indoor pool and sauna, tennis courts, and an adjoining restaurant. Breakfast is included with your room Monday through Friday. Free shuttle to Newport summer evenings.

Inn at Newport Beach (401-846-0310), Memorial Boulevard (east end, at junction of Aquidneck Avenue and Purgatory Road). ($$–$$$) Beach-type hotel above the inn's restaurant-and-lounge operation. Good location for those who want to walk to the beach and still stay no more than a mile or so from downtown Newport. Room includes continental breakfast.

Inn at Shadow Lawn (401-847-0902), 120 Miantonomi Avenue, off Two Mile Corner. ($$$) In Middletown, but not all that far from downtown, this is a stately Victorian manor fronted by an expansive lawn. The main house (circa 1853) has eight guest rooms on the second and third floors; the first floor has a dining room and parlor. Rooms are nicely decorated (the Anniversary Room with its queen-sized four-poster bed is a favorite) and named for Victorian authors—Louisa May Alcott and Elizabeth Barrett Browning, for example. All rooms come with a TV, small refrigerator, and coffee. Continental breakfast is included. If you don't want to drive to town, the inn runs a shuttle bus.

♿ **Newport Ramada Inn** (401-846-7600; 1-800-846-8322), 936 West Main Road. ($$–$$$$) Just a few minutes north of the Newport city line, the remodeled motor inn has 142 rooms and six suites; heated indoor pool, exercise room, restaurant, and lounge.

♿ **Royal Plaza Inn** (401-846-3555; 1-800-825-7072), 425 East Main Road. ($$–$$$) Similar to the Courtyard in concept, the 117-room Royal Plaza caters to vacationers as well as business travelers.

Sandpiper Cottages (401-847-9726), 985 East Main Road. ($) Open April 15 through November 15. Old-fashioned motor court, with individual cabins and rooms for two.

🐾 **Sea View Motel** (401-847-0110), 240 Aquidneck Avenue. ($$$) Forty rooms (including two that accommodate dogs), all with an ocean view; continental breakfast. There's also a coffee shop on the premises.

Sea Whale Motel (401-846-7071), 150 Aquidneck Avenue. ($$) There are just 16 rooms in this motel, but all overlook Easton's Pond; the motel itself is within walking distance of First Beach.

☙ **Travelodge** (401-849-4700), 1185 West Main Road. ($$–$$$) Several miles north of Newport on RI 114, with 70-plus rooms. Nothin' fancy, but the price is right—and pets are welcome.

West Main Lodge (401-849-2718; 1-800-537-7704), 1359 West Main Road. ($$) This hotel offers 55 rooms on the outskirts of town, less than 3 miles from downtown Newport.

CAMPGROUNDS Meadowlark Recreational Vehicle Park (401-846-9455), 132 Prospect Avenue, off RI 138A. Write: 132 Prospect Avenue, Middletown 02841. Hook-ups and picnic tables provided on 40 trailer sites.

Middletown Campground (401-846-6273), Second Beach. Write: Town Hall, 350 East Main Road, Middletown 02841. This popular town-run spot right across from the beach offers 36 trailer sites with toilets, hot showers, and sewer hook-ups.

Paradise Mobile Home Park (401-847-1500), 459 Aquidneck Avenue (RI 138A). Write: 265 Prospect Avenue, Middletown 02841. Trailer sites for 16 self-contained units. Full hook-ups.

✳ Where to Eat

DINING OUT ♿ **Atlantic Beach Club** (401-847-2750), 55 Purgatory Road, at the far end of First Beach. ($$) Open daily for lunch and dinner. A popular beach hangout in summer, the Atlantic also has gained many fans for its fare, emphasizing pasta dishes and fresh seafood (stuffed sole, shrimp scampi, broiled scallops), but with some meat entrées as well. Try one of the big salads, filling enough to

suffice for lunch. Excellent desserts are made fresh daily.

♿ **Coddington Brewing Company** (401-847-6690), 210 Coddington Highway. ($–$$) Open daily for lunch and dinner. A brewpub, this joint offers a menu of beer-compatible food and lots of freshly brewed beer.

♿ **Glass Onion** (401-848-5153), 909 East Main Road, at Newport Vineyards. ($$–$$$) Open daily for lunch and dinner. Basic American fare in a pleasant setting just out of busy Newport. Baked sole and scrod, baked stuffed shrimp, poached salmon, New York sirloin. Try the crabcake side dish topped with shrimp and spiced with a chili mayonnaise sauce.

♿ **Hisae's** (401-848-6262), 21 Valley Road, which connects RI 138 and RI 114. ($–$$) Lunch and dinner. The restaurant's previous life as a no-frills pizza joint enhances the minimalist atmosphere at the island's latest Asian restaurant, which insiders say serves authentic Japanese food. Aside from sashimi (slices of octopus, raw yellowtail, tuna, and the like) and sukiyaki, Hisae's serves bento boxes—combination dinners that in Japan provide workers with a meal in a lunch box. Beer, wine, and hot sake help the squid go down. The ginger ice cream is a great way to finish the meal.

♿ **Newport Beach Club** (401-846-0310), Memorial Boulevard, at Wave Avenue. ($$–$$$) Lunch and dinner. Seafood, steaks, chicken—"American cuisine"—in a nice setting, close by the beaches. Locals come here as an alternative to overcrowded downtown restaurants.

Rhea's Family Restaurant (401-841-5560), 120 West Main Road, between One and Two Mile Corners.

($–$$) Open daily for lunch and dinner. Rhea's delivers just what its name suggests—simple, uncomplicated family seafood and meat dishes. The menu may state "pasta and meatballs," but it's good old spaghetti and meatballs that you get.

& **Sea Shai** (401-849-5180), 747 Aquidneck Avenue. ($$) Lunch and dinner. Pleasant restaurant with a varied Japanese and Korean menu. Popular with local diners for its sushi bar.

EATING OUT & **Anthony's Seafood Restaurant** (401-848-5058), 963 Aquidneck Avenue. ($) Open 11–8 weekdays, until 8:30 on weekends. Formerly located on the Newport waterfront, this is casual shore dining-hall seafood fare minus the shore. Small outside dining area, too. You know the food's fresh here— the restaurant adjoins Anthony's seafood store.

Atlantic Grille (401-849-4440), 91 Aquidneck Avenue. ($) Open for breakfast and lunch daily 6–3. A no-frills place located close to First Beach that serves excellent omelets and other breakfast dishes 7 days a week.

Flo's (401-847-8141), 4 Wave Avenue, at the base of Memorial Boulevard, across from Newport Beach. ($) A new addition to the popular Portsmouth clam shack, this Flo's also offers sit-down eating and full seafood dinners. Very popular.

Gold's Wood-Fired Grill & Café (401-849-3377), 21 Valley Road. ($$) The stylish but casual atmosphere here draws locals as well as tourists for excellent wood-grilled pizzas as well as sophisticated entrées and salads. Lunch and dinner daily except

Monday; breakfasts on weekends from 7.

& **Med Cafe** (401-847-8900), 52 East Main Road, across from Aquidneck Shopping Plaza. ($) Lebanese owners serve up ethnic specialties: hummus and baba ganoush for dipping fresh pita, salads, and such sandwiches as shish taouk—marinated chicken with spices and vegetables. Good place to pack a picnic.

Ocean Coffee Roasters (401-848-0441), 510 East Main Road, at the junction of Aquidneck Avenue. ($) Open early. Popular spot for coffee drinkers and pastry eaters. Also sandwiches.

🐾 🐕 & **Tito's Cantina** (401-849-4222), 651 West Main Road. ($) Good selection of traditional Tex-Mex favorites and a special "Little Amigos" menu. Tito sells his own brand of tortilla chips and salsa, which are worth taking home.

Tommy's Diner (401-847-9834), East Main Road. ($) Classic trailer-style diner that was nicely restored for a TV commercial a few years back. Lots of Formica and chrome and good diner food, from soups and sandwiches to full meals.

☀ Selective Shopping

🐾 **Christmas Tree Shop** (401-841-5100), Aquidneck Shopping Center, just past Two Mile Corner. One of a chain of wildly popular discount stores that began on Cape Cod some years back. The shop gets its merchandise from surplus, discontinued lines, and distress sales. Some surprisingly good stuff, including brand names, at very good prices.

Kitchen Pot Pourri (401-847-5880), 42 West Main Road, just north of One

Mile Corner. One definition of a civilized community is that it has a good kitchen supply shop, and this place fills the bill. Top-of-the-line pots, pans, and cutlery as well as glassware, bowls, dishes, and other accessories. There's also a good selection of cookbooks, including recipe collections of various local charitable groups. If you like cooking, you could spend hours in here.

Newport Vineyards and Winery (401-848-5161), Eastgate Shopping Center, 909 East Main Road. Open daily. Formerly Vinland, which began with plantings in 1977, the vineyard offers some excellent local wines, which include a Vidal Blanc, Seyval Blanc, Viking Red, and other varieties. Visitors can sample the wines at this retail store and also arrange for a tour of the winery. You can even buy wine here on Sunday because it falls under the category of "farm produce."

BOOKSTORE Island Books (401-849-2665), 575 East Main Road (RI 138). One of the better new-book shops for browsing on the island. Hard-to-find literature as well as good sections on art, cooking, and children's books, both fiction and nonfiction.

FARM STANDS Aquidneck Growers' Market (401-848-0099), 909 East Main Road (RI 138). June to mid-October, Saturday 9–1. At Newport Vineyards, this popular market has dozens of vendors selling everything from artisan breads and pastries to organically grown vegetables and fruits.

Simmons Farm Stand (401-848-9910), 91 Greene Lane. Farm produce, fresh eggs, and flowers at this family-run operation.

Sweet Berry Farm (401-847-3912), 19 Third Beach Road. Breezy, hilltop location overlooks fields where you can pick your own strawberries, raspberries, and more in-season. Also fresh herbs and baked goods.

GARDEN CENTER Chaves Gardens (401-846-9623), 935 East Main Road

NEWPORT VINEYARDS AND WINERY HAS BEEN IN BUSINESS SINCE 1977.

Kim Grant

(at the traffic signal). Flowers, plants, and garden tools and accessories.

✳ Special Events

Early October: **Harvest Fair** (401-846-2577), Norman Bird Sanctuary, 583 Third Beach Road. This annual event is designed to resemble a country fair, with hayrides, sack races, a rope walk, and greased-pole climbing (or slipping). There are baked goods and vegetable competitions and lots of locally made crafts and produce for sale. Continuous entertainment from a slew of fine local performers. You can tour the grounds while at the fair, whose proceeds help support this important bird and wildlife sanctuary.

PORTSMOUTH

Oldest (1638) and largest (23.3 square miles) of the Aquidneck communities, Portsmouth at one time was the most populated of Rhode Island's towns. Called Pocasset by the Narragansetts, its current name was proposed by residents a year after their arrival and approved by the General Court at Newport in 1640. Now a suburban bedroom community, Portsmouth once relied on agriculture, and to a lesser extent fishing, for its existence. Portsmouth also operated some coal mines in the north part of town during the 19th and early 20th centuries, but the coal was extremely hard and difficult to ignite and became an early casualty as the demand for the fossil fuel waned. One of the town's more prominent residents over the centuries was early settler Anne Hutchinson, who was noted for her feminism and outspokenness in Rhode Island but tried and hanged as a witch in Boston.

GETTING THERE *By car:* From Providence take either RI 114 or RI 138 to the Mount Hope Bridge in Bristol. Also accessible from the north via RI 24, which connects with a second bridge leading onto the island at its northern end. From Newport and points south, both RI 114 and 138 (West and East Main Roads) are the paths to, and through, Portsmouth.

MEDICAL EMERGENCY The statewide emergency number is **911.**

✳ To See

HISTORIC BUILDINGS Portsmouth Historical Society (401-683-9178), in the Old Union Church, corner of East Main Road and Union Streets. Open Memorial Day through Columbus Day, Sunday 2–4. Free. There are several interesting historical buildings on this site, including what may be the one of the oldest one-room schoolhouses in the country, the original Portsmouth Town Hall, and the Old Union Church, home to a 19th-century fundamentalist sect whose church provided a forum for such abolitionists as Julia Ward Howe and William Ellery Channing. The original church was built in 1821, burned, and was rebuilt during the 1860s. Recently restored, it also houses an eclectic array of Portsmouth artifacts, including coal fossils from the town's once-operating coal mines, stone tools and arrowheads from area Native American tribes, and a large collection of possessions from Julia Howe's Union Street house, including her writing desk and one of her lace caps. The former town hall contains a carriage collection and old farm implements, including an apple press. The schoolhouse was started in 1716 and completed in 1723.

HISTORIC SITES Black Regiment Memorial, at the junction of RI 114 and RI 24. During the battle of Rhode Island, in which Continental troops were attempting to retreat after an unsuccessful siege of Newport, the Americans had to hold off several attacks by the British while awaiting boats to remove them from Aquidneck. It was here on August 29, 1778, that the First Rhode Island Regiment, composed entirely of slaves earning their freedom through military service, whipped the Hessian allies of the British. Lafayette later called the battle "the best-fought action of the war" and wept because he had missed most of it. The retreating regiment inflicted heavy casualties on the enemy in rearguard fighting without losing a single soldier. A flagpole and a stone monument now mark the spot where America's first black troops earned their glory.

Hessian Hole, Cory's Lane, on the grounds of Portsmouth Abbey. After the battle of Rhode Island, according to legend, 30 dead Hessian soldiers (Germans fighting as mercenaries for the British) were buried in a pit just west of where the abbey now stands. Nearby flows Bloody Run Brook, so named because it supposedly ran red for days after the burial. There's some doubt about where the actual burial site is, but you may want to follow the brook and look for a noticeable depression in the land.

Portsmouth Abbey Chapel (401-683-2000), Cory's Lane. Open to the public daily 8–4:30; call ahead for a tour. The Chapel of St. Gregory at this Benedictine abbey and prep school is beautifully contemporary. Designed by Pietro Belluschi, it contains a wire sculpture by Richard Lippold.

WINERY Greenvale Vineyards (401-847-3777), 582 Wapping Road. Open Thursday through Sunday noon–5 for free tours and tastings.

✳ To Do

FOR FAMILIES ✍ Green Animals (401-683-1267), 380 Cory's Lane, off RI 114. Open April through October; admission $10. This splendid topiary garden, started by Thomas Brayton about 1880, contains some 80 sculpted trees and shrubs, formal flower beds, and fruit and vegetable patches. The animal figures—carved from California privet—are the best part. There's a camel, a giraffe, a bear, and many others to pick out as you wander down intricate pathways. A garden shop sells various herbs, plants, and flowers. The adjacent Brayton House overlooking Narragansett Bay contains a child's Victorian toy museum.

GOLF Green Valley Country Club (401-847-9543), 371 Union Street, between RI 138 and RI 114. Eighteen holes, public driving range. Fees are $42.

Montaup Country Club (401-683-0955), Anthony Road, Portsmouth, at the

GREEN ANIMALS TOPIARY GARDEN

northern end of Aquidneck Island and adjacent to Sakonnet River Bridge on RI 24. Eighteen holes. Fees are $44 for 18 holes.

HORSEBACK RIDING Glen Farm (401-846-5321), 163 Glen Farm Road, off East Main Road. Indoor/outdoor riding; jumping and riding lessons.
Sandy Point Stables (401-849-3958), Sandy Point Lane, off East Main Road. Indoor and outdoor rings; hunt-seat instruction.

SWIMMING ♂ **Sandy Point Beach,** Sandy Point Avenue, off RI 138, about 15 minutes from Newport. This is a pleasant family beach with no surf and warm Sakonnet River water. Sandy Point opens Memorial Day weekend and closes Labor Day, with lifeguards on duty 9–6. There are restrooms with an outside shower, picnic benches, and charcoal grills. No concession stand, but a snack truck stops by regularly.

✳ Green Space

Narragansett Bay National Estuarine Research Reserve (401-789-3094), Prudence Island. North and South Prudence Islands, in upper Narragansett Bay, are part of a three-island research preserve. About 60 percent of Prudence, some 2,100 acres, is part of the reserve, which offers hiking and naturalist programs to the public in summer. You can get to Prudence by private boat (some public moorings are available in Potter's Cove on the northeast side) or by ferry from Bristol (401-245-8303). However, the ferry landing is 2 miles from the nearest reserve. Prudence Island, which has a large deer population, is prime deer tick territory, and visitors should dress accordingly to avoid the possibility of contracting Lyme disease.

✳ Lodging

Note: Unless otherwise indicated, the zip code for Portsmouth is 02871.

MOTELS Bay Point Inn (401-683-3600), 144 Anthony Road (Anthony Road exit off US 24). ($$) There are 85 rooms, with an indoor pool, health club, and full-service restaurant, **Bridges,** serving breakfast, lunch, and dinner. Less than 20 minutes from Newport but a big savings on room prices—and close to several golf courses.

✎ **Founder's Brook Motel** (401-683-1244), 314 Boyd's Lane, at the junction of RI 138 and 24. ($$ rooms; $$–$$$ suites with kitchenette) Good location at the north end of Aquidneck, near the Sakonnet River Bridge. The suites, which have a foldout bed in the living room, are handy for couples traveling with children.

CAMPGROUND Melville Ponds Campground (401-682-2424), 181 Bradford Avenue, off RI 114. Write: 181 Bradford Avenue, Portsmouth 02871. Spots for 66 trailers, 57 tents; full hook-ups and facilities.

✳ Where to Eat

DINING OUT ♿ **Fifteen Point Road** (401-683-3138), 15 Point Road, Island Park. ($$$) Open for dinner Wednesday through Sunday. Tiny but elegant, this restaurant (in a former hamburger joint) boasts nouveau California decor and a great view of the Sakonnet River. The cuisine is classic American; seafood dishes, especially the lobster casserole, are the way to go.

Oyster Bar & Grill (401-683-5700), 380 East Main Road. ($$) Open daily for dinner. Seafood steaks, pasta, and excellent appetizers in a casual atmosphere; the locals love it, and Newporters use it as an escape during tourist season.

Sakonnet Fish Co. (401-683-1180), 657 Park Avenue, Island Park. ($$$) Open for dinner daily, for lunch Tuesday through Sunday. This seafood grill and raw bar overlooks the Sakonnet River and serves steaks and chicken dishes as well as fresh-caught fish.

Schooners on the Bay (401-683-2380), 1 Lagoon Road, at Bend Boat Basin. ($$) Open daily for lunch and dinner. Situated as it is between two of the largest marinas in Rhode Island, Schooners attracts a diverse clientele, from former navy personnel (this area of Portsmouth was home to a torpedo station in World War II) to international sailboat racers. Hamburgers and sandwiches to full dinners.

♿ **Sea Fare Inn** (401-683-0577), 3352 East Main Road, just before Island Park. ($$$–$$$$) Open for dinner Tuesday through Saturday. Fine dining in an 1887 Victorian mansion. Owner-chef George Karousos, who has won numerous culinary awards, says he follows the tenets of Archestratios, a famous chef in ancient Greece. He uses only fresh foods (no freezing or marinating) in-season, presented simply. That translates into dishes like Chicken à la Grecque and swordfish stuffed with crab and lobster. Try the chef's salad topped with feta cheese. Wheelchair access via the ballroom door on the side.

EATING OUT **Claire's Roadside Cafe** (401-683-5134), 1324 West Main Road, just past Melville. ($) Breakfast and lunch daily. Hearty home-cooking/diner fare at very reasonable prices. Breakfast runs from 6 to about 11:30 and involves the usual egg and pancake dishes as well as combination plates such as the The Portuguese, which consists of chourico (a Portuguese sausage), eggs, and cheese, with beans and home fries. Lunch plates include great soups and such sandwiches as tuna melts and The Popeye—a cheeseburger with spinach.

& **Flo's** (401-847-8141), Park Avenue, Island Park. ($) Open Thursday through Sunday in summer. CLOSED HURRICANES, according to its sign. A classic clam shack by the shore that draws huge crowds in-season. You place your order, receive a stone with your number on it, and wait as impatiently as a child for your clams, stuffies, or fish-and-chips. You can eat them in the car, or take them across the street to the seawall overlooking the Sakonnet River.

& **Food Works** (401-683-4664), 2461 East Main Road. ($) Open daily for breakfast and lunch. Sandwiches, salads, light lunches. Outdoor patio.

& **North End Pizzeria** (401-683-6633), 3030 East Main Road. ($) This former pizza joint has an expanded Italian menu in cozy quarters in Portsmouth Village.

& **Reidy's Family Restaurant** (401-683-9802), 3351 East Main Road, RI 138, just before Island Park. ($) Open daily from breakfast until 8 PM.

Club sandwiches, meat loaf dinners, fish-and-chips, all done in good diner style and served at the counter or booths. This is the kind of place where you find yourself ordering a slice of chocolate cream pie for dessert. Raucous and informal as the wait staff and regulars engage in friendly banter.

Steve's Famous Pizza (401-683-1505), 2460 East Main Road, on Quaker Hill. ($) Pizza, subs, and sandwiches as well as a good feta-covered Greek salad that serves two.

✱ Selective Shopping

Corner Consignment (401-683-1771), 980 East Main Road. Rated highly by thrift-shop devotees, Corner Consignment carries men's, women's, and children's clothing and also jewelry.

Eagles Nest (401-683-3500), 3101 East Main Road, just north of Portsmouth Village. Open daily. Several floors of antique furniture, jewelry, knickknacks, and that stuff from the 1950s they like to call "collectibles."

Ma Goetzinger's (401-683-9400), 2918 East Main Road. Comfortable, stylish women's clothing and Dansko shoes are attractively displayed in an antique farmhouse in Portsmouth Village. A destination shop for its devotees.

Old Almy House (401-683-3737), 980 East Main Road. The anchor for the Old Almy Village shopping center. This restored 1750 house is filled with cookware, pottery, gourmet items, artwork, fine crafts, and gifts. You can spend a lot of time browsing here (don't miss the penny-candy section), then find yourself segueing into the adjoining Christmas Shop, which sells all kinds of Santas and ornaments, many of the collectible variety. Other shops in the complex sell antiques and clothing.

Yankee Hearths (401-682-2301), 2538 East Main Road. Windsor chairs, period furniture, various antiques, and Oriental rugs.

FARM STANDS The following road-side farm stands offer fresh produce in-season: **W. De Castro & Sons Farm** (401-683-4688), 1780 East Main Road; **Mello's Flower Center** (401-683-6262), 444 Boyd's Lane, between East and West Main Roads at the Sakonnet Bridge; **Stone Wall Stand,** Quaker Hill, East Main Road (look for its sign on a tree); and **Quonset View Farm** (401-683-1254), 895 Middle Road, a pick-your-own berry farm, in-season.

GARDEN CENTERS **Island Garden Shop** (401-683-2231), 54 Bristol Ferry Road, off West Main Road near the Mount Hope Bridge. Perennials, annuals, shrubs—this is one of the largest garden centers in the region.

Mello's Flower Center (401-683-6262), 444 Boyd's lane. Nice selection of annuals and perennials, plus garden gizmos and adornments.

The Potting Shed (401-847-2183), 711 Union Street, which runs between East and West Main Roads. With 350 varieties of perennials and 230 of herbs, it's no surprise that owner Jim Pemble is a major resource for Newport's fussy gardeners. If you like gardening, you'll enjoy poking through the greenhouses and seeing the water garden out back.

✳ Special Events

End of June: **Annual Church Fair** (401-849-4332), St. Barnabas Church, 1697 East Main Road.

July: **Glen Farm Polo Productions** (401-847-7090), 163 Glen Farm Road, off East Main Road. Weekend polo matches between international teams. **4-H Country Fair** (401-847-0287), Glen Road, off RI 138.

August: **Annual Lawn Party** (401-846-9700), St. Mary's Episcopal Church, 324 East Main Road.

JAMESTOWN

Jamestown (Conanicut) is Newport's neighbor island to the east, connected to Aquidneck Island by the Newport Bridge and to South County by the Jamestown-Verrazano Bridge. The island was bought in 1656 by William Coddington, Benedict Arnold, and other Newport settlers, incorporated as a town in 1678, and named in honor of King James II. Among the early residents were Quaker farmers and shepherds, and the island also had its share of shipwrights, sailors, and privateers. Captain Kidd spent much time here visiting with fellow pirate Thomas Paine and supposedly buried some of his loot in the area. He was lured to Boston in 1699, where he was arrested, taken to England, tried, and hanged. His treasure has never been found.

The island's strategic importance, at the mouth of Narragansett Bay, was recognized early, and it was fortified by the colonists in 1776. British troops invaded the island in December 1776, burned many of the buildings, and held possession until the French allies of the colonists arrived in 1778. The British continued to bombard Jamestown periodically, and the colonists, in turn, sniped at passing British ships. During the Gilded Age, Jamestown, like the shoreside communities of South County, became something of a secondary resort, playing host to summer visitors who were either unable or unwilling to make their way in Newport society. Many of these families were from Philadelphia, and their descendants still summer on the island. Until 1969 Conanicut was connected to Newport only by ferry service, and the island retains its sense of separateness, of being its own community.

Jamestown is one of the few Rhode Island communities that hasn't blocked off its waterfront with development. Conanicus Avenue, which leads into town from the Newport Bridge, brings you to the East Ferry Landing, where the harbor is in full view. You can walk the docks, take a bench by the seaside, and enjoy an ice cream from a nearby shop. On a summer afternoon or evening, it's hard to do better than this.

GETTING THERE *By car:* Jamestown is reached via RI 138 from east and west. From the west, the new Jamestown-Verrazano Bridge links the island to mainland North Kingstown. The structure resembling an erector set beside it is the old Jamestown Bridge. In the east, the Newport Bridge (officially the Claiborne

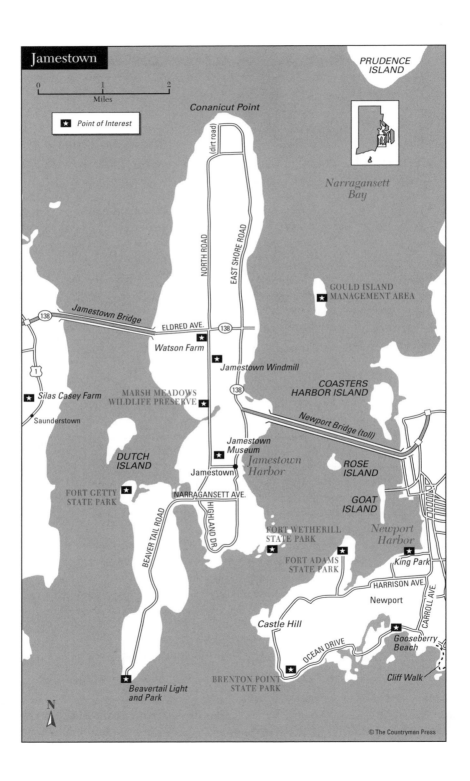

Pell Bridge, for the state's venerable former senator) connects the town to New-port. The toll is $2 per car (a dollar a mile), and the view of Narragansett Bay is spectacular.

MEDICAL EMERGENCY The statewide emergency number is **911.** **Jamestown Rescue** is 401-423-0062.

✳ To See

Beavertail Lighthouse Museum (401-423-3270), Beavertail Road, at the southern tip of Conanicut. Donations. Open daily 10–4 mid-June through Labor Day, weekends spring and fall. One of the oldest lighthouses on the Atlantic Coast (the original was built in 1749), this still-active beacon that marks the way into Narragansett Bay has spawned its own museum, with displays and artifacts depicting the history of lighthouses in the region. Exhibits include models of 33 Rhode Island lighthouses and various artifacts, including the lens used at Beavertail from 1897 to 1991 and a vent ball used to divert heat and fumes from the lantern room in the days when beacons were fired with whale oil and kerosene. The museum is housed in the former assistant lighthouse keeper's cottage (you can't ascend the existing granite tower, built in 1856), and the view from Beavertail Point—considered one of the best ocean vistas in the state—alone is worth the trip.

Jamestown Fire Memorial (401-423-0062), next to the fire department, 50 Narragansett Avenue. Open Monday through Friday 8–3 (check with the fire department to see who has the key). Interesting display of the town's early firefighting equipment, including a horse-drawn pumper.

Jamestown Museum (401-423-0784), 92 Narragansett. Open early June through Labor Day, Tuesday through Saturday 1–4. Free. This tiny museum contains memorabilia from the 300-year-old Jamestown ferry system, the island's only link to Newport until the Newport Bridge opened (still a traumatic event for islanders on both sides) in 1969. There are also other Jamestown historical items.

Jamestown Windmill (401-423-0784), North Road. Open mid-June through mid-September, Saturday and Sunday 1–4. Free but donations welcome. The mill, which operated between 1789 and 1896, was called a

THE JAMESTOWN WINDMILL IS RHODE ISLAND'S LAST SUCH STRUCTURE IN WORKING CONDITION.

Kim Grant

smock mill for its appearance, based on a popular English design of the 16th and 17th centuries. Rhode Island once was dotted with these mills, but this is the last in working condition. Inside, you can view the gears, the stone for corn grinding, and the granary.

Sidney L. Wright Museum (401-423-7280), North Road, in the Jamestown Philomenian Library. Open Monday through Saturday during library hours. Native American artifacts from prehistoric to colonial times are on display. Jamestown was inhabited by the Narragansett tribe, who used the island as a summer camp, when the Europeans arrived. Archaeologists are still researching the many centuries of Narragansett life on the island.

✳ To Do

FOR FAMILIES ✇ **Jamestown Playground,** North Road, near the public library. Imaginative and award-winning playground made from recycled materials. An environmentally friendly place that is also a lot of fun for kids.

✇ **Watson Farm** (401-423-0005), North Road. Admission is $4 for adults, $2 for children. Run by the Society for the Preservation of New England Antiquities, this is a working farm complete with sheep, cows, and agricultural equipment. The mid-1800s farmhouse was relocated here, and the farm, 280 acres of rural haven, offers views of the sea in several directions.

GOLF Jamestown Country Club (401-423-9930), 245 Conanicus Avenue, near the Newport Bridge. Nine holes in a nice island setting. The fee is $16 for nine holes, an additional $8 if you want to go around again. One of the best golf bargains in the area.

WATSON FARM, A WORKING FARMSTEAD, MAKES A GREAT STOP FOR CHILDREN.

Kim Grant

KAYAKING **Ocean State Scuba** (401-423-1662), 79 North Main Street. Kayaks for rent at East Ferry landing (south basin at Conanicut Marina).

SWIMMING **Mackerel Cove,** Beavertail Road. Conanicut's only town-run beach is a family beach at the tip of a cove and fairly well protected from waves. Parking and entrance fee for nonresidents.

✳ Green Space

Beavertail State Park, Beavertail Road. Lots of places to hike, picnic, and just enjoy the scenery in this 153-acre park at the southern tip of Conanicut. Great spot to watch a sunset (or sunrise) and one of the best ocean views you'll find in the Ocean State.

Fort Wetherill (401-423-1771), Ocean Street, off East Shore Road. The fort, set on the highest point of the island, overlooks the East Passage of Narragansett Bay (some feel the Sakonnet River is the true East Passage and not a river at all). The first fortification here was Fort Dumpling, built in 1776. The federal government built Fort Wetherill later, parts of which remain. Now run as a state park, the area is in the wild, and it's a good place for hiking, picnicking, and just plain viewing. You can pick out Newport's Trinity Church to the east, Point Judith and the outline of Block Island to the south. Somewhere down along the shore is where Captain Kidd, who stayed here with friend and fellow pirate Thomas Paine in 1699, supposedly buried some of his treasure. Again, beware of deer ticks.

✳ Lodging

INN **Bay Voyage Inn** (401-423-2100; 1-800-225-3522), 150 Conanicus Avenue, Jamestown 02835. ($$$–$$$$) Formerly a country house in Newport, this Victorian structure, once called Rhoda-Ridge, was transported across the bay by barge to Conanicut Island in 1899 and renamed Bay Voyage. There are 31 one-bedroom suites, some with a balcony overlooking the harbor, with Pullman kitchen and private bath. Continental breakfast is included.

CAMPGROUND **Fort Getty Recreation Area** (401-423-1363), Fort Getty Road. Write: P.O. Box 377, Jamestown 02835. Open Memorial Day through Columbus Day. Good location toward the south end of the island. Sites for 100 trailers, 25 tents; boat ramp.

✳ Where to Eat

DINING OUT **Bay Voyage Inn** (401-423-2100), 150 Conanicus Avenue. ($$–$$$) Open daily for dinner. Best known for its bountiful Sunday brunch, which is consistently voted the best in Rhode Island in local polls. The inn's dining room, overlooking the harbor, also dishes out such standbys as filet mignon, rack of lamb, lobster thermidor, and scallops. Chances are you will get a good meal here anytime, but you can't miss with the waffle- and omelet-intensive, fixed-price brunch.

🏆 ♿ **Jamestown Oyster Bar** (401-423-3380), 22 Narragansett Avenue. ($$) Open daily for lunch and dinner. Probably the most popular dining-out spot in town for local residents, the Oyster Bar serves mostly fresh fish—swordfish, tautog, flounder, tuna—often blackened, always a treat. Burgers, soups, sandwiches, fried calamari, and stuffed quahogs are also available.

♧ **Trattoria Simpatico** (401-423-3731), 13 Narragansett Avenue. ($$–$$$) Open daily for lunch and dinner. Classy Italian restaurant that has gained a reputation for consistently excellent food beyond Jamestown. Antipasti include miniature flatbread pizzas, grilled portobello mushrooms, mussels steamed in tomato broth with wine and olive oil, and duck and radicchio salad. Main dishes include grilled Atlantic salmon, oregano-marinated shrimp, and various pasta/seafood combinations. In warmer weather you can dine out in the yard, on weekends to the accompaniment of soft jazz.

Tricia's Tropi-Grille (401-423-1490), 14 Narragansett Avenue. ($$) Open daily for lunch and dinner. Bright Caribbean-inspired colors and an open-air patio on one side set the tone for this recent addition to the Jamestown dining scene, which features such specialties as Jamaican jerk chicken, blackened seafood, key lime pie, and other spicy dishes from southern climes.

EATING OUT ♧ **Chopmist Charlie's** (401-423-1020), 40 Narragansett Avenue. ($) Open daily for lunch and dinner. Chowder, seafood in an informal setting.

East Ferry Market & Deli (401-423-1592), 47 Conanicus Avenue. ($) Open daily 6 AM–5 PM. Sandwiches, soups, and snacks. The outside patio, across the street from the old ferry landing and harbor, is the best spot in town to people-watch.

BAKERIES **Slice of Heaven** (401-423-9866), 32 Narragansett Avenue.

Breads, pastries, and cookies round out the deli selections at this pleasant café with outdoor seating.

Village Hearth Artisan Bakery (401-423-9282), 2 Watson Avenue. Just a block north of Jamestown village, this homey place makes excellent country-style loaves and baguettes, as well as pastries and (on Sundays only) wood-grilled thin-crust pizzas to take out.

✱ Entertainment

Narragansett Cafe (401-423-2150), 25 Narragansett Avenue. The Narragansett may look like a dive, but it's really a friendly neighborhood bar whose patrons in summer include local residents, area fishermen, and bluebloods from out of state. The draw for all is the same: cheap drinks and lively rock-and-roll bands. The crowd is of all ages, and it's an active one: Narry customers come to dance.

✱ Selective Shopping

The Boutique at East Ferry (401-423-2828), 47 Conanicus Avenue. Chic women's clothing and accessories are sold at this small shop overlooking the ferry landing and harbor.

Conanicut Marine Ship Store (401-423-1556), 20 Narragansett Avenue. A well-stocked ship's store and chandlery is conveniently located for boaters on Jamestown's main drag. Marine hardware and gear, too.

Jamestown Designs (401-423-0344), 17 Narragansett Avenue. Frame store and upscale gift shop. There are also paintings and prints of local scenes by local artists for sale, including Jamestowner John Mecray, whose marine paintings enjoy a national reputation.

The Secret Garden (401-423-0050), 12 Southwest Avenue, just around the corner from Narragansett Avenue at the flashing light. This pleasant shop sells flowers and plants as well as dried flowers, wreaths, candles and candlesticks, and other little odds and ends. It also offers its own brand of scent oils and, of course, *Secret Gardens,* the locally published book about the gardens in Newport's historic Point section.

✳ Special Events

Early August: **Swim the Bay** (401-272-3540). Potter's Cove, near Newport Bridge, is the finish point for this cross-bay swim of about 2 miles. Swimmers of all ages compete for the benefit of Save the Bay, a statewide environmental watchdog group, and there is usually a big crowd on shore to cheer them on.

✧ *Mid-August:* **Fools Rules Regatta** (401-423-1492), Jamestown Harbor. Fun race for charity in which contestants build their own boats on the beach (no marine gear allowed) and attempt to race them across a short course just offshore. The result is sort of a floating (sometimes) Mardi Gras parade.

Mid-October: **'Round the Island Bike Race** (401-423-7260). Okay, so it's only 18 miles around the circumference of Conanicut, but it's still a fun race for young and old as well as a chance for participants to raise money for island charities.

Southern Rhode Island

NARRAGANSETT

SOUTH KINGSTOWN AREA

NORTH KINGSTOWN AREA

CHARLESTOWN AND RICHMOND AREA

WESTERLY AND WATCH HILL

Kim Grant

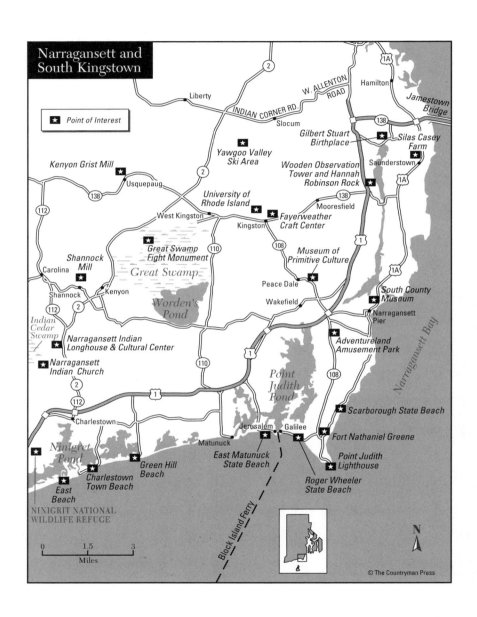

Narragansett and South Kingstown

★ Point of Interest

Liberty
INDIAN CORNER RD.
W. ALLENTON ROAD
Hamilton
Jamestown Bridge
138
Slocum
Gilbert Stuart Birthplace
★ Silas Casey Farm
Kenyon Grist Mill ★
Yawgoo Valley Ski Area ★
Wooden Observation Tower and Hannah Robinson Rock ★
Saunderstown
2
Usquepaug
138
112
University of Rhode Island
West Kingston
Kingston
Mooresfield
138
★ Fayerweather Craft Center
1A
1A
Great Swamp Fight Monument ★
110
108
Museum of Primitive Culture ★
Shannock Mill
Carolina
Great Swamp
Peace Dale
1A
Shannock ★ Kenyon
Worden's Pond
Wakefield
South County Museum ★
112
2
Narragansett Pier
Indian Cedar Swamp
★ Narragansett Indian Longhouse & Cultural Center
Narragansett Bay
★ Narragansett Indian Church
110
★ Adventureland Amusement Park
2
112
1
Point Judith Pond
108
Charlestown
1
Jerusalem Galilee
★ Scarborough State Beach
Ninigret Pond
★
Matunuck
East Matunuck State Beach ★
★ Fort Nathaniel Greene
Green Hill Beach ★
★ Point Judith Lighthouse
East Beach ★
Charlestown Town Beach ★
Roger Wheeler State Beach
NINIGRIT NATIONAL WILDLIFE REFUGE

Block Island Ferry

0   1.5   3
Miles

N

© The Countryman Press

NARRAGANSETT

With its miles of beautiful beaches and rocky cliffs overlooking the ocean, this town is the essence of Rhode Island. Narragansett Bay, as lovely as it is, does not project the awesome power of the open sea. Here it's the ocean that you see, and the ocean that imparts its unique light to the lower sky. While Narragansett was settled early, it gained its own identity relatively late by Rhode Island standards, separating from sprawling South Kingstown only in 1888. A popular beach resort area near the end of the 19th century, with many large oceanfront hotels, the town reached its peak with the construction of the Narragansett Pier and the Stanford White–designed Towers Casino in 1883. Then a devastating fire in 1900 wiped out much of the ocean district; the big stone towers and arch were saved, but the town returned to a fairly small (population: less than 13,000 in 14 square miles), rural, and sleepy state, except when summer crowds from upstate filled the beaches. Extensive urban renewal in the 1970s rebuilt a major portion of the Narragansett Pier area, and what the downtown lost in character, it gained in an influx of new shops and a resurgence of tourism. Today Narragansett offers the resortlike atmosphere along its east coast and the salty aspect of Galilee, the state's major fishing port, on the west, where Point Judith Pond slices inland. *Spartina*, the excellent novel by John Casey, who spent time here working the fishing boats, evokes the spirit of this special place.

GUIDANCE Narragansett Tourist Information Center (401-783-7121), Ocean Road, at the Towers, Narragansett Pier. This office dispenses information and brochures about Narragansett and all of South County.

South County Tourism Council (401-789-4422; 1-800-548-4662), 4808 Tower Hill Road (US 1), Wakefield.

Two local biweekly newspapers, the *South County Independent* and the *Narragansett Times*, provide listings of events and entertainment.

GETTING THERE *By car:* From points south, take US 95 to RI 138 east, to US 1—then follow the signs to Narragansett. If you prefer the scenic route, take exit 92 in Connecticut, and follow CT 2 to CT 78 until you reach US 1 north in Westerly, Rhode Island. It's about 20 miles to the first Narragansett exit. From points north, take US 95 south to RI 4 east, to US 1 south. It's about 8 miles to the first exit.

GETTING AROUND Local taxi service is provided by **Wakefield Cab** (401-788-0007) in Peace Dale, **Wright's Taxi** (401-789-0400) in Narragansett, and **Eagle** (401-783-2970), also in Narragansett.

MEDICAL EMERGENCY The statewide emergency number is **911.**

✳ To See

South County Museum (401-783-5400; www.southcountymuseum.org), Strathmore Street off RI 108, Narragansett. Open Wednesday through Saturday 10–4, Sunday noon–4 in July and August; the same hours Friday through Sunday in May, June, September, October. $5 admission fee. The museum houses almost 10,000 items relating to rural life in Rhode Island from 1800 to 1930—everything from a general store and cobbler shop to antique carriages, a blacksmith's forge, and a country kitchen sink. The museum holds a quilting festival each August and a harvest festival at the end of September.

✳ To Do

BOAT EXCURSIONS Block Island Ferry (401-783-4613), State Pier, Galilee. Departs hourly 8–7; check for current schedule and prices. Carries cars. The trip to "the Block" takes about 1 hour and 10 minutes.

Island Hi-Speed Ferry (401-877-9425), State Pier, Galilee. May through October. Five trips daily that take about 30 minutes. Check for current schedule and prices.

Gail Frances (401-783-4988), Galilee. Whale-watch cruises and half-day fishing trips on this 90-foot motor vessel

AT REST IN GALILEE

Kim Grant

Seven B's V (401-789-9250), Periwinkle Road, Narragansett. This 80-foot motor vessel is available for fishing, whale-watching, and special events.

Southland Riverboat (401-783-2954), State Pier, Galilee. Regular 1.75-hour narrated tours of the harbor and adjoining areas; sunset tours on Saturday and Sunday.

CANOEING/KAYAKING **Narrow River Kayaks** (401-789-0334), 94 Middle-bridge Road, Narragansett 02882. Kayak instruction and rentals.

FISHING There's great bluewater fishing in these parts—blues, cod, and pogies—and plenty of charter fishing (party) boats operating out of Galilee. Some are individually chartered with a crew by groups of six or eight splitting expenses, while others make regular trips for a set fee. Most depart from Galilee's charter boat dock. For information about area fishing charters, write to the R.I. Party & Charter Boat Association, P.O. Box 3198, Narragansett 02882; 401-737-5812.

Misty (401-789-6057), 102 Kimberly Drive, Wakefield. Captain Andy Ambrosia.

Old Salt Charters (401-783-4805), 12 Amancio Street, Wakefield. Captain Bill Della Valle.

Persuader (401-783-5644), 110 Avice Avenue, Narragansett. Captain Dennis Dillon.

Sakarak Sport Fishing Charters (401-783-9015), 42 Exeter Boulevard, Narra-gansett. Captain Mitch Chagnon.

Sea Fox (401-789-0514), 3 Barnacle Road, Narragansett. Captain Donald Slater.

FOR FAMILIES ✐ **Adventureland** (401-789-0030), Point Judith Road. Open Saturday 11–6, Sunday noon–6. Miniature golf, bumper boats, go-carts, and batting cages.

✐ **Narragansett Ocean Club** (401-783-1711), 360 South Pier Road. Phone for hours. Indoor roller skating—loud, and lots of fun.

SURFING It's not exactly California, but Narragansett offers tolerable East Coast–style surfing. **Gansett Juice** (401-789-7890), 74 Narragansett Avenue, offers rentals and gives lessons. **Warm Winds** (401-789-9040), 26 Kingstown Road, has rentals and gives lessons.

SWIMMING Narragansett boasts some of the state's best beaches, ranging from the jam-packed, surf-heavy sands of Scarborough to the quiet waters of Roger Wheeler and Salty Brine State Beaches. For information about state beaches, call 401-222-2632.

Narragansett Town Beach (401-785-6430). Parking, walk-on fees. Half a mile of beach right at the Pier. Good wave action makes this one of the best surfing spots in the state. Best of all, you're right downtown.

Salty Brine State Beach. Named for a legendary Rhode Island deejay and per-

NARRAGANSETT BEACH

Kim Grant

sonality, the former Galilee State Beach is a short stretch of sand to the west of Roger Wheeler.

Scarborough State Beach (401-783-1010), Ocean Road. This 300-plus yards of sand and dunes is a major summer attraction, especially for young adults and teens, who spend equal time checking out each other and the surf. Busy, busy, busy. The lot holds almost 3,000 cars and still fills up quickly on weekends.

✒ **Roger Wheeler State Beach** (401-789-3563), Sand Hill Cove Road, near Galilee. Families with children will like the calm, protected waters of this beach. There are also cabanas and playground equipment.

✴ **Green Space**

Black Point, Ocean Road, near Scarborough State Beach. Environmentalists and state officials fought hard to keep this cliffside pathway a public right-of-way. Park your car in the adjoining beach lot and walk back a few yards to the walkway entrance. The path is less than 0.5 mile long, but the view—to the horizon across Rhode Island Sound—is spectacular. To the northeast you can see the outlines of Beavertail on Jamestown and Brenton Point in Newport. Inland, there's nothing but brush and brambles. Well worth the trip.

✴ **Lodging**

Note: Unless otherwise indicated, the zip code for Narragansett is 02882.

HOTELS AND MOTELS Lighthouse Inn of Galilee (401-789-9341; 1-800-336-6662; wwwlighthouseinnri.com), 307 Great Island Road, Galilee. ($$–$$$) This is a full-service hotel with 100 rooms right across from the docks and ferry landing on the waterfront. Indoor pool.

Ocean Rose Inn (401-783-4704), 113 Ocean Road, Narragansett. ($$$) Recently restored, this is one of the surviving structures from Narragansett's glory days as a beach resort. This inn consists of a 1900s three-story house (which served as a speakeasy and gambling house in its time) and an adjacent, motel-like structure. All rooms have a private bath and all, especially those in the main house, enjoy an ocean view. Restaurant and lounge on the premises.

BED & BREAKFASTS While you won't find as many inns and bed & breakfasts in South County as on Aquidneck, the number is growing. South County B&Bs, whether on the sea or in the country, have a quiet, calming charm of their own. About two dozen are members of a reservation service, **Bed & Breakfast Referral Service of South Coast Rhode Island** (1-800-853-7479), which will help you find a room if the inns are full.

Dunmere (401-783-3797; www.virtual cities.com), 500 Ocean Road, Narragansett. ($$$–$$$$) The approach to this elegant 1880s stone house with a sweeping view of pond and ocean is through a fairy-tale turreted gateway. The one suite, accommodating two, is equipped with a mini kitchen. A continental breakfast with home-baked goods is served.

Four Gables (401-789-6948), 12 South Pier Road, Narragansett. ($$$) One suite accommodating four in this pleasant Arts and Crafts house built by an architect in 1898. View of Narragansett Bay. Full breakfast. Close to the beaches and the Pier shopping area.

1900 House (401-789-7971; www.1900houseri.com), 59 Kingston Road, Narragansett. ($$$) There are two bedrooms and one suite in this restored Victorian. It is furnished with Victorian-era antiques but brought up to date with air-conditioning and cable TV. Screened-in porch. No children under 10. Gourmet breakfasts. A block and a half from the ocean.

The Richards (401-789-7746), 144 Gibson Avenue, Narragansett. ($$) Located in a quiet area about a mile from the Pier, this 1884 guest house is surrounded by English gardens. Each of the four spacious rooms, three with private bath, boasts a working fireplace. Nicely furnished with antiques and Oriental rugs, this is one of the oldest B&Bs in town.

Summertime House (401-782-2274), 24 Cedar Street, Narragansett. ($$$) A pretty little house on a quiet side street with three air-conditioned rooms, cable TV, fireplaces, continental breakfast. There is also one air-conditioned suite with fireplace, cable TV, and kitchen facilities (no breakfast included here) in the main house.

CAMPGROUNDS Fishermen's Memorial State Park (401-789-8374), 1011 Point Judith Road, near Galilee. Write: Division of Parks and Recreation, 2321 Hartford Avenue, Johnston 02919. Season runs from April through October. Reservations required. Sites for 147 trailers, 35 tents, with varying hook-ups. Recreational facilities include tennis and basketball courts as well as playground equipment.

Long Cove Marina Family Campsites (401-783-4902), Long Cove Marina, RR 9, off Point Judith Road. Write: Point Judith Road, #325, Narragansett. Open May through October. Spaces for 155 trailers, 25 tents. Because this is a marina, you also get the benefit of a boat ramp, plus shower and head (toilet) facilities.

✳ Where to Eat

DINING OUT Basil's (401-789-3743), 22 Kingstown Road, at Narragansett Pier. ($$$–$$$$) Open Wednesday through Sunday for dinner. As the French Provincial decor suggests, this small but elegant restaurant specializes in fine French cuisine: steak Diane, rack of lamb Dijonnaise, and the chef's choice, Veal à la Basil's. Lots of spicy cream sauces and fresh and flavorful herbs. Chocolate mousse makes an excellent finale. Basil's also has a comprehensive wine list.

Casa Rossi (401-789-6385), 90 Point Judith Road. ($$) Open daily for dinner. The exterior—a plain white Cape in an overdeveloped stretch of town— is nothing special, but the authentic Italian cooking at this "family-kitchen" restaurant is a real draw. Homemade pastas and sauces (you can buy some to take home) and breads. Fresh ingredients all around and good-sized portions—make sure to save some space for the cannoli.

Coast Guard House (401-789-0700), 40 Ocean Road, at Narragansett Pier. ($$$) Open daily for lunch and dinner. Perched on the edge of the Atlantic, this former Coast Guard station serves up seafood, meat dishes, and one of the best (and closest) ocean views in the state. Busy at dinner but perhaps best known for its Sunday brunch. The upstairs bar and deck are popular in summer.

♿ **La Bodega** (401-782-4013), 140 Point Judith Road, Mariner Square. ($$–$$$) Open for dinner daily, except Tuesday. Formerly the Spanish Tavern, this restaurant offers paella and other Spanish dishes as well as Italian fare.

❖ **Spain Restaurant** (401-783-9770), 1144 Ocean Road. ($$–$$$) Open daily for lunch and dinner. Heaps of Iberian-inspired food—shrimp, swordfish, snapper, and paella—draw summer crowds to this large, informal dining spot. The prices are reasonable; the portions, enormous. Spain's large deck overlooking Narragansett Pier (and the margaritas) makes waiting a pleasure.

♿ **Turtle Soup** (401-792-8683), 1 Beach Street, Narragansett, in the Ocean Rose Inn. ($$–$$$) Open daily except Monday in summer, for both lunch and dinner. In winter open for dinner all weekdays except Monday, and for lunch as well on weekends. Even though there's no turtle soup on the menu, there are plenty of fin and shellfish dishes like Cod Zuppa Doo, a cod fillet in a piquant wine and tomato sauce, or salmon with walnuts and a balsamic raspberry glaze. Lighter fare might be a vegetable pizza. In warm weather, dining out on the shady porch with a view of the bay is especially pleasant. There are French as well as Italian touches in the kitchen.

1200 Ocean Grill (401-782-1777), 1200 Ocean Road, Narragansett. ($$–$$$) Open daily for dinner in summer, and in winter on Thursday, Friday, Saturday. Seafood is the specialty, and the scallop dishes, in all sorts of forms, are favorites.

Wiley's South Shore (401-789-2864), 629 Succotash Road, East Matunuck. Open for breakfast, lunch, and dinner daily except Monday in summer; for dinner Wednesday through Saturday and for breakfast Friday through Sunday off-season. Good healthy food with a Louisiana and a southwestern flavor, served in a location as delectable as the food, right on The Gut between the ocean and Potter's Pond.

♿ **Woody's** (401-789-9500), 21 Pier Market Place. ($$–$$$) Open for dinner Wednesday through Sunday. Chef Ted Monahan's small, upscale restaurant offers an interesting mix of tapas, salads, fresh seafood, and grilled dishes. Very popular with customers from throughout the state.

EATING OUT ✔ ♿ **Aunt Carrie's** (401-783-7930), 1240 Ocean Road, near the tip of Point Judith. ($) Open June through Labor Day, daily except Tuesday for lunch and dinner. Quintessential clam shack by the sea. Fried clams, clam cakes, french fries, and other seafood dinners (plus kids' dinners) eaten the old-fashioned way— outside at picnic tables, in a semi-enclosed, porchlike area, or in your car. Eating here is a summer ritual for many Rhode Islanders.

Champlin's Seafood (401-783-3152), 256 Great Island Road. ($–$$) Open daily for lunch and dinner. You have your choice of seafood operations in Galilee, but you won't go wrong with Champlin's, overlooking Point Judith Pond. Your basic Rhode Island menu of fried clams, stuffed clams ("stuffies" to natives), and lobster rolls enjoyed indoors or out. Good for take-out, too.

♿ **Crazy Burger** (401-783-1810), 144 Boon Street, one street up from Ocean Road. ($–$$) Open daily from breakfast to 9 or 10 PM. A fun place that serves excellent food—real burgers, along with turkey, chicken, and salmon burger concoctions. Plenty of vegan dishes, too, as well as Rhode Island standards like fried calamari. There's a nice patio (partly covered with a canopy) out back for fresh-air dining.

♿ **Gale Warnings Food & Spirits** (401-789-1725), 945 Boston Neck Road, Narragansett. ($–$$) Open daily except Monday for dinner. A cozy log cabin restaurant serving American fare with flair.

Jim's Dock (401-783-2050), 1175 Succotash Road, Jerusalem, across the harbor from Galilee. ($) Open daily for breakfast, lunch, and dinner until Labor Day. Chowder, clam cakes, and local fish dishes.

The Picnic Basket (401-782-2284), 20 Kingstown Road, Narragansett. ($) Open 10:30–5 daily except Monday. Sandwiches, soups, salads, pizza, and

Kim Grant

chili—and the sandwiches range from a simple turkey club to an extravagant honey-maple turkey, roasted peppers, lettuce, tomato, and melted mozzarella combination put together on basil focaccia.

& **Twin Willows** (401-789-8153), 865 Boston Neck Road (RI 1A). ($–$$) Open daily for lunch and dinner. The willows are long gone, but this bar and restaurant seems to have been around forever. Chowder, stuffies, sandwiches, and seafood dinners at reasonable prices. Extensive beer menu and an outside deck with great views of the ocean at Bonnet Shores.

✳ Entertainment

As in many beach communities, there's a variety of entertainment— from jazz to dancing—in Narragansett's restaurants and hotels.

Coast Guard House (401-789-0700), 40 Ocean Road. Piano bar, offering everything from TV theme songs to dance music.

Tequila's at Charlie O's (401-783-1608), 2 Sand Hill Cove Road, just off Point Judith Road. Restaurant, sports bar, and lounge, with dance music

more suitable for aging rock-and-rollers.

✳ Selective Shopping

Francesca's Design Company (401-792-8693), 12A Pier Marketplace, Narragansett. Handmade puppets and china dolls, hand-painted Italian pottery, and assorted other gifts.

The Hope Chest (401-783-8840), 124 Point Judith Road. Consignment shop with everything from knick-knacks to art to major pieces of furniture. Almost exclusively good-quality stuff. Two floors of browsing heaven.

✳ Special Events

End of June: **Narragansett Art Festival** (401-789-4422), Veterans Memorial Park.

Mid-July: **Concert on the Beach** at Narragansett Town Beach. Bring a blanket and a picnic for this annual evening of classical pops.

End of July: **Blessing of the Fleet** (401-789-9491), Galilee.

Mid-September: **Summer's End Festival** at Narragansett Town Beach with rides, a chowder cook-off, and evening band music.

SOUTH KINGSTOWN AREA

South Kingstown, the Ocean State's largest town, occupies roughly 62 square miles in its southwest corner. Surrounding South Kingstown are some of the state's most inviting beaches—East Matunuck, Roy Carpenter's Green Hill, and more sheltered spots like Sand Hill Cove and Galilee State Beach.

Roads wind inland past woods and ponds, and through villages of virtually untouched 18th- and 19th-century houses and gray stone mills. There are turf and potato farms, pick-your-own strawberry patches, a wildlife refuge rich in bird and animal life, and a picturesque 1875 railroad station. Here you'll find 1,075-acre Worden's Pond, the largest body of fresh water in the state, and, abutting it, the historic Great Swamp, the site of the colonists' 1675 attack on King Philip.

Oliver Hazard Perry and his brother Matthew were born in South Kingstown. The former was a naval hero in the War of 1812 battle of Lake Erie; the latter, also a navy man, negotiated the first modern commercial treaty with Japan in 1854, opening that nation to the world.

The principal villages in the town are Kingston, Wakefield, and Peace Dale. Except for its beaches and University of Rhode Island campus, South Kingstown is a quiet, slow-moving part of the state, well worth exploring on a sunny summer or fresh spring day, or when the Great Swamp's maple, sumac, and oak have turned crimson and gold.

Although Kingston today is the site of most of the University of Rhode Island campus, it remains a quiet, tucked-away place, untouched by commercialism. Along RI 138, its main street, green- and black-shuttered clapboard houses stand just as they did in the 19th century. Then known as Little Rest, the village was one of the seats of the Rhode Island General Assembly. That, some say, was the reason for its original name, for when the assembly was in session it was, indeed, a place of little rest. Another story, however, attributes the name to a brief stop that soldiers made in the village on their way to the Great Swamp battle.

Wakefield, the administrative center of South Kingstown, grew up around the Narragansett Mills, a textile manufacturing company established in 1800. Later the Wakefield Mill, it is long since defunct. There are some fine old houses along US 1 plus a main street of 19th-century commercial storefronts, art galleries, and a fish ladder below the Main Street bridge. In spring you can watch the alewives climbing upstream. A pedestrian bridge across the Saugatucket River affords a pretty view downstream.

Peace Dale owes its beginning to the Peace Dale Manufacturing Company, a woolen mill founded in 1800 by Isaac and Rowland Hazard. In its heyday it was known for its shawls and worsted. The mill is still operating, although the gray granite buildings are of later-19th-century construction, the name has changed to Palisades, Ltd., and it does finishing and dyeing.

GUIDANCE South County Tourism Council, Inc. (401-789-4422; 1-800-548-4662), 4808 Tower Hill Road (US 1), Wakefield. Monday through Friday 9–5. Situated in the Government Center office building on the right side of US 1 heading north.

GETTING THERE *By train or bus:* You can take **Amtrak** (1-800-USA-RAIL) to Kingston or a **Rhode Island Public Transport Authority** (RIPTA; 401-781-9400) bus from Providence to Kingston and to the beaches (ask for the Beach Run). All public transportation, however, is infrequent, and by far the best way to explore this part of the state is by car.

GETTING AROUND Local taxi service is provided by **Wakefield Cab** (401-788-0007) in Peace Dale, **Wright's Taxi** (401-789-0400) in Narragansett, and **Eagle** (401-783-2970), also in Narragansett.

MEDICAL EMERGENCY The statewide emergency number is **911.**

South County Hospital (401-782-8000), 100 Kenyon Avenue, Wakefield. Emergency room and regular hospital care to the entire southern portion of the state.

✳ To See

MUSEUMS Kenyon Grist Mill (401-783-4054), Glenrock Road, Usquepaugh, South Kingstown. Corn, wheat, rye, oats, and assorted other grains are ground here, but the mill is open to the public only by appointment. Though a variety of grains is produced at the mill, it's the white cornmeal used to make Rhode Island jonny cakes that brings it fame. These thin, flat, crisp, dollar-sized cornmeal cakes made of Rhode Island–grown hard native flint corn were called journey cakes in colonial days. Rhode Island travelers always packed them in their saddlebags for on-the-road eating. Today native flint corn is usually unavailable, and white dent corn from the Midwest is generally substituted.

The Museum of Primitive Art and Culture (401-783-5711), Peace Dale Office Building, Kingstown Road (RI 108), Peace Dale. Open by appointment in summer and Tuesday, Wednesday, and Thursday 10–2 in other seasons. This is a small collection of tools belonging to New England Native Americans and baskets, pottery, bows and arrows, and weaving from other native North American cultures; boomerangs from Australia; an Inuit kayak; East African lion-hunting spears; and South Sea Island headhunter shields, among others. The museum was opened in 1892 by Rowland G. Hazard II, who urged local residents to donate the objects that are the basis of the present collection.

Pettaquamscutt Historical Society (401-783-1328), RI 138, Kingston. Open year-round Tuesday, Thursday, and Saturday 1–4, or by appointment. This gray granite building beside the Kingston Congregational Church served as the Washington County Jail from 1858 to 1956. A guide shows visitors the downstairs convicts' cells with their cast-iron doors. The debtors' cells on the second floor are now filled with a fine collection of quilts and costumes and a re-creation of a 19th-century Wakefield women's finery and millinery shop. There are also re-creations of a one-room schoolhouse, of 18th- and 19th-century rooms, and a collection of local toys from 1800 to the 1950s. Among the particularly interesting exhibits are a mural, formerly in the Wakefield Post Office, of 18th-century South County planters, and the temporarily closed but soon to be reopened Civil War Room that contains the desk of Julius Booth. He was the actor-brother of Abraham Lincoln's assassin, John Wilkes Booth, and a onetime South Kingstown summer dweller. Nominal admission fee.

University of Rhode Island Rock, Mineral, and Fossil Collection (401-874-2265), Woodward Hall, Kingston campus. Open year-round, Monday through Friday 8–4.

HISTORIC SITES **Congregational Church** (401-789-7313), High Street, Peace Dale. Open in summer, Monday through Thursday 9:30–11:30, Sunday 10–11:30. The stained-glass windows in this impressive granite building are the work of John La Farge, designer of the stained glass in New York City's Cathedral of St. John the Divine.

George Fayerweather House (401-789-9072), RI 138, Kingston. Open May through September, Monday through Friday 10–4; Saturday, special exhibits; October through April, Tuesday, Thursday, and Saturday 10–4—but call to verify hours. This little white Cape was built in 1820 by George Fayerweather, the son of a slave from one of the plantations that stretched along the Rhode Island shore in the 17th century. It now houses the Fayerweather Craft Guild, which displays crafting techniques and sells the finished products.

Great Swamp Fight Monument, RI 2 (South County Trail), 1 mile south of the junction with RI 138 in West Kingston. Unfortunately the historic marker designating the road to the Great Swamp Fight Monument is old and weathered, so travelers seeking to find this memorial of the bloodiest battle ever fought on Rhode Island soil must keep a keen eye out for it. Reaching the monument requires a 0.25-mile trail walk through the swamp maple and oak to the obelisk. It's surrounded by stone markers that commemorate the troops of the Massachusetts, Plymouth Bay, and Connecticut Colonies, who fought in the December 19, 1675, battle.

Colonial forces attacked the winter camp that the Narragansetts had built here in the center of the swamp. The targets were the warriors of the Wampanoag chief King Philip, who was seeking to oust the settlers from Native American lands. Ordinarily the fort would have been inaccessible because of the swampy lands around it, but December 1675 was unusually cold, and the swamp had frozen. So despite a blizzard and relentless Native American arrows, the colonists managed to set fire to the fort. It turned out that it sheltered not only

Wampanoag warriors but also their wives and children. Mercilessly, the colonists slaughtered all who escaped the fire, and by nightfall virtually all the Native Americans within the fortification had been wiped out. The colonists' losses numbered 70 men dead and 150 wounded.

Hazard Memorial Hall (401-789-1555), Kingstown Road, Peace Dale. Call for hours. This gray granite 1891 Richardson Romanesque structure now houses the town library. It was built by the Hazards to be a community cultural center, and inside there are still reminders—like the plaster casts of Florentine singing boys—of when part of the structure was a music hall. Richly polished cypress, oak, and ash wainscoting are other highlights of the interior. On the lawn outside, the bronze relief *The Weaver* is the work of Daniel Chester French, whose *Abraham Lincoln* sits in the Lincoln Memorial. This is the only sculpture by French in Rhode Island.

Helme House (401-783-2195), 2587 Kingstown Road (RI 138), Kingston. Open Wednesday through Sunday 1–5, during shows. Now a gallery for the South County Art Association (see *Selective Shopping*), this inviting yellow-clapboard structure was a center of village activity in the 18th century, when it was two separate buildings, housing a saddler's shop and a lodging house.

Kingston Congregational Church (401-783-5330), Kingstown Road (RI 138), Kingston. This simple, 1820 Federal-style church with a three-story clock tower and steeple is open on Sunday for the 9:30 AM service.

Kingston Free Public Library (401-783-8254), Kingstown Road (RI 138), Kingston. Open Thursday noon–8, Friday and Saturday 10–5, but in summer, Saturday hours are 9–noon. Tan and gray and imposing with its cupola, this building served as the Kings County Courthouse when Rhode Island was a colony. Later, from 1776 until 1853, it was one of the five statehouses of Rhode Island. (The other communities where the legislators met, in addition to Providence and Newport, were East Greenwich and Bristol.) Since 1890 the courthouse, now completely renovated, has been a library.

In the small stone building beside it, Kingston's most notorious criminal, 18th-century silversmith Samuel Casey, was imprisoned for a time. After suffering severe financial losses, Casey tried to recoup by melting down his wife's spoons and making counterfeit money. He was tried and sentenced to be hanged. While he awaited execution in the little jailhouse, his friends managed to engineer his escape.

Kingston Inn, Kingstown Road (RI 138), Kingston. This white-clapboard former inn, which stands on the same side of the street as the church and diagonally across from the Kingston Free Public Library, now houses university students. But in the 18th century when it was constructed and the General Assembly was sometimes gathering in Kingston, it was a center of public activity. Legislators, travelers, and tradesmen all stopped to wet their whistles there in those tavern days. Later, after the railroad was built in 1837, it became a mail and stagecoach stop, and after that, when the citizen-soldiers of the militia held training exercises in Kingston, it was from its porch that the crowds viewed them. One day, when too many viewers were assembled there in high hilarity, the porch collapsed. The inn was reconstructed without a porch.

Kingston Railroad Station, Railroad Avenue, West Kingston. This picturesque, old-time railroad station—a famous Kingston landmark—has been restored and moved back to make way for high-speed Boston–New York trains. A bicycle path to Peace Dale starts here.

Pettaquamscutt Rock, Middlebridge Road, off Bridgetown Road near Tower Hill Road, South Kingstown. A bronze plaque marks the way to this rock that juts from the eastern slope of Tower Hill. This is where, in 1658, Native American sachems agreed to sell the land that today is South Kingstown, Narragansett, part of North Kingstown, and Exeter. From the top of the rock there are views out across the Narrow River to Jamestown, Newport, and lower Narragansett Bay.

Joe Reynolds' Tavern, Kingstown Road (RI 138), Kingston. Built in the mid-18th century, this was the principal village hostelry in the first half of the 19th century. Both Benjamin Franklin and George Washington are said to have been guests here, and a famous local story recounts how Franklin, arriving on a particularly cold night and not offered a seat by the fire, asked one of the servants to take some oysters to his weary, hungry horse for dinner. The whole assemblage in the tavern followed the houseboy to see the oyster-eating horse, giving Franklin plenty of room by the fire. The tavern is now a private residence.

The University of Rhode Island (401-874-1000), North Road, Kingston. At the corner by the Kingston Free Public Library, a sign points the way to the leafy campus of the state university. Founded in 1887 as a state agricultural school, the university still owns an extensive agricultural tract and the 1790 **Oliver Watson Farmhouse** (401-792-8296), which contains furnishings of

THE HISTORIC KINGSTON RAILROAD STATION

Kim Grant

1790–1840. Located on Watson Road, it is open by appointment. On the edge of the campus is the **International Athlete-Scholar Hall of Fame** (401-874-5088) with Olympic flags, pictures, and memorabilia housed in the impressive new Feinstein Building. Open 9–5 weekdays, and weekends by appointment.

SCENIC DRIVES **Curtis Corner Road.** Although development is beginning to scar this laurel-edged road from RI 108 in Peace Dale to Ministerial Road, it still retains considerable sylvan charm.

Middlebridge Road. From Tower Hill head east to reach this road, which crosses the Narrow River and wends its way through marshland rich in birds.

Ministerial Road. Controversy has been considerable about keeping this narrow, winding road—where rhododendron bloom in spring and native laurel in summer—from being widened. Local residents have won the battle, but the result is a road that, though lovely, is bumpy and must be traveled with care. All the same, it's worth it. The road begins at RI 138 in Kingston and ends at US 1 in Matunuck.

Saugutucket Road. This woodsy road, crossing rivers and streams, joins US 1 in Wakefield to RI 108.

Shannock Road. This winding country road passes an attractive horse farm; it starts at US 1 in South Kingstown and ends at RI 2 in Charlestown.

South Road. Stone walls edge this tranquil road from Scenic RI 1A in Wakefield to RI 138 in Kingston. It is, however, beginning to fall to developers.

✳ To Do

BALLOONING **Kingston Balloon Co.** (401-783-9386), 31 Fortin Road, Kingston. Sunrise balloon rides over the neighboring countryside.

BICYCLING **South County Bicycle Path.** Six miles of an eventual 8-mile path around the Great Swamp and the village of Peace Dale. Starting at the Kingston Railroad Station.

CANOEING AND KAYAKING In early spring, before the blackflies arrive, and again in late summer and fall after they have left, the Great Swamp is an inviting area for canoeists. The **State Division of Fish and Wildlife** (401-789-3094) in Wakefield can provide information.

Sand Shack and Sky Toys (401-789-2828), 797 Succotash Road, Wakefield. Kayak rentals. Also see *Canoeing* in "North Kingstown" for more rental companies.

FRESHWATER FISHING Largemouth bass, northern pike, catfish, and yellow perch swim in the freshwater ponds and rivers of the state; trout and salmon are stocked.

Barber's Pond, RI 2. There is a gravel boat ramp. The pond is stocked with trout annually on March 1 and cannot be fished until the second week in April.

Tucker's Pond on Tuckertown Road off Ministerial Road is equipped with a flat stone-and-gravel boat ramp; there is a 10-horsepower limit. Trout are stocked here in spring, so there is no fishing from March 1 until the second week in April.

Worden's Pond, Tuckertown Road off Ministerial Road. Fish for pickerel, bluegills, catfish, yellow perch, and bullheads. There is a flat stone-and-gravel boat ramp.

SALTWATER FISHING *Jessie M.* (914-229-8468; 1-888-537-8299), 134 Salt Pond Road, Wakefield. Flounder, shark, and tuna fishing along the Rhode Island shore from a 38-foot twin-diesel sportfisherman.

Old Salt Sport Fishing Charters (401-783-4805), 10 Amanco Street, Wakefield. Cod fishing in spring, summer, and fall off Cox Ridge, Block Island.

FOR FAMILIES ♪ **Old Mountain Lanes** (401-783-5511), 756 Kingstown Road, Wakefield. Bumper bowling.

GOLF **Laurel Lane Golf Course** (401-783-3844), Laurel Lane, West Kingston. This is an 18-hole par-71 course with a snack bar and lounge.

Rose Hill Golf Club (401-788-1088), 222 Rose Hill Road, South Kingstown. This rolling nine-hole par-3 course is made prettier with a little pond. Restaurant and snack bar.

SWIMMING **East Matunuck State Beach** (401-222-2632), Succotash Road, South Kingstown. Matunuck, as it's known, is one of the state's finer beaches.

TENNIS **Brusseau Park,** Succotash Road south of US 1, Wakefield. Old Mountain Field Courts, Kingstown Road, Wakefield (lit courts at night). **Tuckertown**

JETTY AT EAST MATUNUCK STATE BEACH

Kim Grant

Park Courts, Tuckertown Road, Wakefield. **Village Green Courts,** Kingstown Road, Peace Dale (lit at night). **West Kingston Park Courts,** Route 138 between the University of Rhode Island and RI 2.

The **South Kingstown Recreation Department** (401-789-9031) reserves all tennis courts, with preference given to local children.

✷ Green Space

Great Swamp Management Area (401-789-0281), off Liberty Lane, West Kingston. This is a 2,895-acre swampland of holly and rhododendron, white oak, red maple, tupelo, and pin oak. There are berries of all sorts and more than 5 miles of walking trails. Mink, raccoons, deer, foxes, ospreys, owls, black and wood ducks, pheasants, woodchucks, and grouse are among the swamp inhabitants, and there are both hunting and trout fishing in-season. A canoe is a good way to explore the area.

Observation Tower and **Hannah Robinson's Rock,** intersection of RI 138 and US 1. From the top of this 100-foot wooden observation tower, there is a fine view of the waters of lower Narragansett Bay and its surrounding countryside. One of South Kingstown's favorite legends concerns Hannah Robinson's Rock, which rises just adjacent. Rowland Robinson was a prospering 18th-century Narragansett planter whose lovely daughter fell in love with her French music teacher. When her father frowned on the romance, she eloped but was soon left high and dry by her husband. Her father refused to look after her in any way until she became seriously ill. Relenting finally, he agreed that she could come home to the family house just south of Saunderstown to die. On her way there, she asked the bearers carrying her litter to bring her to this site for a last look at her beloved Narragansett Bay.

THE TOWER NEAR HANNAH ROBINSON'S ROCK OFFERS SPLENDID VIEWS OF NARRAGANSETT BAY.

Kim Grant

Trustom Pond National Wildlife Refuge, off Matunuck Schoolhouse Road. The refuge protects more than 640 acres of fields, shrubs, and woods. In May the white blossoms of the shadbush and the beach plum are everywhere; least terns come to nest, and the songs of prairie warblers and bobolinks are in the air. Summer brings the fragrance of honeysuckle and sweet pepperbush and shorebird migration in August. In September the eyes can feast on the velvet orange and black of migrating monarch butterflies. From mid-September into early October the hawk migration dominates, and ruddy ducks and scaup begin to raft on the pond. Even in winter there is much for the visitor to see—gray foxes, river otters, raccoons, and here and there the nests of great horned owls. Observation platforms along the 3 miles of trails allow viewing without disturbing the birds.

✳ Lodging

INNS AND BED & BREAKFASTS

While you won't find as many inns and bed & breakfasts in South County as on Aquidneck, the number is growing. South County B&Bs, whether on the sea or in the country, have a quiet, calming charm of their own. About two dozen are members of a reservation service, **Bed & Breakfast Referral Service of South Coast Rhode Island** (1-800-853-7479), which will help you find a room if the inns are full.

The Admiral Dewey Inn (401-783-2090; www.admiraldeweyinn.com), 668 Matunuck Beach Road, South Kingstown 02879. ($$–$$$) Nicely restored early-1900s beach boardinghouse; 10 rooms with private bath. When the inn was first opened, rooms cost 50¢ a night; another 50¢ bought three meals per day. Classic laid-back South County living.

Brookside Manor (401-788-3527; www.brooksidemanor.net), 380-B, Post Road. Wakefield 02879. ($$$–$$$$) In the 17th century this was a simple saltbox farmhouse, but additions and refurbishing in the 1920s, '30s, and '60s transformed it into a manor house. Now it's a sumptuous five-room bed & breakfast with, among other attractions, an Ottoman suite whose ceiling has been painted to resemble a Turkish tent and a Cotswold room overlooking landscaped gardens, a brook, and a pond.

Stuffed French toast is one of the breakfast specialties.

🐾 ❧ **The King's Rose** (401-783-5222; www.virtualcities.com), 1747 Mooresfield Road (RI 138), South Kingstown 02879. ($$$) The King's Rose is a large, old-fashioned house in a lovely garden. It offers a welcoming host and hostess, tennis courts, five rooms, a willingness to take children over 7 (and pets off-season, though guests should be aware that there are resident cats), and a full breakfast. Most baths are private.

🐾 **Larchwood Inn** (401-783-5454; www.larchwoodinn.com), 521 Main Street, Wakefield 02879. ($$–$$$) A pleasantly appointed country inn surrounded by the loveliest of trees, which make fall—when the elms and beeches are golden, the maples crimson—a fine time for a visit. The 12 rooms are homey. Most have a private bath, although a few share a bath. The dining room serves breakfast, lunch, and dinner, and there is a cocktail lounge. The six-room bed & breakfast across the street, **Holly House,** is run by the same owners.

Silver Lake Cottage Bed & Breakfast Inn (401-782-3745), 361 Woodruff Avenue, Wakefield. ($$$$) Built in the early 1900s, this elegant lakefront "cottage" was the summer home of the Welch family, renowned for their grape juice. Painstakingly restored, there are five rooms—the Wiamea with a Hawaiian touch; the Huntington Sound with a flavor of Bermuda in its antique wicker furnishings; the Marne decorated in French fabrics; the Narragansett Bay with a nautical flair; and the exotic Far East. There are no TVs or radios, but they're hardly needed with the garden and water view from the cottage's porches.

CAMPGROUNDS **Long Cove Marina Family Campsites** (401-783-4902), off Point Judith Road (RI 108), 1 mile south of the intersection of US 1 and RI 128, Narragansett 02882. Open May through October 15. Water, electricity, a dumping station, hot showers, flush toilets, picnic tables, and a boat ramp serve 25 tent and 155 trailer sites.

Wakamo Park Resort (401-783-6688), 697 Succotash Road, East Matunuck 02879. Open April 15 through October 15. There are 30 trailer sites here with electricity and sewers, a gift store, dock space, canoes to rent, a game room, and planned activities.

Worden's Pond Family Campground (401-789-9113), 416A, Worden's Pond Road, Wakefield 02879. Open May through October 15. This campground offers 75 tent and 125 trailer sites. Water, electric hook-ups (but not at campsites), toilets, showers, dumping station, and play area and equipment.

✴ Where to Eat

DINING OUT 🦞 🗘 ᕦ **Hanson's Landing** (401-782-0210), 210 Salt Pond Road, Wakefield. ($–$$) Open year-round for dinner; in spring, summer, and fall (and sometimes winter) for lunch as well. Call for winter hours. The view of Salt Pond and the

Wakefield Marina from this restaurant couldn't be better, and items from the sea play a key role in the menu. There are not only appetizers like littlenecks and clams casino, but also battered fish bites, Greek calamari sautéed with spinach and olives, and a lobster cheesecake made with three kinds of cheese. The lunchtime menu includes lobster bisque and pesto shrimp sandwiches as well as regulation hamburger and hot dog fare. At dinner there's a wide choice of meat, fish, and chicken dishes. A good-sized bar looks out over the pond and has a rather pubby atmosphere. Outside, there's a splendid deck for casual dining.

ᕦ **Larchwood Inn** (401-783-5454), 521 Main Street, Wakefield. ($$) Open year-round for breakfast, lunch, and dinner. Early-bird specials are available weeknights 5–6:30. Prime rib is the specialty at this pretty inn restaurant. Since Rhode Island is the Ocean State, it is appropriate that after the roast beef the menu emphasizes seafood. Day or evening, there is light fare, too—like spinach salads, quiche, and open-faced roast beef sandwiches. Chicken and lobster pies are favorites.

🗘 ᕦ **Pinelli's Cucina and Twist** (401-789-5300), 2095 Kingstown Road (RI 108), South Kingstown. ($–$$) Open nightly for dinner. Veal dishes and such creative pizzas as one topped with grilled chicken, fresh spinach, roasted red peppers, and Gorgonzola, mozzarella, and Romano cheeses are among the specialties at this big, casual, fine-for-the-whole-family restaurant.

ᕦ **The Pump House** (401-789-4944), RI 108, Peace Dale. ($$–$$$) Open Tuesday through Friday 11–11, Saturday 4–11, Sunday noon–9, Monday 4–9. In 1888 this stone structure was built as a pumping station for the water system of Peace Dale, Narragansett, and Wakefield. Today it's a friendly dining place where baked stuffed shrimp and the catch of the day are highlighted on the menu. There are also several steak and chicken dishes. All entrées are accompanied by soup or salad from the salad bar as well as potato and vegetable.

EATING OUT Camden's Restaurant and Coffee Shop (401-782-2328), Kingstown Road (RI 108), Wakefield. ($–$$) Open daily for breakfast, lunch, and dinner. Here you're dining right at Old Mountain Lanes Bowling Alley, where you can work up an appetite rolling a string or two before ordering a boiled lobster or plateful of steamers, clam cakes or fried calamari, prime rib or steak. The dining is more formal in the restaurant than in the coffee shop, and prices are only a dollar or so more.

Cap'n Jack's (401-789-4556), 708 Succotash Road, Wakefield. ($$) Open daily, except Monday, for lunch and dinner. The denizens of the deep are the specialty of this waterfront restaurant overlooking Point Judith Pond. For homespun American tastes there are fisherman's and seafood platters, and for the more adventuresome such Italian seafood specialties as squid, snails, and mussels in marinara sauce. Clam or lobster rolls and fried clam strips are on the menu, too. For those who don't like fish, veal, chicken, beef, and pasta entrées are offered, of course.

Caylilly's Bistro (401-789-0914), 333 Main Street, Wakefield. ($$) Open Tuesday through Saturday for lunch and dinner and Sunday for brunch. For the hungry at lunchtime, there's such satisfying fare as lobster and avocado salad, littlenecks and chorizo, or an open-faced steak sandwich with crimini mushrooms. Evenings, fresh fish and shellfish are ever-popular.

🦞 ✒ ♿ **Chelo's of South County** (401-783-0008), RI 108, 515 Kingstown Road, Wakefield. ($) Open weekdays 11:30–10, or 11 Friday and Saturday; Sunday 8:30–10. This isn't the place to go for quiet dining. It's busy and noisy, but the prices are right for such Rhode Island favorites as fish-and-chips, clam cakes, and chowder. Burgers, chicken any way you like it, and Italian dishes are always on the menu.

✒ **Giro's Spaghetti House** (401-783-7865), 501 High Street, Peace Dale. ($–$$) Open daily for lunch and dinner. Giro's is comfortable and not grand. It's been around for a long time, and URI alums become quite nostalgic about it. In addition to the Italian dishes, Giro's prides itself on the twin lobster entrée. Fine for the family.

International Pockets Cafe (401-782-2720), 99 Fortin Road, University of Rhode Island campus, Kingston. ($–$$) Open daily 10–10. An energetic young Syrian American and an equally energetic Lebanese American have teamed up to run this fast-food operation that serves such dishes as hummus, gyros, falafel, spinach pies, stuffed grape leaves, tabbouleh, and beef kebabs. The ingredients couldn't be fresher nor the unsquelchable owners more entertaining. The paper-thin-crusted baklava comes from the oven of one of the owners' mothers. Unpretentious but with food that is oh, so delicious.

✐ **Italian Village Restaurant** (401-783-3777), 195 Main Street, Wakefield. ($–$$) Open for lunch and dinner weekdays; on weekends open for brunch as well, 8–noon. Plentiful portions of American-style Italian food and the best pizza around, all at reasonable prices, make this an attractive family restaurant.

The Mews Tavern (401-783-9370), 456 Main Street, Wakefield. ($–$$) Open daily 11 AM–1 AM. There's never a dull moment in this sprawling tavern-restaurant where mixed drinks, wine, and appetizers are served in a sophisticated setting upstairs; there are 69 draft beers on tap in the tavern and wood-fired pizza in the Pizza Bar. In the center of the spacious Tree Room, a giant light-festooned beech tree spreads its limbs. The burgers and fried squid are some of the best around if you're not watching your waistline.

✳ **Entertainment**

Theatre-by-the-Sea (401-782-8587), 364 Card Pond Road, Matunuck. For more than 60 years this summer theater, through which sea breezes blow, has been offering the best of Broadway to vacation audiences from the end of May through Labor Day. As this book went to press, however, its future was uncertain. The old weathered-shingled theater building itself is on the National Register of Historic Places.

University of Rhode Island (401-874-2431), South Kingstown. The university offers frequent concerts (see *Special Events*).

✳ **Selective Shopping**

ANTIQUES SHOP **Dove and Distaff** (401-783-5714), 383 Main Street,

Wakefield. Open Monday through Friday 8–5, Saturday by prior request. Genuine antiques rather than collectibles. Furniture restoration and reupholstery.

ART GALLERIES **The Courthouse Center for the Arts** (401-782-1018), 3501 Kingston Road (RI 138), West Kingston. Call for hours. At this gray granite early-20th-century former Washington County Courthouse, the South County Center for the Arts offers art exhibits, community theater, and concerts. Handicrafts and art are sold at an artisan's shop.

Hera Gallery (401-789-1488), 327 Main Street, Wakefield. Open year-round, Wednesday through Saturday. This lively, modern art gallery displays the work of Rhode Island— and other—artists.

South County Art Association (401-783-2195), 2587 Kingstown Road (RI 138), Kingston. Located in the historic Helme House (see *To See*) and open occasionally for exhibitions by area artists.

ARTISANS **Thomas Ladd Pottery** (401-782-0050), 352 High Street, Wakefield. Salt-glazed stoneware and Raku. Open Tuesday through Saturday 9–6.

Peter Pots Pottery (401-783-2350), off RI 138, down Dugway Bridge Road, Usquepaugh, South Kingstown. Open Monday through Saturday 10–4, Sunday 1–4. Since 1948 Peter Pots Pottery has created dishes in muted tones with subtle designs, making it a popular spot for gift buying in Rhode Island. The only problem is finding it, down a road that is exceptionally lovely in fall.

BOOKSTORES **Rhode Island Book Co., Inc.** (401-789-8530), 99 Fortin Road, Kingston. Reference and instructional books, including a wide selection of computer manuals.

University of Rhode Island Bookstore (401-874-2721), Memorial Union Building, URI campus, Kingston. Textbooks and general books.

Walden Books at the Wakefield Mall (401-783-0554), 160 Old Tower Hill Road, Wakefield. Open daily including Sunday afternoons.

SPECIAL SHOPS **Bird Watchers' Nature View** (401-789-8020; 1-800-270-8020), 484 Main Street, Wakefield. Open daily, though the hours vary. There's everything from binoculars, birdseed, bird and guidebooks, and bird feeders to singing flannel bluebirds and cardinals in this charming little shop for ornithologists.

Folk Art Quilts (401-789-5985), 344 Main Street, Wakefield. Open Tuesday through Saturday 10–5. Everything the quilter needs—fabric, patterns, thread, lessons, and expert advice.

The Glass Station (401-788-2500), 318 Main Street, Wakefield. Open 7 days a week in summer, every day but Sunday in winter, with glassblowing on the premises. It may be of vases or bowls or drinking glasses, jewelry or Christmas tree ornaments. It's wise, however, to call ahead to find out what time the glassblowing is being done.

Kenyon Grist Mill Store (401-783-4054), off RI 138, Usquepaugh, South Kingstown. Open 9–5 weekdays in summer; after Labor Day, weekends noon–5. Flour and grain of all sorts,

mixes for Rhode Island clam cakes, cookie cutters, and fine soaps are all here in this picturesque little shop across from the Kenyon Grist Mill.

Purple Cow (401-789-2389), 205 Main Street, Wakefield. Handmade jewelry, pottery, whimsical gift items.

Saywell's (401-783-0630), 344 Main Street, Wakefield. Open year-round, Monday through Saturday 9–5, and most Sundays until 2. The work of some 300 craftspeople, including many from Rhode Island, is sold here. In addition there are the usual souvenirs and a few books, but all have been selected with good taste.

Sweenor's Chocolates (401-783-4433; 1-800-834-3123), 21 Charles Street, Wakefield. For more than 50 years three generations of Sweenors have been making delectable chocolates, almond brittle, and fudge here. On the first Sunday in December there is always an open house noon–5. Candy making—in particular candy cane making—can be watched in the kitchen. Other outlets are in Charlestown and Cranston.

Zero Wampum (401-789-7172), 161 Old Tower Road, Wakefield. Open weekdays 10–8, Saturday until 5, and Sunday noon–5. There's a little bit of everything in this cheerful gift shop—colorful ceramics and glass, Japanese paper lanterns, handcrafted Rhode Island jewelry, note cards.

FARM STANDS **Carpenter's Farm** (401-783-7550), North and South Matunuck Beach Road, Wakefield. Open June through October, daily 9–6.

John and Cindy's Harvest Acres Farm (401-789-8752), 425 Kingstown

Road, West Kingston. Open May through December, daily 10–6.

✳ Special Events

April: **Spring Concerts** (401-874-2431), Fine Arts Center, URI, Kingston. **Wakefield Mall Spring Arts and Crafts Show** (401-943-3808). **Richmond Grange Roast Beef Dinner** (401-783-8665), West Kingston. **South County Chamber Singers Concert** (401-782-6379), Fine Arts Recital Hall, URI, Kingston.

May: **Spring Concerts** (401-874-2431), URI Symphony Orchestra, Fine Arts Center, URI. **Arbutus Garden Annual Plant Sale,** South Kingstown American Legion Hall, Wakefield. **Kingston Village Fair,** Kingston Congregational Church and Fayerweather Craft Center, Kingston. **Memorial Day Parade,** Wakefield.

May–October: **Farmer's market** (401-789-1388), held at the University of Rhode Island, off RI 138, Saturday 9–noon, on Flagg Road near Keaney Gymnasium. A **farmer's market** (401-789-1388) is also held in Marina Park off Route 1, South Kingstown, Tuesday 3–6.

June: **Summer Chamber Music Festival** (401-789-0665), Fine Arts Recital Hall, URI, Kingston. **Laurel Day Festival,** Ministerial Road, Kingston. **Striped Bass Tournament**

(401-783-7766), Snug Harbor Marina, Wakefield.

July: **Fourth of July Fireworks,** Wakefield. **Kingston Chamber Music Festival** (401-789-0665), Fine Arts Recital Hall, URI. **South County Hot Air Balloon Festival,** Athletic Field, URI, Kingston. **Snug Harbor Shark Tournament** (401-783-7766), Snug Harbor Marina, Wakefield. **Block parties** of music, singing, and vendors on Main Street in Wakefield.

July–August: **Neighborhood Guild Concerts** (401-789-9301), village green, Peace Dale.

September: **Firemen's Memorial Parade** (401-783-1214), Peace Dale. **Narragansett Great Swamp memorial service** (401-364-1100), at the Great Swamp, 1 mile south of RI 138 in West Kingston. **Jonnycake Storytelling Festival** (401-789-9301), village green, Peace Dale.

October: **Block parties** with music, dancing, and vendors along Main Street in Wakefield. **Snug Harbor Striped Bass and Bluefish Tournament** (401-783-7766), Snug Harbor Marina, Wakefield.

November: **Richmond Grange Roast Beef Dinner** (401-783-8665), West Kingston.

December: **Tree lighting and carol sing,** village green, Peace Dale.

NORTH KINGSTOWN AREA

North Kingstown, on the west side of Narragansett Bay, has a most happy situation, stretching as it does along the Narragansett Bay shore. Woodsy roads wind inland past amber ponds. In North Kingstown's principal village of Wickford, yellow- and white-clapboard 18th-century houses line Main Street and the narrow waterfront lanes. Its cozy harbor of working quahog boats still looks much as it did in the late 1800s. Indeed, much of Wickford remains as it was then, which is what makes it a prime tourist attraction.

A mile and a half north of Wickford at Cocumscussoc—"Marked Rock"—Rhode Island founder Roger Williams was given a tract of land by the Narragansett sachem Canonicus, where he built a trading post. It was in a garrison near the trading post that, after Williams's return to England and the souring of relations with the Native Americans, soldiers of the Massachusetts and Plymouth Bay Colonies and of Connecticut, with a handful of Rhode Islanders, laid plans for the Great Swamp Fight.

The abutting rural townships of Exeter and West Greenwich hold three-quarters of the Arcadia Wildlife Management Area. With 13,817 acres of woods, ponds, rivers, and streams, crisscrossed by dirt roads, it is the state's largest area of its kind and one of the most attractive to hunters, trout fishers, and birders.

GUIDANCE **South County Tourism Council, Inc.** (401-789-4422; 1-800-548-4662), 4808 Tower Hill Road (US 1), Wakefield. Situated in the Oliver Stedman Government Center building on the right side of US 1 heading north. Open weekdays 9–5, as well as Saturday and Sunday 9–3 in summer.

North Kingstown Chamber of Commerce (401-295-5566), 245 Tower Hill Road, Wickford. Monday through Friday 9–5.

GETTING THERE *By train or bus:* You can take **Amtrak** (1-800-USA-RAIL) to Providence and a **Rhode Island Public Transport Authority** (RIPTA; 40-781-9400) bus from Providence to Wickford. Exeter and West Greenwich, however, are accessible only by car. Even to Wickford, bus service is infrequent, and there is no local taxi company. Automobile is distinctly the best way to see this southern part of the state.

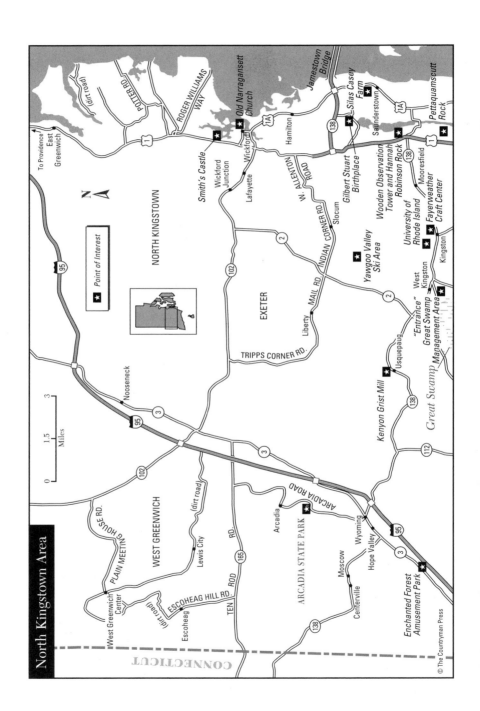

North Kingstown Area

© The Countryman Press

South County Hospital (401-762-8000), 100 Kenyon Avenue, Wakefield. Emergency room as well as regular hospital care to the entire southern portion of the state.

✳ Villages

Wickford. In this pretty, 1-by-1.5-mile village, there are believed to be more fine examples of 18th-century architecture than in any other community of its size in New England. Colonial and Federal houses with fanlights over the doors, shiny black shutters, and gleaming brass door knockers line Main Street. More of the same is found on streets and lanes with names like *Washington, Fountain, Friend, Gold, Bay,* and *Church.* Tree-lined Pleasant Street, bordering the harbor, offers a blend of the village's earliest homes and 1890s shingle-style summer "cottages" from the days when Wickford was a summer resort. Where West Main Street meets Brown Street—today's commercial center—rise two 19th-century business blocks: the redbrick **Avis Block,** with its elaborate facade, and the brick, stone, and terra-cotta 1890s **Gregory Block.**

Wickford has largely been spared the encroachment of development over the centuries, though the village has not always been so happy about it. In pre–Revolutionary War days, when it thrived on trade with the West Indies, it was a bustling place. But when the Revolution closed down the bay to commercial traffic, it languished gloomily. After the war, a revival of trade lasted until 1825. Then came the era of steam vessels and trains, and Wickford was bypassed by both. Nowadays residents recognize that it was this very stagnation that preserved the old-fashioned streets and lanes that visitors so enjoy.

✳ To See

MUSEUMS Quonset Aviation Museum (401-294-9540), 488 Eccleston Avenue, Quonset Point. Open Friday, Saturday, and Sunday 10–3. A Russian MIG-17, a TBM Avenger, an A-4 Skyhawk, and an F6F-5 Hellcat are among the airplanes and airplane memorabilia housed and displayed here. $5 admission for adults.

Tomaquag Indian Memorial Museum (401-539-2786; 401-539-7213), 300 Summit Road, Exeter, at Dovecrest Cultural Center. Open Wednesday and Sunday 1–3 or by appointment. Small admission fee. Pottery, beadwork, and baskets of northeastern Native Americans are on display in this little museum.

HISTORIC SITES Silas Casey Farm (401-295-1030), Scenic RI 1A north of Ferry Road, Saunderstown. Open June through October 15, Saturday 11–5. Draft horses, cows, sheep, and chickens enjoy the barns and the 330 acres that surround this early-18th-century farm. There are also 9 acres of vegetables, fruits, and flowers. The farmhouse itself is appropriately furnished in period pieces. In Revolutionary days, when a few colonial militias spent nights here, the British learned of their presence and fired on the house. A musket-ball hole can still be seen in the parlor door.

Old Narragansett Church (Old St. Paul's; 401-294-4357), 60 Church Lane, Wickford. Open for tours in summer, Thursday through Monday 11–4. Off-season by appointment. Constructed in 1707, this simple white structure with gracefully arched windows flanking its double doors is the oldest Episcopal church north of Virginia. Its restored 1680 organ is the oldest church organ in use in North America today.

The approach to Old Narragansett Church is down the Greenway from May Street, a flagstone walk into which the names of many past church pastors and benefactors have been cut. The church is noted for its box pews, an upstairs gallery for slaves from the plantations, the silver communion service and baptismal font presented to St. Paul's by Queen Anne, and its wineglass pulpit, which was enlarged by pre-Revolutionary wardens to accommodate the girth of one of its preachers.

It was in the silver baptismal font that the infant Gilbert Stuart, the renowned portrait painter famous for his paintings of George Washington, was christened. Originally the church stood about 7 miles south of town on Shermantown Road. In 1800 it was moved to its present site so that its parishioners would not have to travel so far. Since this was a controversial idea in those days and many were in opposition, 24 yoke of cattle hauled it into the village on a dark January night when the snow was crusted with ice and when, it was hoped, parishioners opposed to the move were unlikely to be out. Today **New St. Paul's,** built in 1847 in Romanesque Revival style at 76 Main Street, is used primarily for winter services.

Smith's Castle (401-294-3521), US 1 (Post Road), Wickford. Open June, July, and August, Thursday through Monday noon–4; May, September, and October,

A REVOLUTIONARY-ERA MUSKET-BALL HOLE IS STILL VISIBLE INSIDE THE SILAS CASEY FARM.

Kim Grant

Kim Grant

THE PAINTER GILBERT STUART LIVED IN THIS FARMSTEAD UNTIL HE WAS SEVEN YEARS OLD.

Friday through Sunday noon–4. On spacious grounds above Mill Pond stands the red-clapboard plantation house called Smith's Castle. This impressive house replaced a garrison trading post that Richard Smith had built about 1640 on land sold to him by Roger Williams. It was in the original structure that in December 1675 the colonists planned their attack against King Philip of the Wampanoags, who was seeking to drive the settlers out of the area. After the bloody battle, the weary soldiers returned to Smith's Castle carrying their dead and dying. A tablet at the site marks the common grave of the men who were killed.

Within a few months of the battle, the Native Americans set fire to the hated garrison, damaging it severely. The base of the present structure was erected two years later, using materials from the damaged building. Smith's great-great-grand-nephew, Daniel Updike, eventually inherited the three-room house. A lawyer and a socialite, he needed more room for entertaining and built on extensively.

Smith's Castle is the only surviving example of the plantation houses that once existed all across the southern part of the state.

Gilbert Stuart Birthplace (401-294-3001), 815 Gilbert Stuart Road, Saunders-town. Open April through October, Thursday through Monday 11–4. Small admission fee. In this barn-red, hip-roofed building constructed by Gilbert Stuart Sr. to be a snuff mill, the painter Gilbert Stuart lived until he was 7. The elder Stuart, an able millwright, had come to Rhode Island at the urging of a Scots-born Newport physician, James Moffat. Tobacco was growing well in the area in those days, and Moffat and Stuart hoped that construction of a snuff mill would make them wealthy. Unfortunately the enterprise was not a success, and the Stuarts left Saunderstown for Newport.

Though furnishings in the house are of the Stuart period, they were not there during the painter's lifetime, and the house contains only a reproduction of one of the 111 portraits that Stuart painted of the first president. A genuine child-hood drawing of a dog may be seen in Newport, however.

Wickford Town Dock, foot of Main Street. Broad-beamed Rhode Island qua-hog skiffs vie for attention with sleek sailing yachts off this dock, where small boys fish and seagulls wheel. Nowadays this is a tranquil spot for watching small boats come and go, but both before and after the Revolution, Wickford Harbor was a bustling waterfront. The village thrived on trade with the West Indies, sending cargoes of grain, pork, beef, geese, turkeys, horses, and renowned Rhode Island cheese from the plantations of South County to the Caribbean, returning with sugar and spices, molasses and tobacco.

SCENIC DRIVES An interesting excursion off Scenic RI 1A in Saunderstown is down **Ferry** and **South Ferry Roads,** affording an attractive view of Narra-gansett Bay, then along Old Boston Neck Road, site of several plantation houses including the 18th-century Hannah Robinson House.

Annaquatucket Road off Scenic RI 1A in Saunderstown edges pretty Annaquatucket Pond, with its swans and wild ducks.

Gilbert Stuart Road between Scenic RI 1A and US 1 in Saunderstown dips down through deciduous and piney woods. It passes ponds and the Gilbert Stu-art Birthplace, then crosses streams and climbs hills before reaching US 1.

Both **Mail Road** and **Liberty Road** off RI 2 in Exeter are routes through the typical rural Rhode Island countryside of woods, streams, and ponds.

Shermantown Road, an extension of Gilbert Stuart Road, is, similarly, a wind-ing, wooded, country road, though houses are springing up along it. It was on

A GIANT SCARECROW OFF RI 2

Kim Grant

Shermantown Road that Old St. Paul's stood before it was spirited away (see *Historic Sites*).

South County Trail (RI 2) begins in Exeter and continues through Charlestown to the Connecticut border, passing through woods and nurseries and crossing farmland.

Ten Rod Road (RI 165) meanders from RI 3 to the Connecticut border through the Arcadia Wildlife Management Area's deciduous and white pine woods. Many dirt side roads penetrate deeper into the woodland, past the rivers, ponds, scrub, wetlands, and swamps that are part of the preserve.

Waldron Avenue off Scenic RI 1A in Hamilton offers a panoramic view of the bay, including Fox Island and several rocks to its south that are visited by harbor seals in winter.

✳ To Do

BICYCLING **Wilson Park,** West Main Street, Wickford. This short but pleasant bike path winds through the underbrush along Wickford Harbor.

CANOEING AND KAYAKING **Kayak Centre** (401-295-4400), 9 Phillips Street, Wickford. Canoe and kayak rentals and guided trips.

Quaker Lane Bait & Tackle (401-294-9642), 4019 Quaker Lane, North Kingstown. Canoe and kayak rentals.

FISHING **Beach Pond,** Exeter. Boat launching is possible on the Connecticut side of the pond. Fish for yellow perch, pumpkinseed sunfish, black crappies, largemouth and smallmouth bass, and brook, brown, and rainbow trout, among others.

Breakheart Pond, Arcadia Management Area, Exeter. Brook, brown, and rainbow trout, chain pickerel, largemouth bass, yellow perch, bluegill sunfish, and more.

FOR FAMILIES 🐾 **Yawgoo Valley Water Park** (401-295-5366), Yawgoo Valley Road, Exeter. Open June through Labor Day, with a swimming pool and a kiddie pool as well as water slides.

GOLF **Exeter Country Club** (401-295-1178), Victory Highway, Exeter. This is an 18-hole course with flat terrain and ponds, a covered bridge, plus breakfast and luncheon facilities and golf carts.

North Kingstown Municipal Golf Course (401-294-4051), Callahan Road, Quonset, on the former naval air base. Eighteen holes, flat terrain. Golf carts, hand carts, and golf supplies are available. There is a restaurant at the 19th hole.

Rolling Greens Golf Course (401-294-9859), 1625 Ten Rod Road, North Kingstown. Nine holes, well-maintained hilly terrain, a pond, and a clubhouse serving largely sandwiches and drinks. Golf carts and hand carts.

Woodland Greens Golf Course (401-294-2872), 655 Old Baptist Road, North Kingstown. Nine holes, mixed terrain. Golf carts, hand carts, and a bar and grill.

HIKING **Arcadia Wildlife Management Area,** West Greenwich and Exeter. There are innumerable hiking trails and gravel roads through woods and scrub, past ponds, marshes, and wetlands, and along the Wood River. Among the most popular is the 3.5-mile **Arcadia Trail,** which is maintained by the Appalachian Mountain Club (AMC) and links Dawley State Park in Exeter to the John E. Hudson Trail.

The **Mount Tom Trail,** also cared for by the AMC, passes through the Arcadia Management Area in West Greenwich. It is reached from RI 165 via the **John B. Hudson Trail.** More than 5 miles long, the Mount Tom Trail travels through a pine forest and along the banks of the Wood River, climbing ridges and over-looking cliffs. The **Breakheart Trail** is another 5-mile-long AMC trail beginning off RI 165, with the entrance into Arcadia on Bliven Road. Here and there stone walls rest among the pine and oak, maple and birch.

The **Tippecansett Trail** links Beach Pond State Park with Yawgoo Pond in Exeter. This AMC-maintained trail begins off RI 138 about 5 miles west of exit 3 from I-95. The trail runs back and forth across the Connecticut line through farmland and forest.

HORSEBACK RIDING **Legrand G. Reynolds Horsemen's Camping Area** (401-539-2356; 401-277-1157), Escoheag Hill Road, Exeter. Open May through September. This is a campground for horseback riders, equipped with picnic tables, fireplaces, a horse-show ring, a corral, water, pit toilets, and riding trails.

Stepping Stone Ranch (401-397-3725), 201 Esccoheag Road, Exeter. Riding lessons, trail rides, lunch, overnight and lobster bake rides.

Tower Hill Equestrian Center (401-294-8190), US 1, Tower Hill Road, North Kingstown. Trail rides, pony rides, hayrides, and riding lessons year-round. Indoor and outdoor rings, cross-country course.

SKIING ✧ **Yawgoo Valley Ski Area** (401-295-5366), Yawgoo Valley Road, Exeter. Open December through March 15, weekdays 10–10, Saturday 8:30–10, Sunday 8:30–5. This is Rhode Island's only ski area. The longest of the 12 ski trails is 2,300 feet; the greatest vertical drop is 245 feet. Two double chairlifts and a surface tow serve the trails; half-day, full-day, and evening tickets are sold; and skis may be rented. Tubing down a slope on the ice is also offered for those 4 and up.

TENNIS **Wilson Park,** West Main Street, Wickford. Two outdoor courts available on a first-come, first-served basis.

✳ Green Space

Both West Greenwich and Exeter are largely rural, with endless expanses of green space. Listed below is only a sampling of the most frequented. Information about other areas available for public enjoyment may be obtained from the state's **Department of Environmental Management, Division of Fish and Wildlife,** at 401-789-0281.

Arcadia Wildlife Management Area (401-789-3094; 401-539-7117). The main entrance to this 13,817-acre wildlife preserve—the state's largest—is off RI 165 in Exeter. It offers endless opportunities to the outdoor enthusiast, birder, hunter, angler, hiker, and bicyclist. Its many trails (see *Hiking*) and gravel roads crisscross the preserve, providing access to the woods and scrub growth, ponds, marshes, wetlands, and the trout-filled Wood River. Pheasants and bobwhites are stocked by the state for hunting, and there are also ruffed grouse and wild turkeys, white-tailed deer, cottontail rabbits, and snowshoe hares. Frosty Hollow Pond is stocked with trout for youngsters under 14.

Big River Wildlife Management Area, West Greenwich. This wildlife refuge protects 8,319 acres of forest, wetlands, and agricultural lands. There is access from Division Street and RI 3 (Nooseneck Hill Road), principally for hikers, cyclists, hunters, birders, and anglers, with many roads closed off to vehicles. Both stocked and native trout abound in the Big River, and in addition to ruffed grouse and wild turkeys, there is a variety of waterfowl.

Wickaboxet Wildlife Management Area, Plain Meeting House Road, West Greenwich. Songbirds and birds of prey populate this woodland area, which is rich in upland game such as deer and rabbits as well as other wildlife such as coyotes, foxes, and raccoons.

Wilson Park, West Shore Road, Wickford. This park offers both bicycle and walking trails, a boat ramp, picnic tables, outdoor tennis courts, and a playground.

✻ Lodging

BED & BREAKFASTS **Crosswinds Little Farm** (401-294-3031; 1-888-349-3105; www.crosswindsbnb.com), 800 Boston Neck Road, North Kingstown 02852. ($–$$) Three homey rooms with private bath in a Federal-style farmhouse with a porch and pretty gardens.

Mount Maple of Wickford (401-295-4373), 730 Annaquatucket Road, North Kingstown 02852. ($$) In this farmhouse outside Wickford are three sunny, air-conditioned rooms with private bath.

The Haddie Pierce House (401-294-7674; wwwhaddiepierce.com), 146 Boston Neck Road, Wickford 02852. ($$$) This spacious Victorian house sits virtually in the heart of waterfront Wickford village. It has three rooms with a shared bath and a fourth with a private bath. The first-floor double parlor is furnished with

period antiques, and there's a front porch for rocking on warm summer days.

MOTEL ♿ **Hamilton Village Inn** (401-295-0700), 642 Boston Neck Road, North Kingstown 02852. ($–$$) This 36-room motel—open April through Christmas—has its own restaurant, open for breakfast, lunch, and dinner, just across from the motel itself.

CAMPGROUNDS **Oak Embers Campground** (401-397-4042), Escoheag Hill Road, West Greenwich 02817. Open February through December. There are 60 sites at this privately owned campground, with freshwater fishing, swimming, boating, and horseback riding nearby. Facilities include water and electric hook-ups, hot showers, a swimming pool, picnic tables, a game room, restrooms, a dumping station, a laundry, and a grocery store.

☻ **Peeper Pond Campground** (401-294-5540), Liberty Road, Exeter 02822. Open May through September. This privately owned campground has a total of 31 sites— wooded tent and trailer sites, tent decks, pull-throughs, and primitive sites. There are water and electric hook-ups, a dumping station, flush toilets, hot showers, fireplaces, and a camp store. Pets are allowed on a leash.

Also see Legrand G. Reynolds Horsemen's Camping Area under *To Do*.

✳ Where to Eat

DINING OUT ☻ ♿ **HOOFFIN-FEATHERS** (401-294-2727), 1065 Tower Hill Road, North Kingstown. ($–$$) Open Tuesday and Wednesday for dinner, Thursday through Sunday for lunch and dinner. Shrimp, scrod, scallops, roast duck in port wine sauce, and prime rib are regular offerings at this architecturally interesting restored old stone barn. Meals are prepared and presented with care. Good value.

♿ **Seaport Tavern** (401-294-5771), 16 West Main Street, Wickford. ($–$$) Open daily for lunch and dinner. There's a Mediterranean emphasis at this casual restaurant with a waterfront deck for summer dining, but New England clam chowder, lobster rolls, and a lobster salad plate are also on the menu.

EATING OUT **Brown Street Deli** (401-294-1150), 85 Brown Street, Wickford. ($) Open daily 7–6, except Friday when closing time is 8. Locals find this a cozy, comfortable place for breakfast, coffee, or lunch, and particularly acclaim the soups.

The Wickford Gourmet (401-295-8190), 21 West Main Street, Wickford. ($$) Open for breakfast, lunch, and a teatime sandwich (until 6 PM). Seating is limited, but the fare is delicious at this gourmet take-out that specializes in coffee, muffins, and scones. Cheeses of the world are sold here and can go into the imaginative sandwiches prepared on fresh breads.

SNACKS **Allie's Doughnuts** (401-295-8036), 3661 Quaker Lane (RI 2), North Kingstown. ($) Open Monday through Friday 5–5, Saturday and Sunday 6–1. From all across the state, Rhode Islanders make expeditions here for the fresh old-fashioned homemade doughnuts ($5.40 a dozen), which are a far cry from ordinary chain-store doughnuts. There's take-out coffee, too, but no place to sit down.

The Inside Scoop (401-294-0091), 30 Ten Rod Road, Wickford. Open March to mid-October, noon–9. ($) Homemade ice cream in such offbeat flavors as pumpkin, apple and blueberry pie, and ginger—along with all the old favorites, of course.

Sugar Shack (401-667-0529), 11 Brown Street, Wickford. ($) Open daily 10:30–5:30, except closed winter Mondays. Gelato and sorbeto from Milan, Italy, are refreshing delights on a sultry summer's day. In fall and winter the fudge, the chocolates in nautical shapes, and the candy-jar licorice in this cozy little shop are energizing for walkers.

✳ Selective Shopping

ANTIQUES SHOPS **Mentor Antiques** (401-294-9412), 7512 Post Road (US 1), North Kingstown. English and American furniture of the past.

Wickford Antique Center (401-295-2966), 16 Main Street, Wickford. Furniture, paintings, and bric-a-brac.

BOOKSTORE **Bassett Books** (474-8225), 7456 Post Road, North Kingstown. Used books and a few new books in both hardcover and paperback, including some local authors.

SPECIAL SHOPS **Allie's Tack Shop** (401-294-9121), 3710 Quaker Lane (RI 2), North Kingstown. A top-notch supply of boots, jeans, and horseback-riding gear.

And the Beadz Go On . . . (401-268-3899), 1 West Main Street, Wickford. Everything for the beader—glass beads, ceramic beads, bead kits, and instructions. There is yarn for the knitter, too, as well as an assortment of handmade jewelry.

Askham & Telham, Inc. (401-295-0891), 12 Main Street, Wickford. A pretty gift shop filled with needlepoint pillows, fine picture frames, throws, and similar quality decorator items for the home.

Canvasworks (401-295-8080), 10 Main Street, Wickford. Canvas bags of all sizes and shapes, printed with designs in a variety of colors.

J. W. Graham (401-295-0757), 16 Brown Street, Wickford. Designer pillows, pottery, and glass are among the items in this upscale gift shop.

The Grateful Heart (401-294-3981), 17 West Main Street, Wickford. This New Age store specializes in spiritual and environmental books, crystals, New Age jewelry, tarot cards, greeting cards, and candles. You can

have a photograph taken of your "aura" and learn the colors of your spiritual energy.

Green Ink (401-294-6266), 17 Brown Street, Wickford. Style is important in this women's clothing and accessories boutique, and the South County woman with Fifth Avenue tastes might well shop here.

The Hour Glass (401-295-8724), 15 West Main Street, Wickford. There are big clocks and small ones, cuckoo clocks, mantel clocks, reproduction clocks, and sundials—virtually every kind of timepiece ticking and ringing the hours in the Hour Glass.

Juleez (401-294-8546), 10 Phillips Strret, Wickford. Funky handblown fused glass jewelry; handcrafted, hand-painted colorful furniture; ceramics and acrylic paintings fill this shop whose contents are largely family-made.

Village Reflections (401-295-7802), 5 West Main Street, Wickford. Women's clothing that is "way out" as well as pieces meant for office wear.

Wickford Gourmet Factory Outlet (401-294-8430), 656 Ten Rod Road, Wickford. In the gatehouse of the former Lafayette Textile Mill, seconds and discontinued china, glassware, cutlery, and kitchenware are offered at reasonable prices.

Wickford Gourmet Kitchen & Table (401-295-9790), 31 West Main Street, Wickford. Anything and everything for the kitchen is for sale in this attractive barn shop that is an annex to the Wickford Gourmet.

The World Store (401-295-0081), 16 West Main Street, Wickford. The merchandise in this shop emphasizes a better environment and appreciation of the world around us. There are stained-glass window decorations, balloon globes, fossils, bird- and bat houses.

Nautical Impressions (401-295-5303), 16 West Main Street, Wickford. Find gifts aplenty for the yachter and the wannabe sailor— anchor andirons and bookends, globes and telescopes, galley signs and books on sailing—in this second-floor shop that is an adjunct to the World Store.

FARM STANDS **The Farm Stand** (401-885-4804), 445 North Quidnessett Road, North Kingstown. Open July through October, daily 10–6.

Healey's Farm (401-295-0912), 1100 Lafayette Road, North Kingstown. Open mid-July through October, daily 11–dusk.

The Little Tree Farm (401-294-4148), 7470 Post Road, North Kingstown. Open daily 9–6 year-round.

Schartner Farms (401-885-5510), RI 2, Exeter. Open March through December, daily 8–dusk.

✳ Special Events

June: **Rhode Island Air National Guard Quonset Air Show,** Quonset State Airport, North Kingstown. **Lafayette Band Concerts** (401-295-

0072), Band Shell, North Kingstown Town Beach, Wickford. **Strawberry Festival and Crafts Fair** (401-294-3521), Smith's Castle, off US 1, Wickford.

June–August: **Summer Concert Series** (401-294-3331), behind the Town Hall Annex, 55 Brown Street, Wickford.

July: **Wickford Art Festival** (401-294-6840). Paintings, photographs, sculptures, and food on the sidewalks of Wickford. **Lafayette Band Concerts** (401-295-0072), Band Shell, North Kingstown Town Beach, Wickford, and St. John's Chapel, Willett Road, Saunderstown.

August: **Lafayette Band Concerts** (401-884-8579), North Kingstown Free Library, Boone Street, Wickford.

September: **Annual Dahlia Show** (401-294-3486), Cold Spring Community Center, Beach Street, Wickford.

October: **Plantation Day** (401-294-3521), Smith's Castle, off US 1, Wickford.

December: **Festival of Lights** (401-295-5666), Wickford village, North Kingstown. An old-fashioned Christmas celebration with hayrides, storytelling, caroling, and house tours.

CHARLESTOWN AND RICHMOND AREA

The tribal lands of the Narragansett Nation extend over 1,800 acres of woods and fields in rural Charlestown, which was named for Charles II, who gave Rhode Island its charter in 1663. Each summer and fall Native American musicians and dancers perform in celebrations open to all. Here are the Cup and Saucer Rocks—huge boulders, balanced on a ledge, that the Narragansetts rolled together centuries ago so that the rumbling would send messages. This area also holds the Narragansett Coronation Rock, church, and royal burying ground.

The level land here was once dominated by potato farming. That gave way to turf farming in the 1970s after a potato bug infestation caused crop failures at the same time that housing developments and businesses multiplied, which increased the demand for ready-made patches of lawn.

Along the ocean Charlestown is edged with long barrier beaches, ever-popular with neighboring Connecticut residents, and windswept salt ponds rich in crabs, quahogs, and steamers. In the Charlestown woods, freshwater ponds sparkle, and its swamps are rich in bird life. Charlestown is one of the Ocean State's most laid-back areas, and its appeal is largely to visitors who are laid back, too.

In the town of Richmond to the north, white-clapboard mill villages like Carolina, Kenyon, Shannock, Woodville, and Wyoming suddenly appear at the end of long, bosky roads, and the Wood River, Rhode Island's best trout stream, winds among maple and oak, laurel and birch.

GUIDANCE **Rhode Island Welcome Center** (401-539-3031), I-95 north, 6 miles north of the Connecticut line in Richmond.

Charlestown Chamber of Commerce (401-364-3878), Ninigret Park exit off US 1 and Scenic RI 1A northbound. Open limited hours mid-June through September. Sells tickets to such events as the Big Apple Circus, as well as providing travel information.

GETTING THERE *By car:* Charlestown lies about 6 miles northeast of the Connecticut border and about 40 miles southwest of Providence. From Mystic take

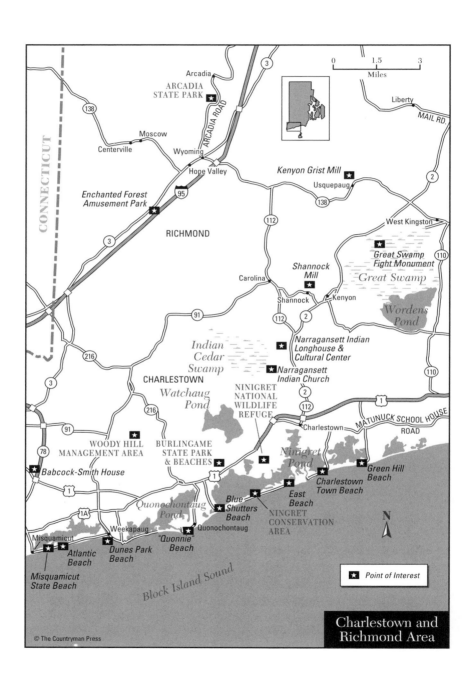

Charlestown and Richmond Area

US 1 east. From Providence take I-95 to exit 9 to RI 4, and then follow US 1 into Charlestown. Automobile is really the only convenient way to get to Charlestown.

By rail: **Amtrak** (1-800-USA-RAIL) has service from both Boston and New York to Kingston and Westerly. From either point, a taxi must be taken the rest of the way.

By bus: **Rhode Island Public Transport Authority** (RIPTA; 401-781-9400) has bus service to Kingston and Wakefield, but a taxi must be taken from both towns into Charlestown.

By taxi: **Wright's Taxi** (401-596-TAXI; 1-800-698-2941), 23 Bradford Road, Westerly.

MEDICAL EMERGENCY The statewide emergency number is **911.**

Westerly Hospital (401-506-6000), 25 Wells Street, Westerly. **South County Hospital** (401-782-8000), Kenyon Avenue, Wakefield.

✳ Villages

Ashaway, Hopkinton. Here on the banks of the Ashaway River in 1824, Captain Lester Crandall, a local fisherman, began twisting his own fishing lines with the help of a wooden wheel. Industrious and entrepreneurial, Captain Crandall was soon making fishing line for others. He built a dam to provide the waterpower to run the machinery for his production, and before he died he was selling fishing line worldwide. Today Crandall Field is a charming village green, and pretty Victorian houses line the village streets.

Carolina, Richmond and Charlestown. This little community straddles the town lines. In the mid–19th century Rowland G. Hazard bought the gristmill that stood here and turned it into a cotton mill; he named the village Carolina for his daughter, early Wellesley College president Caroline Hazard. Most of the Greek Revival and Victorian houses in Carolina were constructed by the early 20th century. The mill then closed during the Depression, and little Carolina has been largely frozen in time ever since. Among the grander homes here, all on RI 112, are the hilltop house with touches of gingerbread that once belonged to the owners of the mill; the octagon-shaped house; the imposing Italianate house; and, set back next to it, the Greek Revival house with an encircling porch. There is also the white-clapboard and Westerly-granite Carolina Free Will Baptist Church, built in 1845, with a well-restored interior.

Hopkinton City, Hopkinton. Its impressive name notwithstanding, this is barely a crossroads on RI 3 in the town of Hopkinton, but it has a handful of handsome 18th- and 19th-century houses, including Federal, Greek Revival, and Colonial structures. In the mid–19th century this was a carriage- and sleigh-manufacturing town.

Shannock, Richmond. This pretty little village of white-clapboard houses near the Pawcatuck River is situated on a road as tortuous as the river itself. In the 18th century there was a gristmill and a sawmill here. Toward the end of that century a woolen mill was constructed. Virtually abandoned years ago, the village was more recently discovered, purchased in its entirety by a developer, and restored. The project, which was planned to attract upwardly mobile young couples, largely went sour. But the restored Shannock has remained, a gem of a rural Rhode Island mill village.

Wyoming, Richmond. There was an ironworks in this village in the 18th century; in the 19th century it became the site of two textile mills, and its handsome Greek Revival houses were built in this period. An old horseshoe-shaped dam here spans the Wood River.

✳ To See

HISTORIC SITES Charlestown Historical Society (401-364-6211), Old Post Road (Scenic RI 1A), Charlestown. Open July and August, Wednesday 2–4 and Saturday 10–noon. Small donation required. This one-room 1838 schoolhouse, which was in use in neighboring Quonochontaug until 1918, has an 1856 map on its wall, period primers, and a potbellied stove.

THE HORSESHOE FALLS IN WYOMING

Kim Grant

Fort Ninigret, Fort Neck Road, Charlestown. Boats bob in a sheltered cove below this grassy park, where an iron railing marks the site of what is believed to have been an early Dutch trading post. For many years the earthworks here were thought to have been part of a Niantic tribe stronghold. The rough stone in the center of the site is a memorial to the Niantics and the Narragansetts.

Narragansett Indian Church (401-364-1100), off RI 112, across from the Charlestown Police Station. This Greek Revival granite church burned down some years ago, but it has been rebuilt and is open for Sunday services. Further information is available from the Narragansett Tribal Council's administrative offices, situated at the junction of RI 2 and RI 112 and open weekdays 8:30–4:30.

✳ To Do

CANOEING Hope Valley Bait and Tackle Shop (401-539-2757), RI 3 and RI 138, Wyoming. Canoe rentals.

FRESHWATER FISHING A license is required for all freshwater fishing in

the state, except for fishing in **Watchaug Pond** (401-322-7337), US 1,
Burlingame State Park.

241

CHARLESTOWN AND RICHMOND AREA

Ashville Pond, Canonchet Road, Hopkinton. Trout, bass, perch, bullheads, and pickerel are all found here.

Biscuit City Landing, access to Pawcatuck River. The Biscuit City Road is directly off RI 2. Angle for northern pike, largemouth bass, bullheads, pickerel, trout, and sunfish.

Dow Field, Main Street, Hopkinton, and **Grantville,** Hope Valley Road, Hopkinton. These are two of the best access points for Wood River trout fishing. There is also the **Wood River Access** in Wyoming.

Locustville Pond, Fairview Avenue, Hopkinton. Although there are no trout in this pond, calico bass are a good catch here.

Richmond Landing, Pawcatuck River, RI 91, Richmond. Catch northern pike, largemouth bass, pickerel, trout, and bullheads.

Wyoming Pond, off I-95, Wyoming. Bullheads, trout, largemouth bass, and pickerel are all here.

SALTWATER FISHING Saltwater fin fishing requires no license, but the take is limited. Information on limits is available from **Rhode Island Fish and Wildlife** at 401-789-3094 or 401-783-2304.

Charlestown Breachway, Charlestown Beach Road. Striped bass, bluefish, tautog, and winter and summer flounder can be caught here.

Ningret Conservation Area, East Beach Road, Charlestown. From this long stretch of beach that extends to the Charlestown Breachway there is fine fishing for striped bass, bluefish, tautog, and winter and summer flounder.

Quonochontaug State Beach, West Beach Road, Charlestown. Striped bass, bluefish, and winter and summer flounder are the prizes along this stretch of beach, too.

FOR FAMILIES ✿ **The Enchanted Forest** (401-539-7711), RI 3 in the Hope Valley area of Hopkinton. Open May through Labor Day, daily 10–5. Tucked away in a wooded setting, as its name implies, this fairyland theme park is for youngsters 2–12 years old. Here are a merry-go-round and a variety of nursery-tale attractions for toddlers, like the brick cottage of "The Three Little Pigs," the yellow shoe of "The Old Woman Who Lived in a Shoe," and "The House That Jack Built." Older children will find a Ferris wheel, roller coaster, batting cages, jeep and boat rides, and miniature golf. For all-day visitors, there are picnic tables and a snack bar. Virtually all rides are included in the entrance fee charged for those over 2 years old.

✿ **The Fantastic Umbrella Factory** (401-364-6616), Ninigret Park Tourist Information exit off US 1, Charlestown. Open mid-June through Labor Day, daily 10–6; Wednesday through Sunday the rest of the year. The whole family will enjoy this potpourri of shops, gardens, and a 19th-century farmyard with ducks, geese, sheep, goats, chickens, and peacocks. In an untamed backyard garden grow many flower varieties, including lilies, cannas, hibiscus, dahlias, and phlox. An art gallery with collectibles and vintage clothing, books, and paintings is also on the Umbrella Factory's extensive grounds. The International Bazaar sells kites, cards, and small toys, and when you tire of exploring, relax in the small café serving sandwiches, salads, Mexican specialties, and desserts. The Umbrella Factory is distinctly reminiscent of the 1960s, when it had its start.

GOLF **Beaver River Golf Club** (401-539-6022), 343 Kingstown Road, Richmond. This inviting 18-hole course with a restaurant, bar, and pro shop is just 3 years old.

Fenner Hill Golf Club (401-539-8000), 33 Wheeler Lane, Hope Valley. Rolling hills and rambling stone walls are part of the setting for this challenging 18-hole golf course that has a restaurant and lounge.

Foxwoods Golf & Country Club (401-539-0300), Kingstown Road (RI 138 east; exit 3A, I-95), Richmond. This is an 18-hole golf course on rolling terrain.

Laurel Lane (401-783-3844), 309 Laurel Lane, West Kingston. There's a driving range and two practice greens along with a snack bar, pro shop, and lounge at this well-maintained 18-hole course.

Lindhbrook Executive Golf Club (401-539-8700), Alton-Woodville Road (exit 2, I-95), Hope Valley, Hopkinton. This is an 18-hole golf course on flat terrain with brooks and ponds.

Pinehurst Golf Club (401-364-8600), Pinehurst Drive, Richmond. This is a 2-year-old impeccably maintained nine-hole course set among pines and oaks. It has a grill, bar, and snack bar.

Richmond Country Club (401-364-9200), 79 Sandy Pond Road, Richmond. An 18-hole, well-maintained golf course among the pines with a pond.

HORSEBACK RIDING **Old Coach Farm** (401-783-6555), 410 Old Coach Road, Charlestown. Riding lessons and horse boarding, but no trail rides.

Willow Valley Farm (401-539-2742), Hillsdale Road, Richmond. Half-hour and hourlong lessons, but no trail rides.

STARGAZING ✺ **Frosty Drew Observatory** (401-364-9508), Ninigret Park, off Scenic RI 1A, Charlestown. On clear Friday nights in summer, the astronomically inclined can study the stars at this observatory.

FRESHWATER SWIMMING ✺ **Burlingame Picnic Area** (Watchaug Pond), Burlingame State Park, off RI 1, just 2 miles north of the Burlingame Camping Area. Shallow water and a clean beach make this an attractive spot for small children. Lifeguards are on duty in midsummer. Restrooms, fireplaces, picnic areas.

✺ **Ninigret Park,** off Scenic 1A, Charlestown, has a pond that is ideal for children.

SALTWATER SWIMMING **Blue Shutters Beach** (401-364-7000), East Beach Road, off RI 1.

Charlestown Town Beach (401-364-7000), Charlestown Beach Road, off RI 1. Small but nicely set-up beach, with surf and room for volleyball.

East Beach/Ninigret (401-322-0450), end of East Beach Road.

TENNIS Ninigret Park, off Scenic RI 1A, Charlestown. Several courts, with no fee.

✳ Green Space

Arcadia Wildlife Management Area (401-789-3094; 401-539-2356). This 13,817-acre habitat is the largest wildlife preserve in the state, offering trails through fields and evergreen forests, past wetlands and marshes. The wildlife of Arcadia includes foxes, deer, mink, snowshoe hares, ring-necked pheasants, ruffed grouse, and wild turkeys. Pheasants and bobwhites are both stocked during hunting season, and Arcadia's ponds contain warm- and cold-water fish. The Wood River, which flows through Arcadia, is Rhode Island's most impressive scenic wild river, renowned for its trout. The management area extends not only into the towns of Hopkinton and Richmond but also into Exeter and West Greenwich. Access in Richmond is off the K-G Ranch Road or off Old Nooseneck Hill Road, which leads to Wildlife Management Headquarters.

Burlingame Wildlife Management Area (401-322-7994), Charlestown. Here there are 1,390 acres of forest, wetland, marsh, and agricultural land with rabbits, deer, foxes, raccoons, muskrats, and coyotes among the resident mammals, and ruffed grouse, wild turkeys, woodcock, and waterfowl also in evidence. Access is north of Buckeye Brook Road at Clawson Trail.

Carolina Wildlife Management Area (401-364-3483), Richmond. Foxes, deer, woodchucks, muskrats, otters, ospreys, and owls are just a few of the animal and bird species you might encounter on a hike through this 1,875-acre area of woodland, wetland, and agricultural land. A segment of the Pawcatuck River

CHARLESTOWN TOWN BEACH

Kim Grant

flows through the area. Access is possible at three locations: the hunter check station on Pine Hill Road, along Shippee Trail off Hope Valley Road, and along Meadowbrook Trail north of Pine Hill Road.

Kimball Wildlife Refuge (401-251-6444), off Prosser Trail, Charlestown. The Audubon Society runs this area, which is especially attractive to waterfowl and migrating birds.

Long Pond Woods (401-949-5454), Canonchet Road, Hopkinton. Trails wind through hemlock and around rock outcroppings at this Audubon refuge.

✔ **Ninigret Conservation Area, Ninigret Park** (401-364-0890), and **Ninigret National Wildlife Refuge** (401-364-9124), off Scenic RI 1A, Charlestown. These three separate areas edge both sides of Ninigret Pond. Along the conservation area on the ocean side stretch 2.5 miles of barrier beach, where walking and sailboarding are popular. At the town-owned park, lifeguards watch over a spring-fed beach with freshwater swimming that is ideal for children. The park also offers a playground, 10-speed-bicycle course, and tennis and basketball courts. In the refuge you can walk through beach plum and honeysuckle that shelter birds and deer, and there is access to Ninigret Pond for swimming, wading, and shelling.

✳ Lodging

HOTELS AND INNS **The General Stanton Inn** (401-364-8888; 1-800-364-8011; www.GeneralStantonInn.com), 4115 Old Post Road, Charlestown 02813. ($$–$$$) Open year-round. A small, old-fashioned establishment that had its beginnings in 1647, this is a spot for those who cherish old inns. Its low ceilings, brick ovens, and hand-hewn timbers attest to its origin. Some rooms have bath; some without. Not all have closets. The room decor, however, is summery and attractive. Most beds are four-posters—and there's even one that actress Julia Roberts is said to have slept in for one of her films. It has its own restaurant and bar.

& **The Stagecoach House** (401-539-9600; 1-888-814-9000; www.stagecoachhouse.com), 1136 Main Street, Wyoming 02898. ($$) Back in the 18th century this inn above the Wood River in the village of Wyoming was a stagecoach stop. Over the years it fell on hard times, but it has now been refurbished to offer 12 air-conditioned rooms with fireplaces for travelers to rent—not elegant, but comfortable. A continental breakfast is served.

Willows Resort Hotel (401-364-7727; www.willowsresort.com), 5310 Post Road, Charlestown 02813. ($–$$$) Open Memorial Day through Columbus Day. It would be hard to beat the setting of this hotel-motel, on 20 acres above Ninigret Pond. Added attractions are a tennis court, pool table, swimming pool, and small boats for sailing on the pond. The accommodations—a motel for single-night stays, plus apartments, efficiencies, and a cottage for stays of a week or more in summer—are more ordinary than their surroundings. There is also a restaurant.

BED & BREAKFAST **King Tom Farm** (401-364-9535; www.kingtomfarm.com), 4740 Old Post Road, Charlestown 02613. ($$$) Named for Tom Ninigret, the last crowned king of the Narragansett Indians, King Tom Farm was buit in 1880 and for many years was a potato farm of more than 500 acres. Today there are three cozy guest rooms with ceiling fan and private bath in the former foreman's house and two guest cottages on 8 shady acres with colorful gardens.

CAMPGROUNDS **Burlingame State Park** (401-322-7994; 401-322-7337), US 1, Charlestown. Write: Division of Parks and Recreation, 2321 Hartford Avenue, Johnston 02919. Open April 15 through October. Situated on the banks of Watchaug Pond, there are 755 campsites in this 2,100-acre state park, which is equipped with water, fireplaces, washrooms, showers, toilets, picnic tables, and a dumping station. Both boating and fishing are possible on the pond, and Atlantic Ocean swimming is only a few miles away.

Charlestown Breachway (401-364-7000 in-season; 401-322-8910 year-round), off Charlestown Beach Road, Charlestown. Write: Division of Parks and Recreation, 2321 Hartford Avenue, Johnston 02919. Open April 15 through October. Sites for 75 self-contained trailer units. There are flush toilets, a boat ramp, fishing, and swimming in the Atlantic or in Ninigret Pond.

☙ **Greenwood Hill Campground** (401-539-7154; 1-800-232-7154), Newberry Lane, Hopkinton. Write: Box 141, 13A Newberry Lane, Hope Valley 02832. Open May 15 through October 15. Situated on a spring-fed pond, this facility offers 10 tent sites and 40 trailer sites with water/electric hook-ups as well as a sports field, recreation hall, and playground. There are hot showers, picnic tables, fireplaces, and a dumping station.

Pets are allowed on a leash. Camping equipment can be rented on the premises.

Whispering Pines Campground (401-539-7011), RI 138, Hope Valley. Write: Saw Mill Road, Box 425, Hope Valley 02832. Open May 15 through October 15. There is space in this private campground for 30 tents and 150 trailers. Water, electricity, and sewage hook-ups are available, as are a dumping station, hot showers, picnic tables, firewood and fireplaces, a store and coin-operated laundry, and playground facilities. Activities offered include movies and miniature golf.

✷ Where to Eat

DINING OUT **The General Stanton Inn** (401-364-8011), 4115A Old Post Road (US 1), Charlestown. ($–$$) This 200-year-old inn is open year-round for breakfast, lunch, and dinner. The breakfast pancakes are scrumptious, and the poultry dishes are ever-popular.

Josie's (401-322-9200), 5259 Old Post Road (US 1), Charlestown. ($$$) Open Tuesday through Sunday for dinner. The dishes are mainly Italian, with such entrées as veal with shrimp and saffron cream, and veal with lobster and shallots, among the specialties at this formal-for-the-seaside-style restaurant.

Richmond Country Club (401-364-9292), Sandy Pond Road, Richmond. ($–$$) Open daily for lunch and dinner almost the whole year, but call for hours in winter. You can overlook the 18-hole championship golf course here and satisfy your hunger with a fat hamburger or a grilled chicken sandwich, or, in the dining room, feast on roast beef, filet mignon, or roast chicken at surprisingly moderate prices.

& **Wilcox Tavern** (401-322-1829), Old Post Road, Charlestown. ($$–$$$) Open Tuesday through Saturday from 4:30 for dinner; Sunday from noon on. Since 1850 generation after generation of the Wilcox family has operated either an inn or a tavern in this 1730s house. The present tavern is a comfortable place decorated with fare that is American or Italian American. The lobster bisque, clear Rhode Island clam chowder, and peppery clam cakes are all worth trying.

& **Willows Resort and Foster Pier Restaurant** (401-364-7727), Old Post Road, US 1, Charlestown. ($–$$) Open mid-May through Columbus Day for breakfast and dinner. The dining room view of Ninigret Pond is a beauty; the fare is seafood and Rhode Island favorites like clam cakes and jonny cakes (though, of course, there is charcoal-broiled steak, too). Nothing fancy. Plain American cooking in a so-so (but for the view) dining room.

EATING OUT **The Cove** (401-364-9222), 3963 Post Road, Charlestown. ($–$$) Open daily for lunch and dinner. Such typical ocean fare as fried clams and scallops and fish-and-chips are on the menu, along with pasta, sandwiches, and burgers.

Nordic Lodge (401-783-4515), 178 East Pasquisset Trail, Charlestown. ($$$$) Open for dinner mid-April through December. At this stone hunting lodge set on a pond in the woods, you get all you can eat on Friday, Saturday, and Sunday—lobster, shrimp, filet mignon, prime rib, salad, shortcakes, pies, cookies, and cakes from a buffet table.

The Rathskeller (401-783-7839), 489 Old Coach Road, Kenyon. ($) Open daily 11 AM–1 AM except Monday. University of Rhode Island students, years after graduation, come back for the Rathskeller's french fries and oyster stew. Once a speakeasy, the Rathskeller is big and noisy and beery, with plentiful servings.

♪ **Spice of Life Natural Foods Cafe** (401-364-2030), the Fantastic Umbrella Factory, Ninigret Park Tourist Information exit off US 1, Charlestown. ($) Open daily in June, July, and August. Call for hours. There are Mexican and vegetarian dishes and snacks served in this little café on the grounds of the Fantastic Umbrella Factory.

🍴 ♪ **West's Bakery** (401-539-2451), 999 Main Street, Hope Valley, Hopkinton. ($) Open Wednesday through Saturday 6–3, Sunday 6–1. It's for the bismarcks—raised doughnuts filled with raspberry jelly and whipped cream—that locals flock to this little bakery, but the steak-and-cheese and cold-cut grinders are worth sampling, too.

🍴 & **Wood River Inn** (401-539-9800), intersection of RI 138 and US 3, Wyoming. ($–$$) The prices are surely right at this bustling, friendly, noisy inn restaurant by the side of the road. There's a special menu for seniors with smaller appetites as well as for children, and there are plenty of old favorites like shepherd's pie, fried smelts, and Grape-Nut pudding.

✳ Selective Shopping

ANTIQUES SHOPS **Hope Valley Antiques** (401-539-0250), 1081 Main Street, Hope Valley, Hopkinton. Open year-round, Wednesday through Sunday 10–4. In this sizable shop with furniture, glassware, lamps, and china, mahogany furniture is something of a specialty.

Richmond Antiques Center (401-539-0350), 320 Kingstown Road, Richmond. Open daily 10–5. Dealers rent space to show off and sell their antiques. An eclectic collection.

ART GALLERY **Charlestown Gallery** (401-364-0120), Matunuck Schoolhouse Road, Charlestown. Open daily in summer; call for spring and fall hours. Paintings and graphics for small spaces by Rhode Island artists, along with hand-painted jewelry and hand-painted furniture.

SPECIAL SHOPS **Galapagos Collection** (401-322-3000), 5193 Old Post Road, Charlestown. Open year-round, daily 8–6. This family business had its start in Ecuador—hence the name *Galapagos,* for those Ecuadoran Islands renowned for their birds and animals. Occasionally there are one-of-a-kind Ecuadoran knitted sweaters, hats, and scarves in bright designs, but the regular stock is boutique clothing, largely from France, Italy, and England. There are also hand-made cards, blown glass, and tabletop accessories. A café serving coffee and sandwiches is a hospitable touch.

Hack and Livery General Store (401-539-7033), 1006 Main Street, Hope Valley, Hopkinton. Open daily 10–5 July through January. Closed Monday and Tuesday in winter. A century ago this was a genuine livery stable. Nowadays it's full to the rafters with gift items that range from cards and Christmas decorations to dolls and miniature decorative houses, table linens, baskets, ribbons, and bows.

Hope Valley Bait & Tackle (401-539-2757), Main Street, Wyoming. Open daily year-round 6 AM–8 PM,

Sunday 5 AM–6 PM. Anything anyone could want in the way of fishing, hunting, camping, or canoeing equipment.

The Lily Pad (401-364-7710), 4202 Old Post Road, Charlestown. Open daily 10–4:30 mid-June through mid-September; after that, weekends through Christmas. Closed January through March. In this original Charlestown school building, erected in the 1830s, there is now an upstairs gallery of New England paintings and a downstairs shop of fine jewelry and pottery, elegant dresses and hats.

Meadowbrook Gardens (401-539-8711), 93 Kingstown Road, Richmond. Open Monday through Saturday 9–6, Sunday 11–5. This is a gold mine of seeds and plants, books of plant lore, old-fashioned teas like nettle and wormwood, herbs, and natural perfume oils like lavender and rose—and children's books and toys, too.

Simple Pleasures (401-364-9852), 5000 South County Trail, Charlestown. Open daily 9–5:30. In this garden-themed antiques and gift shop are such items as topiaries and birdhouses, potpourri, dried flowers and herbs, handwoven balsam-filled pillows.

URE Outfitters (401-539-4050), Main Street, Hope Valley. Open daily; call for hours. Hikers and backpackers, hunters and anglers, birders and canoeists—all nature lovers—will find stock to explore here. In addition, there's a fine collection of books for the outdoorsperson.

FARM STANDS **Jackson's Farm Cart,** Pat's Power Equipment parking lot, Scenic RI 1A, Charlestown. Open daily in summer.

Peaches (401-364-5949), 47 Charlestown Beach Road, Charlestown. Open year-round, daily 9–6, except closed Mondays in fall and winter.

✳ Special Events

March–November: **Flea Market** (401-364-8888), grounds of the General Stanton Inn, US 1, Charlestown. Saturday and Sunday 7–4.

May: **Charlestown Memorial Day Parade** (401-364-9715). Sponsored by the American Legion and featuring the Girl Scouts, the parade starts in the morning at the Carolina Fire Station.

Mid-July: The **Big Apple Circus** (401-364-0890), sponsored by the Charlestown Chamber of Commerce, performs in Ninigret Park, Charlestown.

August: The annual **August Meeting of the Narragansett Indian Tribe** (401-364-1100) is held on the second weekend in August at the Narragansett Indian Church grounds on Indian Church Road in Charlestown and includes music and dance, foods and storytelling. The **Charlestown Seafood Festival** (401-364-4031) features clam cakes and chowder, a seafood cook-off, and live music in Ninigret Park. The **Washington County Fair** (401-539-7042) is a Thursday-through-Sunday midmonth event at the fairgrounds on Townhouse Road in Richmond. **Swamp Yankee Days** are held at the end of the month or the beginning of September at Ninigret Park in Charlestown: Music, food, events, and crafts celebrate the local country Yankee.

September: At the **Hopkinton Colonial Crafts Festival** (401-377-7795), handmade colonial crafts are on sale, and crafts demonstrations are offered at Crandall Field, ordinarily in early September. On the fourth Sunday in September, the Narragansett tribe holds the **Great Swamp Pilgrimage** (401-364-1100) at the Great Swamp Fight Monument on RI 2 in West Kingston, followed by special ceremonies at the Longhouse off RI 112 in Charlestown.

October: The **Fall Thanksgiving Festival of the Narragansett Indians** (401-364-1100) is held the first Sunday in October with a traditional dinner, including jonny cakes, plus an arts and crafts sales at the Longhouse off RI 112 in Charlestown.

Thanksgiving–January 1: **Christmas Nostalgia** (401-364-6616), the Fantastic Umbrella Factory, 4830 Old Post Road, Charlestown. An exhibition of toys, Christmas cards, and decorations of the past is held in the barn.

WESTERLY AND WATCH HILL

Westerly, as the name implies, is the most westerly part of the state of Rhode Island. It shares the meandering Pawcatuck River as well as its main post office and railroad station with Pawcatuck, Connecticut.

In the 19th century, textile mills and a quarry producing good construction-grade granite and fine-grained, easily carved granite for monuments brought Westerly considerable wealth and renown. That heyday is long gone, reflected now only in a few imposing houses and public buildings, but the beach resorts of the township continue to bring it fame. And increasingly, artists from New York and Connecticut are opening studios in renovated old buildings.

Watch Hill is, after Newport, Rhode Island's most select beach resort, with arcaded shops and turn-of-the-20th-century "cottages" (less pretentious than those of Newport) set on hills overlooking Little Narragansett Bay and the Atlantic. Weekapaug, with a salt pond and a combination of rocky and sandy beaches facing the ocean, remains a place of largely remote, private, untouched natural beauty, while Misquamicut is the Coney Island of Rhode Island: young, noisy, effervescent, crowded.

When the English arrived in the 17th century, this was all Native American land (as names like *Weekapaug* and *Pawcatuck* and *Misquamicut* suggest). The Niantic sachem Ninigret, memorialized in Fort Ninigret and by a Watch Hill statue, was then the ruler.

The first permanent white settlers are said to have been an eloping couple—John Babcock from the Plymouth Bay Colony and Mary Lawton of Newport—who fled Mary's father's wrath in an open boat that they took from Newport across Narragansett Bay. Later, other Newporters began speculating in land in the area, and Connecticut residents began making land claims. In the 18th and early 19th centuries, shipbuilding became important in Westerly on the Pawcatuck. Soon came cloth manufacturing and, in the middle of the 19th century, quarrying.

Today's Westerly township is a 36-square-mile area in which, as in much of Rhode Island, it is the countryside rather than the cityscape that is most appealing.

GUIDANCE **Greater Westerly-Pawcatuck Area Chamber of Commerce** (401-596-7761; 1-800-SEA-7636), 1 Chamber Way, Westerly 02891. Publishes an

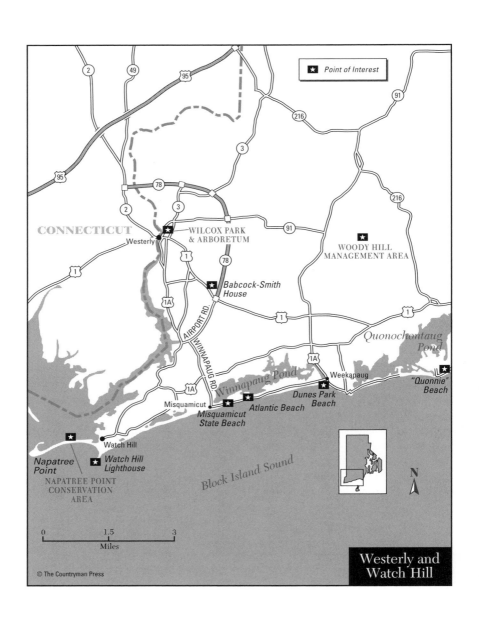

Point of Interest

CONNECTICUT

WILCOX PARK
& ARBORETUM

Westerly

WOODY HILL
MANAGEMENT AREA

Babcock-Smith
House

AIRPORT RD

WINNAPAUG RD

Quonochontaug
Pond

Winnapaug Pond

Weekapaug

"Quonnie"
Beach

Misquamicut

Dunes Park
Beach

Misquamicut
State Beach

Atlantic Beach

Watch Hill

Napatree
Point

Watch Hill
Lighthouse

NAPATREE POINT
CONSERVATION
AREA

Block Island Sound

0   1.5   3
Miles

N

Westerly and
Watch Hill

annual tourist guide listing restaurants, accommodations, recreational facilities, and so on.

Rhode Island Welcome Center (401-539-3031), I-95 north, 6 miles north of the Connecticut line in Richmond.

South County Tourism Council (401-789-4422; 1-800-548-4662), 4808 Tower Hill Road, Wakefield 02879. This office in the Oliver Stedman Government Center can supply information about the Westerly area.

GETTING THERE *By car:* Westerly is 128 miles from New York City and 100 miles from Boston. Coming from New York, take I-95 to exit 92 in Connecticut, then CT 2 less than 5 miles to the intersection with US 1. There, turn into downtown Pawcatuck, Connecticut, and Westerly, Rhode Island. Coming from Boston, take I-95 south to RI 3, and leave it at exit 1 for Westerly.

To get to Watch Hill from I-95, take exit 92 onto CT 2, and continue to RI 78. Take RI 78 all the way to US 1, cross US 1 onto the Airport Road, and at the junction with Scenic RI 1A, turn left and proceed to downtown Watch Hill.

To get to Weekapaug, continue on Atlantic Avenue, crossing over the Winnapaug Breachway, and go right on Wawaloam Avenue, which leads into Ninigret Avenue and Weekapaug Beach.

By rail: **Amtrak** (1-800-USA-RAIL) has service from both Boston and New York to Westerly.

By bus: **Rhode Island Public Transit Authority** (RIPTA; 401-781-9400) offers one late-afternoon weekday bus from Providence to Westerly.

By taxi: **Wright's Taxi** (401-596-TAXI; 1-800-698-2941), 283 Bradford Road, Westerly. **Eagle Cab** (401-596-7300), 55 Beach Street, Westerly.

MEDICAL EMERGENCY The statewide emergency number is **911.**

Westerly Hospital (401-596-6000), 25 Wells Street.

✳ To See

MUSEUM ✐ **Lighthouse Museum,** Lighthouse Road, Watch Hill. Open July and August, Tuesday and Thursday 1–3. This granite lighthouse was built in 1856 to replace an earlier wooden light. The most notable rescue took place in 1872 when the steamer *Metis,* en route to Providence from New York, collided with a schooner and sank in less than an

THE LIGHTHOUSE MUSEUM IN WATCH HILL MARKS THE SITE OF MANY NOTABLE SHIPWRECKS.

Kim Grant

hour. Volunteers manning the one lifeboat from the lighthouse managed to save 33 of the more than 100 passengers on board. Another wreck off this site, frequently remembered because of the importance of the commanding officer, was that of a coastal patrol boat under Oliver Hazard Perry that ran onto rocks in a fog. Even when the museum is not open, its grounds are pleasant to visit.

HISTORIC SITES Babcock-Smith House (401-596-5704), 124 Granite Street, Westerly. In July and August, open Sunday and Wednesday 2–5; in May and June, September and October, open Sunday only. Small admission fee. A two-story gambrel-roofed handsomely paneled home filled with old Connecticut and Rhode Island furniture, this 1734 house was built by Westerly's first physician, Dr. Joshua Babcock. Also a chief justice of Rhode Island and a major general in the Revolutionary army, he was a friend of Benjamin Franklin. Franklin was a frequent visitor and supposedly provided the lightning rods for the house roof. An engraving of the diplomat-inventor at the French court hangs over the dining room mantelpiece. An avid angler, Franklin frequently fished off Weekapaug Point. The exterior of the house is particularly notable for the hand-carved pilasters and the broken-scroll pediment over the main entrance. A 19th-century owner of the house, Orlando Smith, discovered Westerly granite. In addition to much local use, this high-grade granite was used for the Roger Williams statue in Providence and for the Rhode Island block in the National Monument in Washington.

✎**Flying Horse Carousel,** end of Bay Street, Watch Hill. The colorful, hand-carved wooden horses with real tails and manes virtually do fly through the air with their little passengers, for the animals are suspended from a center frame. Local residents claim that this carousel, built by the Charles W. Dere Company of New York City in 1879, is the nation's oldest. Outdoors and on the beachfront as it is, however, the carousel operates only in summer.

WEEKAPAUG HARBOR

Ninigret Statue, Bay Street, Watch Hill. The "Guardian" of Watch Hill, legend has it, is the Niantic sachem Ninigret. Sculpted by Edith Yandell, an American artist of the early 20th century, this bronze statue kneels with a fish in each hand, in a little park in the heart of the village.

River Bend Cemetery, Beach Street, Westerly. Extending along the banks of the Pawcatuck, this sylvan cemetery dating from 1844 contains many a grand monument of Westerly granite.

U.S. Post Office (401-596-2755), Broad and High Streets, Westerly. It is hard for the visitor to miss this late-Beaux-Arts building with its curved white marble facade and columns. The interior contains bronze, cast-iron, and marble decoration.

Westerly Hospital (401-586-6000), 25 Wells Street. Mementos of Crimean War nurse Florence Nightingale, who is largely responsible for modern nursing methods in military hospitals, are on display and include photographs and one of her letters. The exhibition was the gift of Westerly relatives.

Westerly Public Library (401-596-2877), Broad Street opposite Wilcox Park. Built in 1894 as a memorial to veterans of the Civil War, this yellow-brick Romanesque Revival structure houses not only one of the largest book collections in the state but also an art gallery upstairs, with changing collections in a new wing.

Wilcox Park, opposite the Westerly Town Hall on Broad Street. Open in summer, dawn–11 PM. This 18-acre park was laid out by the Olmsted architectural firm from Boston at the turn of the 20th century. It is the site of frequent outdoor musical and theatrical events.

✳ To Do

AIRPLANE RIDES **New England Airlines** (401-596-2460; 1-800-243-2460), Westerly State Airport, Westerly Airport Road off US 1, 3 miles east of downtown Westerly. Fifteen-minute flights over Block Island are offered year-round. Flights are usually in 10-seat, two-engine planes and cost $76 per person.

FISHING **Billfish Sport Fishing** (401-860-741-3301), Avondale Boatyard, Westerly. Charter boat fishing.

Bonito II (401-596-6433), 13B Maybrey Drive, Westerly. Charter boat fishing for striped bass and bluefish.

Don's Bait and Tackle (401-322-0310), Post Road, Westerly. Striped bass and bluefish expeditions for a maximum of three people in a 22-foot charter boat. There are also kayak, rod-and-reel, and fresh- and saltwater tackle rentals; hunting, fishing, and clamming licenses provided.

Heffernan Charters (401-364-9592), 8 Scot Circle, Charlestown. Charter boat fishing for striped bass, bluefish, scup, and fluke in a 25-foot runabout.

FOR FAMILIES ✐ **Atlantic Beach Park** (401-322-0504), Atlantic Beach Park, Misquamicut. Open Memorial Day through Labor Day. Batting cages, bumper and go-carts, miniature golf.

❦ **Bay View Fun Park** (401-322-0180), Atlantic Avenue, Misquamicut Beach. Memorial Day through Labor Day. Batting cages, bumper boats, mini golf, and go-carts.

❦ **Carousel** (401-322-0504, Atlantic Beach Park, Misquamicut. Some of the horses on this cheerful merry-go-round were hand carved in 1917, others in the 1930s, but from Memorial Day through Labor Day—age notwithstanding—they all spin merrily for the young in heart to music from the original organ.

❦ **Water Wizz** (401-322-0520), Atlantic Avenue, Misquamicut Beach. Open weekends Memorial Day to mid-June, then daily until Labor Day. Water slides, serpentine slides, kiddie slide, high-speed slides swoop through the air and the water.

GOLF **Weekapaug Golf Club** (401-322-7870), 265 Shore Road, Westerly. This nine-hole golf course is largely on level terrain and borders Winnepaug Pond. A restaurant with outdoor seating and a fine view of the course and the pond is one of its attractions.

Winnapaug Golf & Country Club (401-596-9164), Shore Road, Westerly. This is an 18-hole course on both flat and hilly terrain with a number of ponds. There's also a restaurant.

SWIMMING **Misquamicut State Beach** (401-596-9097), Atlantic Avenue, Westerly. Raucous, crowded, with the feel of an old-time beach. For geographic as well as aesthetic reasons, this beach is a favorite of out-of-staters eager to bathe in the ocean rather than Long Island Sound. Surfing. To reach Misquamicut Beach from the Watch Hill bathing beach, drive up Bluff Avenue, turn right onto Wauwinet, then make another right onto Ninigret to Ocean View Highway. At its end, turn right again onto Shore Road to Winnapaug Road. Turn right, then left onto Atlantic Avenue.

TENNIS **Airport Road Public Tennis Courts** (401-828-4450), Westerly Airport Road off US 1, approximately 3 miles from downtown Westerly. Outdoor asphalt courts, open to the public. There is no charge for their use.

Pond View Racquet Club (401-322-1100), Shore Road, Westerly. These indoor tennis courts are open to the public for a fee.

✳ Green Space

Napatree Point, Watch Hill. Before the 1938 hurricane, houses stood along this 2-mile-long finger of sand. Today only the beach grass remains where seabirds wheel and Block Island Sound thunders on stormy days. The finest spot for a Watch Hill outing, it invites the beachcomber and the birder to explore at sunrise or sunset or when the moon is rising. On the inland side, small boats bob snugly at anchor in Little Narragansett Bay, and at the tip of the point a few walls remain of the Spanish-American War's Fort Mansfield. Access is from Watch Hill Beach, where there is limited parking.

Potter Hill Open Space Area, Westerly. A network of walking trails winds through the woods and over the fields of this 100-acre conservation area. Access is from Old Potter Hill Road off RI 3, in the northern section of town.

Wilcox Park, Westerly. Scotch elm, ginkgo, black walnut, buttonwood, and umbrella pine shade the walks and jogging paths of this pretty, 18-acre Victorian strolling park. There is a duck and water lily pond, fountain, statues, and manicured gardens (a fragrant garden for the visually impaired among them).

Woody Hill Wildlife Management Area, Westerly. This 819-acre state management area is open only to hikers and cyclists. Much of the land is forested, but there is also hardwood swamp. Wood ducks, black ducks, mallards, and green-winged teals can be found during the hunting and fall migration season as well as wild turkeys, woodcock, and ruffed grouse. Rabbits, squirrels, white-tailed deer, foxes, coyotes, raccoons, muskrats, and mink also inhabit the area. Access is along South Woody Hill Road, off US 1.

WATCH HILL

Kim Grant

✳ Lodging

Note: Unless otherwise indicated, the zip code is 02891.

INNS ✐ ♿ **Shelter Harbor Inn** (401-322-8883), 10 Wagner Road (US 1), Westerly. ($$–$$$) Open year-round. In the early 1800s this site was a working farm. The property then became a music colony in 1911. Today the old farmhouse, barn, and carriage house all have been converted into a laid-back, comfortable 23-room country inn, furnished in cozy early American style. There's an enclosed porch-lounge, a library, paddle tennis and croquet courts, a pretty garden, and a private 2-mile-long ocean beach. Three meals a day are served year-round.

✐ ♿ **Weekapaug Inn** (401-322-0301), 15 Spring Avenue, Weekapaug. ($$$) Open mid-June through Labor Day. This sprawling weathered-shingled 62-room inn set on 3-mile-long Quonochontaug Pond just a stone's throw from Block Island Sound is a charming, old-fashioned resort. Though guest rooms may be small, the public rooms are spacious and airy, and an inviting porch looks out on both pond and sound. The inn has its own 2 miles of beach, and there are tennis courts plus sailboats, canoes, and sailboards to use on the pond. For rainy days or quiet evening entertainment, a big living room is available for bingo and bridge or for films and slide shows. Three meals a day are included in the room rates.

BED & BREAKFASTS Grandview Bed & Breakfast (401-596-6384; 1-800-447-6384; www.grandview-bandb.com), 212 Shore Road, Westerly. ($–$$) Comfortable and casual, built in the early 1900s, this 12-room bed & breakfast has ocean views from some of its cozy bedrooms. There's a wraparound stone porch for taking the air in the shade and a garden for sunning. A continental buffet breakfast is included in the price of the rooms, some of which have shared baths. Both tennis and golf are walking distance away.

Langworthy Farm (401-322-7791; 1-888-355-7083; www.langworthy farm.com), 308 Shore Road, Westerly. ($$–$$$) This handsome 1875 farmhouse with local scenes painted on its dining room walls and a faux-book-lined library rises just opposite the entrance road to Misquamicut Beach.

There are four guest rooms and a pair of two-room suites; some offer a splendid view of the Atlantic Ocean half a mile away. Eggs Langworthy—ham, eggs, cheddar cheese, and to-mato on whole wheat toast—is among the breakfast offerings.

The Villa (401-596-1054; 1-800-722-9240; www.thevillaatwesterly.com), 190 Shore Road, Westerly. ($$–$$$$) There are suites with Jacuzzi, suites with balcony, suites with fireplace, and suites with sheer curtains and mahogany woodwork in this flamboyant complex of six suites. The Villa's Italian porticos won't be to everyone's liking, but suites are equipped with microwave, coffeemaker, and refrigerator, and there's a backyard swimming pool and a hot tub. Breakfast is served either poolside, in the dining room, or in your suite.

Woody Hill Bed & Breakfast in the Country (401-322-0452; www.woodyhill.com), 149 South Woody Hill Road, Westerly. ($$–$$$)

THE WEEKAPAUG INN IS AN OLD-FASHIONED RESORT.

Kim Grant

Open year-round, but rates vary according to the season. It would be hard to find a lovelier setting than this hilltop with informal gardens and miles of rolling fields in the distance. For an escape from summer heat, there is a swimming pool. Though the house itself is new, it has been built like an old-fashioned farmhouse, and its four rooms with private bath are furnished largely with antiques. Far off in the quiet countryside as it is, it's easy to forget that the mad world exists. Full breakfasts with items like French toast and waffles are a highlight.

MOTOR INN & **Winnapaug Inn** (401-348-8350; 1-800-288-9906; www.winnepauginn.com), 169 Shore Road, Westerly, between Dunn's Corners and Misquamicut. ($$–$$$) A three-story motor inn overlooking the Winnepaug Golf Course, with shuffleboard, a pool, and a restaurant. About a mile from a private beach.

✳ Where to Eat

DINING OUT **Dylan's** (401-596-4075), 2 Canal Street, Westerly. ($$–$$$) Open daily for dinner from 5. Casual dining in a rustic atmosphere. The all-you-can-eat pasta bar Tuesday night is a local favorite. For grander dining, there's a crustacean filet mignon topped with rock shrimp and lobster.

✐ & **Olympia Tea Room** (401-348-8211), Bay Street, Watch Hill. ($$–$$$) Open Easter through November for lunch and dinner. Once upon a time this was a circa-1918 tearoom with a marble-topped soda fountain that sent forth such delights as a puff pastry swan filled with ice cream and swimming in fudge sauce. But now the soda fountain has become a bar stocked with (among other things) an award-winning selection of wines. You can still get the Avondale swan and other old favorites like raspberry bread pudding, but only as desserts after more substantial fare that includes entrées like griddled flounder with champagne grapes, baked seafood casserole, and littlenecks and sweet Italian sausage on penne. For lunch there's an elegant lobster salad.

✐ & **Shelter Harbor Inn** (401-322-8883), 10 Wagner Road, Westerly. ($$–$$$) Luncheon 11:30–3; dinner 5–10 nightly. At this charming inn, the imaginative dishes include mustard pumpkin crusted salmon, as well as hazelnut chicken (with Frangelico liqueur). Homey fare might include sautéed calf's liver with bacon and onions, and finnan haddie. Traditional Rhode Island jonny cakes are always on the menu, too. Since this is an inn as well as a restaurant, diners can work up an appetite with a stroll on the beach (or walk off a hearty repast). Breakfasts with banana-walnut French toast or apple buttermilk pancakes are also inviting.

& **The Up-River Cafe** (401-348-9700), 37 Main Street, Westerly. ($$–$$$) Call for hours. The Pawcatuck River flows by this quietly elegant restaurant in an old stone building that in the 19th century was an addition to Westerly's Woolen Mills Company. Served in quiet dining areas are such handsomely presented and skillfully prepared entrées as fresh Stonington sea scallops with a lobster potato pancake; swordfish with preserved lemon, olives, coriander, and couscous salad; and grilled filet mignon with port wine, onion, and Gorgonzola mashed potatoes. The desserts are not to be missed.

♂ ♿ **Venice Restaurant** (401-348-0055), 165 Shore Road, Westerly. ($$–$$$) Open daily 4–9 for dinner, Saturday for lunch from noon on. As its name suggests, this is a restaurant that serves Italian specialties—chicken breast stuffed with Italian sausage, veal saltimbocca, rigatoni with broccoli and sweet Italian sausage. There is also a children's menu and a bar menu and early-bird specials.

Weekapaug Inn (401-322-0301), 15 Spring Street, Weekapaug. ($$) Open mid-June through Labor Day. Prix fixe menu in a bright and sunny dining room; in the evening, its spaciousness makes it attractive. Seafood is something of a specialty—sea scallops with mushrooms, baked salmon with mango. A special favorite is the Thursday-evening cookout on the beach, where the choices include grilled chicken, steak, or fish and a cold buffet.

EATING OUT ♞ ♂ **Bay Street Deli** (401-596-6606), 110 Bay Street, Watch Hill. ($–$$) Open May through Columbus Day, 8–8. Overstuffed sandwiches, fresh as can be, and first-rate soups and pies (the apple is wonderful).

♿ **The Cooked Goose** (401-348-9888), 92 Watch Hill Road, Westerly. ($–$$) Open year-round for breakfast and lunch. Call for hours. Lobster salad and poppy seed coleslaw, Thai sesame noodles and grilled vegetables and goat cheese in a wrap are among the offerings at this bright and cheery little eatery where the desserts—linzer cookies, jam bars, and succulent lemon squares—are too tempting to be overlooked.

Deck Seaside Grill (401-348-6300), 38 Bay Street, Watch Hill. ($$–$$$) Open in-season for lunch and dinner. There's no better view of the boats on Little Narrangansett Bay and the Watch Hill sunset than from the deck of this restaurant.

♂ ♿ **84 High Street Café** (401-596-7871), 84 High Street, Westerly. ($–$$) Open for lunch Monday through Saturday and for dinner Wednesday through Sunday. A casual, friendly eatery with Formica tables and a counter. Grilled chicken focaccia and various pastas are among the popular evening dishes.

♞ ♂ ♿ **FRA Italian Gourmet** (401-596-2888), Shore Road and Crandall Avenue, Misquamicut. ($) Open March through November for lunch and dinner; call for hours. Vegetarian delights as well as soups, salads, and sandwiches for carnivores. Mouthwatering Italian pastries like cannoli and cream-filled, shell-shaped sfogatelli.

♂ **Kelley's Deli** (401-596-9896), 14 High Street, Westerly. ($) Open Monday through Friday 8 AM–3 PM; in summer, also open Saturdays 10:30 AM–2:30 PM. There are such homemade soups as baked potato, bayou chicken and shrimp, and tomato-based chicken at this friendly little deli. Specialty sandwiches include the hefty Ninigret: turkey, ham, Swiss cheese, avocado, and a special sauce on pumpernickel bread for under $6. Homemade scones fresh from the oven are on the breakfast menu.

♿ **Maria's Seaside Cafe** (401-596-6886), 132 Atlantic Avenue, Westerly. ($–$$) Open April through November; weekends in spring and fall, daily in summer. Although it isn't really by the seaside, this pleasant little café-restaurant serves many dishes from the sea, along with a wide variety of pastas. Veal-filled Ravioli Maria in a cognac sauce is ever-popular.

♪ ♿ **Modesto's Pizza and Pasta Family Restaurant** (401-596-8686), 49 Beach Street, Westerly. ($–$$) Open daily except Monday for lunch and dinner. Extravagant pizzas made with the freshest of ingredients, Mexican nachos and tostados and fajitas, fish-and-chips, and a children's menu all combine to make this little eatery an ideal place for casual family dining.

♪ ♿ **Rafters** (401-596-5709), 55 Beach Street, Westerly. ($$) Open Saturday and Sunday for lunch and dinner; weekdays for dinner only. Entrées include French and Italian dishes and plenty of dressed-up fish and seafood. Once part of an old farm building, Rafters gets its name from the beams overhead.

♪ **St. Clair Annex Ice Cream Sandwich Shop** (401-348-8407), 141 Bay Street, Watch Hill. ($) Open Memorial Day through Columbus Day, in summer 7:30 AM–9 PM; in spring and fall 8–2 for breakfast and lunch, then till 5 for ice cream. This little ice cream and sandwich shop began as a candy kitchen in Westerly well over a century ago and has been in the same family ever since. Today its specialty is homemade ice cream in more than 30 flavors. Sandwiches, clear Rhode Island clam broth chowder, and pies (strawberry-rhubarb among them) are also on the menu.

CAFÉS **The Bean Counter** (401-596-9999), Riverside Building, Broad Street, Westerly. ($) Open Monday through Friday 7–5, Saturday 8–5, Sunday 8–3. Homemade pastry twists, scones, and muffins accompanied by cappuccino, espresso, or caffé latte for a satisfying breakfast.

♪ ♿ **Green Marble Coffee House** (401-596-2010), 55 Beach Street (in Merchants Square), Westerly. ($) Open Monday through Friday 7–5, Saturday 7–4, Sunday 8–3. Coffees and teas from around the world, fat bagel sandwiches, and homemade cookies, brownies, scones, and muffins are on the menu at this laid-back coffeehouse.

✳ Entertainment

Chorus of Westerly (401-596-8663). Several times a year this choral group holds concerts in its performance hall in the early-20th-century, former Immaculate Conception Church. The structure is noted for its exceptional acoustics. In summer the chorus offers pops in Wilcox Park.

Colonial Theatre (401-596-0810), 1 Granite Street, Westerly. In the Greek Revival, former Broad Street Christian Church, four or five theatrical performances are given annually, using some Equity actors. The company puts on Shakespeare-in-the-Park productions in Wilcox Park during summer.

♪ **Musica Dolce** (401-348-9453), Box 732, Westerly. This chamber music orchestra performs concerts for (and including) children and for adults from time to time during the year at the Chorus of Westerly Performance Hall.

✳ Selective Shopping

ANTIQUES SHOPS **Fine Consignments** (401-348-1818), 41 High Street, Westerly. More than 300 consignors from all parts of New England display and sell their jewelry, china, and furniture—some very good, others not so good—in room after room of an upstairs display hall.

Riverside Antiques (401-596-0266), 8 Broad Street, Westerly. Many dealers display 18th-, 19th-, and early-20th-century furniture, china, glass, silver, and more.

Westerly Enterprises (401-596-2298), 28 Canal Street, Westerly. Rare coins, estate jewelry, and antique military items from around the world are to be found in this funky little shop.

ART GALLERIES Artists' Cooperative Gallery of Westerly (401-596-2020), 12 High Street, Westerly. Exhibitions by artists from all over the state.

Black Duck Gallery (401-348-6500), 25 Broad Street, Westerly. Antique decoys. Prints and paintings of marine scenes, wildlife, sporting, and aviation events.

Hoxie Gallery (401-596-2877), 44 Broad Street, Westerly. There are changing exhibits by a wide variety of artists in this attractive gallery wing of the Westerly Public Library.

Lily Pad Gallery (401-596-3426), 1 Bay Street, Watch Hill. Oils and watercolors by New England artists. Some antiques and rugs.

BOOKSTORES Book & Tackle Shop (401-596-1770), 7 Bay Street, Watch Hill. Open June, July, and August, and weekends in September and October. Bernard L. Gordon, a geology professor whose specialty is marine science, owns this cozy little shop filled with "retired" books, including many on seafaring subjects and on Westerly and its environs. New books, too. The perfect browser's bookstore.

Book & Tackle Antiquated Book Store (401-596-1770), 166 Main Street, Westerly. Out-of-print books and local history are for sale year-round in this annex to Watch Hill Book & Tackle.

Book Tales (401-348-8253), 116 Granite Street, Westerly. Hardcover and paperback books.

The Other Tiger (401-596-2200), 90 High Street, Westerly. Open Monday through Saturday 9–6; Wednesday, Friday, and Saturday until 9. A wide selection of hardcover and paperback books.

SPECIAL SHOPS Bay Breeze Interiors (401-348-0722), 84 Bay Street, Watch Hill. Open April through Christmas. Anything and everything decorative for summer cottages, including contemporary hand-painted furniture and antiques.

The Candy Box (401-596-3325), 14 Fort Road, Watch Hill. Open April through Columbus Day. Saltwater taffy, Turkish delight, candied ginger, pecan patties, fudge, and sailboat-shaped lollipops—all the favorites, domestic and imported, of a childhood of yesteryear to satisfy the sweet-toothed in summertime.

Gabrielle's Originals (401-348-8986), 1 Fort Road, Watch Hill. Open April into December. A charming collection of children's summer clothing,

Sun-Up Gallery (401-596-0800), 95 Watch Hill Road, Avondale. Handmade glass, wood carving, and pottery by American artists as well as sophisticated, subdued women's clothing make this gallery set on the banks of the Pawcatuck River a worthwhile stop for the gift shopper.

Woodmansee's Boutique & Gifts (401-596-2310), 27 Broad Street, Westerly. Handmade wreaths, tie-dyed clothes, gifts.

FARM STAND Manfredi Farms (401-322-0027), 77 Dunn's Corners Road, Westerly. Open daily June through October and November 25 through December 24.

✳ Special Events

January: **A Celebration of Twelfth Night** (401-596-8663) is offered by the Chorus of Westerly in the Performance Hall. **Westerly Artists Night** (401-596-2020). The first Wednesday of each month, year-round, Westerly artists open their studios and galleries to the public. Some are in lofts; one occupies a former bank building; some have Pawcatuck River views. Music sometimes accompanies the open houses.

February: **Washington's Birthday Celebration** (401-596-7761). Sales by downtown Westerly merchants.

March or April: **Easter Egg Hunt** (401-596-7761). Easter eggs are hidden throughout Wilcox Park, and an Easter Bunny puts in an appearance. **Chorus of Westerly annual auction** in the performance hall.

May: **Memorial Day Parade** (401-596-7761) with marchers from neighboring Connecticut as well as Rhode Island. **Scottish Highland Festival** (401-596-7761) with Scottish music, games, and dancers in Wilcox Park. **Virtu Art Festival** (401-596-7761), celebrating all the arts in Wilcox Park. **Spring Concert** (401-596-8663) by the Chorus of Westerly with the Boston Festival Orchestra in the Performance Hall.

June: **Westerly Firemen's Memorial Parade** (401-596-7761). **Annual Summer Pops and Fireworks** (401-

596-8663) in Wilcox Park fills the park grounds with musical enthusiasts in mid- to late June as the Chorus of Westerly joins the Boston Festival Orchestra.

July: Three weeks of live performances of **Shakespeare-in-the-Park** are given in Wilcox Park by the Colonial Theatre (401-596-0810).

August: **Westerly Band Concerts** in Wilcox Park.

October: **Columbus Day Parade** from Westerly High School, with marchers from Connecticut as well as Rhode Island (401-596-7761). **Pasta Challenge** in Wilcox Park.

November: The 180-voice **Chorus of Westerly Fall Concert** (401-596-8663) with the Boston Festival Orchestra is preceded by a candlelight dinner. On Veterans Day the **Veterans Day Parade** (401-596-7761) begins in downtown Westerly, saluting veterans of all wars with marchers from Connecticut as well as Rhode Island. **Santa Arrives** (401-596-7761) on the steps of the Westerly Post Office, and there is an old-fashioned tree lighting with Christmas caroling.

December: A **Christmas Pops Concert** (401-596-8663) with the Chorus of Westerly and the Boston Festival Orchestra. **Christmas Crafts Bazaar at the Babcock-Smith House** (401-596-5704). A **Luminaria and Downtown Stroll** (401-596-7761) is held in Wilcox Park. Hundreds of small white candles line the downtown streets before they are carried to the park. **First Night** (401-596-7761) fireworks and dancing in downtown Westerly to celebrate the arrival of the New Year.

Block Island

Kim Grant

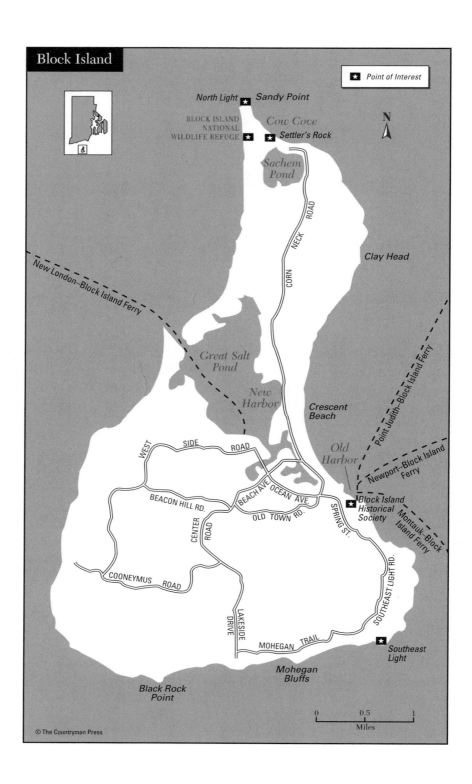

Block Island

★ Point of Interest

North Light ★ Sandy Point

BLOCK ISLAND
NATIONAL
WILDLIFE REFUGE ★

Cow Cove

★ Settler's Rock

N

Sachem
Pond

CORN NECK ROAD

Clay Head

New London–Block Island Ferry

Great Salt
Pond

New
Harbor

Crescent
Beach

Old
Harbor

Point Judith–Block Island Ferry

WEST SIDE ROAD

BEACON HILL RD.

BEACH AVE. OCEAN AVE.

OLD TOWN RD.

CENTER ROAD

SPRING ST.

Newport–Block Island
Ferry

★ Block Island
Historical
Society

Montauk–Block
Island Ferry

COONEYMUS ROAD

LAKESIDE DRIVE

MOHEGAN TRAIL

SOUTHEAST LIGHT RD.

★ Southeast
Light

Mohegan
Bluffs

Black Rock
Point

0   0.5   1
Miles

© The Countryman Press

BLOCK ISLAND

Twelve miles off the Rhode Island shore, Block Island—the Bermuda of the North—rises out of the Atlantic. It is 10.8 square miles of bayberry and blackberry tangles, moors and rolling hills, cliffs and coves. There are 365 ponds—one for each day of the year, residents say proudly—and 300 miles of stone walls rise and fall, edging the fields.

Red-roofed farmhouses perch on the hilltops, though nowadays few of them belong to farmers; Block Island has been a summer resort since the start of the 20th century. Once sultry summer days arrive on the mainland, the island's winter population of 850 more than doubles. Day-trippers on bicycles and mopeds wend their way along the winding roads; swimmers sun on Old Harbor's sandy beaches; yachters put into New Harbor. Pink and white wild roses tumble along the roadsides that lead to towering 1880s and 1890s hotels and inns, their turrets and wraparound porches overlooking the sea, open to yet another generation of visitors seeking respite from the frenetic pace of the mainland.

Block Island's history is a long one. Giovanni da Verrazano, sent in 1524 by Francis I of France to find a shorter route to the Orient, is said to have been the first European to sight Block Island. He likened its green, undulating landscape to that of the Greek island of Rhodes, thereby giving Rhode Island its name. Block Island acquired its name from the Dutch explorer Adriaen Block, who in 1614, while sailing in Long Island Sound, stopped for a time on the island, calling it Adriaen's Eylandt.

Tranquil getaway that Block Island is for many, it has not always been so peaceful a spot. In the days of the Manisseans, the Narragansett tribe that first inhabited it and called it Manisses—"Little God's Island"—there were bloody internecine Native American as well as white–Native American conflicts. Accompanied by two white youths and two Native Americans, Connecticut trader John Oldham put into Block Island in 1636 and was murdered; his companions were taken prisoner. White men and mainland Native Americans, seeking to avenge the trader's death and free the prisoners, burned the Native tribe's island encampment to the ground. Later, privateers and mooncussers came to the island to lure unsuspecting mariners onto the rocks and shoals of its waters and then loot the ships. In the 19th century a kettle of pirate gold is said to have been found, and treasure hunters still search for the chest that notorious Captain Kidd supposedly buried in a Block Island field.

For almost two centuries, from the arrival of the first English settlers in 1661 until the first hotel was built in 1842, Block Island was an out-of-the-way place where fishermen seined for mackerel and cod, shellfished, and harpooned swordfish and where farmers' cows roamed the stone-wall-bordered fields.

After 1842, visitors flocked to the summer hotels erected on hilltops and promontories, the dining rooms filled with the freshest of fish and vegetables supplied by island fishermen and farmers. In 1870 the breakwater that created Old Harbor was built, luring yachters as well as tourists.

Tourism declined after World War I, however. First came the Great Depression, followed by the 1938 hurricane that dealt the island a murderous blow. The tempest virtually cut the island in two and destroyed the entire fishing fleet.

Today tourism is regaining its former vitality. Old Harbor energetically seeks to enthrall tourists. On sunny summer days when the beach roses are in bloom or on crisp autumn days when the bittersweet is crimson and gold—and the striped bass are biting—Block Island is for sheer enjoyment.

GUIDANCE The Block Island Chamber of Commerce (401-466-2982; 1-800-383-BIRI; www.blockislandchamber.com). In summer, open daily 9–5; in the off-season, Monday through Saturday 10–3. Information is provided at its offices on the Old Harbor dock where the ferry comes in.

GETTING THERE *By boat:* Year-round ferry service is provided by the **Interstate Navigation Company** (401-783-4613; www.blockislandferry.com) from the State Pier in Galilee, Rhode Island. The sailing time is approximately 1 hour and 10 minutes. Car reservations must be made in advance. It costs $25.95 one way to bring a car over. A one-way adult passenger fare is an additional $8.30; it's $13.65 for a same-day round-trip ticket. Children under 12 pay $4.05 one way,

FISHING BOATS IN BLOCK ISLAND'S OLD HARBOR

Kim Grant

$6.40 for a 1-day round trip. Bicycles are $2.25 each way, motorcycles one way $15.20. Prices are, however, subject to change on all Interstate Navigation Company routes. For those not wishing to take a car across, there is parking in Galilee for $5 a day. Bus service to the ferry from various parts of the state is provided by the **Rhode Island Public Transit Authority** (RIPTA; 401-781-9400). **Amtrak** (1-800-USA-RAIL) stops at Kingston, where taxi service to Galilee is available.

From late June through Labor Day, Interstate Navigation Company also operates a passenger ferry from Newport. The one-way sailing time is about 2 hours. Fares are comparable to those charged for the Galilee ferry.

From mid-June to mid-September, a daily ferry departs from New London, with an additional evening ferry on Friday. Dock-to-dock sailing time is approximately 2 hours. Car reservations must be made in advance (401-783-4613) and cost $28 one way. Adult one-way tickets are an additional $15, $19 for a 1-day round trip; $9 one way for a child or $11 for a same-day round trip. Motorcycles cost $16 one way, and bikes $3.50. **Amtrak** (1-800-USA-RAIL) offers train service to New London.

High-speed 30-minute passenger ferry service is offered from Galilee from mid-May to mid-October by the **Island Hi-Speed Ferry** (1-877-733-9425; islandhi speedferry.com) and is approximately $27 round trip, with bicycles $3, but prices are subject to change. Reservations are recommended.

From Montauk, New York, *Viking Star* (401-631-668-5700) carries passengers and bicycles and surfboards—but no cars—to Block Island once a day, leaving Montauk at 9:30 and returning at 4:30 from May 23 through September 21. Earlier in May and in October there is weekend-only service. The crossing is approximately 1 hour and 45 minutes and costs $45 round trip for adults, $25 for children, $10 for surfboards or bicycles. All fares are subject to change.

By air: Year-round air service is provided from Westerly, Rhode Island, by **New England Airlines** (401-596-2460; 401-466-5881; 1-800-243-2460; www.block island.com/NEA) for $45 one way, $76 round trip, adult fare. Children are $34 one way, $57 round trip, but all fares are subject to change. Parking is available in Westerly. **Action Airlines** (1-800-243-8623) offers charter service to Block Island from Groton/New London Airport in Connecticut.

GETTING AROUND *By taxi:* Taxis are generally on hand at the dock when ferries arrive. Among those operating year-round are **Oscar Berlin** (401-741-0500), **Kirb's Taxi** (401-466-2928), and **McAloon's Taxi** (401-741-1410).

By rental car, bike, or moped: In New Harbor, **Block Island Bike & Car Rental** (401-466-2297) and **Aldo's Boat Basin Rentals** (401-466-5811) offer rental cars and bikes; in Old Harbor, the **Old Harbor Bike Shop** (401-466-2029) has bikes, cars, and mopeds. For more bike and moped rentals, see *To Do*.

MEDICAL EMERGENCY The statewide emergency number is **911.**
Block Island Medical Center (401-466-2974), Payne Road.

BENSON TOWN BEACH IN OLD HARBOR IS GOOD FOR SWIMMING OR STROLLING.

Kim Grant

✳ To See

MUSEUMS The Block Island Historical Society (401-466-2481), Old Town Road and Ocean Avenue, Old Harbor. Open Memorial Day to mid-June, weekends 10–4; mid-June through Labor Day, daily 10–4; minimal admission fee. In Block Island's 19th-century heyday of tourism, this weathered-shingled structure was an inn called the Woonsocket House. Now its little rooms are furnished with 19th-century furniture, and there are displays of the geology of the island and of pottery and beads of the Manisses tribe. Youngsters will enjoy the birds stuffed by the late island teacher and naturalist Elizabeth Dickens.

North Light Interpretive Center, Sandy Point. Open daily mid-June through Labor Day 10–5, and Labor Day through Columbus Day 11–4. Small admission fee. Exhibits here are of the island's maritime history and old lifesaving equipment.

Southeast Light (401-466-5009), Mohegan Bluffs. Call for hours. For many years this redbrick lighthouse atop Mohegan Bluffs was the strongest light on the New England seacoast, blinking its warning to mariners as far as 35 miles away. Erosion of the bluffs finally forced its relocation 400 feet back several years ago. In its new location a museum of lighthouse history is open.

HISTORIC SITES Beacon Hill. Most of this 210-foot-high hill that is the island's highest point is privately owned today, but there are walking trails nearby. In Revolutionary days, when Block Island was fiercely anti-Tory, it is said that a barrel of tar was kept on top of the hill and set on fire whenever a watchman saw what looked like an "unwelcome" boatload of deserters from the mainland heading toward shore. Then it was up to the islanders to drive off the questionable visitors.

Block Island Historical Cemetery, overlooking New Harbor. Many stones here mark the graves of 17th-century settlers. On later markers, decorations include the polished black granite ball that is the emblem of part of the island's Ball family, and the pick and shovel of an islander who took part in the gold rush.

Indian Burial Ground, near the intersection of Center Road, Lakeside Drive, and Cooneymus Road. Here are the headstones and footstones of a number of Native American graves. The Manisseans were buried in a sitting position, which explains the closely set gravestones.

Mohegan Bluffs, to the west of the Southeast Light. These sandy cliffs rising 150 feet above the sea get their name from that of a war party of 40 invading members of the Mohegan tribe, who were cornered there by the local Manisseans. A wooden stairway leads down to the water.

New Harbor. Its name notwithstanding, this was Block Island's earliest harbor, but keeping the breachway open between Great Salt Pond and Block Island Sound became too difficult and expensive for the early settlers, so in 1705 New Harbor was abandoned in favor of Old Harbor. However, in 1897 a permanent cut was made, and today this is the port of call for most yachters visiting the island as well as for the new high-speed ferry. On the hilltop above it sits the Victorian Narragansett Inn, and there are restaurants and facilities for yachters at Payne's Dock.

Old Harbor. Most ferries dock in this Victorian seaport. Sprawling early-1900s hotels, with turrets, gingerbread decoration, and wraparound porches, and the 0.5-mile-long lifeguarded Fred Benson Town Beach makes this an inviting spot for the day-tripper. Restaurants offer take-out fish-and-chips, lobster and clam rolls, and chowder. Little shops sell souvenirs, T-shirts, and bric-a-brac. There are also art galleries offering jewelry, stained glass, and pottery as well as paintings.

Rebecca, center of Old Harbor. This statue of the biblical Rebecca, wife of Isaac and mother of Jacob and Esau, was erected by the Women's Christian Temperance Union in 1896. At its foot sit basins kept supplied with fresh water for dogs and horses—either in memory of the gentle Rebecca's kindness to animals or because the WCTU promoted the drinking of water rather than spirits.

Settlers' Rock, Cow Cove. It is at this spot, according to legend, that Block Island's first settlers—from Braintree and Taunton in the Massachusetts Bay Colony—landed in 1661. The tale is that they pushed their cows overboard and made them swim ashore—hence the cove's name. You can walk along a sandy road from here to the North Light, but take care to stay on the road to prevent damaging the birds' nests at Sandy Point.

Smilin' Through, Cooneymus Road above Rodman's Hollow. Private. It was in this little house, one of the island's oldest farmsteads, that composer and lyricist Arthur Penn wrote in post–World War I days, "There's a little white road winding over the hill, to a little white cot by the sea. There's a little green gate, by whose trellis I wait, where two eyes of blue come smilin' through at me."

✳ To Do

AIRPLANE RIDES **New England Airlines** (401-466-5681 on Block Island; 401-596-2460 in Westerly; 1-800-243-2460) takes sightseers on 15-minute flights over the island, year-round, in single-engine Piper Cherokees that carry up to five people. The rate is $50 for one or two passengers.

BICYCLING/MOPED RENTALS Block Island is the ideal spot for leisurely cycling. Though it is hilly and the roads are winding, the hills are never arduous. The vistas invite cyclists to stop and rest a while at the side of the road and look out across the stone walls to the sea. Because the roads are narrow and tortuous, automobile drivers tend to travel at a reasonable speed. Mopeds are an alternative—though considerably less safe—means of transportation. Rental rates for all modes of transportation—cars, bikes, mopeds—tend to be higher on weekends than on weekdays.

Breakwater Rentals (401-466-2478), Old Harbor.

Island Moped & Bike (401-466-2700), Payne's Dock, New Harbor. A wide selection of bicycles and single and double mopeds may be rented by the day or the hour.

The Moped Man (401-466-5444), 435 Water Street, Old Harbor. At this shop located diagonally across from the ferry landing, mopeds, mountain bikes, child seats, and assorted gear for moped riders are available.

Old Harbor Bike Shop (401-466-2029), to the left of the ferry landing as visitors arrive in Old Harbor. Single and double mopeds, bikes, cars, and vans available by the day or the hour.

Seacoast Inn Bicycle Rentals (401-466-2882), at the Seacoast Inn on High Street in Old Harbor. Mountain bikes, dual-suspension bikes, 7- and 21-speed bikes, children's bikes and carriers.

BIRDING Block Island is situated under the Atlantic Flyway. It is said that more birds, heading north in spring and south in fall, pass by Block Island than anywhere else in New England. This, combined with the low vegetation, makes Block Island an excellent birding spot. From August to early November is exceptionally good for birding, and the **Audubon Society of Rhode Island** (401-949-5454) offers a special weekend trip annually in late September or early October.

CANOEING AND KAYAKING Oceans & Ponds (401-466-5131), Ocean Avenue, Old Harbor. Open May through Columbus Day, daily 9–6. Both kayaks and canoes are available to rent.

CARRIAGE RIDES Seaside Carriage Rides (401-466-2195), Box 602, Block Island. Off-season hayrides are offered.

DIVING Island Outfitters (401-466-5502), 239 Ocean Avenue, Old Harbor. Diving advice and gear.

FISHING Striped bass and bluefish bite close to the Block Island shore. Offshore there are tuna, bonito, shark, and marlin; in the island's wealth of freshwater ponds, pickerel and bass are likely catches. A number of charter boats take sportfishers out to the fishing grounds in summer.

Kahuna Sports Fishing (401-466-2184), 206 Water Street, Old Harbor. Inshore and offshore fishing trips of half or full days aboard a 37-foot, six-passenger sportfishing boat.

G. Willie Makit (401-466-5151), Captain Bill Gould, Box 1010, Block Island. Inshore and offshore fishing trips range in length from 3 to 10 hours, with a six-passenger minimum.

Persuader (401-783-5644), Captain Denny Dillon, 110 Avice Street, Narragansett. This six-passenger mainland-based boat takes anglers out into Block Island waters on trips of 4 to 10 hours.

Oceans & Ponds (401-466-5131), Ocean Avenue, Old Harbor. Open May through Columbus Day, daily 9–6. Offshore fishing trips are also offered by this fishing equipment company.

HIKING ✍ **The Greenway** (see *Green Space*) is a 30-mile system of trails through both public and private lands. It crosses 600 acres of the island—from Great Salt Pond to Black Rock—and is open to hikers, birders, and other nature lovers, but not to cyclists. A map of the trails is available at **The Nature Conservancy** (401-466-2129) opposite Payne's Dock in New Harbor. The Conservancy also offers guided tours and children's nature programs in summer.

HORSEBACK RIDING ✍ **Rustic Rides Farm** (401-466-5060), West Side Road. Open May through October 9–6. There are guided trail and beach rides, pony rides for children, and carriage rides through the countryside available at this stable.

KAYAKING AND CANOEING **New Harbor Kayak Rental** (401-466-2890), Ocean Avenue, New Harbor. Kayaks and motorboats available by the day or hour.

Oceans & Ponds (401-466-5131), Ocean Avenue, Old Harbor. Kayak, canoe, and rod rentals.

Old Harbor Bike Shop (401-466-2029), to the left of the ferry landing in Old Harbor. Kayaks for rent.

PARASAILING **Block Island Parasail** (401-466-2474), Box 727, Block Island. Parachute flights, which rise up to 600 feet above island and sound, take off and land all summer long.

SAILING **The Block Island Club** (401-466-5939), Corn Neck Road, Old Harbor. Open late June through August 9–4. For 30 years this club has been providing instruction in sailing, swimming, and tennis for families and individuals. The club has J-prams, JY15s, Lasers, keel boats, and Sunfish available to members. Two-week and full-season single and family memberships are available, with instruction in sports for an additional fee, but use of boats and courts is included.

Sail Block Island (401-466-7938), Smugglers' Cove Marina, Old Harbor. In summer and into fall, sailing lessons are offered and JY15s, Pearson Ensigns, Herreshoff Bullseyes, and Hobie 16s are available for rent, while the 70-foot brigantine *Black Pearl* can be chartered.

SWIMMING **Ballard's Beach,** to the left as you leave the Old Harbor ferry landing. This is a clean, sandy, private beach adjacent to Ballard's Inn but open to the public and supplied with food, beverages, and toilet facilities.

Fred Benson Town Beach (formerly Block Island State Beach; 401-466-2611), Corn Neck Road, Old Harbor. The town decided to name this section of Crescent Beach for longtime resident, raconteur, historian, and all-around favorite citizen Fred Benson. It boasts a concession stand, a bathhouse with cold showers made for rugged New Englanders, and a lifeguard.

🎣 **Sachem Pond,** at the north end of the island near Settlers' Rock. A fine place for youngsters to have a freshwater dip (with a touch of salt remaining from the 1938 hurricane), but there is no lifeguard on duty.

TENNIS **The Atlantic Inn** (401-466-5883; 1-800-224-7422), High Street, Old Harbor. Tennis courts for inn guests are available to the public for $20 an hour when guests are not using them.

The Block Island Club (401-466-5939), Corn Neck Road, Old Harbor. Access to the courts is available to members (see *Sailing*).

Champlin's Marina (401-466-2641), New Harbor. Use of the tennis courts by the public is possible when guests are not using them. The fee is $20 an hour.

✴ Green Space

BEACHES **Black Rock Beach,** on the south shore at the end of Black Rock Road. Accessible to only the hardiest. The beach is stony, and the water is rough with an undertow. No facilities or lifeguard.

Charlestown Beach, Dead Man's Cove, down Coast Guard Road off West Shore Road. A west-facing beach that gets sun in the afternoon. Pebbly, so wear sneakers or beach shoes. There are no facilities or lifeguards, but the water is clear and you can often have the beach almost to yourself.

Coast Guard Beach, farther down Coast Guard Road at the entrance into New Harbor. Friday and Saturday afternoons this is a fine place to watch the boats coming and going into the Great Salt Pond. Good fishing, too.

Crescent Beach, Corn Neck Road (northeasterly from Old Harbor). Two-plus miles of sand, surf, and (cold) blue water. A must if you visit the island.

Mansion Beach, 0.5 mile down dirt Mansion House Road off Corn Neck Road. No facilities or lifeguards, but a pleasant stretch of beach in a pretty area of bayberries and wild roses. There is often more surf here than at Benson and Scotch Beaches.

Mohegan Bluffs, south shore at the foot of the steep bluffs. Not a bad climb down, but it's a long, hard climb up. Rocky beach with rough surf. No lifeguard.

Pebbly Beach, southeast shore. Off Spring Street. A sandy little beach in a cove. No lifeguard.

Scotch Beach. Beyond Fred Benson Town Beach, farther to the right, opposite the Great Salt Pond. Pebbly, but a pleasant, generally uncrowded beach. No facilities or lifeguards.

Vail's Beach, south shore. Stony beach with rough water.

Also see *Swimming.*

WALKS Clay Head, off Corn Neck Road. A dirt trail called Bluestone leads to and along briar-clad Clay Head, which once was faced with good, usable clay in shades of blue, ocher, white, and red. Unfortunately rain and sea have eroded the clay surface. This headland is the perfect spot for watching the events of June's Block Island boat race, and hikers here will find 9 miles of trails known as the Maze that wander above the surf and past shimmering blue ponds and through pine groves.

AMBLING THROUGH THE FIELDS WITH NORTH LIGHT
IN THE BACKGROUND

Dickens Farm. This 40-acre bird sanctuary of stone-wall-edged fields begins on Cooneymus Road. Pheasants strut and swallows wheel over its grasses, and this is a favorite spot for viewing the marsh hawk. In the interests of conservation, all visitors are urged to stay on the marked paths.

The Greenway. Thirty miles of Greenway walking trails begin on Beacon Hill Road and continue to Cooneymus Road, through pastures and heath and the Enchanted Forest of Japanese black pine planted by conservationists in the 1930s and 1940s. Guided nature tours are offered twice daily in summer, and a map is available for self-guided tours from **The Nature Conservancy** (401-466-2129) in New Harbor, across from Dead-Eye Dick's. Entry points onto the Greenway from main roads are marked with posts.

Rodman's Hollow. This glacial depression that stretches down to the sea is particularly spectacular in spring, when the snow-white shadbush is in bloom, and in fall when the bayberry and poison ivy are crimson. A Greenway path meanders through the brush from Cooneymus Road to the water.

Sandy Point. One of the largest gull rookeries in Rhode Island—frequented by black-backed and herring gulls as well as yellow- and black-crowned night herons—is nestled in these dunes. Tall blond swamp grasses lie flat in the wind against the gold-brown sand. Beachcombers stroll the water's edge gathering the round, smooth gray and white stones that rumble in from the waters of the sound. It was at this northernmost point of the island, legend has it, that the 18th-century Dutch ship *Palatine,* filled with immigrants seeking religious freedom in the New World, drifted ashore between Christmas and New Year's Day in 1752. A mutiny had left the captain and many of the officers dead and the passengers in the merciless hands of the mutineers. When they had extracted all the gold they could from the hapless immigrants, the mutinous crew abandoned ship, leaving the vessel to drift ashore at Sandy Point. In a poem criticized by Block Islanders as historically inaccurate, John Greenleaf Whittier described Block Island "wreckers" hustling down to the shore to further strip the vessel. In any case, they apparently brought 16 passengers ashore, but when a storm threatened to break up the craft, they set it afire and adrift, unwittingly leaving a woman on board—and her screams as the flames rose around her have haunted Block Islanders ever since, warning of danger.

✳ Lodging

Note: Unless otherwise indicated, the zip code is 02807.

INNS Atlantic Inn (401-466-5883; 1-800-224-7422; www.atlanticinn.com), High Street, Old Harbor. ($$$–$$$$) Open Memorial Day through Halloween. This 21-room white-clapboard hotel has sat like a grande dame on its hill above Old Harbor and the sea since 1879. Though close to town, it seems far away from the hustle and bustle of summer crowds. The pleasant rooms are more or less Victorian in style and include a continental buffet breakfast. There is a minimum 3-night stay required on weekends in high season. Two tennis courts and croquet are available for guests, and the inn's location makes its porch the ideal island spot for sunset viewing.

Nicholas Ball Cottage, Spring Street, Old Harbor. ($$$$) Open year-round. A re-creation of the 1888 St. Anne's Episcopal Church, which was blown down in the 1938 hurricane, this inn offers three rooms equipped with fireplace and Jacuzzi. Some baths are shared, and all rooms have fans. This is part of the Hotel Manisses.

Blue Dory Inn (401-466-5891; 1-800-992-7290; www.blockisland inns.com), Dodge Street, Old Harbor. ($$$) Open year-round. This 10-room Victorian-style inn, with five beach cottages, is only minutes away from the beach and from the heart of Old Harbor. There is a view of the sea through the white-curtained windows of many of the rooms. Floral bedspreads and antique furniture are part of the ambience; rockers and rattan adorn the rear deck and patio. A continental breakfast with home-baked breads is included. All rooms have private bath; some, air-conditioning.

✔ **Gables Inn** and **Gables Inn II** (401-466-2213; 401-466-7721; www.GablesInnBlockIsland.com), Dodge Street, Old Harbor. ($$–$$$) Open late May through November. A 2-minute walk from Crescent Beach, this is an ideal spot for families with children (although the inn cannot accommodate very large families). There are barbecue and picnic facilities in the yard, and rooms have access to a refrigerator. Apartments are available by the week. The room decor is Victorian, and some rooms have a shared bath. Ceiling and dresser fans help blow away the midsummer heat.

✔ **Hotel Manisses** (401-466-2063; 401-466-2421; 1-800-MANISSES; www.blockislandresorts.com), Spring Street, Old Harbor. ($$$–$$$$) Open year-round. The turreted Victorian

Manisses has 17 rooms named for ships wrecked in Block Island waters. Guest rooms are small, but the spacious, sunny common rooms are filled with summery white rattan furniture and stained glass, and there is a Boston-style saloon bar. Complimentary tours of the island are offered daily by the inn, and an attraction for families with children is the little animal farm of donkeys, llamas, goats, geese, and ducks.

♿ **Payne's Harbor View Inn** (401-466-5758; www.paynesharborviewinn .com), 111 Beach Avenue, New Harbor. Open April through November. This brand-new hilltop inn with an old-fashioned look has eight rooms and two suites through which cool breezes blow. A continental breakfast is served.

Sea Breeze Inn (401-466-2275; 1-800-786-2276; www.blockisland .com/seabreeze), Spring Street, Old Harbor. ($$–$$$$) Two rooms are open year-round; the other eight, mid-May through mid-October. Overlooking Spring House Pond and a field of wildflowers with a view of the sea in the distance, the weathered-shingled Sea Breeze is an idyllic honeymoon getaway. The main building was once an old-fashioned boardinghouse. There are four rooms, each in its own airy, sunny cottage with antique furnishings, pastel decor, porch, and private bath; five rooms with shared bath are in the main house. A continental breakfast of juice, coffee, and home-baked pastries is delivered to guests' doors in a basket each morning.

Sheffield House (401-466-2494; 1-866-466-2494; www.thesheffield house.com), High Street, Old Harbor. ($$–$$$$) Open year-round. The

Sheffield House is a turreted six-guest-room Victorian in the heart of Old Town. It is pleasantly furnished with patchwork quilts and family antiques and has a welcoming home-spun look, There are some shared baths. A full breakfast is included. Fans are available.

1661 Inn and Guest House (401-466-2063; 401-466-2421), Spring Street, Old Harbor. ($$$$) Open year-round. Cottages and efficiencies, in addition to the main inn. Set on a hill-top overlooking the sea, this nine-room inn has an unbeatable view of sunsets over the ocean. The inn gets its name not from the year it was built—that's 1890—but from the year Block Island was settled. To further keep a historical perspective, each room is named for a notable Block Islander. The decor is eclectic, with lots of antiques to give it a tranquil, old-fashioned air, but there are also sliding glass doors in rooms where they improve the view, Jacuzzis for the aching bones of cyclists, and fans as required. Breakfast is a bountiful buffet. Dinner is offered from the third week in May to the third week in October in the imposing old Hotel Manisses across the street.

Spring House Hotel (401-466-5844; 1-800-234-9263; www.springhouse hotel.com), Spring Street, Old Harbor. ($$$$) Open from April through mid-October. Since 1854 the sprawl-ing Spring House on its promontory above Block Island Sound has been receiving guests—one of the most famous in its early days was Ulysses S. Grant. Fifteen acres of hills and dales surround the inn, and there are con-certs on the grounds every other Sun-day in July and August. Among the attractive public rooms are the dining room done in a restful pale pink and a sitting room furnished in Victorian fashion. The cool bar off the dining room is **Victoria's Parlor.** Rooms, studios, and suites are all available, and Victorian again tends to be the theme. If sea breezes don't blow through the rooms sufficiently, there are ceiling fans to help out. A complimentary continental break-fast is served in the dining room or on the porch, and lunch and dinner are offered daily in the dining room in summer, with drinks on the porch.

🍴 **Surf Hotel** (401-466-2241), Dodge Street, Old Harbor. ($–$$) Open Memorial Day through Columbus Day. This weathered-shingled beach-front hostelry with rockers on its porch is truly vintage. It will especially please families with young children and those looking for early-20th-century Block Island. The lobby is darkly Victorian with maroon Nau-gahyde chairs, a tin ceiling, a giant-sized chess set for guests enjoying the comfort of the hotel on stormy nights, and an equally dark nook of a library. These rooms belong in an Agatha Christie movie set. The bedrooms (most with a shared bath) are fur-nished in Victoriana, too. Its slightly down-at-the-heels funkiness will be memorable for some—and the last thing others will want. But with its location virtually on the beach and near a playground, it is ideal for youngsters. There are ceiling fans in all rooms, and a light buffet breakfast is included. A 6-night minimum book-ing is required in summer.

BED & BREAKFASTS Barrington Inn (401-466-5510; 1-888-279-9400; www.thebarringtoninn.com), Beach and Ocean Avenue, New Harbor. ($$$) Open early spring through mid-November. There are six sunny, airy rooms with bath and two complete apartments in this cozy, newly refurbished hostelry on the quieter part of the island. It's about 0.75 mile to Old Harbor and 0.25 mile to New Harbor. From the back deck there are views of New Harbor and Trim's Pond. The apartments are $820–1,200 a week. Fans are available.

Hygeia House (401-466-9616), Beach Avenue, New Harbor. ($–$$$$) Open year-round. This handsomely restored, mansard-roofed house was built in 1886 by Dr. John C. Champlin, a Block Island physician who named it for a minor Greek goddess of health. It was given a new lease on life in 1999. Its 10 rooms with private bath are appointed with the Victorian furnishings that have been in the house since the beginning, All rooms have a view out over either Old or New Harbor. A continental breakfast is served.

Rose Farm Inn (401-466-2034; www.rosefarm.com), Roslyn Road off High Street, Old Harbor. ($$–$$$) Open May through late October. Because the Rose Farm Inn is set on a rise above 20 acres of rolling hillside, the ocean can be seen in the distance from this Block Island getaway vacation spot. The original farmhouse dates back to 1897, but there is also a new Captain Rose House with an old-fashioned look. While the deluxe rooms have fringed canopy beds, a modern touch is the Jacuzzis in the rooms themselves. An expanded continental breakfast is served on an enclosed porch with flowers all around outdoors. Fans are in all rooms.

Hardy Smith House (401-466-2466), High Street, Old Harbor. ($$–$$$) Open Memorial Day through October. The Hardy Smith

THE VENERABLE SPRING HOUSE HOTEL IN OLD HARBOR

Tom Gannon

House was built in 1826, as a sign on its door announces proudly. Prettily painted, it has a most inviting look inside and out and is close to where the Old Harbor action is, but still quiet. Summer weekends require a 2-night minimum stay. All rooms have ceiling fans.

Sullivan House Bed and Breakfast (401-466-5020; www.sullivanhousebi .com), New Harbor. ($$$–$$$$) Open early spring until Columbus Day. This recently restored 1904 house, situated above Trim's Pond and acres of sweet-smelling bayberries, opened as an inn in 1994. The owners are descendants of the original 1904 builder, who constructed the interior walls of knotty pine and the exterior walls of stone. Its sweeping grounds make it an ideal spot for wedding receptions, but the five rooms and spectacular situation would satisfy just about anyone's idea of a Block Island retreat.

The Weather Bureau Inn (401-466-9977; 1-800-633-8624; www.weather bureauinn.com), Beach Avenue, New Harbor. ($$$) Open May through October. Built as a U.S. Department of Commerce weather station in 1903, the inn has fine views of both Old and New Harbor from its hilltop location. Wood paneling, wainscoting, and Victorian decor contribute to a cozy ambience in this hostelry, which opened in 1994. Enjoy a continental breakfast on the front porch, back porch, or rooftop deck, which all afford views of the ocean and the sound. All rooms have private bath. Fans are available.

✳ Where to Eat

DINING OUT The Atlantic Inn Restaurant (401-466-5883), Old Harbor. ($$$$) Open Memorial Day through mid-October for dinner. Fish, of course, is a specialty of the elegant prix fixe dinner here, but all dishes are prepared with flair. A typical menu might include a terrine of wild mushrooms followed by seared salmon and lemon cake for dessert. Service is impeccable. For fine dining, it's a favorite with local residents. The hilltop location overlooking the water affords the best of sunset views. Dress may be casual.

Harborside Inn (401-466-5504), Water Street, Old Harbor. ($$$$) Open daily mid-May through mid-September, for breakfast 8–11, lunch 11:30–4, and dinner 5:30–10. You can eat indoors or out on the porch. Outdoors, you can watch the ferry and the passing crowds come and go. The menu includes fish and shellfish in all forms—lobster ravioli sautéed in garlic and served with a pink brandy cream sauce, flounder with a lemon butter sauce, a seafood pasta with shrimp, clams, mussels, and scallops, a veal chop with fresh sage, prosciutto, and mozzarella. The salad bar is a favorite with one and all.

♿ **Hotel Manisses** (401-466-2836), Spring Street, Old Harbor. ($$$–$$$$) Open April to mid-November, serving dinner daily 5:30–10. You can start your dinner here at the raw bar, then have your main course on the outside deck or in the dining room proper. Entrées may include a bouillabaisse of local fish or a honey-braised pork shank with vegetable and potato. Among the desserts are a Cambozola cheese apple tart and hot Indian pudding. A fine way to end a Block Island evening out—whether or not you dine at the Manisses—is sipping an after-dinner drink or a flaming coffee at the **Victo-**

rian **Top Shelf Bar** with its cool and comfortable wicker furniture.

Spring House Hotel (401-466-5844), Spring Street, Old Harbor. ($$$–$$$$) Open daily, except the occasional Saturday, June through Labor Day 11:30–3:30 and 6–10. In the light and airy dining room overlooking Rhode Island Sound, the baked stuffed lobsters will put you in the Block Island mood; there are chicken and meat dishes, too, of course. The entrée price includes potato or rice and a vegetable.

Winfield's (401-466-5856), Corn Neck Road, Old Harbor. ($$–$$$) Open Memorial Day through Labor Day, daily 6–10 PM. Probably Block Island's most sophisticated fare, making good use of local seafood but still including rack of lamb, Angus steaks, and tempting pasta dishes. Meals are nicely prepared and presented. Portions tend to be small.

EATING OUT Ballard's Inn (401-466-2231), on the Harbor in Old Harbor. ($$$) Open May through September, daily 11:30–10. Lobster family-style—two 1.25-pound lobsters, corn on the cob, and potatoes—is just one of the meals this longtime Block Island shore dinner hall (in the same location since the 1880s) is famous for. The fish-and-chips with corn on the cob is another. You can eat under an umbrella on the patio after your swim at the beach or in the big shore dinner hall itself.

The Beachhead (401-466-2249), Corn Neck Road, Old Harbor. ($) Open daily 11:30–9. Fat, juicy hamburgers are the specialty at this casual little roadside eatery, but you can have chili or sandwiches, fish-and-chips, and bountiful salads as well.

✐ **Bethany's Airport Diner** (401-466-3100), Block Island Airport. ($) Open Memorial Day through Labor Day, daily 6–3; off-season, 6–2. Should you want a $2.95 bowl of homemade corn chowder or a $3.95 bowl of chili—literally, to fly—the Airport Diner is the place to go. If your preference is to stay on the ground and watch the hundreds of small private planes that take off and land on Block Island on summer weekends, you might want to try the Airport Diner's most popular dish, Crab Cake Benny: poached eggs on an English muffin topped with hollandaise sauce and a crabcake.

Dead-Eye Dick's (401-466-2654), New Harbor. ($$) Open for dinner late May through Labor Day. A favorite with the yachters who put into New Harbor and are weary of galley dishes, Dead-Eye Dick's is right on the water, and you can eat on its deck and watch the boats sail by while you enjoy the likes of crabcakes or swordfish, sea scallops or pasta. À la carte entrée prices are in the low to middle teens.

✐ & **Eli's** (401-466-5230), 458 Chapel Street, New Harbor. ($$–$$$) Open weekends in March and April and from Columbus Day to mid-November, 5:30–10; daily in summer, also 5:30–10. For years it was the pasta that mattered at Eli's, but now this bistro-like restaurant that receives kudos from Block Islanders for its fine quality also has such grand entrées as rack of lamb and pesto-crusted grouper and such desserts as chocolate bread pudding and pumpkin cheesecake.

🐾 ✐ & **Ernie's Breakfast Restaurant** (401-466-2473), Water Street, Old Harbor. ($) Open 6:30–noon May through Columbus Day. Situated on the deck above Finn's, this breakfast eatery is the perfect place to wait for a ferry and enjoy coffee and home-made muffins for under $3, or more exotic lox and cream cheese omelets for under $10.

✍ ♿ **Finn's Seafood Restaurant** (401-466-2473), Water Street, Old Harbor. ($–$$$) Open Memorial Day through Columbus Day, Sunday through Thursday 11:30–10, Friday and Saturday until 11. New arrivals to Block Island can't miss Finn's, facing as it does the ferry parking lot. Go there for the memorable clam chow-der, fried clams, fish-and-chips, baked fish sandwiches, lobster rolls, and broiled fish. The dining room decor is plain and simple, but there's also a deck and a take-out window.

✍ ♿ **Mohegan Cafe and Brewery** (401-466-5911), Water Street, Old Harbor ($–$$) Open daily for lunch and dinner mid-March to November. There's a definite nautical, masculine look to the Mohegan Cafe and Brew-ery where four to six homemade brews are always on tap and range from pale ales to Irish ambers and nonalcoholic ginger beer. The café is largely but not entirely casual. There's prime rib and fresh seafood on the menu along with Tex-Mex and Thai dishes. Luncheon favorites include a veggie wrap and a fried clam plate. It's noisy at night—not suited for inti-mate dining but a fine place for a rol-licking good time.

The Oar (401-466-8820), New Har-bor. ($$) Open May through Labor Day 6:30 AM–1 AM for breakfast, lunch, and dinner and serving every-thing from twin lobsters to hot dogs. The blueberry pancakes are a break-fast favorite; Rhode Island clam

cakes, lobster rolls, chowder, and veggie burgers are inviting lunch-time fare.

✍ **Pizza Plus** (401-466-0039), Corn Neck Road, Old Harbor. Open Memorial Day to Christmas noon–9. The pizzas and calzones, hearty salads and broccoli pie, heroes and hoagies and grinders and subs offered here will surely satisfy the appetite of any mariner in from the sea.

✍ ♿ **Sharky's Restaurant** (401-466-9900), Corn Neck Road, Old Harbor. ($–$$) Open 11:30–10 May through November. At this down-home restau-rant, sandwiches, fish-and-chips, and burgers are always on the menu, but there are also more substantial entrées.

Smuggler's Cove (401-466-2828), New Harbor. ($$) Open 11:30–4 and 6–10 PM June through Labor Day. Though set right on Smuggler's Marina, there is a parking lot between the restaurant and the water, which is too bad. But the atmosphere is warm and friendly, indoors and out. The cooking isn't all gussied up, making this the perfect place for when you just want a plain broiled salmon or swordfish steak or a piece of broiled chicken. There is a good, though not extensive, wine list.

Three Sisters (401-466-9661), Old Town Road across from the Block Island Historical Society, Old Harbor. ($–$$$) Open April to mid-November 10–3 and in summer for evening babecues. The homemade soups, meat loaf, and turkey, bacon, and avo-cado sandwiches are among customer' favorites.

SNACKS AND ICE CREAM **Aldo's Bakery & Homemade Ice Cream** (401-466-2198), Weldon's Way, Old

Town. Open 6:30 AM–11:30 PM May through September. Twenty-four flavors of ice cream and many frozen yogurts to choose from at the end of a long day of bicycle riding. At breakfast or teatime, you might want to sample Aldo's Portuguese sweetbread, blueberry muffins, cinnamon twists, cupcakes, and turnovers, or any kind of doughnut you can think of. For yachters, Aldo's delivers baked goods to boats in the harbor each morning and afternoon.

✔ **The Ice Cream Place** (401-466-2145), through the archway beside the Harborside Inn, Old Harbor. Open 10 AM–11 PM daily May through Labor Day, weekends until Columbus Day. The ice cream, made to order in Connecticut for the Ice Cream Place, comes in delectable flavors like French Silk (light chocolate with bittersweet bits in it) and coconut. You can have it scooped into a homemade waffle cone or topped with homemade hot fudge or butterscotch sauce and real whipped cream. There are also cookies, muffins, fresh lemonade, and fat-free and sugar-free frozen yogurts. The Ice Cream Place prides itself on being Block Island's original ice cream parlor. You can sit outside in the shade and enjoy your delicious confection.

Juice 'n' Java (401-466-5220), Dodge Street, Old Harbor. Open 7 or 8 AM–11 PM Memorial Day through Columbus Day. This was Block Island's very first coffeehouse, and it specializes in rich desserts and international coffees. There are books and magazines to read, artwork on the walls to admire, Scrabble and chess to play, an Internet connection, and storytellers and musicians performing live as the nights wear on.

✳ **Entertainment**

Club Soda (401-466-5397), in the basement of the High View Hotel, Connecticut Avenue, on the way to the airport. Open year-round 4 PM–1 AM weekdays, and Sunday noon until 1 AM. Bar and lounge with occasional live entertainment.

The Empire Theatre (401-466-2555), Old Harbor. First a roller-skating rink back in 1882, then a theater for plays of stage and screen, the Empire fell on hard times in the 1980s when the old structure began to give way and appeared destined for demolition. But in 1993 it got a reprieve, and now the theater is all spruced up and showing first-run films.

McGovern's Yellow Kittens (401-466-5855), Corn Neck Road, Old Harbor. Year-round. This is where you go for live music on the weekends, and dancing to jukebox tunes any night of the week. There are pool tables, Ping-Pong, darts, and video and pinball games to keep you occupied from 11 AM until the wee hours in summer; from 4 PM until 1 AM in winter. Lunch, and dinner until 10, are also served in summer.

✔ **Oceanwest Theatre** (401-466-2971), Champlin's Marina, New Harbor. First-run films are offered in this little theater, and on rainy days there are often matinees for the small fry. Bear in mind, though, that it has a tin roof and can be noisy.

Payne's Dock (401-466-5572), New Harbor. Once upon a time this was where the New London boat and the steamers from New York came in. Now it's a marina for private boats. But the live Irish song on Wednesday and weekends at little **Mahogany**

Shoals, the bar down on the dock, is open to everyone.

✷ Selective Shopping

ANTIQUES SHOPS **Eylandt Fine Antiques & Furnishings** (401-466-9888), first floor, Payne's Harbor View Inn at Beach and Ocean Avenues, New Harbor. Open Memorial Day through October, Wednesday through Sunday. This one-room antiques shop whose walls are covered with antique maps and seascapes gets its name from the island's old name, *Adriaen's Eylandt.* When its owner isn't on the island, he's traveling the world, collecting African carvings and Russian icons, old globes and inlaid boxes to squeeze into his inviting shop.

ART GALLERIES **Jessie Edwards Gallery** (401-466-5314), second floor, New Post Office Building, Water Street, Old Harbor. Open mid-June through Columbus Day, daily 10–6, Sunday 10–5; other times by appointment. Woodcuts, watercolors, prints, baskets, and pottery by Jessie Edwards and other New England artists.

Eisenhauer Gallery (401-466-2422), second floor, New Post Office Building, Water Street, Old Harbor. Landscapes, seascapes, figurative work by established and emerging artists, handmade furniture and jewelry. Open May through Columbus Day, daily 10–5.

Encore Gallery (401-466-2770), Figurehead Building, Water Street, Old Harbor. Open 11–6 daily mid-June through Labor Day. A gallery showing contemporary painting, sculpture and drawings, ceramics and glass by Rhode Island artists.

Malcolm Greenaway Gallery (401-466-5331), Water Street at Fountain Square, Old Harbor. Open 9–9 daily in-season; until 5 after Labor Day. At other times by appointment. Color photographs of Block Island by Malcolm Greenaway.

Mixed Media Gallery (401-466-2910), second floor, New Post Office Building, Old Harbor. Open June through Labor Day, Monday through Saturday 10–6, Sunday 11–4. From Labor Day through Columbus Day, Thursday through Saturday 10–6, and Sunday 11–4.

The Spring Street Gallery (401-466-5374), Spring Street, across from the Manisses Hotel, Old Harbor. Open daily Memorial Day through Columbus Day. The artists and crafters represented here are all year-round or summer Block Islanders, and the works they are showing and selling include paintings, photographs, jewelry, decoupage, quilting, and folk art.

BOOKSTORES **The Book Nook Inc.** (401-466-2993), Water Street, Old Harbor. Open April through November daily, 10:30–4. Paperback books of all kinds. Special-order hardcovers.

Island Bound (401-466-8878), New Post Office Building, Water Street, Old Harbor. Open daily year-round, 9–9 in summer; call for hours in winter. Hardcover, paperback, Block Island books. Books aplenty to keep you occupied on stormy days.

SPECIAL SHOPS **Beach Plum** (401-466-8844), 596 Corn Neck Road, Old Harbor. Open Memorial Day through Columbus Day, daily 9–8. Origami paper, pretty gift wrapping paper, exotic candles, and natural bath salts are among the offerings in this pleasant little gift and art supply store.

The Bird's Nest (401-466-5080), Dodge Street, Old Harbor. Open April through Columbus Day, daily 10–5 and weekends until 9; from Columbus Day until Christmas, open weekends. Cheerful ceramics, art glass, aprons and tea towels nautically decorated with seagulls and shells and fish.

Block Island Blue Pottery (401-466-2945), Dodge Street, Old Harbor. Open July through August, daily 10–6, and weekends until Columbus Day. Joan S. Mallick of Trumbull, Connecticut, has been fashioning island clay into fanciful, blue-glazed pottery for years now. You can find dinnerware and dresserware, ceramic jewelry and mobiles with a marine air. Prices are moderate.

Block Island Kite Company (401-466-2033), Corn Neck Road. Open June through September, daily 1–5; in spring and fall, open weekends 10–5. Block Island beaches and winds lend themselves to the carefree world of kite flying, and there's a kite to suit every fancy either here or in the sister shop next door, The Boatworks. You'll also find hammocks, French sailor shirts, and toy boats to send sailing on the island's 365 ponds.

Blocks of Fudge (401-466-5196), Chapel Street, Old Harbor. Open mid-May through Columbus Day 10 AM–10:30 PM at the height of the season, and until 5:30 before July 4 and after Labor Day. For 13 years they've been stirring the kettle making penuche and peanut butter, chocolate, chocolate walnut, and turtle fudge (with caramel and pecans in the center) in this little shop for the sweet-toothed.

Lazy Fish (401-466-2990), 235 Dodge Street, Old Harbor. Open 10–6 mid-May through Columbus Day. Vintage home accessories, estate jewelry, and Block Island photographs by K. C. Perry.

The Mad Hatter (401-466-5264), Chapel Street, Old Harbor. Open May 15 through Labor Day, daily 10–9; weekends in spring and fall. Straw hats, beribboned hats, hats decorated with this and that, canvas hats, wacky hats, bonnets, and caps for grown-ups and children can all be found in this creative little shop.

Oceans & Ponds (401-466-5131), Ocean Avenue, Old Harbor. Open Memorial Day through Columbus Day, daily 9–6. Anything and everything for salt- and freshwater anglers and for yachters can be found at this Orvis dealership, as well as a fine collection of swimwear, sportswear, foulweather gear, and yachting flags and pennants. Sailing charters and kayak rentals are also offered.

Old Salt Taffy Co. (401-466-5005), 457 Chapel Street, Old Harbor. Open Memorial Day through Columbus Day 10–7. There are 20 flavors of taffy to be sampled here and to watch being pulled, cut, and wrapped mornings.

The Scarlet Begonia (401-466-5024), Dodge Street, Old Harbor. Open July through September, daily 10–9; in spring and fall, open weekends 9–6. Tasteful table linens, pottery, and bric-a-brac; Block Island beeswax candles and honey; and interesting decoupage plates decorated with flowers, fruits, and beachfront scenes. A cozy, friendly gift shop.

The Star Department Store (401-466-5541), Water Street, Old Harbor. Open April through October, daily

10–5; November 1 until Thanksgiving, open weekends. In this cavernous, old-fashioned department store you can find shoes and socks, T-shirts and sweatshirts, stockings, guidebooks and maps, and sunglasses—just about every "essential" you left behind on the mainland, plus souvenirs.

Watercolors (401-466-2538), Dodge Street, Old Harbor. Open May through October, daily 10–9; in fall, early winter, and spring, weekends only 10–6. The handcrafted jewelry, blown- and stained-glass items on sale here are more than just the ordinary souvenirs of a summer holiday.

✳ Special Events

Unless otherwise noted, further information can be obtained from the **Block Island Chamber of Commerce** (401-466-2982), Old Harbor.

February: **Groundhog Day Winter Census,** Albion Inn.

March: **St. Patrick's Day Dinner** (401-466-5855), Yellow Kittens. **St. Patrick's Day Brunch** (401-466-5519), St. Andrew's Parish Center.

April: **Ecumenical Choir Concert** at Harbor Baptist Church.

May: **Annual Beach Cleanup. Islandwide Shad Bloom Festival. Bake, Bloom, Book Sale** (401-466-3233), held on the Block Island Free Library lawn.

June: **Fred Benson Picnic** (401-466-2641), Champlin's Marina, New Harbor. **Race Week,** New Harbor.

July: **Fourth of July Weekend Parade and Fireworks** at Crescent Beach. **Arts and Crafts Guild Fair,** Esta's Park. **Steak Fry,** Fire Barn, Beach and Ocean Avenues. **Barbershop Quartet Concert** (401-466-2555), Block Island School. **Ham and Bean Bake and Harbor Baptist Church Fair** (401-466-5940), Harbor Baptist Church lawn.

August: **Arts and Crafts Guild Fair,** Esta's Park. **Block Island Arts Festival,** Ocean Avenue. **Block Island Recreation Department Triathlon** (401-466-3200) starts at the Coast Guard station. **Crop Walk** (401-466-5940), Harbor Baptist Church. **Harbor Baptist Church Fair.**

September: **Run Around the Block,** Isaac's Corner. **Heritage Dinner** (401-466-5940), Harbor Baptist Church.

October: **Audubon Birding Weekend. Roll Call Dinner** (401-466-5940), Harbor Baptist Church.

November: **St. Andrew's Christmas Bazaar** (401-466-5519). **Christmas Shopping Stroll,** Harbor Baptist Church. **Ecumenical Church Concert** (401-466-5940), Harbor Baptist Church or St. Andrew's Church.

December: **Islandwide Holiday Window Decorating Contest. Ecumenical Choir Christmas Concert** (401-466-5940), Harbor Baptist Church or St. Andrew's Church. **Islandwide Christmas Light Decorating Contest.**

INDEX